HOT SECTOR
INVESTING
Profit from Over 100 Emerging Opportunities

David Wanetick

DEARBORN™
A **Kaplan Professional** Company

This publication is designed to provide accurate and authoritative information in regard to the subject matter covered. It is sold with the understanding that the publisher is not engaged in rendering legal, accounting, or other professional service. If legal advice or other expert assistance is required, the services of a competent professional person should be sought.

Editorial Director: Cynthia A. Zigmund
Managing Editor: Jack Kiburz
Interior Design: Lucy Jenkins
Cover Design: Scott Rattray, Rattray Design
Typesetting: Elizabeth Pitts

Library of Congress Cataloging-in-Publication Data

Wanetick, David.
　　Hot Sector Investing : profit from over 100 emerging opportunities
　/ David Wanetick.
　　　　p.　cm.
　　Includes index.
　　ISBN 0-7931-3023-9 (paper)
　　　1. Investments—United States.　2. Industries—United States.
　　3. Corporations—United States.　I. Title.
　HG4910.W314　1999
　332.6′0973—dc21　　　　　　　　　　　　　　　　99-24924
　　　　　　　　　　　　　　　　　　　　　　　　　　CIP

Contents

Preface

The future is impossible to predict. But Yogi Berra is remembered for saying, "You can see a lot just by looking." You can enhance your returns by purchasing shares of companies that are participating in major trends. And to discover those trends, you only have to observe your surroundings—how people live; the industries in which the most jobs are being created; what people are buying, eating, and wearing; and how people are spending their time.

I chose industries that I believe will offer investors substantial profit potential for at least the next three to five years. Each of the industries discussed in this book is driven by real world factors, such as demographics, technological change, lifestyle changes, and legislation—and each is destined for rapid and sustainable growth.

I wanted to give you a leg up on other investors by introducing you to many industries that are not followed or are little followed by Wall Street securities analysts. Indeed, few if any analysts follow many of the industries featured on these pages. It is very difficult for investors to locate investment research on holograms, food inspection, candles, electronic interference, and noise pollution. While I wanted to chart new paths in the discovery of investment opportunities, I did not include some exciting industries because of a lack of legitimate investment candidates. For instance, telemedicine is a promising technology, but there are few, if any, ways for investors to play this emerging industry.

I tried to thoroughly substantiate my contentions using statistics and expert opinion related to issues like demographic trends and legislative decrees. However, because I did not want to repeat similar statistics and quotes throughout the book, I often refer to chapters with more information regarding the issues at hand. For example, when reading about the dental industry, you will see that I refer to the growth of nonfluoridated bottled water as contributing to dental decay. And to achieve a better understanding of professional employer organizations, you'll want to read about employment practices liability insurance.

Although the merits of all investments change with market conditions at the time of investor action, I wanted to provide as many actionable investment ideas as possible. To that end, I provided the names of hundreds of companies that are beneficiaries of the trends that I have illuminated. The vast majority of the companies mentioned are public, but some will inevitably merge, be acquired, or return to private ownership. On the other hand, new companies will arise (and go public) to seize the dynamic opportunities discussed throughout this book.

One theme that recurs is the extraordinary importance of time. I believe that time is the most valuable commodity—it is non-negotiable, perishable, constant. Less than ten minutes spells the difference between life and death for sudden cardiac arrest victims in need of automated external defibrillation.

Time is not renewable as Benjamin Franklin said: "Lost time is never found again." Another dimension to time is its relative speed. Just as we try to fit more into each hour, those hours pass the fastest. Companies that help their customers save time or use their time more efficiently will prove to be the source of solid investment opportunities. Corporate jets save executives great amounts of time; interactive voice response systems save phone callers time; and corporate-sponsored child care providers save employees time in dropping off and retrieving their children.

Time is money now more than ever. Or as Jim McCann, CEO of 1-800-FLOWERS, has said: "Time is the currency of the nineties." As a result, millions of people are saving time by conducting their financial transactions with online brokers. Even more people are increasingly committed to electronic commerce.

The crux of the entire $1 trillion U.S. health care industry is to expand the time and quality of human life. Industries I discuss that pursue this objective include alternative drug deliverers, clinical research organizations, and vaccine manufacturers.

The penultimate variation of the time theme relates to where and how people are spending their time. Older people are spending more of their years in assisted living facilities, and more children are spending time under the supervision of child care providers. People the world over are traveling as never before, and a growing number of people are engaging in extreme sports.

The final time-related theme that resonates throughout this book is the importance of security and safety. These investment opportunities range from food inspection firms and fingerprint providers to prison management companies and surveillance camera manufacturers. Security service providers are important in that by keeping their clients safe they help increase their protectees' longevity.

Each chapter presents at least one investment opportunity; most chapters provide several. I believe that *Hot Sector Investing: Profit from Over 100 Emerging Opportunities* will direct you to many timely and profitable investment niches.

David Wanetick

CHAPTER 1

Education Services

As the nation continues to migrate from a manufacturing economy to an information economy, and more recently to a knowledge economy, education takes on increasing importance. In growing numbers, Americans are realizing that attaining higher educational diplomas unlocks doors to success and provides the keys to realizing more lucrative careers. Distance learning is proving to be a tool well-suited to meet the needs of ever more-harried professionals striving to climb the rungs of upward mobility. Also, parents are more determined to place their toddlers in child care centers that are committed to nurturing youngsters' cognitive processes. Finally, parents across the socioeconomic spectrum—confronted with a growing choice of elementary schools—refuse to enroll their children in schools that fail to meet high standards.

Child Care Providers

Child care providers are perfectly positioned to benefit from demographics, fundamental shifts in the composition of the workforce, a continuation of the full-employment economy, and a variety of legislative initiatives. Judging from the way that politicians are talking, child care may soon become America's next Great Entitlement.

The child care industry's growth into the next millennium will be fueled by high birth rates. In recent years, the number of births in the United States has surpassed 4 million each year, birth rates that had not been achieved from 1965 to 1988. One reason for the nation's fecundity is that immigrant mothers have been bearing more children than initially estimated. Also, birth rates for women in their 30s have been higher than anticipated as more than 35 percent of all children born in the U.S. are born to mothers in their 30s, compared with only 19 percent in 1976. The chief of fertility statistics at the Census Bureau reports that women aged 30 through 34 who have given birth are more likely to return to work faster than did mothers in previous decades, which fuels demand for child care. There

1

also has been a consistent decline in infant mortality as a result of education, advances in medical care, and more inclusive health coverage.

Not only are women bearing more children but an unprecedented number of these children are being placed in child care centers. Sandra L. Hofferth, Ph.D., from the Institute for Social Research at the University of Michigan, says that "child care is no longer an experience for a few children; it is rapidly becoming the norm." More than 12 million children under the age of six are in the care of someone other than their parents. And because the birth rate in the United States has been below the population replacement rate of 2.1 children born per woman, parents have a shrinking constellation of family members to rely on. Since grandparents, aunts, and uncles are more geographically dispersed, the logistics of placing children under the care of relatives becomes increasingly infeasible. Thus, it is no surprise that almost one-third of children under the age of five are enrolled in a child care center.

Working Mothers Rely on Child Care

The demand for child care is being propelled by rising rates of working mothers and a growing incidence of single mothers. In 1998, women represented over 46 percent of all persons in the civilian labor force and demographers predict that women will comprise 48 percent of the total U.S. labor force by 2005. The percentage of married mothers with children under six years old who worked increased from nearly 19 percent in 1960 to nearly 63 percent in 1996. Looking ahead, the U.S. Bureau of Labor Statistics estimates that the number of working women of childbearing age who work outside the home is expected to reach 44 million by 2000, up from 41 million in 1990. More important, the demographic data that I have reviewed suggest that 93 percent of this group will become pregnant during their working careers.

TIP: Another way to play the fact that many single-parent and dual-career families cannot go anywhere unless they take their children along is to invest in such companies as Koala Corporation that manufacture indoor and outdoor playground equipment (the likes of which McDonald's has long championed). Companies are often willing to make investments toward diverting children's attention, because doing so allows salespeople to cater to parents.

Another demographic trend that is of benefit to child care providers is single parenthood. Even though women being abandoned by the men who fathered their children is nothing new, more adults are consciously deciding to raise children without a spouse. Also, the incidence of single-parent families resulting from divorce will remain high, as the number of divorces is estimated to remain at the annual rate of 1.2 million until 2008. As a result of these factors, the Census Bureau has reported that the percentage of single-parent families climbed to 28 percent of all families in 1997, a full four percentage points more than the 24 percent in 1990, and 2.5 times the 11 percent level recorded in 1970. Single-parent families are highly likely to require child care services because the parent must almost always work but there's no spouse to provide child care.

Whether married or single, more mothers than ever are working outside the home. The U.S. Census Bureau estimates that by 2005, eight out of ten American children under the age of 12 will have mothers that work. These mothers are becoming increasingly comfortable entrusting their offspring to child care centers. This is becoming increasingly true as the media continue to devote considerable attention to cases of unmonitored, in-home child care arrangements where children have been either abused or neglected. Driven by fears of those arrangements and unable to find professional child care services, many parents have resorted to cameras in their home to monitor baby-sitters' behavior. One New York–based company called Communications Control Systems International inserts a phone line and a camera into children's toys. These mechanisms are designed to allow parents to check on their children in real time through a personal computer.

TIP: Child care centers are preferable to nannies because when nannies provide child care, parents have to assume the responsibilities of an employer—offering health care benefits, providing vacation time, and withholding taxes, for example. Employer responsibilities carry administrative burdens, and failure to comply with legal requirements often results in severe penalties. In fact, it was Zoe Baird's employing an illegal alien to care for her child that resulted in her withdrawing her nomination as U.S. attorney general.

Quality Counts

According to a 1998 study by the YMCA of the USA, parents are more concerned about the quality of child care than about either its cost or availability. The benefits from parents' willingness to pay for quality accrues to publicly traded child care providers, such as Children's Discovery Centers of America and Nobel Education Dynamics, which have accreditations, a history of sound operations, name recognition, and multiple references. Moreover, the better-funded child care providers can afford to offer more generous compensation to their staffers (which results in higher retention rates) and to invest in child development activities.

In a report released by the White House in April 1996, neuroscientists found that good stimulation in the first three years of a child's life activates more neural pathways in the brain that might otherwise atrophy. Early nurturing may even permanently increase the number of brain cells. Separately, a study sponsored by the National Institute of Child Health and Human Development has shown that high-quality child care improves children's scores on cognitive and language tests. This study also indicated that children in child care centers tended to score higher in intellectual and verbal skills than children left at home with relatives, nannies, or sitters.

Several of the publicly traded child care companies such as Childtime Learning Centers offer a variety of other value-added services to older children and their parents. Some of these services include summer camps, backup care programs (to which parents resort when their primary child care providers are unavailable), parent's night out, expectant mother courses, wellness programs, and parent counseling.

Another area of activity consists of offering after-school programs to older children. Those services are increasingly in demand as student populations outgrow their classrooms and political pressures are exerted to reduce class sizes. The strain on classroom space is resulting in the elimination of on-site extracurricular programs. A September 1997 report compiled by the Federal Bureau of Investigation found that half of all violent youth crime occurs between 2 PM and 8 PM. According to U.S. Attorney General Janet Reno, the report confirms the need for effective after-school programs and has generated growing support for an extended school year—both proposals presenting opportunities for child care providers.

Political Support

Realizing their constituents' demand for child care services, politicians have arranged for various governmental bodies to collect taxes that are used to fund the child care industry's growth. Already, sales and property taxes in the form of tax credits, deductions, and exemptions are used to finance child care facilities. A federal income tax credit of 20 to 30 percent of certain child care expenses is available for qualifying individuals with maximum credits ranging from $480 to $720 for one child, and from $960 to $1,440 for two or more children.

Child care operators have also worked with many states in securing general obligation bonds, tax-exempt bonds, grants, and direct loans to finance child care centers. Similarly, governments at the federal, state and local level have generated significant revenues for early education from general fees and lotteries. The following are examples of the initiatives that have already been undertaken or proposed:

- The Georgia state lottery generates $185 million annually for full-day pre-kindergarten programs for all families who desire these services.
- County voters in Florida have established special taxing districts similar to school districts to levy property taxes for children's services; the districts have raised an average of $10 million annually for a range of children's services, including child care.
- U.S. Representative Carolyn Maloney has proposed the "Kiddie Mac," under which the Department of Housing and Urban Development would offer guaranty insurance to lenders that wish to build or invest in child care facilities. The Kiddie Mac would also provide small purpose loans to operators who need to bring existing facilities up to code.

The White House and many members of Congress seem determined to make child care the next entitlement program. The Clinton administration has proposed spending at least $21.7 billion over five years to double the number of children—to 2 million—receiving subsidized day care. This spending package would increase tax credits to eligible families, expand child development programs by reauthorizing Head Start, provide scholarships to students working towards child care credentials, and encourage companies to offer child care by expanding corporate child care tax credits.

Another driving force behind the subsidization of child care costs is in the form of the hundreds of thousands of welfare recipients who are migrating from welfare to workfare. Under federal law, 30 percent of all mothers on welfare were required to participate in work activities by September 30, 1998. That required percentage is mandated to rise 5 percent each year and stops at 50 percent. The government realizes that one of the biggest challenges for parents trying to make the transition from welfare to work is the availability of affordable child care. Thus, many of the state welfare-to-workfare programs provide for welfare parents to receive subsidized child care.

Corporate-Sponsored Child Care

Perhaps the most exciting investment opportunities found within the child care sector are the corporate-sponsored child care providers. According to Jerry Herman of EVEREN Securities, while the overall child care industry grew at a 5 percent annual rate, from $23 billion in 1992 to $30 billion in 1997, the work-site child care subsector grew at a 25 percent annual rate, from $700 million in 1992 to $2 billion at the end of 1997. Although expanding rapidly, worksite child care providers have a great deal more room to grow; the Child Care Information Exchange, in fact, reported that these providers account for only 1 percent of the total child care services market. However, the concept is clearly catching on as about 10 percent of large companies provided worksite child care by 1995, compared with only 6 percent in 1990.

Corporate-sponsored child care offers parents convenience in terms of delivering their children to—and retrieving them from—child care centers. The close proximity that parents have to their children during the day facilitates parents spending time with their children during breaks, at lunchtime, and after school.

Worksite child care is a competitive weapon for the companies and organizations that offer it. This is especially true when the labor market is tight; employers realize that the provision of child care is an effective tool in recruiting and retaining workers. One of the studies indicating that working parents value child care and early childhood education was conducted by the Simmons Graduate School of Management in Boston in 1997. The study indicated that 42 percent of parents cited child care as an important factor in deciding to join a company. The same study reported that 19 percent of prospective employees decline job offers or do not pursue job offers because of a lack of child care benefits.

The following are examples of the benefits that worksite child care confers upon the sponsoring companies:

- At AlliedSignal, Inc., the availability of its Family Center reduced absenteeism of employees using the center by 89 percent.
- Chase Manhattan Corporation calculated that its back-up child care services generated net savings of approximately $800,000 over a one-year period as a result of the reduced absenteeism and greater productivity of employees using the program.
- Union Bank estimated that its annual savings from reduced turnover and absenteeism were double the yearly cost of subsidizing its child care centers.
- An internal study by Johnson & Johnson disclosed that 71 percent of the employees who used its corporate-sponsored family support system attributed their decision to remain with Johnson & Johnson to the availability of such programs.

Corporate-sponsored child care providers enjoy several structural operating advantages that often result in healthy profitability. These advantages include the following:

- Because companies such as Bright Horizons Family Solutions operate on corporate sites, their facilities are heavily subsidized by their corporate partners, which substantially reduces their occupancy costs.

- Companies providing child care benefit from built-in demand for their services and therefore do not have to aggressively market their services. Rather, marketing can be directed through the corporate partners' internal channels, such as their newsletters and bulletin boards.
- The preceding factors allow the worksite child care providers to more generously compensate their employees, which is a very effective tool in reducing employee turnover—an enormous cost for an industry that has a 42 percent annual turnover rate. Also attractive to workers is that they can often avail themselves of the corporate partners' subsidized gyms and cafeterias as well as other vendor discounts that partners enjoy.
- The high switching costs that preexisting child care centers present for their corporate sponsors result in extremely long-term contracts, which lend stability to the child care providers' revenue streams.
- Locating child care centers at a company's facilities rather than in a given neighborhood reduces the risk of adverse changes in the neighborhood. Thus, companies like Bright Horizons Family Solutions have little exposure to a neighborhood's maturing children, deteriorating demographics, or changes in traffic flows.

Investment Vehicles

The following are among publicly traded child care providers: Bright Horizons Family Solutions, Childtime Learning Centers, Children's Discovery Centers of America, and Nobel Education Dynamics.

Distance Learning

Distance learning—the electronic distribution of instruction in applications ranging from elementary school to universities and from telemedicine to corporate training—is projected to continue to grow at torrential rates. According to International Data Corporation, U.S. spending on Internet and intranet training should soar from less than $100 million in 1995 to $1.8 billion in 2001, and Web-based information technology training alone is estimated to grow to a $1.75 billion market by 2004.

Such dramatic growth is not difficult to fathom when reviewing the recent past. For example, online software-enabling companies, including CBT Group and Centra Software, doubled their revenues each quarter in 1997 and 1998. Strayer Education's enrollment for its online courses soared from 300 students in the fall of 1997 to 1,000 students in the fall of 1998. Many analysts believe that companies involved with employee training via the Internet or intranets, such as UOL Publishing, could grow at annual rates of more than 100 percent past the turn of the century.

Computer-based learning is especially important as more jobs require high levels of education and as the increasingly mobile workforce is ill suited to attend site-based courses for long periods of time. Remote learning is appealing to students because it greatly expands the curricula available to them: they can learn at their own pace, and the tuition is much more affordable than campus-based education. Universities are attracted to distance learning because it enables them to attract students beyond their campuses. Finally, corporations appreciate the tremendous reduction in training costs that distance learning makes possible.

Education Grows Increasingly Important

Distance learning will grow as a result of Americans placing greater emphasis on education. The heightened focus on education is due to the realization that more, and higher-paying, jobs beckon a well-educated workforce. The U.S. Labor Department estimates that by 2000, 85 percent of the nation's jobs will require education or training above the high school level, compared with 65 percent of the jobs at the beginning of the 1990s and only 40 percent of the jobs in 1950. These knowledge-based jobs are much more lucrative as the U.S. Census Bureau reported that the average annual earnings of individuals possessing a bachelor's degree was 85 percent higher in 1994 than those with high school diplomas, while earnings of those with graduate or MBA degrees were 45 percent higher still.

The rapid proliferation of ever more powerful technology and the lack of job security as the result of corporate downsizings, restructurings, and transformations brought about by the Internet induces workers to keep their skills fresh and growing. Workers understand that they must embrace new skills as they realize they cannot expect to perform the same tasks indefinitely. (The Bureau of Labor Statistics reports that the typical peripatetic American holds 8.6 different jobs between the ages of 18 and 32.) Thus, education is becoming a lifelong process that an increasing number of workers are integrating into their careers. In fact, the percentage of U.S. college and university students over age 25 increased from 28 percent in 1972 to 45 percent in 1997.

Employers are largely supportive of their workers pursuing formal education—important because employers must grant their employees time to pursue their studies. According to an International Foundation of Employee Benefits survey, more than 90 percent of companies surveyed offered continuing education as an employee benefit in 1997, and 97 percent planned to offer this benefit by 2000. In addition, a 1996 survey conducted by *Training* magazine indicated that approximately 134,000 organizations in the United States with more than 100 employees spent $60 billion to provide education and training to 59 million of their employees. Employers have been demonstrating a growing commitment to their employees' education as 93 percent of those surveyed by *Training* magazine expected to spend an equal or greater amount in 1997 relative to their 1996 budgets.

TIP: Some analysts have argued that the gap between the skills that jobs require and the skills that workers possess is being driven by the rising power of computer chips. Because microprocessors sit at the core of computer technology, Moore's Law can be used as a proxy for the increasing complexity of the workplace. Moore's Law states that circuit density, or the number of transistors per square inch on a computer chip, doubles every 18 months. The increasing number of transistors per chip enables each chip to perform ever more complex operations. In addition, the decreasing distance between transistors enables the chips to process data more quickly. Both factors combine to produce computers that every 18 months double the number of calculations per second they can perform, but the nation's workforce is not increasing its skills nearly as rapidly.

The importance of education on career development is realized not only by the nation's workforce and employers but also by high school students. College participation rates (the percentage of high school graduates matriculating in colleges and universities) have risen from 53 percent in 1987 to 63 percent in 1993. These rising enrollment rates complement the soaring population of teenagers. (Data supporting the rising number of American teenagers is found in Chapter 3.) The number of high school graduates should increase by one-third, from 2.5 million in 1997 to 3.3 million in 2008. Thus, according to the National Center for Education Statistics (NCES), enrollment in postsecondary institutions is expected to reach 16.4 million by 2006, and could reach 17.8 million under NCES's "high-alternative-projection" scenario.

TIP: The federal government has taken action to spur the development of distance learning. For example, the Federal Communications Commission vowed to provide all elementary schools (through high school) and public libraries up to $2.25 billion a year in discounts for telecommunications services, which will reduce companies' infrastructure costs for distance learning.

Part-Time Enrollment Rises Faster Than Full-Time Enrollment

Although the aggressive growth in the number of postsecondary students provides a general indication of rising demand for distance learning, I believe that the soaring enrollment of students in part-time programs is a more direct leading indicator of participation in cyberlearning because distance learning offers the flexibility that part-time students require.

Part-time education is preferred to full-time matriculation for working and learning adults. Between 1970 and 1995, the number of part-time students enrolled in higher education programs had grown from approximately 3.0 million to 6.7 million, or 139 percent, while full-time enrollment grew only 44 percent over the same period. In 1995, over 76 million adults, or 40 percent of all Americans over 16, participated in some form of part-time educational program.

Part-time education is favored by workers because their careers are not interrupted. Also, the astronomical costs of full-time tuition can be mitigated. Full-time education has become extremely expensive as postsecondary tuition costs have undergone an eightfold increase from 1965 to 1997. Members of the workforce who pursue part-time programs receive remuneration and often reimbursement from their employers. Because they take fewer courses than full-time students each semester, their tuition obligations are more dispersed.

Universities Embrace Distance Learning

Universities have been growing increasingly receptive to distance learning. According to the Department of Education, the number of four-year colleges offering cybercourses increased from 645 in 1994 to 1,218 in 1996. The number of distance learning schools tallied by Peterson's, the esteemed purveyor of college guides, was only 93 in 1993; but Peterson's 1997 Distance Learning guide included 762 distance learning schools.

The underlying factors driving demand for distance learning at the postsecondary level include the growing importance of education and training, the inadequacy of site-based learning in a highly mobile society, and the high quality of interactive instruction available to students without regard to where they reside. One statistic supporting my second contention is that some 200 college campuses closed permanently between 1987 and 1997, twice the number that closed in the previous decade.

The primary limitations of modern universities are their expense and their inflexibility with regard to where and at what pace learning takes place. Peter Drucker has gone as far as to say that "universities will not survive. The future is outside the traditional campus, outside the traditional classroom. Distance learning is coming on fast." And Nobel laureate economist Milton Friedman, a long-time advocate of stripped-down vcollege education, has said: "There are many activities at universities that have very little to do with higher education—ranging from athletics to research."

Many of these activities are wasteful of students' time and money. Moreover, even though most of American industry has become extremely efficient in arranging to have its inventories delivered just when they are needed, the nation's current pedagogical system is not geared toward delivering education when it's needed. However, Douglas Van Houweling, chief executive of the University Corporation for Advanced Internet Development, has predicted that "education will change from a place-centered enterprise to education where you need it."

The following are among the most notable advantages of interactive learning over campus-based learning:

- People can log onto the Internet when they wish to learn about a subject or when they need to develop new skills. Students can start learning almost as soon as their payment has been accepted. In contrast, students at universities must wait until the particular course is offered and can only enroll in that course if there is room.
- Remote learning allows students to listen to lectures and work on assignments when they believe they can devote the most attention to them. In contrast, students enrolled in campus-based courses can only attend courses when they're scheduled.
- Asynchronous learning (e.g., listening to a lecture after it has been delivered) allows students to rewind and review difficult points or fast-forward past obvious ones. Students who do not understand their classroom lectures either do not ask the instructor for more clarification or, if they do, risk diluting the academic rigor of the course for the remainder of the class.

Students enrolling in university-sponsored distance learning courses do not compromise the quality of their education. Effectiveness studies have been quite consistent in showing that—whether in business, military training, or adult learning—there is no significant difference in effectiveness between distance learning and traditional instruction methods. In fact, on administering a standard achievement test to graduate students, Apollo's University of Phoenix found that its online students scored 5 to 10 percent higher than their traditionally educated peers.

Another endorsement of distance learning programs stems from the fact that most have achieved accreditation because they are already part of accredited institutions. In fact, the vast majority of the degrees granted by the distance learning programs are identical to the degrees granted by the corresponding campuses.

The legitimacy of distance learning is rising further as some of the nation's most prestigious institutions of higher learning are offering courses over the Internet. Even the Harvard Business School and the Wharton School of Business have offered business courses through the Internet since 1998.

Benefits of Distance Learning to Students

Internet-facilitated learning is really nothing more than a technologically sophisticated form of correspondence course that has appealed to students for well over 100 years. Distance learning—both correspondence and Internet-based—continues to be appreciated for being less disruptive than site-based learning, allowing students to pursue other professional or personal goals while pursuing an education.

Skeptics of distance learning argue that computers fail to engage students in intellectual exchange as well as the traditional classroom setting does. However, technology and computer users' intense obsession with their computers is disproving this concern. The reality is that computers have proven to hold people's attention—just ask the spouse of a computer enthusiast! Separately, online instructors often try to compensate for their own feelings of isolation by trying more earnestly to engage their cyberstudents.

In addition, many distance learning packages have tools aimed at keeping students engaged. Some software facilitates personal attention from the teacher as students can type questions directly to the teacher without the rest of the class seeing them. Software from Interactive Learning International allows a teacher to send pop-quiz questions to the class. The answers are instantly tallied and inform the instructor which students understand the material.

Moreover, the students are not completely unsupervised as most packages allow the instructor to glimpse the students' screens from afar. Thus, the teacher can check to make sure the students are completing their assignments properly. Strayer Education introduced an innovative technique to compel student participation. By utilizing a synchronous lecture format—much like an online chat room—teachers lead discussions from broadcast booths so students actually hear the lectures. Because students can also respond via audio, more dynamic dialogs are likely to ensue; speaking is easier and faster than typing.

The following are among the other advantages that distance learning confers on students:

- Students are able to satisfy their craving for knowledge much more effectively when choosing from a menu of courses from the Internet than choosing from the selection offered at their local community college or university. Many community colleges do not offer courses in Greek mythology, for example, but students willing to learn via the Internet will find that this medium offers an array of esoteric courses.

- The ability to connect by modem from the home, office, or mobile locations makes accessibility greater. Enhanced accessibility also makes remote learning attractive for people who travel extensively, live in rural communities, are in the military, are disabled, or are senior citizens.
- Distance education is typically much less expensive than campus-based learning. For instance, the Washington Post's Kaplan Educational Centers unveiled its Concord University School of Law in mid-1998, offering online law degrees at substantial discounts from the price of traditional law schools. According to Jack Goetz, dean of Concord, tuition covering the four-year program is about $17,000, less than the $23,900 tuition for a single year at Harvard Law School—and this does not include the $12,200 in annual charges for room and board at Harvard.
- Nearly endless hyperlinks to other resources on the Web enrich the learning experience.
- Distance learning safeguards students from feeling embarrassed by asking questions that their classmates might deem to be unenlightened.

Benefits of Distance Learning to Universities

Distance learning enables universities to increase their revenues, broaden their geographic reach, and enhance their reputation. An additional revenue stream (achieved with the relatively limited increases in fixed costs associated with offering distance learning) is appealing to college administrators in light of 200 college campuses closing from 1987 to 1997 and parents more aggressively resisting paying higher tuition. Also, because universities can market their Internet-based curricula internationally, they stand to attract a more diverse student body to their campuses.

Universities offering Internet-delivered courses can build a more extensive array of course offerings than can solely campus-based universities. The Internet's reach can attract enough students from around the nation (or from around the world) to make a niche course economical to run, while the same may not be true for a traditional site-based institution of higher learning. For example, if an instructor wanted to offer a course on Tibetan culture, there might not be sufficient enrollment on campus to make the course profitable. However, by offering the same course to the entire nation through the Internet, it is more likely that the university would receive enough registrations to make offering the course economically feasible.

The following are among the additional advantages that distance learning confers on universities:

- Greater storage capacity of the Internet host, compared with a user's hard drive, allows users to access more products and allows instructors to mix and match courseware activities to fit specific needs. Students can preview presentations of different courses before selecting one, or they can access a specific slide from thousands in the university's intranet library.
- Offering courses through the Internet is controllable—the university can decide which of its courses will be offered to distance learners. Thus, renowned professors can take solace from the fact that their lectures will not be commoditized, for only a limited number of students in the classroom will be privy to their thoughts.
- Enrollments in Internet-based courses are expandable with virtually no obstacles to allowing more students to enroll through the Internet. On the contrary, universities eschewing the Internet have space constraints, and professors can teach only a limited number of sections of popular courses.

Benefits of Distance Learning to Businesses

Faced with retraining 50 million American workers, corporate America is adopting distance learning for all aspects of internal and external training. Many major corporations such as Hewlett-Packard and Staples save millions of dollars each year using distance learning to train employees more effectively and more efficiently than with conventional methods.

Companies utilizing distance training are able to save substantial sums of money because the Internet allows companies to eliminate the paper, postage, and packaging associated with distributing manuals and software nationally or internationally. Also, META Group, a leading information technology consultancy, reports that 45 percent of the cost of classroom training goes toward travel. Of course, the Internet eliminates these expenditures.

One deficiency associated with traditional classroom training is that it almost always lasts for five days—not the seven or eight days that may be better suited to learning the skills being demonstrated. As a consequence, people less familiar with the course content may not have sufficient time to absorb the material.

On the other hand, an advantage associated with Internet instruction is that training classes can be pared into shorter sessions and spread out over a number of days or weeks—meaning companies do not lose an employee for entire days at a time. Shorter training sessions are also beneficial for students as studies show that retention levels fall significantly after two hours. Even better, qualified

Information Technology Training

Training people to program, remediate, analyze, and operate information technology (IT) systems is a burgeoning industry. The Labor Department predicts the number of job openings that require information technology skills will soar by 5.9 million between 1994 and 2005. Similarly, International Data Corporation (IDC) estimates that IT training revenues will rise from $16.4 billion in 1996 to $28 billion in 2002. IDC also estimates that the U.S. market for Web-based training alone will grow from $197 million in revenue in 1997 to $6 billion in 2002.

One of the avenues open to investors riding the bullet train up the exponential revenue curve in information technology training is to invest in companies such as Sylvan Learning Centers, New Horizons Worldwide, or The Learning Tree that offer certification courses in a host of information technology disciplines. More than 1 million IT certification tests were delivered in 1997 yielding a market worth $1.3 billion in revenue. The following increases are among the reasons that corporate managers and IT professionals valued information technology industry certification in 1998:

- A 12 percent increase in the number of IT professionals seeking certification for career advancement
- A 16 percent increase in certification as a criteria for promotion
- A 95 percent increase in the number of corporations willing to spend more than $200 to train candidates for certification

The following are among the reasons for IT professionals' continued interest in certification testing:

- *Emerging technologies:* As new technologies emerge, standards to assess new job skills needed to implement these new technologies must be developed. Certification is a way to create such benchmarks, and individuals need to get these credentials to increase their value in the marketplace.
- *Multiple certifications:* There was a 55 percent increase in the number of IT professionals seeking multiple certification in 1998 in contrast with the number in 1997. IT professionals realize they need to be skilled and certified on a variety of platforms because the trend is toward system integration.

instructors can train employees in multiple locations simultaneously, yielding the company "first-mover" advantages. In contrast, a significant drawback for companies using traditional classroom instruction for a large number of employees is that they often have to deputize unqualified trainers.

The following are among the additional advantages associated with using the Internet as a training tool:

- Data management can be simplified. The rapid rate at which new products are introduced and older products outdated creates a management nightmare for individuals charged with updating product-training libraries. However, if a single version of each course is kept on the host server, users have instantaneous access to updated components.
- Monitoring usage by students is simple because the number of downloads can be measured. This helps training managers evaluate cost-effectiveness as well as negotiate licenses with software developers that assess charges on the basis of estimated usage.
- Individual education programs can be generated from a combination of the historical record of the students, prior training (from monitored usage), and the vast database stored on the server. As students progress through training, information is delivered based on what they have learned and how they have performed in previous training. For example, a student could sign on to a course and enter previous training he has had and what types of information he wants into a user profile, and a customized course could be generated from the content database. This dimension focuses the training curriculum on gaps in skills only, thus saving organizations both time and money.*

Resistance to Distance Learning

Distance learning allows instructors to increase their reach and possibly their compensation when their remuneration is based on the total number of students being taught. In addition, the outlook for Internet-based learning should improve as younger instructors become more accustomed to using technology.

Investors, however, should be aware of the challenges that confront distance learning. Many professors simply do not want to be bothered with Internet-based instruction. For instance, the University of California at Los Angeles found that just 30 percent of its faculty complied with a 1997 requirement that each of over

---

*Howard M. Block, *Workplace Learning,* Volume 2: *Bridging the Skills Gap* (Boston: Bank-Boston Robertson Stephens, June 9, 1998), p. 41.

3,800 courses have some material on the university's intranet sites. More than 900 professors at the University of Washington signed a letter to Washington Governor Gary Locke protesting calls for more instruction by computer. Also, unionized faculty struck Toronto's York University in 1997, in part over Internet teaching requirements, which were later dropped.

The following are a few of the reasons that some academicians oppose distance learning:

- Instructors may feel that distance learning is excessively time-consuming. In fact, the American Association of University Professors has complained that courses taught via a school's intranet demand too much teaching time.
- Many instructors are compensated on the basis of the number of students that enroll in their live classes. Thus, beaming courses out of classrooms is often perceived as cannibalizing their efforts.
- Dissention crops up over ownership of course materials. Some colleges contend they own the material that teachers post on their school's internal Web sites, a change from current practice, under which teachers own class materials.

Investment Vehicles

Educational institutions involved with distance learning include Apollo Group, DeVry Inc., ITT Educational Services, Computer Learning Centers, and Strayer Education.

Companies that provide the enabling technology to facilitate distance learning include Systems and Computer Technology Corporation, CBT Group, Centra Software, Educational Video Conferencing, UOL Publishing, Caliber Learning Network, and RWD Technologies.

Other companies that develop training programs for information technology professionals include Analysis & Technology, Canterbury Information Technology, and ITC Learning Corporation.

Private Elementary Schools

The public is growing increasingly dissatisfied with the quality of the nation's public schools. Politicians across the ideological spectrum are pushing for legislation that makes it easier and less expensive for parents to send their children to nonpublic elementary schools. And an expanding cast of wealthy individuals are funding private schools. These trends accrue to the benefit of private school operators such as The TesseracT Group, The Edison Project, and Nobel Learning Communities.

Public Schools Fail to Make the Grade

Indications abound that America's public schools are simply inadequate. Research from the late 1990s by the Organization for Economic Cooperation and Development noted that U.S. students from ages 9 to 14 made the least reading progress of children in 16 countries. Also, only students from Cyprus and South Africa scored worse than American high-school seniors in the 1998 Mathematics and Science Study.

Many make the argument that many of these problems are attributable to underqualified teachers. Such arguments are based on findings that include the following:

- A full 75 percent of the teaching applicants that were given an 11th-grade-level reading comprehension test in Suffolk County, New York, in July 1997, failed.
- The Massachusetts Board of Education announced that almost 60 percent of aspiring teachers flunked the state's certification exam in April 1998, the first time the exam was ever required.
- According to the National Commission on Teaching and America's Future, more than 20 percent of high school teachers do not have so much as an undergraduate minor in the subject they teach.
- In California, one-half of the state's math and science teachers have no background in their field. And 12 percent of all newly hired teachers enter the classroom without any pedagogical training at all.

Politicians Are Calling for Education Reform

Politicians became increasingly focused on educational issues in the 1990s, partly because the breakup of the Soviet Union, a rising stock market, and a plummeting urban crime rate shifted attention away from traditional front-runner issues. Because the demographically powerful baby boom generation has children throughout the school system, the boomers' attention is focused on education. Women are often heavily involved in educational issues, so focusing on these issues is a way to appeal to them as voters.

On reviewing the state of the nation's education, politicians representing a variety of ideological bents have expressed their interest in reforming education.

One of the first efforts made in this direction has been the replacement of the tenure system with methods that ensure teacher competency. For instance:

- Former Republican presidential candidate Robert Dole blasted the teachers' unions for "protecting the perks and privileges of the members" and called for replacing tenure with renewable five-year contracts.
- California's Democratic Governor Gray Davis supports evaluations of public school teachers by their peers and the testing of teachers in their subject every five years.
- Massachusetts Senator and Democratic presidential hopeful John Kerry said in June 1998 that "no teacher should have a lock on any job."
- The head of the National Education Association made the following admission before the National Press Club in Washington in February 1998: "The fact is that in some instances we have used power . . . to protect the narrow interests of our members and not to advance the interests of our schools."

Charter Schools Catch Fire

A major step beyond screening for teacher proficiency is allowing parents the right to send their children to schools they—the parents—choose. Democrats such as Milwaukee Mayor John Norquist and former New York Congressman Floyd Flake have joined Republicans in advocating school choice. Since 1988, at least 16 states have passed school choice laws granting students permission to attend schools beyond the geographic borders of their local school districts tuition-free. More than 4,000 magnet schools allow students to select schools with special teaching or curricular themes within their school systems.

Of particular appeal, in view of the deficiencies associated with public schools, are charter schools run by companies such as The TesseracT Group. Charter schools are public schools that are financed by the same per-pupil funds that traditional public schools receive. Unlike traditional public schools, however, they are held accountable for achieving educational results. In return, they receive waivers that exempt them from many of the restrictions and bureaucratic rules that shape traditional public schools.

Thirty-three states, the District of Columbia, and Puerto Rico have enacted laws authorizing the creation of charter schools, and by 1998, there were about 1,200 charter schools. In 1997, President Clinton called for quadrupling the number of charter schools to 3,000 by the year 2000. Subsequently, the Clinton administration requested $100 million in its fiscal 1999 budget to meet the growing demand for starting these schools.

One impetus for charter schools is that more schools are being evaluated, which will lead to more parents deciding to transfer their children out of schools that perform poorly. According to the Education Commission of the States, 16 states had comprehensive school report cards in the fall of 1998. These report cards rated the schools on such categories as discipline problems, dropout rates, teacher salaries, and SAT college entrance scores. Another 24 states reported at the least their schools' test scores and attendance.

Private schools should become more affordable. This is because Congress passed legislation in 1998 that allows parents to put as much as $2,000 a year into tax-free savings accounts for elementary and high school expenses, including private school tuition.

Another boon to private school operators was delivered by the Supreme Court in November 1998, when it declined to hear a challenge to a Wisconsin program that allows some Milwaukee youngsters to attend private or religious schools at public expense.

Private Schools Gain Popularity

Even though the concept of charter schools is relatively new, it has been well received. In the vast majority of cases, once charter schools are established, they have remained open. Also, more than 70 percent of the charter schools sampled by the Education Department in 1998 reportedly had more applicants than could be admitted.

TRAP: One of the primary challenges that private schools face is their ability to attract and retain qualified teachers. First, with record numbers of students projected to enroll in grade schools and high schools; with politicians slashing class sizes; with a generation of teachers on the verge of retiring; and with the possibility of teachers being disqualified, American schools may face a deficit of as many as 1 million teachers by the early 2000s. In addition, because private school teachers are not unionized, their compensation is less than that of public school teachers, which results in higher teacher turnover in private schools.

In addition to government grants, many sources of financial support are available for private schools. Members of the National Association of Independent Schools awarded $464 million in scholarships to be used at private schools in 1997, up $38 million over 1996.

Investment banker Ted Forstmann and Wal-Mart heir John Walton initiated the $200 million Children's Scholarship Fund, which provides scholarships for

50,000 children to attend private or parochial schools. Donald and Doris Fisher, the founders of The Gap, endowed a foundation with $25 million to spur school reform. Alfred Taubman, chairman of Sotheby's, launched the Leona Group, a Michigan-based, for-profit operator of charter schools.

Investment Opportunities

While most other American industries have made tremendous progress over the past several decades, public elementary education clearly has not. Parents, politicians, wealthy benefactors, and energetic entrepreneurs are driven to reinvigorate the delivery of education with private market alternatives. Companies positioned to benefit include The TesseracT Group, The Edison Project, and Nobel Learning Communities.

School Uniforms

Uniforms are the fastest growing segment of the children's clothing industry. School districts in more than 20 states already have uniform requirements. Uniforms are worn in some of the nation's largest school districts, including those of Detroit, Los Angeles, Miami, Milwaukee, New Orleans, Phoenix, and Nashville. In Chicago, 391 of the 557 public schools require uniforms as do 81 of the 147 elementary schools in Dallas. New York City, the nation's largest school district, began requiring uniforms in 670 schools in 1999.

According to research conducted by Land's End, 8 percent of all public schools had uniform programs in 1997 and another 15 percent were likely to follow suit. This would mean nearly 25 percent of the nation's students will don uniforms in the beginning of the 21st century. Uniforms are becoming pervasive because they are warmly embraced by all of the affected constituents: students, teachers, parents, administrators, and juvenile corrections professionals. In fact, less than 1 percent of the students at the Long Beach, California, Unified School District, one of the first public school systems to adopt uniforms, have elected to opt out of the uniform policy. Separately, the growing number of voucher schools will be a boon to uniform manufacturers and retailers, for 60 percent of voucher students attend Catholic schools, where uniforms are standard. (For more on the growing popularity of voucher schools, see the section "Private Elementary Schools" in this chapter.)

Uniforms are credited with reducing school violence, decreasing peer pressure, and focusing students on learning. These objectives are relatively easy to achieve with uniforms because school policies prescribing uniforms are easy to implement and monitor, and noncompliance is easily detectable. As Bill Modze-leski, director of the Safe and Drug-Free Schools program at the U.S. Department of Education, says, "The beauty of uniform programs is that they are simple, doable, and easy."

Modular Classroom Manufacturers

Manufacturers of portable classrooms represent an interesting investment opportunity. First, classrooms are overcrowded: The Census Bureau reports that the number of Americans under age 18 was higher in 1998—70.2 million—than it was in 1966, when the number of baby boomers reached 69.9 million. Second, impressive political support exists for limiting class sizes; the Clinton administration, in mid-1998, proposed $12 billion in investments designed to limit the number of students in a classroom to 18. And in 1998, at least 25 states started or were considering some sort of initiative for class-size reduction.

Third, many communities have been balking at funding school construction. For instance, a 1995 study by the National School Boards Association found that proposed bond issues or tax hikes had failed over the previous five years in one of every four urban school districts surveyed. The result is that classrooms do not get built and that classes must be conducted in modular facilities. For instance, in Houston in 1996, voters rejected a $390 million bond proposal to build 15 schools and repair 84 others. Thus, about 47,000 Houston public school students were taking classes in 1,500 temporary classrooms outside existing schools. Fourth, the growing popularity of charter schools drives demand for modular classrooms because charter schools often need to find inexpensive facilities.

The primary modular classroom manufacturers positioned to benefit from the convergence of these trends are McGrath Rentcorp and Modtech.

Uniforms Build Self-Esteem and Foster Learning

More children are growing up in homes without the love and attention of a mother and a father. In even the best of such situations—when both parents, although living apart, want to share in the rearing of their children—children's sense of self-worth is diminished when they are shuttled back and forth from one parent to the other while never feeling like an intrinsic part of the fabric of either household. Many parents try to compensate for the breakdown of their household or their unavailability by indulging their children with designer wardrobes.

This parental-inspired materialism, compounded by incessant advertising by apparel designers and unrelenting peer pressure, has contributed to children judging their self-worth based on the clothes they wear. As New York City's schools chancellor, Rudy Crew, has said, "These young people have literally gotten the notion of human worth confused with the notion of material worth. It's time for us to clear this notion up. You are not what the label says in the back of your shirt."

Forward-looking educators want youths to base their self-image on academics, not fashion. School uniforms encourage students to develop their individuality and creativity through the use of their minds, attitudes, actions, and abilities, not merely through how they look. During the years that adolescents experience hormonal and anatomical development, they are physiologically destined to be extremely conscious of their appearance. However, an atmosphere in which all of their peers dress the same way creates a constant in adolescents' lives and removes one layer of distraction.

In addition to reducing lasciviousness, uniforms induce children to learn. As Linda Wells, editor in chief of *Allure* magazine, wrote, "When you wake up in the morning and put on your uniform, it's almost like sitting up straight in your chair. It's a really useful way to psychologically tune into a different environment. I think that appearance affects behavior and that looking neat and tidy fosters self-respect." To the extent that uniforms build confidence and self-esteem, students will refrain from crime and will instead take pride in their studies, extracurricular activities, and their school.

Uniforms Lead to Reduced School Violence

In a landmark 1996 speech, President Clinton said: "I challenge all our schools to teach character education, to teach good values and good citizenship. Our public schools should be able to require students to wear uniforms if that means that teenagers will stop killing each other over designer jackets." President Clinton subsequently directed the Department of Education to distribute a manual to the nation's 16,000 school districts suggesting how they could make school uniforms mandatory.

Support for using uniforms to reduce school violence has also come from the U.S. Conference of Mayors, which, at a national summit on school violence in October 1998, endorsed uniforms even for high school students; and from most school principals, who, according to a 1998 survey by the Educational Testing Service, believe that uniforms improve school discipline.

One of the tenets of a school uniform policy is to frustrate gangs, which require members to wear special colors or insignias that instill fear among students and teachers. Gang identification clothing has proven to be very disruptive at best and, at worst, results in children killing children to steal designer jackets or expensive basketball shoes.

Reducing violence at schools is the key to eradicating violence endured by the nation's youth. More than half of all crimes against teenagers occur on or near school property, and almost a fourth of all violent crimes against teenagers occur at school. According to the Justice Department, no other setting, except for prisons, experiences such a concentration of violence. In response to those findings, President Clinton reiterated his stance on school uniforms in a July 1998 speech before the American Federation of Teachers by saying that "mandatory uniforms would help reduce crime and violence, freeing children from danger."

The recent school uniform wave got its start when the Long Beach Unified School District in 1994 mandated simple blue and white outfits for pupils in kindergarten through eighth grade. After only two years the results of this policy were compelling. School violence, vandalism, and even drug possession fell precipitously. In fact, chemical substance possession fell 66 percent; weapons possession was down 80 percent; assault and battery offenses dropped by 34 percent and vandalism fell by 18 percent. Overall, crime in these schools fell from 3,222 incidents to just 920—a 71 percent drop even as enrollment rose 8 percent.

Even if not all of the improvements can be attributed to school uniforms, the correlation is more than coincidental. Crime rose 28 percent over the same two-year period in Long Beach high schools, which had no uniform policy. Although both the high school and elementary school students came from the same families and the same neighborhoods, a delineation of which students became deviant was clear. Other school districts have documented the reduction in violence that follows the implementation of school uniform programs. For instance, in Birmingham, Alabama, drug and weapon incidents dropped 30 percent in the two years after the school board required uniforms, and violent crime plunged 38 percent two years after Houston's schools adopted uniforms. Separately, private and parochial schools have long demonstrated a correlation between the use of uniforms and a lack of behavioral problems.

Moreover, school uniforms do more than just stem violence. One of the positive influences of uniforms surfaced when Long Beach's elementary attendance rates reached 94.5 percent in the 1995–1996 school year, the highest level in that district's 15 years of recordkeeping.

Uniforms Are an Inexpensive Crime Buster

School uniforms cost far less than the ad hoc uniforms children create for themselves and that often consist of Tommy Hilfiger and Calvin Klein ensembles.

Knight-Ridder newspapers calculated the cost of one typical urban public school teenager's school outfit for one day at $140; and that didn't include the cost of a $150 down jacket. If the cost of getting the right look for today's teen can be astronomical, the cost in stigmatization and peer pressure for *not* having the right clothes can be even higher.

On the contrary, the average cost for a whole uniform can be as low as $25 because the uniforms are plain, unadvertised, and mass produced. Many districts with mandatory uniform policies make the price comparison even more dramatic by buying uniforms in bulk at discounted rates and then selling them at reduced cost to their students. School officials believe that durability, reusability, and year-to-year consistency increase the economy of uniforms.

The administration at South Shore Middle School in Seattle found that the average cost of clothing a child in a school with a prescribed wardrobe is as much as 80 percent less than in schools without such a program. Many parents find that school uniforms represent savings in total clothing expenditures, and they further decrease these costs by arranging for hand-me-downs. For instance, schools in Washington, D.C., opened clothing banks so students can turn in old uniforms for their younger peers. Also, at some elementary and middle schools in Baltimore, 98 percent of graduating junior high school students donate their uniforms to the school.

Even when all of these initiatives fail to bring the cost of school uniforms within the budgets of all of the affected families, then states, school districts, and businesses are often willing to subsidize and donate uniforms. In one recent year alone, some 500 business partners donated more than $120,000 worth of clothing to help provide Long Beach students with uniforms. Disadvantaged students at George Washington Carver Elementary School in Kansas City, Missouri, receive their uniforms at no cost because the state and school district pay for the uniforms. Parents in San Antonio receive between $350,000 and $400,000 in uniform vouchers each year; and New York City Schools Chancellor Rudy Crew announced that his plan for school uniforms provides financial aid to families who cannot afford the uniforms.

The following are among the other attractions that uniforms offer students, parents and teachers:

- Uniforms help instill discipline. When children arrive at school in their uniforms, they begin the day with a mind-set focused on learning rather than playing. When a school is able to dictate its students' dress code, it conveys the message that the administration calls the shots on other issues, such as discipline. Uniforms also teach lessons in responsibility because children are held accountable for wearing complete uniforms maintained in good condition.

- Uniforms help bridge economic differences and make equal treatment more likely. Uniforms discourage clothes competition, make rich and poor students look more alike, and wean children from crass consumerism. Also, many educators believe that children from low-income families are short-changed in the classroom by teachers who have low expectations for them. Uniforms make treatment based on outward appearance almost impossible and forces teachers to know their students for their academic acumen and other attributes.

- Uniforms keep unwanted, often troublesome, youths off campus by making outsiders easily identifiable.

- Uniforms identify who should be in school. Because easily recognizable uniforms reduce truancy, strict dress codes help fund schools with pre-scribed dress codes as federal funds are distributed on the basis of a school's average daily attendance.

- Uniforms make it easier and faster for time-starved students to get dressed in the morning. Parents find less friction in preparing their children for school because there are no debates over what to wear.

Investment Vehicles

The drivers behind implementing school uniforms are more than academic. They are producing real results. Federated Department Stores' Macy's West reported that its school uniform business tripled from 1995 to 1997, and school uniform sales at Sears, Roebuck & Co. rose 50 percent in 1997. Other beneficiaries of the growing popularity of uniforms are such uniform manufacturers as Kettmann's School Uniforms, Active Knitting Ltd., and Ibiley School Uniforms. Although known primarily for its catalog business, Land's End is also a leading producer and distributor of school uniforms. And providing uniforms to school districts would be a natural progression for industrial uniform providers such as Unitog, G&K Services, and Cintas Corporation.

CHAPTER 2

Business Services

America's manufacturing sector has been extremely lean and mean since the early 1990s. However, a growing portion of the nation's output derives from the service sector, which has lagged the efficiency gains of manufacturing. Several business services providers are beginning to close this efficiency gap. For instance, document management software providers enable offices to automate their workflow, enhance collaboration, and make knowledge more accessible through expedient document retrieval. Also, professional employer organizations save small business owners incalculable time by handling their human resource responsibilities. Finally, government bureaucracies are outsourcing more of their administrative and disbursement responsibilities to highly efficient, for-profit companies such as Lockheed Martin and MAXIMUS.

Professional Employer Organizations

Red tape spewing uncontrollably out of Washington, D.C., threatens to strangle the economy's primary job creation machine. Small businesses (those employing fewer than 100 employees) have been responsible for roughly 90 percent of the job creation in the 1990s. Concurrent with this growth has been, and will continue to be, a torrential flood of labor regulations. The tragedy is that the smallest businesses are the employers least equipped to comply with the deciduous application of these onerous statutes. I believe the most promising solution to this problem lies with professional employer organizations (PEOs).

PEOs such as Barrett Business Services relieve small businesses from their personnel burdens. By acting as coemployers with their small business clients, PEOs contractually assume substantial employer rights, responsibilities, and risks. Some of the responsibilities and liabilities PEOs assume include actual disbursement of payroll, payroll tax compliance, human resources compliance, risk management, and personnel management. Even though PEOs provide comprehensive administrative services relating to employee matters, business owners retain complete control over their business, including the right to hire, promote, and terminate workers.

PEOs Spell Exciting Opportunities

PEOs have a long history of explosive growth. Although the PEO industry did not exist in the early 1980s, it generated over $27 billion in revenues in 1998, up from $5 billion in 1991. The PEO industry grew at a 30 percent annual rate for more than a decade, ending in 1997. From 1984 to 1997, the number of PEOs soared from roughly 50 to more than 2000 while the number of employees coemployed by PEOs skyrocketed from fewer than 50,000 to approximately 2.4 million.

TIP: Because PEOs serve such fertile markets, their management teams do not feel that it is necessary to try to grow by assuming risks (and charging higher fees) for their clients' noncompliance with discrimination, sexual harassment statutes, and the like. (For further discussion of employment discrimination and sexual harassment, please refer to the section on "Employment Practices Liability Insurance" in this chapter.)

The PEO industry should be able to accelerate its torrential growth rate as it has achieved critical mass in many geographic markets and is confronted with monumental opportunities. The primary market—but not the only market—for PEOs are businesses that have 100 or fewer employees. The number of workers employed by these small businesses reached 52 million in late 1998. At that time Loren Hulber, president and chief executive officer of NovaCare Employee Services, stated that PEOs had captured less than 5 percent of their primary market.

Even more exciting is research from the National Association of Professional Employer Organizations indicating that the number of workers employed by small businesses will expand from 52 million in 1998 to 63 million in 2002 and that if PEOs maintain their 30 percent growth rate, they will still serve only 10 percent of their primary market in 2002. One reason that I believe these heady growth rates will continue is that the industry is gaining more credibility as such respected business service companies as Fidelity Investments, Automated Data Processing, CNA Insurance, Paychex Inc., American Express, Wackenhut Corp., and Kelly Services enter the PEO market. The underlying reason that PEOs should enjoy rapid growth far into the future is that they yield very important benefits to all parties involved—small business owners, worksite employees, and the government.

TIP: The Small Business Administration reported that a record 885,000 small businesses were created in 1997, up from 758,000 in 1993. Other companies that will benefit from small-business creation include office supply stores such as Staples, Office Depot, and OfficeMax as well as New England Business Service, a major supplier of business forms and related products to small businesses. Factors that ensure future growth in small business creation include the following: (1) corporate downsizings and restructurings result in the dismissal of many white-collar workers who decide to strike out on their own; (2) efforts to outsource various government services (e.g., the collection of fines and child support payments) should result in a reduction of bureaucrats; (3) the price performance of personal computers doubles every 18 months and reduces the expense of starting a business; and (4) the venture capital market remains a vibrant source of capital for developing businesses.

PEOs Are the Salvation of Small Businesses

Small businesses are clearly receptive to outsourcing their increasingly complex employee-related issues. (Perhaps customer satisfaction with PEOs was best demonstrated when 60 percent of Staff Leasing's new clients in 1997 came from existing clients' word-of-mouth references.) The extent of the hassle and expense of matters such as personnel management, health benefits, workers' compensation claims, payroll, payroll tax compliance, and unemployment insurance claims is exemplified by the following:

- According to the U.S. Small Business Administration, the average annual cost of regulation, paperwork, and tax compliance for firms with fewer than 500 employees is roughly $5,000 per employee.
- The average cost of administering benefits to an employee is $1,000 a year, but the cost for small businesses is closer to $1,700.
- Average small business owners spend between 7 and 25 percent of their time handling employee-related paperwork, leaving owners with as little as 75 percent of their time to run their businesses. Many small business owners report that the benefits realized from being able to devote more of their time and energy to managing their businesses are even greater than the substantial dollars saved by subcontracting human resources responsibilities to PEOs.
- According to Jeffries & Company, the human resources function at small firms is often borne by the business owner (which may be the highest relative cost of all because that owner typically drives the core business of a small company) or an inexperienced employee, thus exposing these businesses to the high cost of noncompliance.

Small businesses remain unprepared for meeting the challenges that the administration of employee benefits present. According to a 1998 survey by Employease, only one in four businesses invested in information systems to manage human resources and benefits information. Thus, it is simply more expedient to outsource to PEOs the administration of benefits; the preparation of payrolls; the calculation of withholdings; the payment of insurance premiums; and the formulation of policies covering recruitment, employee conduct, and termination. Outsourcing to PEOs also represents cost savings as studies show that doing so saves between 3 and 5 percent of annual payroll expenses.

Much of this savings is achieved through better management of workers' compensation expenses. First, PEOs such as Staff Leasing are able to obtain more favorable workers' compensation premium rates than small businesses. By aggregating all of their clients' employees into large purchasing pools, PEOs gain negotiating leverage with workers' compensation insurance providers. Second, PEOs help their clients reduce workers' compensation costs by implementing safety processes—such as requiring workers to wear safety goggles or protective glasses—that reduce the overall number and severity of workplace injuries, which results in a corresponding reduction in future insurance premiums. (For more on worker safety, refer to "Protective Clothing" in Chapter 10.) PEOs also reduce costs by fostering worker rehabilitation programs.

TRAP: Many PEOs derive as much as 40 to 50 percent of their income from workers' compensation arbitrage. (Workers' compensation arbitrage entails a PEO's aggregated employee list being used to purchase workers' compensation in bulk and then the PEO sells the same coverage to clients at marked-up prices.) As PEOs continue to cover a growing percentage of the nation's workforce, more state insurance commissioners are likely to scrutinize workers' compensation arbitrage. And as this arbitrage is curtailed (as has already happened in California), the earnings of PEOs could plunge (as has already happened to Employee Solutions).

Such measures by PEOs can lead to substantial savings because worker-related injuries cost employers over $53 billion in medical expenses and lost employee productivity each year. Better management of employers' insurance premiums, workers' compensation contributions, and other worker benefits is very important as these items cumulatively account for 42 percent of gross payroll costs.

A reprieve from administrative burdens as well as cost saving are not the only benefits small businesses realize when they contract with PEOs like TriNet Employer Group. In fact, a National Federation of Independent Business survey of small businesses in 1996 showed that 6 of the top 13 major problem areas for small businesses are issues addressed by PEOs. Some of the other advantages realized by contracting with PEOs include:

- Providing better employee benefits packages, which helps small businesses attract and retain employees
- Providing professional human resources services such as employee hand-books, forms, and the articulation of policies and procedures
- Providing professional compliance with regulations promulgated by govern-ment agencies such as the Occupational Safety and Health Administration (OSHA) and the Equal Employment Opportunity Commission (EEOC)

PEOs Are Beneficial for Worksite Employees

PEOs such as NovaCare Employee Services are attractive to worksite employ-ees for several reasons. First, PEOs ensure that worksite employees are provided with a workplace that is safe, conducive to productivity, and operated in compli-ance with employment laws and regulations. Studies have shown that job satis-faction and productivity increase when workers are provided quality human resource services like employee manuals, grievance procedures, and improved communications with management. Also, enhanced job security results from business owners lowering their employment costs by leveraging PEOs' econo-mies of scale.

Second, PEOs provide worksite employees with Fortune 500–quality em-ployee benefits, including health insurance, a host of retirement savings plans, dental care, and behavioral health care programs as well as many other benefits, such as discounts on health club memberships or warehouse clubs. Interestingly, a study by BT Alex Brown indicated that 40 percent of the companies that have signed with a PEO were able to upgrade their employee benefits package over what they had previously, and one-fourth of those companies could offer health care and other benefits for the first time.

The following are among the additional benefits workers enjoy when their employer affiliates with a PEO:

- Accurate and timely receipt of paychecks
- Professional assistance with employment-related problems that includes up-to-date information on labor regulations and workers' rights
- Efficient and responsive claims processing for health coverage and retire-ment contributions
- Portable benefits that allow employees to move from one PEO client to another without losing their eligibility for benefits

Government Benefits from PEO Growth

PEOs and the government enjoy a symbiotic relationship. As government agencies continue to add layers to the body of employment law, small businesses become more inclined to outsource to PEOs. This is because compliance with such regulations as the Americans with Disabilities Act, the Fair Labor Standards Act, and the Workers Adjustment and Retraining Notification Act is difficult, and penalties for failure to comply are severe. The difficulty of compliance is compounded by a diversity of state statutes, constant legislative revisions, and malleable legal interpretations.

As for penalties, violations of Occupational Safety and Health regulations carry a $7,000 fine per violation in California, and failure to correct violations is punishable by a $7,000 per day fine. In Florida, employers who fail to file the First Report of Injury or Illness form (in workers' compensation–related incidents) are fined $100 to $500 per form.

TIP: The accounting treatment for PEO revenues, required by generally accepted accounting principles (GAAP), is that all of the PEO client's payroll costs—including salaries, wages, and fixed employment taxes of a client's employees—must be recorded as revenues on a PEO's income statement. These noncontrollable revenues are expensed on a dollar-for-dollar basis on the direct expense line of the income statement. Therefore, a PEO's gross profit excludes any amounts billed as salaries, wages, and fixed employment taxes. The result of this revenue "gross-up" is that compared with other business services, PEO revenues appear much larger and margins smaller than they really are.

As a general rule of thumb, Brian Kearns of Salomon Smith Barney assumes controllable revenues are roughly 10 percent of total revenues recorded on the income statement. Therefore, corresponding controllable margins are about ten times the margins calculated from the SEC documents.*

On the other side of the equation, the government benefits from the PEOs' success. First, PEOs such as Administaff professionally prepare, report, collect, and deposit employment taxes with state and federal authorities. Not only are most errors avoided but PEOs consolidate numerous small companies' employment tax filings into one submission and PEOs remit taxes every three days as

---

*Brian J. Kearns–Salomon Smith Barney, *The Wall Street Transcript,* Analyst Interview, Special Healthcare Services Edition, September 1998, p.11.

opposed to quarterly. Second, PEOs allow government agencies to reach multiple businesses through a single-employer entity, which is especially important in communicating government requirements and changes to small business regulation. Other benefits the government derives through PEOs include the extension of medical benefits to more workers and the resolution of many problems before they reach court.

Additional Investor Attractions of PEOs

According to Lehman Brothers' Bernard Picchi, the PEO industry's addressable market will present a $1.5 trillion annual opportunity by 2005, up from the $27 billion in revenues generated in 1998. The explosive growth confronting the PEO industry is due to a combination of rapid small business formation; capturing a larger percentage of existing and new small businesses; benefiting from these small businesses increasing their headcount; selling more ancillary products to clients; and serving larger employers. As for the last point, PEOs served only 1 percent of the businesses that employed between 100 and 500 workers in 1997.

Many aspects of managing PEOs are easier and less risky than managing other businesses. For instance, PEOs have no inventory that can be stolen or burned, out of season, misrouted, or depreciated. After assembling a staff of competent customer care representatives and establishing a robust management information system, PEOs face marginal capital expenditures. The industry rarely has a problem with uncollectible receivables. In fact, PEOs enjoy a positive float as their clients typically remit payments electronically to PEOs on Wednesdays, whereas PEOs usually wait until Fridays to pay their worksite employees.

TRAP: PEOs are responsible for paying their worksite employees regardless of whether they receive payment from their clients. Thus, investors should only invest in PEOs that adequately screen their clients' financial stability.

The following are among the other attractions PEOs—especially the larger PEOs—offer investors:

- Revenues are predictable because PEOs usually retain between 80 and 85 percent of their clients every year.
- Because PEOs have fiduciary responsibilities as employers—payroll, payroll taxes, prepayments on health insurance, and workers' compensation coverage—government overseers require PEOs to have nonleveraged balance sheets.

- Electronic business-to-business commerce and document management are of great help to PEOs. (See "Document Management" in this chapter.) For instance, technology allows PEOs to eliminate most of the paperwork associated with processing paychecks. After clients electronically submit their employees' timesheets (and after the PEO reviews the timesheets for accuracy), direct deposits of workers' paychecks can be accomplished with little more than the press of a button. Also, the Internet allows workers to review their retirement and profit-sharing accounts as well as read about their health coverage whenever they wish. In fact, Paul Sarvadi, president and CEO of Administaff, said that over 30 percent of his company's activity occurs when Administaff's offices are closed.

- PEOs have the opportunity to earn returns on pools of investable capital, including 401(k) plan dollars, workers' compensation insurance reserves, and health insurance reserves.

- The larger PEOs can afford to invest in the technology that will yield economies of scale in processing employee benefits. In addition, larger PEOs are better able to offer enhanced employee portability. With employee portability, worksite employees can move from company to company while their benefits and human resource administration continue to reside with a given PEO.

- PEOs enjoy the opportunity to cross-sell additional services to their worksite employee base. Mark Allen, senior analyst at Robinson-Humphrey, best explained the rationale by saying, "While Americans are inundated with junk mail, the one envelope that everyone always opens is their pay envelope." Examples of products that some PEOs are cross-selling include insurance, mortgages, financial planning, long-distance phone services, online access services, retail club membership programs, and travel services. However, TriNet Employer Group's Martin Babinec issued a perceptive warning to investors about too aggressively projecting the success of such cross-selling efforts: because the PEOs' direct relationships are with companies and not employees, chances of success may be limited.

Leading Industry Players

The leading pure-play professional employer organizations include Administaff, Barrett Business Services, Employee Solutions, NovaCare Employee Services, Staff Leasing, TriNet Employer Group, and Vincam.

Insights into the Employment Staffing Services Industry

Revenues generated by the domestic employment staffing industry rose at a 17 percent compounded annual growth rate, from $25 billion in 1992 to $63 billion in 1998. Mark Marcon of Wheat First Union believes that this industry will grow to at least $138 billion in revenues in 2006.

One of the most important drivers is the appeal of "just-in-time" labor to businesses wishing to convert the formerly fixed-cost nature of payroll into a more variable cost to meet peak demand. Another factor in the growth of staffing services is that employers can audition workers before hiring them on a permanent basis. This helps employers avoid hiring people who are not suitable that in turn reduces the incidence of wrongful termination lawsuits. (A detailed discussion of employment law and liability is found in this chapter in the section "Employment Practices Liability Insurance.") These suits are no small matter as Jury Verdicts Research found that over 50 percent of wrongful termination suits are ruled in the plaintiffs' favor with an average award of $219,000.

The following are among the most interesting investor imperatives vis-à-vis the employment staffing industry:

- Traditional employment agencies such as Manpower, Robert Half International, and StaffMark should prosper from Americans' increasing tendency to job hop. According to the Bureau of Labor Statistics, Americans hold an average of 8.6 different jobs between ages 18 and 32. Going forward, the number of job changes should increase as Aon Consulting found a 2.2-point decline in 1998's workforce commitment index versus the 1997 index.
- Employment agencies such as Alternative Resources, General Employment Enterprises, Metamor Worldwide, and Cotelligent that specialize in placing computer programmers stand to benefit from the voracious demand for such professionals. However, Herbert Imhoff, chairman and president of General Employment Enterprises, indicated that the downside is that atomized computer programmers often resign within the first 90 or 180 days of their employment, which causes the employment agencies to lose large percentages of their placement fees.

- Foreign businesses, particularly in Europe, are increasingly receptive to temporary labor. (The primary reason is that it is nearly impossible to fire full-time employees, and their benefits are extravagant.) For instance, Europe's temporary help market is growing more than 10 percent a year. In the summer of 1998, French Labor Minister Martine Aubry noted that "86 percent of new hires are on short-term contracts, usually for six months, renewable once." The Netherlands is the world leader in temporary workers—it has the biggest proportion in its labor force with 3.2 percent. Spain's temporary labor force is growing the fastest as evidenced by Manpower's deriving 719 percent more revenue from that country in 1997 than in 1996. Even the percentage of Japanese workers expected to stay at one company for their entire career is expected to fall from 81 percent in 1995 to 70 percent in 2000, according to Niekkeren. Companies best positioned to capitalize on these foreign opportunities include Professional Staff plc, Adecco, and Select Appointments.
- As the leading provider of temporary employment for entry-level and manual laborers, Labor Ready represents an interesting vehicle through which investors can play the trend of people moving from welfare into the workforce (see "Government Outsourcing" in this chapter).

Litigation

The United States is easily the world's most litigious nation. Even back in 1995, the market for legal services was estimated at $114 billion. America has more lawyers than any other country and awards are far higher in the United States than anywhere else in the world.

Practicing law is a highly lucrative business. According to *American Lawyer* magazine's survey of the nation's 100 top-grossing firms, average profits per partner increased 14 percent in 1997 to $587,000. The 1997 ranking was the first in which all of the "Top 10" firms paid partners an average of at least $1 million. Overall, billing rates rose by more than 6 percent for partners in 1997 while rates rose 8.2 percent for associates, according to Altman Weil, Inc.

Although investors cannot buy shares in law firms, they *can* gain exposure to the massive litigation in the United States by purchasing shares of companies that support lawyers in their discovery procedures.

Extent of Lawyers and Litigation

According to the American Bar Association, there were 985,900 licensed lawyers in the U.S at the end of 1997. The United States accounts for 70 percent of the world's lawyers. To compare the incidence of lawyers, there was one lawyer for every 274 Americans at the end of 1997, while the ratio of lawyers to citizens in Japan was 1 to 1,319, and 1 to 4,200 in France.

At the end of 1996, there were 87.5 million cases filed in state courts (which accounted for 98 percent of all cases filed in the United States). Liability Consultants found that tort filings involving premises liability have increased over 260 percent in the ten years ending in 1997. At that time, the average negotiated settlement was more than $545,000, and the average jury award was $3.35 million.

The costs of these lawsuits, settlements, and awards are massive. According to Tillinghast-Towers Perrin, liability lawsuits cost corporate America nearly $175 billion in 1997, and they continue to grow 5 percent a year. In addition, consumers have been spending about $45 billion annually on legal services since 1989.

Investment Opportunities

Companies such as Exponent analyze scientific and engineering accidents, failures, and disasters. Such companies offer laboratory and product-testing facilities as well as engineering, automotive, aviation, and marine investigations. Other services rendered by the likes of Exponent include environmental and risk assessment.

Companies such as Exponent and Engineering Animation also provide visualization and animation services in accident reconstruction. Additionally, companies like FTI, Inc., and Decision Quest find expert witnesses, consult in jury selection, and maintain shadow juries (which are composed of individuals who match the same demographic profiles of actual jurors) to understand how actual juries will respond to different legal arguments and tactics. Interestingly, FTI, Inc., has an economic analysis unit that assesses personal injury damages, employment and commercial liability, and business appraisals as well as analyzing claims for insurance companies.

An interesting concept is a legal service plan that offers members reduced rates on such stipulated services as reviewing contracts, preparing wills, or trial defense for a set number of hours in return for a monthly premium. Thus, companies such as Pre-Paid Legal Services enable their clients to receive reputable legal assistance on very reasonable terms and without the worry of ruinous legal expenses.

The final area of opportunity in connection with the proliferation of litigation is computer evidence services offered by companies such as Ontrack Data International. Computer evidence services consist of recovering and analyzing data that may be used as evidence in legal proceedings. Companies like Ontrack Data can determine if data were deleted, tampered with, modified, or destroyed. These companies are able to provide a complete recovery of inaccessible data and find the electronic "smoking gun" used in courtroom settings.

TIP: Another area of opportunity within the litigation theme is structured settlement services offered by companies such as J. G. Wentworth and Enhance Financial Services. These companies arrange to pay a large up-front lump sum of money to people awarded substantial damages that would otherwise be paid over many years. Companies like Enhance Financial Services profit by paying out in one large sum a discounted present value of the structured settlement. The size of the structured settlement market was $40 billion in 1997. Companies like Enhance Financial Services are expanding their services to include paying lottery winners up front, a $33 billion market in 1997 and growing by about $3.5 billion a year.

The data recovery business offers tremendous potential as a result of the proliferation of E-mail. International Data Corporation has predicted that 100 million people will use E-mail in U.S. corporations by 2000, but most business users do not use this method of communication with care. A November 1997 survey of 800 corporate human resource managers found that only 52 percent of the companies polled had written policies governing E-mail use—and of these only a quarter actually were enforcing them. This is problematic because electronic memos are being used against many companies—Microsoft, for example—in trials. According to Computer Forensics, some companies have spent $1 million or more to comply with E-mail discovery requests.

Employment Practices Liability Insurance

In one episode of *Seinfeld,* the star of the TV show had difficulty speaking to his Native American date because he could not think of anything to say that could not be construed as offensive. Today, employers face the same dilemmas. Almost any action they take, or fail to take, could be construed as discriminatory, a form of harassment, fostering a hostile workplace or an infringement of a growing number of employment laws. Not only do current workers file suits for alleged wrongs in employment practices but job applicants and former employees are frequent plaintiffs in these cases. Thus, employers are flocking to purchase employment practices liability insurance (EPLI), which covers liability for employer malfeasance, from insurers such as AIG, Chubb, Exel Limited, and Reliance.

Employment Lawsuits Are Pervasive

According to the U.S. Judicial Conference, 20 to 25 percent of all federal district court cases are employment lawsuits; and polling conducted by the Society for Human Resources Management has revealed that 60 percent of companies become the target of at least one employment practice liability suit every five years. Other indications of the rapid growth of employment-related litigation include:

- Total federal lawsuits charging various violations of employment law are more numerous (19,095) and have increased faster (up 127 percent from 1991 to 1997) than suits in any other civil rights category.
- According to *Business Insurance,* cases involving employment practices have increased by 2,166 percent over the 20-year period ending in 1997.

There are many reasons for such widespread charges of employer wrongdoing. First, the general deterioration of job security caused by aggressive downsizing and restructurings and the diminished sense of employee loyalty makes workers less reluctant to sue their employers. Second, there has been greater visibility of workplace issues resulting from such high profile media events as Anita Hill's alleging that she was subject to sexual harassment by Clarence Thomas in the workplace.

Sexual Harassment Cases Soar

Sexual harassment cases in particular have been exploding. In fact, the number of sexual harassment complaints lodged with the Equal Employment Opportunity Commission (EEOC) alone more than doubled, from 6,883 in 1991 to 15,889 in 1997. Among many examples from the late 1990s of claims for sexual harassment are the suit against Mitsubishi Motor Manufacturing of America by the EEOC for $150 million and a $94 million claim against American Stores' Lucky supermarkets.

Where gender discrimination and sexual harassment claims once consisted overwhelmingly of women accusing men of misbehavior, such claims have turned into a free-for-all. A group of men actually filed suit against Hooters Restaurants for discriminatory hiring practices and a male bank teller at Chase Manhattan Bank sued his employer on the grounds that calendars of male models displayed by his female colleagues fostered a hostile environment. If this were not enough, same-sex lawsuits have already begun to fly with one of the first being filed by a roughneck on an offshore drilling rig who claimed that his supervisor made numerous unwanted sexual advances towards him.

Another driver of sexual harassment cases is the fact that many romances begin in the office and then later sour. According to a Bureau of National Affairs study, nearly one-third of all romances begin at work, meaning that between 6 million and 8 million Americans enter into such relationships every year.

Employment Legislation

The growing volume of employment legislation creates new classes of protected workers. (See the previous section, "Professional Employer Organizations.") Because every worker shares several classifications—gender, race, national origin, religion—with a worker that has won a settlement from an employer, precedent exists for every worker filing an employment practices lawsuit. The following are among the employment acts protecting workers from discrimination:

- The Family and Medical Leave Act of 1993 forbids firing workers who take undue time off to care for family members.
- The Americans with Disabilities Act of 1990 prohibits discrimination on the basis of physical or mental impairment.
- The Older Workers Benefit Protection Act of 1990 protects workers over the age of 40 from discrimination.
- The Equal Pay Act forbids paying workers differently solely on the basis of gender.

Employment Violations Are Exorbitantly Expensive

The following are examples of the expenses that employers can incur for violating employment law:

- On February 12, 1998, a jury awarded $80.7 million to a former United Parcel Service employee who said she was punished for accusing a coworker of poking her in the breast.
- When Astrodome USA settled a $500,000 lawsuit with 25 women from a janitorial service in June 1997, it was proved that one need not even speak English nor know one's rights to successfully bring sexual harassment claims against an employer.

- In September 1998, Mitsubishi Motor Manufacturing of America reached a $3 million settlement with 87 job applicants with disabilities, such as diabetes and asthma, who filed charges under the Americans with Disabilities Act.

Investment Opportunities

The value of EPLI premiums doubled from $100 million in mid-1996 to $200 million in early 1998. According to the *Journal of Commerce,* EPLI premiums should double from $1 billion in 1999 to $2 billion in 2007. Because of greater availability, premiums for EPLI contracts have been falling, which expands the potential market. In 1993, EPLI premiums for companies with fewer than 100 employees were in the $50,000 to $100,000 range, but by early 1998, the premium on the same policy would have been closer to $5,000.

TRAP: One of the drawbacks to purchasing EPLI is that companies dislike losing control over defending themselves to their insurers—a condition usually stipulated under EPLI contracts. Also, some directors' and officers' liability insurers modify their policies to cover employment practices for additional premiums.

Despite the growth of EPLI, the market was underpenetrated in the late 1990s. According to a survey of 1,250 Marsh & McLennan clients in 1997 (with revenues between $200 million and $1 billion), half had less than $50 million in EPLI coverage. The rapid growth of EPLI purchases and the extent of the underpenetrated market bode well for EPLI providers such as AIG, Chubb, Exel Limited, and Reliance.

Document Management

As the late 1990s ushered in the knowledge era, companies began viewing their data as a strategic asset and realized that properly managing their intellectual property enhances their competitiveness. Robert Olson, president of IntraNet Solutions, remarked that "up to 85 percent of the data in the average Fortune 500 company is contained in documents."* To improve competitiveness and reduce

---

The Wall Street Transcript–CEO Supplement, CEO Interview, IntraNet Solutions, December 1998, p. 78.

costs, companies are budgeting increasingly generous resources to document management software to access and harness that wealth of information more easily.

Managing documents is a monumental challenge as roughly 1 trillion copies of documents are generated every year in the United States. To make matters worse, documents are stored in a variety of locations—computers, Web pages, disks, filing cabinets, employees' memories—making it difficult to retrieve information. In manufacturing organizations, up to 40 percent of professionals' time is wasted searching or storing information versus using information to make decisions. And as much as 15 percent of total gross revenue in an organization is spent creating, managing, and distributing information contained in documents. Thus, software companies such as Documentum and FileNET are developing programs to accommodate the demands of document management.

Industry Background

As Robert Kugel of FAC/Equities explains, almost from the start of the computing age, managers tried to determine how information technology could improve the flow of information through their organizations. Because most of the information was in printed form, the initial focus was on eliminating paper. The act of physically moving, processing, storing, and retrieving paper records created numerous problems: A significant percentage are routinely misdirected or lost; moving them from place to place is labor intensive and time consuming; only one person at a time can handle them; they consume a great deal of space; and process management is extremely difficult.

As the 1990s unfolded, the goal of managing physical documents more efficiently evolved into the broader concept of managing unstructured data. The term *unstructured data* was invented to distinguish information that easily fits into standard database architectures (e.g., accounting records, names and addresses, and phone numbers) from information that does not conform to standard database architectures (e.g., marketing intelligence, legal text, regulatory submissions, maintenance manuals, insurance claims, computer-aided design drawings, correspondence, E-mail, video, photographs, and sound).

In the late 1990s, unstructured information made up the largest portion of an organization's knowledge base. However, it was usually still inaccessible, either because it was not in digital form or because it was trapped in isolated files scattered across multiple networks.

The Importance of Document Management

Documents are a critical asset in contemporary business environments. Examples of business-critical documents are aircraft maintenance manuals, drug manufacturing formulas, current and approved standard operating procedures for manufacturing plants, and sales reports. The knowledge such documents contain fuels the productivity of a company's most vital business processes—from product development, engineering design, and manufacturing to marketing, sales, and distribution.

Despite the importance of documents and the value of the information they contain, documents are not user-friendly. In fact,

- in a typical corporate environment, documents are created, modified, distributed, and stored using multiple software programs;
- these software programs operate on a variety of computing platforms that may be geographically dispersed, with little compatibility or data-sharing capability between systems; and
- the above factors, combined with overwhelming amounts of information, increase the risk that relevant information is out-of-date or inaccessible.

Without an effective means of searching for and reusing enterprise information, workers are often forced to recreate documents from scratch, duplicating effort and increasing the margin for error. As a result, important processes are often stalled because the documents on which they depend are out-of-date, inaccurate, or simply unavailable to the people who need them. The inability to access and manage such critical business information hampers knowledge workers' productivity and presents one of the greatest obstacles facing Global 1000 organizations.

In light of these factors, many organizations have begun to recognize that a competitive advantage can be gained from the more effective use of available information, in particular by the rapid searching of text or other unstructured information contained in internal or external databases, including the Internet. For instance, sales representatives for industrial solvents will be more effective if they can quickly research their competitors' product descriptions before making a sales call, and research engineers will be more productive if they can locate solutions to daunting technical problems from seemingly unrelated work performed in a separate division.

Specific Benefits of Document Management

While document management helps companies in a wide array of industries become more efficient in general, the following are among the specific benefits of deploying document management software:

- *Shorter time to market.* This is crucial as pharmaceutical companies forgo as much as $1 million for every day of delay in receiving regulatory approval for a new drug, while high-technology industries are under constant pressure to accelerate their product development cycles. Also, in project industries the inability to access the abundance of information required to submit bids on competitive projects can lead to lost contracts, inaccuracies, and cost overruns.
- *Increased operating efficiencies in manufacturing.* Access to engineering changes for the factory floor requires speedy dissemination of design documentation, and plant maintenance regimens must be easy to retrieve.
- *Decision support in a world of increasing information overload.* Filtering out data that are immaterial during searches is important for making intelligent decisions.
- *Ability to capitalize on the opportunities presented by the Internet.* Since the Internet has emerged as a crucial medium for communications and information publishing, it has dramatically increased the volumes of unstructured information available in organizations. The Internet and intranets are used to distribute information to the public and an enterprise's employees as well as functioning as the medium of electronic commerce. These applications require electronic document creation, modification, maintenance, and storage throughout a document's lifecycle to reduce costs and to increase the effectiveness of the information.
- *Compliance requirements in process industries.* Regulated companies have to provide access to the latest information on manufacturing procedures, plant safety, and disposal procedures for hazardous waste to satisfy such regulations as those of the Occupational Safety and Health Administration.

Growth Drivers for Document Management

The document management business offers enormous opportunity for companies such as OpenText. Providing software to manage unstructured information generated only $700 million in revenues in 1997. By contrast, software applications that manage structured information—data about customer orders, inventory, accounts payable, and the like—generated about $10 billion in 1997. One indication of how far document management companies can grow is that unstructured information exceeds the volume of structured information by a factor of three to four times. Thus, many analysts believe that the market for unstructured information will grow to $1.6 billion by 2000.

TIP: As costs of memory and processing power continue to decline, document management systems, once feasible only for Fortune 100 companies, will be increasingly adopted by smaller companies.

The key trends driving document management include the following:

- The price/performance of both hardware and software are improving. Because unstructured data management is complex, handling it requires ever-growing memory and processing power. The price of both has, and is likely to continue to, plummet.
- Advances in object technology (itself memory and processing-power intensive) are making these types of applications far more powerful, versatile, and easier to create and modify.
- Communications infrastructures such as intranets and the Internet are increasingly robust. Faster electronic networks are important because document management requires the rapid retrieval and sharing of information.
- The proliferation of imaging technology—mainly created by scanners and machines—allows digital image files to be easily entered, indexed, managed, manipulated, stored, and retrieved.

Growing Acceptance of Document Management

Just as industrial America spent much of the 1980s and 1990s prodding the blue-collar sector to become more efficient, the growing service economy will focus on ratcheting up white-collar productivity. An example of contemporary white-collar inefficiency comes from studies showing that in 1998 knowledge workers spent 20 percent of their time searching for, or updating and sharing, documents, and doing paper-based document distribution and storage. The following are among the indications that enterprises are receptive to deploying document management software to improve white-collar productivity:

- In a 1998 survey of 500 chief information officers, Deloitte & Touche found document management software to be the fourth most promising new technology (behind data warehousing, LANs, and intranets), with more than 60

Printing Ink

One of the prime beneficiaries of the proliferation of documents are companies that produce printer consumables such as ink and toner. Ink-jet and laser toner cartridges yielded over $12 billion in sales in 1997, and Cap Ventures, a market research firm, estimates that these two products will generate sales of $17 billion in 2002. Companies such as Hewlett-Packard, Dataproducts, Nu-Kote Holdings, and Nashua Corporation that can meet this torrential demand are growing aggressively as a result of the following trends:

- *The installed base of printers and office machines is expanding very rapidly.* For instance, sales to the small-office and home-office market were about $1.32 billion in 1998 and are expected to grow 10 percent a year through at least 2002. The greater functionality and printing speeds of digital copiers—which International Data Corporation expects will surge from 176,000 units in 1997 to 930,000 units by 2002—should also result in more intense usage.

- *Printers and office machines are printing more pages.* United States sales of office paper reached an estimated $9.23 billion in 1998, up about fourfold over the preceding ten years. The number of pages consumed in United States offices is rising 20 percent each year and is expected to reach 6 trillion by 2000. Every time a United States corporation's revenue increases by $100 million, its employees end up using 8.8 million additional sheets of paper that year, according to the Association of Information and Image Management.

- *The use of E-mail and the Internet is soaring.* Printing skyrockets 40 percent in an office when E-mail is introduced. I have found, too, that I am among those that use the Internet as an electronic filing cabinet: I usually discard reports that I print only to reprint another identical report a few weeks later when I want to review the same information.

- *Color printing consumes much more ink than black-and-white printing.* According to Lyra Research, color-printing technology is expected to grow 20 percent a year. One reason is that page coverage averages 40 percent with color printing versus only 5 percent with black-and-white printing. Another reason is declining cost: Xerox expects to drive down the cost of its color pages—roughly 15¢ apiece in early 1998—to 4 or 5¢ by 2000. In addition, color ink-jet printers have become extremely inexpensive; some cost only $89 in 1998.

- *The craze for digital cameras is growing.* Digital cameras are proving to be wildly popular, with their unit shipments expected to soar from 2.7 million in 1997 to 28.1 million in 2002. Consumers like being able to manipulate pictures by enhancing their own appearance, deleting ex-lovers, and pasting in new friends. Other factors driving sales of digital cameras include plunging scanner and printer costs, unlimited reproducibility, the ability to instantly send pictures over the Internet, enhanced resolution, and the growing ease of connecting the cameras to computers. In fact, some cameras are designed to connect directly to printers—an easy solution for serving the 57 percent of American households that did not have computers in 1997. Not only is the digital photography revolution resulting in more pictures being printed, but ink covers 100 percent of every page on which a digital picture is printed, dwarfing the typical 5 percent page coverage on letters and spreadsheets.

Printing is not only a booming business but a lucrative one as well. According to one industry insider, an ink-jet cartridge that retails for $22 to $30 holds less than 50¢ worth of ink. Even including the other parts, such as the print head and allocated research and development, the cost of producing an ink-jet cartridge sold to a retailer for $18 is less than $5.

Industry Participants

Companies positioned to profit from these trends include ink and toner manufacturers such as Hewlett-Packard, Dataproducts, Nu-Kote Holdings, and Nashua Corporation. As the world's leading wholesale distributor of non-paper computer and office automation supplies, Daisytek International is a good play on the printer consumable business. Standard Microsystems is a leading manufacturer of the print heads that are responsible for cartridges dispersing ink onto printed pages. And Jeff Spetalnick, president of Infinity Financial Group, has pointed out that Cabot Corporation is developing innovative ink-jet printer cartridges based on carbon black.

Derivative plays include the dominant printer manufacturers such as Hewlett-Packard and Lexmark as well as Xeikon, which makes high-speed digital color printers for professional applications. Splash Technology produces software-based color servers that transform printing engines into powerful networked printers. Finally, ENCAD makes wide-format color ink-jet printers that are used in graphic arts, architecture, and mapping.

percent of those responding rating the technology important over the next two years.

- In another survey of intranet users, document management was ranked the number three intranet application, behind E-mail/faxing and corporate communications.
- According to one survey of 500 leading information technology professionals, 98 percent expected a payback on their deployment of document management software in less than two years, and 60 percent expected a payback in less than one year. Projections of such rapid paybacks make it easier to win budgetary approvals for document management software throughout an organization.

Industry Players

The primary players in document management include Documentum, Eastman Software, FileNET, IntraNet Solutions, Lason, and OpenText. In addition, F.Y.I. Inc. specializes in converting paper documents to digital form.

Government Outsourcing

Beginning in the mid-1990s, state and local governments have been striving to become more efficient, and as they have downsized, they have realized they must outsource their responsibilities. Specific programs that are being outsourced include welfare-to-workfare, managed care enrollment, disabilities benefits, and child support enforcement. Governments across the country spend some $30 billion on the administration of these programs annually, but only $2.5 billion of that was outsourced in 1998. Companies—such as MAXIMUS and Lockheed Martin—to which governmental authorities outsource their activities should realize significant opportunities.

The Welfare Reform Act

One of the most significant legislative reforms passed in the late 1990s was the Welfare Reform Act of 1996. This act restructured the benefits available to welfare recipients, eliminated unconditional welfare entitlements, and restructured the funding mechanisms that exist between the federal government and state governments. Recipients must seek work and can only receive welfare benefits for a limited time. States must keep accurate records of their welfare recipients, such as their first enrollment dates, skills training, job interviews, job hires, and reenrollment dates.

Beyond these basic requirements, states are free to take their own approaches to reforming welfare. For instance, Wisconsin favors work programs, Oregon is more aggressive in its casework, and Oklahoma has been investing in interviewing skills for its welfare recipients. The resulting mosaic in welfare reform provides outsourcing companies like EDS with a great deal of work because the data that require monitoring differ.

TIP: Because many states' information technology systems are not up to the challenges presented by government perestroika, or reform, they are compelled to outsource to companies such as MAXIMUS. These outsourcers manage welfare-to-workfare programs by providing eligibility determination, emergency assistance, job referral and placement, transition services such as child care and transportation, job readiness preparation, and selected educational and training services.

Under the Welfare Reform Act, states receive block grants from the federal government and can no longer seek reimbursement in the form of matching federal funds for expenditures in excess of block grants. By 2002, states must prove that 50 percent of their recipients, or roughly 2 million people, are working or they will lose a large amount of federal funding. In 2001, the federal government will stop paying benefits to all families who were on welfare in December 1996. Because states bear the financial risk for the operation of their welfare programs, they are more inclined to outsource much of the administrative work to for-profit companies that are likely to be more efficient in providing these services than are government agencies.

Another potential driver for government outsourcers is the possibility of secession. If more states and city governments come into being, they are likely to contract with government outsourcers to deliver their services. Secession anywhere within the United States sounds impossible, but there are paradigms that can be referred to. For instance, Quebec's secession from Canada has come within one percentage point of voter referendums. The following are examples of secessionist sentiment in the U.S.:

- In California, the San Fernando Valley has been trying to secede from the city of Los Angeles.
- In April 1998, the rural East End of Long Island, New York, filed suit, trying to force the state legislature to allow it to secede from Suffolk County and from Peconic County.

- Maryland State Senator Richard L. Colburn asked the Maryland legislature to let Eastern Shore residents decide if they wanted to form their own state, which would be called Delmarva (after the peninsula shared by Delaware and Virginia).
- In March 1998, people in a sliver of Minnesota called the Northwest Angle enlisted their congressman to propose a constitutional amendment allowing them to secede from the United States and join Canada.

Other Government Services Being Outsourced

The following are among the sources of additional opportunities for government outsourcing companies such as International Business Machines and MAXIMUS:

- The State Children's Health Insurance Program, established in 1997, provides federal matching funds to enable states to expand health care to targeted uninsured, low-income children. Over the five-year period ending in 2002, $20.3 billion will be made available to states with federally approved plans to expand their state Medicaid programs.
- Child support services are becoming more common.
- Child support enforcement services rendered under such programs include outreach to parents of children entitled to child support; the establishment of paternity, obtaining and enforcing child support orders; and payment processing.
- Government outsource companies such as Lockheed Martin provide a variety of project management services for Medicaid programs. These services include recipient outreach, education, and enrollment services; data collection and reporting; collaborative efforts with community-based organizations and advocacy groups; the design and development of program materials; and health plan encounter data analysis and reporting.
- Other programs that government outsourcing companies administer for their clients include vocational rehabilitation, substance abuse/mental health services, and monitoring of disability beneficiaries.

Investor Attractions to Government Outsourcers

Government outsourcing companies are appealing to investors because their business model is inherently more attractive than that of a governmental bureaucracy. First, private companies do a better job of motivating their workers than does the government. Second, private companies are more flexible in hiring people quickly and dismissing them when their projects are completed. Separately, outsourcers' contracts are often for extended periods—in some cases 20 years—which adds stability and predictability to their revenues and earnings.

Significant barriers to entry in providing administrative services to government bodies exist. Outsourcers must have a long track record of successful performance to win contracts from the government. Smaller or less experienced competitors are also handicapped by the difficulty of learning about the requests for proposals that state and local governments advertise, many of which are posted in very obscure places; by the costs of complying with constant government audits and reviews; by the expense of posting large performance bonds at the start of contracts; and by their frequent inability to incur start-up expenses on large, new contracts before receiving funds.

TRAP: One of the biggest obstacles to the growth of government outsourcing is resistance by unionized government workers.

Industry Players

The primary industry players in government outsourcing are EDS, International Business Machines, Lockheed Martin, and MAXIMUS.

CHAPTER 3

Retail Niches

There are many investment opportunities associated with what growing segments of the population are eating and wearing. The natural foods producers and retailers are direct beneficiaries of the trend towards Americans striving to attain healthier lifestyles. Teenage apparel retailers are positioned to prosper from the unprecedented size of the teenage population, as well as from rising disposable income among teenagers. Automotive superstores are steamrolling the independent auto dealerships by offering wider selections, nonconfrontational customer services, attractive pricing, and unbeatable after-sales support. Finally, aromatherapy candles are catching on like wildfire.

Natural Foods

Producers, retailers, and distributors of natural foods offer investors opportunities to benefit from the graying of America, the fear of food contamination, and heightened environmental sensitivity. The growth of natural foods companies will also be driven by increased health consciousness and the trend toward self-medication induced by restricted access to the health care system. Those are among the factors resulting in foods, which not long ago were considered alternative foods, now becoming mainstream. For instance, the Kellogg Foundation commissioned a study that revealed a "diverse majority of consumers appreciate natural foods that defy demographics."

In addition, traditional supermarkets and other food retailers will continue their attempt to take advantage of these recent trends by offering natural foods. Although such efforts will result in higher sales of natural foods (which will benefit producers and distributors of natural foods), traditional retailers will prove not to be competitive with the dedicated natural foods store chains such as Wild Oats and Whole Foods Market.

Natural Foods' Growth Is Already on Solid Footing

According to *Natural Foods Merchandiser* magazine, natural product sales—which includes organically grown fruits and vegetables, frozen meals made with organic ingredients, and products made with natural ingredients and without artificial additives and preservatives—soared from $1.9 billion in 1980 to $14.8 billion in 1997 in the United States. Sales of organic products soared from a mere $178 million in 1980 to more than $4 billion in 1998; and the market for dietary supplements generated about $9 billion in 1997, double the revenues five years earlier. Moreover, growth in the natural products industry has accelerated from a 15 percent annual increase in sales in 1992 to a 29 percent annual increase in 1997.

TRAP: Claims regarding vitamins' ability to preserve health and cure ailments have a tendency to be very aggressive. Further, there is usually little academic research funded by the producing companies to support such claims. Thus, vitamin companies are at risk for having their claims challenged by the Federal Trade Commission and state attorneys general.

Such rapid growth notwithstanding, sales of natural foods are positioned to continue growing at a rapid rate. In fact, *Progressive Grocer* magazine expects sales of natural products to reach $25 billion by the year 2000. This ambitious target is likely to be reached as natural foods retailers increase their same-store sales and as they open increasingly spacious stores. First, same-store sales growth among traditional independent natural product retailers averaged 9 percent during 1997, which was well above the 2 to 3 percent same-store sales growth for conventional supermarkets.

Second, the size of natural foods stores has increased consistently throughout the 1990s. While there were fewer than 90 natural products stores in 1990 with more than 5,000 square feet, there were roughly 600 natural products stores with over 5,000 square feet in 1997. *Natural Foods Merchandiser* expects the number of natural foods stores with over 5,000 square feet to reach 1,000 by the year 2000. Similarly, Whole Foods Market is slated to increase its average store size to 33,000 square feet in its new markets from its traditional 24,000 square feet.

Natural Foods Are Positioned for a New American Ethos

Consumption of natural foods seems appropriate for the growing legions of Americans (and foreigners) who strive for healthier lifestyles, wish to help preserve the environment, and are turned off by consumer products companies' crass marketing. A study conducted by Hartman & New Hope in 1998 found that a fundamental shift in underlying values seems to be occurring across all segments of the American population, with values of personal health and wellness, environmental health, and community involvement rising to the forefront. More than 85 percent of respondents, for instance, stated that they increasingly value good nutrition and exercise; 71 percent stated that they are more concerned about ecology and the health of the planet; and 66 percent stated that they are more concerned about kindness, integrity, and honesty than they were just a few years before.

Because the values expressed by the study's respondents are not as transitory as the attitudes measured in most consumer surveys, the study's professed values have the potential to serve as stable, reliable indicators of general shifts in consumer behavior. That explains why researchers increasingly believe that the desire for natural products is based on deeply held values rather than on superficial faddism.

Demographics and Lifestyles Drive Demand for Natural Foods

The alignment of deep-rooted values with food preferences may be important, but some of the more concrete underlying growth drivers of natural foods' consumption are described in the following paragraphs.

The desire to eat healthier foods, already noted, is widespread. Roughly 79 percent of Americans believe nutrition affects their health, and an estimated 54 percent of grocery shoppers "almost always read the nutrition label before buying a product for the first time." More than 100 million American adults watch their fat intake, and 90 million Americans monitor their dietary cholesterol. According to a poll conducted by Multi-Sponsor Surveys, 43 percent of American adults took some kind of vitamin or mineral in 1997 compared with 33 percent in 1991. More than half of grocery shoppers rate health as their primary concern in making food selections. Americans have indeed been changing their diets. From 1980 to 1995, the per capita consumption of red meat and eggs declined at a compound annual rate of 1 percent. Over the same period of time, per capita consumption of seafood, fresh fruits, and vegetables each grew 1 percent a year. The most dramatic substitution can be seen in milk consumption. Consumption of whole milk fell 4 percent annually from 1980 to 1995, while consumption of low fat/skim milk increased 3 percent annually over the same period. Because consumption of food increases roughly 2 percent a year, a 1 percent change in consumption is indeed significant.

An aging population is another factor in the increasing consumption of natural foods. People become even more concerned about preserving their health as they age. Therefore, the growing numbers of aging Americans are likely to increase their consumption of healthier foods. (This is especially true as the 10,000 Americans that turn 50 every day grew up during the 1960s, when the natural foods industry was born.) In 1990, the percentage of the U.S. population over 50 years of age was about 25.5 percent. The Census Bureau expects that percentage will grow to 27.6 percent in 2000 and to 34.4 percent in 2015.

As a result of the prevalence of managed care restricting Americans' access to the health care system, people are making more concerted efforts to maintain their health, partly through improved nutrition. In mid-1998, some 85 percent of the American workforce had health care coverage through a health maintenance organization (HMO). HMOs and other managed care providers typically limit access to specialists, require a second opinion before approving surgery, and demand preauthorization before their enrollees are admitted to hospitals.

The increasingly widespread phenomenon of self-medication is a precursor to greater reliance on natural foods. People with the confidence to self-medicate certainly believe they have the wisdom to choose the foods that will serve them best. Over-the-counter (OTC) sales of medications were $1.9 billion in 1964, soaring to some $16.6 billion spent on more than 100,000 OTC products in 1997. According to the American Pharmaceutical Association, of approximately 3.5 billion health problems treated annually, some 2 billion, or 57 percent, are treated with a nonprescription drug.

One reason that self-medication is popular is that OTC medicine provides consumers substantial savings. For instance, a study conducted in 1997 by Kline & Company showed that Americans saved $20 billion in 1996 by using OTC medicines. Also, the U.S. Bureau of Labor Statistics reported that the cost of OTC medicines increased only 10 percent during the five-year period ending March 1997. In contrast, hospital care jumped 32 percent during the same period, physician services went up 24 percent, and dental care increased 28 percent. Another driver of OTC spending is aggressive advertising. In 1987, advertising expenditures for OTC remedies totaled $1 billion, while advertising expenditures in 1996 totaled nearly $2 billion.

Underpenetration is a fifth growth driver of natural foods. Despite its history of rapid growth, the natural foods industry accounted for only 2.5 percent of the total food market in mid-1998. Further, the majority of Americans are still not eating as healthily as they should. According to Matthew Patsky, managing director at Adams, Harkness & Hill, nutritional supplements are consumed by only 40 percent of the U.S. adult population, even though a body of medical evidence indicates that they should be consumed by everybody.

Growing concerns about food purity, food safety and the effects food production has on the environment also drive natural foods consumption. (See Chapter 10, "Food Inspection.") Natural foods devotees are disconcerted by the fact that politically incorrect ingredients and processes are increasingly being used in food production processes—hormones to boost milk production, steroids to increase the harvest weight of meats, genetically reengineered animals and plants, and fat substitutes with unpleasant side effects. Pesticide contamination of the water supply and pesticide poisoning of wildlife are additional environmental issues that concern many consumers of organic products.

Heightened concern for the ethical treatment of animals and the growing ranks of vegetarians is leading more Americans to seek nutritious natural foods. There were an estimated 19 million vegetarians in the United States in 1997, more than an eightfold increase from 1987. According to Worthington Foods, that number was growing at a rate of nearly 20,000 new vegetarians a week in 1998. Moreover, some 75 million American adults are actively reducing their red meat consumption. Thus, the market for vegetarian foods is projected to reach $662 million by 2000 as 42 percent of grocery shoppers eat meatless meals at least once a week and 15 percent of shoppers include meat substitutes at least once a week.

With a seeming revival of epicureanism, gourmet cooking is another driver for natural foods. In fact, some of the natural foods chains seek to locate new stores in neighborhoods that have a high incidence of gourmet magazine subscribers. (One reason that many people believe that organic food tastes better is because it is often delivered to its markets faster than processed food.) Three-quarters of the nation's supermarkets have gourmet sections and mail-order sales of gourmet foods are projected to surpass $3.1 billion by the year 2000. Of the country's nearly 300 schools for chefs, one-quarter opened since the late 1980s. According to the National Restaurant Association, about 57 percent of upscale American restaurants (those with entrees costing $25 or more) offer organic items on their menus while about one-third of medium-priced restaurants include organic cuisine. Cooking shows occupy one-third of the Public Broadcasting Services' "how-to" programming and run 20 hours a day on cable's Food Network.

The natural foods industry is winning legitimacy. For instance, one survey conducted in 1998 revealed that doctors' recommendations have become the leading cause of people turning to dietary supplements. Similarly, some HMOs, such as Oxford Health Plans, have already begun paying for herbal remedies. Also, American Home Products' purchase of Solgar Vitamin & Herb and SmithKline Beecham's test-marketing of four herbal remedies in the United States marked the first forays of respectable pharmaceutical companies into the natural remedy market. Even when not developed by leading pharmaceutical concerns, many natural remedies are marketed under respectable categories such as nutraceuticals or phytonutrients. Finally, more credibility is likely to be enjoyed by the industry since the National Institutes of Health established an office of alternative medicines in 1992 and an office of dietary supplements in 1995.*

---

*Paul Klebnikov and Zina Mouheiber, "A Healthy Business," *Forbes,* Sept. 21, 1998, p. 89.

Functional Foods

Americans are increasingly conscious of the foods they consume. However, there seems to be a shift from avoiding deleterious ingredients (such as salt, preservatives, and sugar) to seeking healthy ingredients (natural fat replacers and antioxidants, for instance) in the foods consumers eat. The shift has come about because educational efforts to promote healthy lifestyles have increasingly focused on eating the right foods as a preventive measure for such chronic illnesses as cancer and heart disease. Three prominent U.S. health organizations—the National Cancer Institute, the American Cancer Society, and the American Heart Association—have publicly stated, for example, that a diet rich in fruits and vegetables may reduce the risk of cancer and heart disease.

The desire to avoid life-threatening medical conditions by eating healthy foods has given birth to functional foods. Functional foods are defined by the American Dietetic Association as "any modified food or food ingredient that may provide a health benefit beyond the traditional nutrients it contains." Kalorama Information LLC expects sales of foods bought for their healthy properties to reach $17.6 billion in 2001. In late 1998, a spokesman for DuPont predicted that revenue from its nascent crop biotechnology unit (which produces functional foods) would reach over $45 billion in a few decades.

Examples of companies that are developing functional foods include the following:

- Kellogg began shipping a line of cholesterol-lowering foods (including frozen entrees, bread, cereal, and desserts) under its Ensemble brand in early 1999.
- Monsanto sells an omega-3 fatty acid to dietary supplement makers. Research has indicated that omega-3s are an important factor in the brain's development and that insufficient levels of omega-3s are linked to Parkinson's disease, Alzheimer's and other neurological abnormalities.
- Zeneca PLC is genetically engineering a tomato that has high levels of lycopene, which purportedly reduces the risk of prostrate cancer.
- Northland Cranberries has long benefited from general scientific acceptance that the consumption of cranberry juice reduces the risk of urinary tract infection in women. More recently, studies from the University of Wisconsin have demonstrated that drinking cranberry juice reduces the risk of cardiovascular disease.

TRAP: Despite consumer attraction to companies that can improve health and the financial potential such prospects entail, investors should be aware of three obstacles that confront functional foods companies. First, taste cannot be compromised as Campbell Soup learned when it disbanded its Intelligent Quisine line of frozen entrees after investing $50 million in it. Second, regulatory hurdles are higher when launching food with pharmaceutical characteristics. Third, functional foods companies could be liable if their customers suffer effects from consuming functional foods in excess of daily recommended doses.

Natural Foods Are Sold in More Venues

The widespread interest in natural foods is confirmed by the fact that traditional grocery stores, mass merchants, discount clubs, and mail-order services are among the retail channels that are complementing some 2,000 dedicated natural foods shops. Rather than merely making token efforts at selling natural foods, these stores are aggressively increasing natural foods sales. For instance, U.S. retail sales for herbal remedies at grocers, mass merchants, and drugstores climbed 42 percent to $850 million from 1997 to 1998.

Traditional grocery stores are arguably taking the most ambitious initiatives for selling natural foods. Sales of natural foods in mainstream supermarkets rose 7.9 percent, from $1.65 billion in 1996 to $1.78 billion in 1997. (These totals do not include sales for mainstream brands that contain natural ingredients such as Post Grape-Nuts, Altoids, and Progresso soups.) Conventional supermarkets that offer natural foods run the gamut, from Albertson's in California to Winn-Dixie Stores in Florida. A&P reserves at least 200 to 400 square feet of space for organic foods in each of its stores, and Copp's Corporation supermarkets in Wisconsin set aside at least 1,400 square feet. Also, the natural foods departments at Kroger's stores are as large as 7,000 square feet, which rival the size of many independent natural foods shops.

The proliferation of natural foods outlets is a boon to producers and distributors of natural foods. For instance, these new avenues helped distributors' sales for organic foods reach $3.5 billion in 1996, a 26 percent surge from the previous year. As Norman Cloutier, CEO of United Natural Foods, remarked: "The lines that once defined the boundaries between natural, gourmet, kosher, and ethnic foods are becoming blurred. It's more of a gradient today than a hard line. As a result, [distributor] United Natural Foods serves a wider range of customers and our products reflect that."*

---

*Robin Stanton, "Health Food Thrives," *Investor's Business Daily,* Feb. 12, 1998, p. A4.

Dedicated Natural Foods Stores Reign Supreme

Although the producers and distributors of natural foods will benefit from more venues selling their products, the increased competition in selling natural foods should not imperil the dedicated natural foods store chains such as Wild Oats and Whole Foods Market. Statistics already bear this out. Based on information from the Agricultural Outlook Forum and Chain Store Guide, on a sales-per-square foot basis, the large natural foods stores had average sales of $615 in 1997 versus about $409 for the traditional supermarkets.

Outlets of Whole Foods Market in San Francisco—considered the strongest market for the natural foods industry—have experienced growth despite the challenge posed by virtually all the competing supermarkets, which carry complete selections of organic produce and natural foods. Also, when Wild Oats opened a new unit in the heavily saturated natural foods market in Boulder, Colorado, that store drew 75 to 80 percent of its sales from conventional grocers.

The following are among the reasons that the proliferation of grocery stores offering natural foods will not pose a significant threat to the investment merits of dedicated natural foods retailers such as Wild Oats and Whole Foods Market:

- When natural foods stores were smaller, their selection was limited; customers tended to shop at conventional stores for most of their needs and at natural stores for specialty products. Because most natural foods supermarkets offer almost every category of product that can be found at a conventional supermarket, less need exists today for natural foods aficionados to shop at conventional stores.
- Because traditional grocers lack a credible selection of natural foods, they cannot offer shoppers one-stop shopping. In fact, mainstream retailers derive about 96 percent of their sales of natural foods from just 30 percent of the stock typically carried by natural foods stores.
- Grocery stores cannot offer as much customer service as natural foods stores because they lack educated and knowledgeable sales associates. An educated sales force is important because the majority of natural foods products exist outside our brand-based advertising culture. Also, unionized employees found at grocery stores are less flexible than are the nonunionized employees of natural foods stores.
- Conventional chains lack credibility and integrity in merchandising natural products because of the presence of unhealthy products. Displaying cigarettes, beer, and doughnuts close to natural products does not convey a sense of commitment to natural foods.
- Traditional grocery chains use their aggregate buying power to win concessions from suppliers. However, natural foods are likely to be suitable for

only some of a chain's stores, so retailers are not able to make maximum use of their buying power.

- Natural foods suppliers are too fragmented and unreliable for conventional food chains. As the large grocery chains have invested tens of millions of dollars in electronic replenishment systems, they demand immediate fulfillment of their orders. Because suppliers of natural foods are much smaller and less technologically sophisticated than the suppliers with whom the grocery chains typically contract, they simply cannot satisfy the volume or delivery demands of conventional food chains.
- The low turnover of natural foods in traditional grocery stores causes spoilage problems, particularly true with organic produce, which lack the preservatives and shelf life of conventional products.

Other Advantages of Natural Foods Chains

The following are among the other attractions of the dominant natural foods retailers:

- Retailers of natural foods have captured only a minuscule portion of the food-retailing industry. Whole Foods Market's share of the $470 billion supermarket industry was 0.2 percent and the share for Wild Oats was 0.07 percent in 1997. According to Wild Oats' management, the two largest natural foods retailers—Wild Oats and Whole Foods Market—accounted for only 12 percent of the total dollars spent by consumers in 1998 on natural foods.
- Many natural foods retailers lack business savvy. Most competition for the large chains comes from independents, which are more likely to be health advocates or hobbyists than hard-nosed business people. In fact, about 60 percent of natural foods stores are owned by people that operate only one or two stores.
- Discounting is less likely in the sale of natural foods compared with most other retail sectors. As Danny Wells, a retail consultant, said: "Discounting does not make sense in an industry where the products are based on value and quality. Natural foods companies are selling health, and for most people health is the most important thing they have. They are willing to pay the price for a product that will prevent them from getting sick, reduce their symptoms, or, in the case of the baby boomers, keep them more youthful."
- Natural foods have demonstrated some immunity to recessions. FAC/Equities' Gary Giblen noted in November 1998: Reviewing evidence from severe regional recessions in southern California (early 1990s), New England (late 1980s to early 1990s), and the Texas oil bust (late 1980s to the early 1990s),

natural chains—less developed than today's—maintained positive comparable store sales and healthy profitability. Moreover, retailers have recently developed major natural private label lines, which should minimize or eliminate price differentials versus conventional supermarkets.

A Review of Producers of Natural Foods

I believe that companies such as Balance Bar and Twinlab that make healthy snacks will enjoy robust growth. As people are increasingly pressed for time, they are searching for meal replacements. Balance Bar Company estimates that the number of people who skip meals "very often" or "quite a bit" increased from 21 percent in 1995 to 28 percent in 1997, and that 21 percent of Americans view time as a major barrier to achieving a healthful eating lifestyle. This thesis is supported by data from InfoScan, which indicate that dollar sales of nutrition bars by mass merchandise, grocery, and drug stores increased approximately 47 percent in 1996 and 50 percent in 1997.

There are other vehicles through which investors can gain exposure to the natural foods producers. The largest dedicated natural foods retailers are Wild Oats and Whole Foods Market, and the largest distributor is United Natural Foods. Companies that produce natural foods for babies include Gerber (through its line of organic baby food called Tender Harvest) and H. J. Heinz (through its acquisition of Earth's Best).

Hansen Natural is a purveyor of functional beverages; its D-Stress is supposedly a natural antidepressant and its Anti-ox is said to counter the body's excess free radicals. Vegetarian plays include Gardenburger and Worthington Foods. Celestial Seasonings is the largest herb tea producer. PharmaPrint and Opta Food are manufacturers of natural ingredients for the food industry. Other general natural foods companies include Weider Nutrition, Hain Food Group, and Natural Alternatives.

Teenage Apparel Retailers

Teenage apparel retailers' fortunes will continue to be driven by favorable demographics, teenagers' greater spending power, and the resurgence of fashion among adolescents. Young people will have fewer demands on their discretionary dollars as computers have already been purchased, college costs are moderating, and credit card financing becomes more reasonable. The apparel merchandisers that correctly determine teenage trends will be rewarded with large volumes of sales as, according to the International Council of Shopping Centers, the average teen visits shopping locations 54 times a year compared with 39 times for the typical shopper. I believe that the chains that cater to teenagers will be able to expand their store counts faster because teenagers are becoming increasingly homogenous, and the chains will become more prosperous as a result of reduced competition with the demise of thousands of stores in the early 1990s.

Teenagers Are the Largest Demographic Segment

Teenager apparel chains will continue to grow as a result of the sheer numbers of teenagers. The teenage population is growing at twice the rate of the overall American population. According to the U.S. Census Bureau, the number of people between 13 and 19 years old will increase from 25 million in 1997 to over 30 million in 2006, when the teenage population will be larger than at any time in history, including in 1976 when 28 million baby boomers were teenagers.

At a Retail Industry Conference at The New York Society of Security Analysts, Rowland Schaefer, chief executive officer of Claire's Stores, remarked that the number of teenage apparel buyers is much larger than the actual number of teenagers. This is because (especially) girls as young as eight aspire to look like teenagers. Thus, including aspirational youngsters and people in their early 20s who share similar fashion tastes with teenagers, teen retailers such as Gadzooks and American Eagle Outfitters have a market that is projected to grow from 55 million people in 1998 to 62 million by 2005.

Adolescents Are Flush with Cash

Not only are the large numbers of teenagers a boon to apparel and accessories retailers such as The Buckle and Fossil but teens' unprecedented spending power will prove to be a powerful driver of their revenues. The teenage segment of the population has more discretionary spending power as a result of higher income and greater influence over their families' spending. In fact, disposable income for teenagers rose 12 percent in 1997 to $4,300 per capita, after having increased 40 percent from 1987 to 1996. According to Teenage Research Unlimited, teen spending for ages 12 to 19 reached $141 billion in 1998, up 16 percent from 1997.

Aspirational teenagers are not far behind teenagers in disposable income or discretionary spending. Research by James McNeal, a professor at Texas A&M, indicates that spending directed by children has been accelerating. While the aggregate spending by or on behalf of children 4 to 12 roughly doubled every decade in the 1960s, 1970s, and 1980s, it tripled from January 1990 to December 1997 to more than $24 billion in 1997. Also, the weekly income of a 10-year-old—including allowances, gifts, and cash for household chores—rose more than 75 percent to $13.93 in 1997, from $7.90 in 1991. Further, while children spent almost all of their money on candy in the 1960s, only one-third was allocated to food and drink in the late 1990s, with the balance going to clothing, accessories, playthings, and movies.

What is even more compelling for the teenage apparel and accessories retailers like Claire's Stores and Hot Topic is that substantially all of the money in the hands of children is disposable, because children do not have to provide for their food, clothing, housing, or health care. As Greg Weaver, CEO of Pacific Sunwear of California said: "If you think about 15-year-olds, they are not worried about rent or mortgages. They are not worried about car payments, because they do not have cars yet. Their disposable income truly is disposable."

Drivers of Teenage Income

Teenagers will continue to enjoy more discretionary income as a result of their increasing earnings power and their parents' growing largesse. Because many teenagers' parents have become increasingly wealthy throughout the 1990s, there has been less motivation for children to work. However, the following are among the reasons that I believe teenagers will continue to be handsomely compensated for the work that they perform:

- The federal minimum wage is likely to continue to increase, which is important because teenagers typically begin working at the minimum wage. The federal minimum wage increased to $4.75 in October 1996 and then again to $5.15 an hour in September 1997. President Clinton is in favor of raising the national minimum wage to $6.15 by 2000. Strong precedent exists for continued hikes in the minimum wage; it has already been increased at least 17 times and the minimum hourly wage was increased under every elected president (except for Ronald Reagan) since its establishment in 1938.
- Many states have minimum wages that exceed the federal minimum, and employers must pay their workers the higher of the two. Interestingly, in November 1998, Washington State promulgated legislation that indexed that state's minimum wage to inflation.
- A growing number of cities are adopting living wage legislation. For instance, Boston in 1998 began requiring private companies that conducted business with the city to pay their workers at least $7.49 an hour—a full 45 percent above the federal minimum. Variations of living wage legislation are on the books in cities such as New York, Milwaukee, and Los Angeles. Other cities that were considering such legislation in 1998 included Philadelphia, Denver, St. Louis, and Albuquerque.

- More businesses are hiring teenagers as a result of policies such as the School to Work Opportunities Act of 1994, which provides subsidies to school districts for the purpose of establishing partnerships with businesses. In the 18 months ended June 1997, the number of partnerships between high schools and businesses jumped 270 percent to 1,087 in the 45 states surveyed by the federal school-to-work office. Realizing that teenagers benefit from the work experiences provided by these programs, many state legislators have been passing similar bills.

- As a result of the strong American economy during the 1990s, employers have been desperate for workers. As the unemployment rate reached its 24-year low (by falling to 4.3 percent in May 1998), employers have resorted to aggressively recruiting from all segments of the population—including the youngest possible segment. As a result, 32 percent of teens in 1998 held part-time jobs—six percentage points more than in 1996. Also, youth unemployment has fallen sharply across the nation—from 25.4 percent in the summer of 1996 to 19.6 percent in the summer of 1998.

Adolescents Win Parents' Wallets

Of the $141 billion that teenagers spent in 1998, $47 billion came from their parents. There are several reasons why parents are so generous to their children. First, increasingly time-constrained parents often try to substitute money for time not spent with their children. Second, as couples are having children later in life (when they are more affluent), they can often afford to be more generous with their children.

A third explanation for parents lavishing money on their children is their belief that their children are behaving increasingly responsibly. Several findings support this contention. A survey by the American Academy of Pediatrics of 600 young adults between the ages of 16 and 19 found that roughly 19 percent never drank, and 38 percent had consumed four or fewer drinks in the last month. Teenage drinkers are also heeding society's advice about being careful—64 percent, in fact, said they always designate a driver. Children have not only learned to save their money but millions of children are learning how to invest their money. Merrill Lynch, for example, surveyed 512 teens in February 1998 and found that 28 percent of them save most of the money they receive, 60 percent save about half, and only 12 percent spend everything immediately. Also, Liberty Financial Companies has been pitching a mutual fund to children since 1994. By mid-1998, Liberty's Stein Roe Young Investor fund, whose average investor's age was nine, had assets of $725 million.

Children Gain Control of Parents' Purse Strings

Teenagers have more discretion over their parents' income because of the high incidence of two-career parents, single-parent families, and general parental time pressures. (See the discussion of dual income families and single-parent households in Chapter 1.) Thus, parents are delegating more of family shopping duties to their children. According to Professor James McNeal, 48 percent of children "weigh in" on family purchases and are especially influential when parents are buying such high-ticket electronic items as computers and home entertainment systems. Even children under 13 directly influenced $187.7 billion in family purchases in 1997.

Another effect of children's accepting more of what had traditionally been considered parents' responsibilities is age compression. Age compression means that children are forced to grow up faster than ever before and is attributable to children's being made aware of the harsh facts of life—AIDS, homelessness, and drugs—at very young ages. Thus, children are ceasing to play with toys at younger ages and beginning to emulate teenagers earlier.

TRAP: One segment of the children's apparel industry that may be a casualty of age compression includes retailers such as Gymboree, which sells clothing that makes children look childish (e.g., lots of bright colors and cute designs). The problem is that parents are increasingly dressing their children like miniature adults, which is benefiting companies such as The Gap.

Baby boomer parents are willing to entrust their children with family purchases because they share many of the same values with their children. According to a late 1998 survey commissioned by Clinique, 90 percent of mothers and their teenage daughters were happy with their relationship and in sync on everything from general values to career choices, and 41 percent of teenage girls said their mothers were cool or hip. Although baby boomers and their parents were divided over issues like Vietnam and marijuana use, teens and parents in the late 1990s were more likely to share the same points of view on major issues such as environmentalism and gun control.

The investment implication from children's assuming more control over their parents' spending is that the retailers that appeal to children run less risk that their sales will be vetoed by parents. In fact, only 57 percent of parents in the western United States said they have influence over where their children shop. As children pay for more of their clothing, they will have more control over where they shop and what they purchase. One survey of 1,300 consumers showed that 82 percent of teenagers helped pay for their back-to-school items in 1998.

Teens Can Allocate More Money to Apparel

I believe that Generation Y (those born after 1982) will be able to allocate a larger percent of its money to apparel and accessories than Generation X (the 52.4 million people born from 1965 to 1978). This will benefit the teenage apparel and accessories industry in the first decade of the 21st century.

First, financing purchases will be easier and less expensive for Generation Y. Not only are billions of potential credit card users solicited through the mail and the phone each year, but also solicited every time computer users log on to many of the most popular Internet access providers such as America Online. Generation Y will benefit from falling interest rates, the disappearance of annual credit card fees, and the ease of transferring balances from one card to others in order to take advantage of teaser rates. In contrast, Generation Xers were subject to near usurious interest rates, high annual fees, and a host of penalties for the slightest infraction of their credit card agreements.

Second, college costs—traditionally a source of angst for teenagers and their parents—have already begun to show signs of moderating. According to the College Board, college costs rose at double-digit rates from the early 1980s until 1992 but decelerated to a 5 percent average annual increase from 1992 to 1997.

College costs should become even more affordable as students receive more financial assistance. For instance, scholarships soared to $55 billion for the 1996–1997 school year, up from $32 billion in inflation-adjusted dollars nearly a decade earlier. Congress increased the maximum Pell grant from $2,700 to $3,000 in 1998, and Congress legislated $1,500 in yearly tuition tax credits. Bipartisan political support for educational funding resulted in the 1998 federal budget including $40 billion of tax breaks for college tuition; increased the federal College Work-Study Program; permitted tax-free IRA withdrawals for education; and exempted $5,250 per year of employer-paid tuition. Federal legislators may make college even more affordable as some senators, such as Charles Schumer, favor making all college tuition tax-deductible.

Third, because about 50 percent of American homes had a computer in 1998, many teenage households will not have to reserve money for computers, peripherals, or software. Furthermore, the cost of home computers is declining. For instance, by the fourth quarter of 1998, between 60 and 65 percent of personal computers cost less than $1,000, and one-third of those computers cost less than $800. It is increasingly common for software to be downloaded free from the Internet. The implication for teenage apparel retailers is that this freed-up money can be spent on apparel.

Teenagers Should Have More Confidence to Spend

Children who will become teenagers early in the 21st century should have more confidence to spend than adolescents who became teenagers in the late 1980s and early 1990s. One reason is that society seems to value their well-being more than in the past.

William Strauss, a generation specialist and coauthor of *The Fourth Turning,* argues that there are sharp contrasts between Generation X and Generation Y. Generation Xers grew up in one of the most antichild periods in modern history—a time when divorce rates soared, abortion on demand was a rallying cry for liberals, drug use devastated families, and parenthood was disparaged by feminists. On the other hand, Generation Yers grew up listening to politicians rhapsodizing about providing for a safe and prosperous future for the nation's children; senior corporate executives announcing their retirements to spend more time with their families; protective minivans gaining wide popularity; "Baby on Board" signs proliferating; and supportive movies such as *Three Men and a Baby* becoming box office hits.

TIP: Investors who accept my thesis that society in general and parents in particular are placing more value on youngsters' well-being may be attracted by child safety companies such as Safety 1st. Safety 1st is the manufacturer of the prevalent "Baby on Board" car signs, and it also sells such child protection products as outlet plugs, cabinet latches, stove knob covers, and balcony guards.

Generation Yers should feel much more economically secure than Generation Xers. Generation Xers struggled in an early-1990s economy beset with dead-end jobs, layoffs, and recession. On the other hand, Generation Yers grew up during one of the hottest periods of economic growth. Teenagers in the late 1990s have had a host of jobs to choose from, and their parents thrived.

Other Attractions of the Teenage Apparel Retailers

Retailers that cater to young people should benefit from reduced competition resulting from the demise of thousands of competing stores as well as a resurgence of fashionable clothing and accessories. Moreover, the fact that teenagers throughout the world are becoming homogenized will expand the potential sales of successful teenage-apparel retailers.

Throughout the early 1990s, approximately 4,500 teen apparel retailers were shuttered as a result of unfavorable demographics, previous overexpansion, poor merchandising, mismanagement, and the appeal of the "grunge" look. The most significant event was the Chapter 7 bankruptcy filing of Merry-Go-Round, which resulted in the closing of 1,200 stores. However, other notable closings included Brooks Fashion (800 stores); Foxmoor (625 stores); Edison Brothers (550 stores); Clothestime (128 stores); and Contempo Casuals (40 locations). As a result, the remaining teen retailers should be able to achieve higher profitability as they face significantly reduced competition.

In the early 1990s, many teenagers were attracted to the grunge look that was inspired by several Seattle-area bands popular with teenagers. The grunge look was as antifashion as any apparel trend could be as teenagers tried to look dowdy by wearing old clothes, buying used clothes, and donning hand-me-downs. Of course, these preferences in dress reduced demand for new clothing. More recently, we have seen a renewed emphasis on appearance that was partly inspired by trends in womenswear—more colors, higher heels, and less emphasis on suits. Young girls have also been inspired by the Spice Girls, attractive entertainers who wear a variety of trend-setting clothes. And more attention is being paid to young men's physical condition and pleasing appearance.

TIP: Investors wishing to gain exposure to the body-piercing trend can do so through the shares of Hot Topic. In addition to its more traditional teenage apparel and accessories, Hot Topic sells its Morbid Metals line of body jewelry, which includes sterling lip and nose clips, silver belly clips, tongue barbells, and nipple rings. Although there are no reliable statistics available on the number of people piercing their bodies, it seems that this number could approximate the number that are engaged in self-mutilation. Researchers have found that 2 million Americans are chronic "cutters," and studies have found that as many as one in eight adolescents have tried to mutilate themselves.

Finally, retailers that are successful in predicting teenage trends will benefit from huge markets because teenagers endeavor to fit in with their peers by dressing and acting according to unwritten codes. More than any other segment of the population, teenagers tend to shop together and form a consensus about which clothes are acceptable. And teenagers do not shop in pairs or in threesomes but in packs of 10 or 15 or more. (On a similar note, many of the cognoscenti in the motion picture industry attributed *Titanic*'s box office success to groups of girls flocking to stargaze at young Leonardo DiCaprio, the leading actor.)

The tendency for teens to dress according to consensus is not just a local or regional phenomenon but often has national and global dimensions. Children throughout the world are becoming more homogeneous from the worldwide prevalence of MTV, ESPN, and CNN as well as the appearance of sports, movie, and music stars throughout the media. The more that young people see their role models in the various forms of media, the more they want to dress like their pop culture icons. This universality makes it easier for teen-focused retailers to expand nationally and internationally.

Investment Vehicles

Among the publicly traded retailers geared to teenagers are: American Eagle Outfitters, Claire's Stores, Delias, Gadzooks, Hot Topic, Pacific Sunwear of California, Quiksilver, and Buckle.

Automotive Superstores

Automotive superstores such as United Auto Group and Lithia Motors have achieved a great deal of popularity with vehicle buyers by offering greater selections and friendlier service than traditional auto dealers. Customer satisfaction indexes are nearly universally higher (compared to independent dealers) for the superstores, which set one price on their vehicles, thereby eliminating the customary haggling that has given auto dealers a terrible reputation. When asked by independent surveyors, more than 95 percent of shoppers at both Republic Industries' AutoNation USA and CarMax reported being very satisfied with their customer experience. In addition, one study by Bain & Company found that customers were driving as far as 75 miles (presumably past several dealerships) to shop in a superstore. Moreover, the superstores offer investors the prospect of aggressive earnings growth as a result of rapid expansion and reduced expense structures stemming from economies of scale and returns on their investment in technology.

TRAP: Automotive superstore chains have difficulty expanding when their shares are depressed because it is these shares that are usually exchanged for ownership of the dealers they acquire.

A Fertile Market for Consolidation

I believe investors should be attracted to the U.S. automobile retail market because it is both enormous and ripe for consolidation. The benefit of the market's being ripe for consolidation is that superstores such as AutoNation USA, CrossContinent Auto Retailers, and CarMax can accelerate their growth through acquisitions.

With $661 billion in estimated revenue in 1997, auto sales account for the largest segment of retail sales in the United States. If one were to include auto finance, auto parts, and service, the entire industry would exceed $1 trillion in annual revenues.

Second, according to research by BankBoston Robertson Stephens, the number of superstores was expected to surge from 41 toward the end of 1997 to more than 100 by the end of 1998. Although automakers were initially militantly opposed to selling their vehicles through superstores, they are no longer adverse to doing so. By 1998, Jaguar (with less than 1 percent of vehicle sales) was the only manufacturer to unconditionally oppose public ownership of its dealerships. However, even Jaguar's (which is owned by Ford) automobiles have been sold through the Ford Retail Network stores—which are similar to superstores as they sell all of Ford's cars under one roof—since 1998.

The primary reason for auto manufacturers becoming amenable to selling their cars through superstores is their realization that their dealer networks are "overstored." Largely as a result of the Big Three automakers historically trying to gain market share from one another, there were 22,600 new-car dealerships at the beginning of 1998. This translated into roughly one dealer for every 115,000 people, far more dealerships than the auto manufacturers' target of one dealership for every 250,000 people. General Motors and Chrysler have announced Project 2000 which calls for decreasing their dealerships by 1,500 (18 percent) and 500 (11 percent) respectively. To corroborate, one Ford Motors spokesman with whom I conferred said that one-third of Ford's dealers were inefficient and would not be missed if they decided to leave the industry.

In 1997, Ford began to consolidate its 21 Indianapolis dealers into a few Ford Retail Network superstores. The following factors illustrate the rationale behind Ford's decision to reduce the number of its dealers:

- Ford was "overdealered" in the greater Indianapolis area and did not need 21 dealers for a population base of 1.5 million people (i.e., 1 dealer per 70,000 residents versus a target of 1 dealer per 250,000 residents).
- The 21 Indianapolis dealers were competing against each other on price. On any given Sunday, 21 advertisements for the same Ford Taurus could appear in the *Indianapolis Star* at 21 different prices. This intense price competition among dealers selling identical products resulted in the dealers becoming more aggressive in selling used cars and led many salesmen to make false representations about the vehicles they were selling. Such behavior reflected poorly on Ford's brand equity and adversely impacted repeat purchases.

  On the contrary, Ford believed that reducing the number of dealerships would lead to higher invoice prices that would produce more income for both itself and the remaining dealers. Also, sticker prices closer to the manufacturer's suggested retail prices were expected to result in higher residual values on the manufacturer's leased automobiles.

- Ford believed that adopting a no-haggle selling policy executed by salaried sales associates would eliminate the hostility that car buyers reserve for auto sales personnel and alleviate the apprehension surrounding the car buying process.
- Service locations and repair times were often inefficient for consumers, which generated negative goodwill towards Ford Motors.

Independent Dealers Are Willing to Exit the Industry

Consolidation of automobile superstores will continue to be fueled by the fact that a very large percent of independent dealers are willing to leave the industry. (And even fewer children wish to take control of their parents' dealerships.) This is evidenced by the number of the smallest dealerships (those that sell 149 or fewer cars a year) declining from 13,100 in 1977 to 4,540 in 1997, according to the National Automobile Dealers Association (NADA).

Small dealers will continue to exit the industry because profitability continues to evaporate. According to Tom Webb, NADA's chief economist, the average net profit per car realized by dealers fell from $77 in 1996 to $55 in 1997. Profit deterioration is leading to more dissatisfaction and pessimism on the part of auto dealers. NADA's April 1998 survey of the profit expectations of new-car and new-truck dealers for the following 12 months was 134, down substantially from the 180 level reached in April 1994. Increasingly educated car buyers, higher operating costs, and deterioration of the used car market are just a few of the factors that are resulting in dealerships becoming less appealing small businesses.

Dealers Find It Nearly Impossible to Receive Full Sticker Prices

There is extreme pressure on the selling prices of new cars. For instance, Ford reports that the average sticker price on its 1999 model cars and trucks sold in the United States would be 3 percent lower than prices on its 1998 models. In 1998, the cost of rebates, discounted lease deals, and other incentives jumped 27 percent to an average of $1,400. Also, 1998 witnessed the Big 3 redeeming each other's $1,000 coupons for new vehicle sales.

Chronic overcapacity—the worldwide auto industry had enough capacity to manufacture 70 million cars a year in 1998 but demand was closer to 50 million and falling as a result of Asia's economic deterioration—is certainly a contributor to price concessions. And the growing influence of auto superstores themselves (which sell high volumes of vehicles at reduced prices) puts pressure on new car prices.

A much more daunting problem for the independent dealerships in terms of receiving sticker prices, however, is that car buyers are much better educated. It is no longer uncommon for customers to enter dealer lots with *Consumer Reports'* lists of invoice prices (revealing how much the dealer paid for the cars on his lot) and refusing to pay more than a few hundred dollars above these prices. In addition, professional car-buying services such as Auto-by-Tel charge their customers a set fee to shop for the best price on specific makes and models. Other car-buying services collect profiles of their customers' driving habits and familial situations and recommend cars that best suit the needs of their customers.

The ease with which customers can compare prices of vehicles and search for bargains through Internet sites such as Microsoft's CarPoint poses a critical challenge to dealerships. Two of the most popular Web sites—of the more than 20,000 devoted to automobiles—are Edmund's and Kelley Blue Book, both of which offer data on what dealers pay the factories for their vehicles. These two sites also post up-to-the-minute rebate and incentive lists, some of which are not normally made public.* As such sites uncover the cheapest cars, dealers' profits get squeezed. Other Web sites provide used car valuation guides for people trading in their vehicles. These sites are intended to guard consumers against dealers who lowball prices on new cars only to cut the trade-in prices on used vehicles.

Knowledge truly is power and knowledge of vehicle prices and dealer practices is shifting to a broad cross section of the car-buying public. Robert Eaton, Chrysler's chairman until 1998, estimated that 25 percent of U.S. auto buyers used the Internet at some point during the buying process in 1998 and that by 2000, half of the auto buyers would use the Internet as a research tool. Similarly, a 1998 survey by Dohring Company indicated that 10 percent of those likely to buy a car would be willing to skip the test drive and purchase a vehicle over the Internet. The Internet is terrifying to auto dealers because only 9 percent of Internet car buyers pay the full sticker price compared with 22 percent of the remainder of vehicle buyers.

Dealers Earn Less Money in Other Areas

Not only are profit margins being squeezed on new cars, but dealers are finding that their used car and repair operations are increasingly less lucrative. Used car prices began to decline on a year-over-year basis beginning in 1997. As prices of used cars have been deteriorating, so, too, have the fortunes of auto dealers, because they have come to depend increasingly on used car profits. In 1996, used

---

*Paul Eisenstein, "Buying Cars over the Web," *Investor's Business Daily,* March 3, 1998, p. A7.

vehicle sales contributed 35 percent of dealerships' profits, up from 14 percent in 1986.

The following are among the reasons that used car prices have been weakening:

- Because people on the lower rungs of the economic spectrum have been adversely affected by the reduction of government transfer payments—most notably welfare disbursements—their purchase of used cars has become more difficult.
- Many Americans' credit records are so blemished that they cannot qualify for auto loans. Personal bankruptcy filings reached a record 1.4 million in 1997, up more than 300 percent since 1980. In mid-1998, installment credit was roughly 20.4 percent of disposable income and 3.11 percent of credit card accounts were more than 30 days past due.
- Many subprime auto lenders have ceased to exist, significantly reducing the ability of used car buyers to obtain loans. At a Specialty Finance Conference at The New York Society of Security Analysts, Henry Coffey (managing director of J. C. Bradford & Company) remarked that AutoLend, First Merchants Acceptance, Jayhawk Acceptance, Reliance Acceptance, First Enterprise, General Acceptance, and Western Fidelity filed for bankruptcy protection in the same 1997 period during which the Money Store exited the industry.
- The plethora of leased cars returning to the market presents serious competition for used car prices. The percentage of new-car customers that leased rose from 15 percent in 1992 to more than 33 percent in 1997. Because the leased cars are in extremely good condition when they are returned to the market (they are usually only two years old and severe penalties are attached for such things as driving excessive miles) and are less expensive than new cars, many people prefer these preowned cars over the traditional used cars.

Moreover, American cars are durable, so less repair work by auto dealers is necessary. The median age of registered cars reached 8.1 years in 1997, a record high, and the average age of cars on the nation's roads has been increasing at the rate of two months each year. Also, in mid-1997, the number of vehicles in operation that were more than 11 years old was an amazingly high 75.3 million out of a total 201.1 million cars on the road. These numbers indicate that cars are being driven far past their warranties (under which the manufacturers cover dealer repairs).

Rising Costs Are Squeezing Dealers

In addition to declining revenues, auto dealers are beset with rising costs. First, compensation for mechanics is rising because repairing cars is becoming much more difficult as a result of electronics in cars. Doug Andrey, director of Information Systems at the Semiconductor Industry Association, said that the auto industry increases its organic purchases (which exclude growth in vehicle output) of semiconductors by 12 percent a year. Thus, today's mechanics require much more than on-the-job training. Rather, they are highly trained technicians that must take continuing education courses to remain current in their craft.

Second, auto dealerships are confronted with rising environmental remediation costs as there is increased sensitivity to pollution that may be caused by dealers' oil slicks, battery drainage, and other chemical emissions possibly impacting the property in and around the dealerships. Higher costs associated with compliance and environmental remediation reduce the appeal of remaining in the dealership business.

In the 1980s car dealers had an incentive to stay in business so they could benefit from steady increases in the value of their land. However, by the late 1990s, it became far less likely that dealers would receive windfall profits on the sale of the property on which their dealerships rested. Property values had not fully recovered from their highest points achieved in the 1980s, and environment liabilities threatened to further reduce the value of dealers' land. (If environmental liabilities were extensive, the land could even be appraised at a negative value.)

Third, independent auto dealers realize that they must make substantial investments in technology if they are going to be competitive players in their industry. For instance, customers are demanding computer kiosks in the showroom that allow shoppers to browse the complete inventory of vehicles available at each location. These kiosks also display pricing models that show the consumer the total and monthly payments for any vehicle in inventory under different lease and financing alternatives, and with different accessories, warranties, and other after-market products. Similarly, auto dealers are compelled to invest in management information systems and inventory control software.

In light of all of these obstacles, it is very appealing for many independent auto dealers to gracefully exit the auto retailing industry by agreeing to sell to a consolidator such as Republic Industries. This is especially true when the independent dealer receives shares from a consolidator whose management team enjoys a reputation for increasing shareholder value.

Consolidators Enjoy Advantages over Independents

Consolidators have numerous advantages over independent operators simply because of their larger size. The following are among those advantages:

- The superstore chains are professionalizing auto retailing. With meaningful insights mined from a large number of data points, they can adopt best practices across all of their stores, and they can retain effective managers with the prospect of moving up the ranks.

- Publicly traded auto dealership groups are negotiating preferred vendor arrangements to expand their market reach through national affiliations (e.g., Pep Boys provides discounts on aftermarket parts for Republic Industries) and lower the cost of goods sold through bulk purchase arrangements (e.g., United Auto Group buys its oil at a discount from Quaker State). Some superstores are taking this a step further and offer ancillary benefits such as free roadside towing, cellular phone centers, and discounts at corporate partners.

- Larger auto retailers can achieve more favorable economies of scale when implementing highly capital-intensive reconditioning centers. It is important that auto retailers have legitimate reconditioning centers because customers are increasingly demanding reconditioned used vehicles with service warranties; and most manufacturers have instituted used-vehicle certification programs.

- Big auto retailers can better afford to invest in expensive technology to automate inefficient back-office operations, to install computer kiosks, and to develop Web pages. Making such investments can result in the retailer's becoming enormously more efficient than dealers that fail to make such investments. For instance, computerizing a dealer's inventory is much more efficient than the traditional practice of writing the makes and models of the cars on the lots on index cards and calling other dealers in the network to query the availability of a particular vehicle. Republic Industries indicated that eliminating duplicative accounting, payroll, and management information systems departments would save it roughly $100 per new vehicle retailed in 1999.

- Placing more cars on one lot reduces transportation costs compared with dispersing the same number of cars on multiple lots.

- Publicly traded automotive superstores have access to less expensive capital than do independent dealerships because they can tap the stock and bond markets. This can represent a very substantial cost savings because the auto retailing business is very capital-intensive—real estate and inventory costs consume a great deal of capital.

- Larger auto retailers can better leverage their marketing costs. For example, a 30-second spot on a local radio program costs the same for large and small retailers, but the large retailer is likely to sell more cars from such ads.

Risks and Challenges to Consider

Despite the numerous advantages that automotive superstores enjoy over independent auto dealerships, you should be aware of the risks that confront even the largest auto retailers. Following are some of these risks:

- Superstores are subject to many of the same challenges that plague the independents. For example, deteriorating pricing on both new and used vehicles and reduced repair business as a result of greater durability of American cars are negative developments for all auto retailers. However, the superstores are better able to cope with these challenges.
- In the sale of used cars, it is very difficult to eliminate fraudulent practices by the sales force. When a used car is sold, the dealer typically faxes loan applications for the buyer. In attempting to close sales, the salesperson will often lie on the loan applications (e.g., understate miles on the odometer or underreport the number of dents in the doors) so that the collateral appears higher. The risk for the auto retailer is that some lenders will bar dealers that have lied on loan applications from submitting future loan applications. As buyers learn that they have less chance of securing loans from a particular dealer, they are likely to take their business elsewhere.
- The customer advocate approach to selling cars may be too subtle. Holding customers' hands may be good for building long-term relationships, but it's important that sales actually close, especially when the superstores have extremely high carrying (real estate and vehicles) costs.
- The fact that most auto rental companies are now publicly traded—instead of owned by the auto manufacturers as they were for many years—could result in reduced availability of used cars to sell. (As explained in "The Travel Industry" in Chapter 7, these profit-minded companies are retaining their cars for longer periods of time.) Even though there is pricing pressure in used cars, used car sales are still generally more lucrative than sales of new cars.
- Superstores take great pains to develop amenable relationships with their customers; but when these same stores sell used vehicles, facilitated by auto loans, they must become involved in the repossession business. And the repossession business is inherently anathema to fostering endearing customer relationships.

Investment Vehicles

The following are among the publicly traded automotive superstore retailers: CarMax Group, CrossContinent Auto Retailers, Lithia Motors, Republic Industries (which owns AutoNation USA), and United Auto Group.

Candles

Retail sales of candles in the United States have grown more than 10 to 15 percent annually throughout the 1990s and, according to the National Candle Association, reached $2.3 billion in 1998. Some 52.3 percent of all households own at least one candle, and unit volumes have soared from 40 million in 1992 to 700 million in 1997.

Although more detailed industry statistics do not exist, the rising popularity of candles is evidenced by candle manufacturers' growth. Blyth Industries, for instance, achieved a 42 percent compound annual revenue growth rate for the five-year period ending January 31, 1998. And for the three-month period ending July 31, 1998, Blyth, the largest publicly traded pure candle play, marked its 17th consecutive quarter of sales and earnings in excess of the comparable quarter a year earlier. And, in response to having detected the growing popularity of scented candles in the mid-1990s, Lancaster Colony increased its candle distribution facilities by over 450,000 square feet from 1996 to 1997.

Sales of candles, especially scented candles, are positioned to continue to run on all cylinders. One sign of their wide acceptance and the high level of repeat purchases of candles is that this once highly seasonal (Christmas) business now generates about 65 percent of its sales during the remainder of the year.

Candles Enhance Time Spent with Others

Candles are benefiting from the cocooning effect. Faith Popcorn stated in her book, *The Popcorn Report:* "Anything to do with home indulgences will be a big trend in the '90s and beyond. People are staying home more and people want their home environment to be nurturing and entertaining." Wendy Liebermann, president of WSL Strategic Retail, offers one explanation why people are spending more money on candles by saying, "Apparel is becoming less expensive because of the casual trend, leaving people with more money to spend, and they like to put it into their home." Many of the people that are spending more time relaxing and entertaining at home become accustomed to enjoying the nurturing effects of candles, which in turn encourages repeat purchases.

Ann Raddatz of Door County Candle Company explains: "Consumers are choosing candle fragrances to define the personality of their home much as they choose perfume or cologne to be their signature fragrance." Similarly, executives at Blyth Industries believe that customers "wardrobe" their homes through the use of candles, potpourri, and other fragrance products in different odors, colors, and forms. As a result, Blyth's management believes that candles are replacing scented air fresheners.

One reason home dwellers enjoy the natural light candles provide is that, in addition to reducing electric utility bills, candles reduce one's field of vision and thus allow people to focus more intensely on their conversation partners. This facilitation of more intimate dialog is highly valued in a world in which people are increasingly trying to compress time by multitasking. Shutting out part of a room also allows people to escape reminders of responsibilities, such as dishes to be washed or work to be completed.

Candle Sales Piggyback on the Spirituality Trend

Candle sales are, in part, being driven by the spreading interest in spirituality, mysticism, and inner reflection, a trend forecasters believe is fueled by proximity to the new millennium. While the New Age lifestyle was once believed to be confined to hippies and gypsies, Anne Alexander, editor-in-chief of the bimonthly *Natural Health* magazine, explains that these psychographics are now mainstream: "New Age is no longer an alternative lifestyle."

Although difficult to quantify, Americans are conservatively estimated to spend more than $12 billion a year on so-called unconventional therapies, of which candles are often part. *Forbes* magazine figures that nearly $2 billion more every year goes to thousands of aromatherapists, channelers, macrobiotic food vendors, and assorted massagers of mind and body. Corroborating evidence of growing spirituality is that, according to the Consumer Research Study on Book Purchasing, religious books accounted for 92 million of all of the books sold in 1997, up 53 percent from some 60 million five years earlier. Christian book retailers rang up $3 billion in 1997 versus $1 billion in 1980, according to CBA (formerly Christian Booksellers Association), a trade group of Christian-product suppliers.

The fact that so many dollars are allocated to quench Americans' thirst for spirituality and that so many lives revolve around enhancing their inner selves—despite the lack of virtually any coordinated marketing engines at work—suggests that New Age spirituality is much more than a fad resulting from an ephemeral advertising gimmick. Some trend spotters have even argued that spirituality is going so far as to replace organized religion, the family, and traditional organizations. Adherents feel so strongly about their New Age lifestyles that their beliefs have forged a political movement. The Natural Law Party, a creation of Transcendental Meditation followers, for example, claimed it had signatures to qualify for ballots in 48 states in the mid-1990s.

Soaring Sales of Aromatherapy Candles Have a Strong Foundation

Candles used in conjunction with aromatherapy are among the fastest growing segments of the candle industry. Aromatherapy candles emit specific smells as they burn and are believed to evoke specific psychological and physiologically therapeutic results. A growing legion of candle buyers believe that if a smell is pleasing or stimulating, neurotransmitters in the brain will generate pleasant sensations throughout the body, which will reduce pain and stress, stimulate appetite, arouse sexual feelings, and engender an overall sense of well-being.

TIP: Companies such as Aeron International sell aromatic scent diffusers for installation in vehicles to reduce stress associated with driving.

Aromatherapists rely on history and science to bolster their claims of aromatherapeutic healing. Greek warriors are known to have anointed themselves with oils before going into battle. In the Middle Ages in Europe, aromatic plants such as clove, cypress, sage, and rosemary were burned in an effort to control plagues. Even Hippocrates, the father of medicine, is said to have conducted studies that led him to believe that a daily aromatic bath and scented massage would promote good health.

During the turn of the 20th century, French chemist and author Dr. Rene-Maurice Gattefosse discovered that different natural applications had antiseptic, antiinflammatory and antiviral effects. Because of his work, lavender was used to decrease pain, and lemon, clove, and chamomile were used as disinfectants. These applications were carried on to the Second World War, when doctors used oils to prevent gangrene and to speed healing. Today, many people (especially believers in holistic healing) herald one aromatic fragrance, echinacea, for combating symptoms of the common cold.

Aromatherapies are effective because oils can enter the body through the air via the nose and bronchial passages or can be absorbed through the skin directly into the bloodstream by using massage. Although aromatherapy makes use of both inhalation and absorption, one American neurologist explains that of all the senses, smell has the greatest impact on human emotions. Smell receptors in the nostrils are directly linked to the brain's limbic system. Smell is the only sense that bypasses mental judgment and interpretation and goes straight to the center of emotions. In other words, aromas usually have an immediate effect, which is why smelling salts instantly revive.

The following are additional research findings on the effects of aromas:

- A study at the University of Cincinnati revealed that scent in offices significantly boosted computer operators' alertness and productivity. This study supported earlier findings of Japanese researchers who found that such fragrances as lemon significantly reduced errors among workers by as much as 54 percent and enabled enhanced concentration.
- Studies have been conducted proving that fragrances can reduce the incidence of long-haul truck drivers falling asleep behind the wheel. In one of these experiments, a device was constructed on which mounted sensors in a harness were placed around the driver's neck. If the driver began to nod off, a metered consistency of peppermint essential oil was sprayed into the cabin to stimulate the driver—thus keeping him awake.
- Another study conducted by Philadelphia's Monell Chemical Senses Center and by New York's Sloan-Kettering Memorial Cancer Center on magnetic-resonance-imaging patients proved that the scent of vanilla reduced the level of stress and anxiety patients experienced while undergoing treatment.

Other Drivers of Candle Sales

Candles' increasing utility is also partly responsible for the industry's growth. Many candles made with highly formulated wax burn evenly across and straight down and continue to emit their scents for the more than 150 hours that the candles last. Also, "smoke out" or "odor candles" actually destroy household and other foul odors as they burn, leaving a clean scent. Similarly, kitchen candles neutralize kitchen odors and freshen the air.

The combination of these attributes seems to be especially appealing to women. For example, Ted Forstmann, whose vaunted leveraged-buyout firm—Forstmann Little & Co.—acquired Yankee Candle Company in early 1998, reported that every single one of the women he surveyed said they like scented candles. Even though candle manufacturers' surveys show that 96 percent of all candles are purchased by women, men, too, appear to be warming to candles. Lorelei Kraft of Candles of the Earth has said: "Men are into candles now! The smells of cinnamon, vanilla, etc., give them home memories! We are also supplying the male trend with our outdoor look of embedded candles of pine-and-cone, birch bark, etc."

Foreign markets represents huge potential for candle makers. Candles are an inexpensive indulgence, and because they can be designed in almost any fragrance, shape, or color, they can be molded to suit any cultural preference. Moreover, foreign candle markets, especially for scented varieties, are severely underserved. For instance, even Europe's home fragrance candle market, which is equal in size to that of the United States and Canada, only derives 5 percent of its candle sales from scented candles, even though these candles are preferred by women by a margin of nearly three to one.

Investment Vehicles

Investors can participate in the growth of the candle industry by purchasing shares of candle manufacturers, such as Blyth Industries, which markets candles under the name Colonial Candle of Cape Cod; Eclipse Candles and Ambria brands; or Lancaster Colony Corporation, which sells its candles under the Candle-lite moniker. Investors can also play the candle industry by accumulating shares of candle sellers. Target Stores almost doubled the space allocated to candles through the late 1990s, during which time Caldor cut back its space for fragrances to clear space for scented candles. However, retailers that offer a purer play on candles are the home furnishings accessories retailers such as Bed, Bath & Beyond, Linens 'n Things, and Pier One Imports.

CHAPTER 4

Financial Services and Related Opportunities

The Internet is revolutionizing the delivery of financial services. Growing legions of consumers just cannot resist shopping, banking, and bill paying electronically. Also, online trading is so alluring that it can become addictive. In fact, New Jersey's Council on Compulsive Gambling has been just one sponsor of conferences that address the issue of compulsive online trading. Separately, the unprecedented wealth creation in the United States during the 1990s has resulted in millionaires becoming one of the fastest growing segments of the population. The financial institutions that manage their money are positioned to experience dynamic growth.

Electronic Commerce

Online commerce—particularly online retailing—exploded in the late 1990s and showed no sign of abating in early 1999. According to Boston Consulting Group, North American retailers sold more than $13 billion worth of merchandise online in 1998, up from $2 billion in 1997—absolutely smashing earlier projections of $3.3 billion in sales for 1998. Even Wal-Mart Stores, the largest and most powerful retailer of all, believed that the threat from E-commerce companies was so great that in its lawsuit against Amazon.com, Wal-Mart asserted that Amazon.com caused it economic damage.

Consumers are flocking to Internet retailing, primarily because of cost savings and convenience. Internet retailers have embraced and extended these advantages by offering a steady stream of innovations that not only make online shopping easy but actually fun. Despite the amazing growth posted by Internet retailers, the best is yet to come, for less than 1 percent of total retail sales were transacted over the Internet in 1998. The advantages of Internet retailing accrue to the benefit of companies that facilitate Internet commerce (e.g., America Online and Yahoo!) as well as to pure Internet retailers, such as Amazon.com, CDnow, Cyberian Outpost, and Barnes & Noble Online.

Growth of Consumer Electronic Commerce

Online retail sales are positioned to remain on their explosive upward trajectory. Consumers spent $4 billion buying goods and services in the fourth quarter of 1998, up from $1.1 billion during the same period in 1997. Forrester Research projects that cybershoppers will spend $108 billion by 2003, which will still only account for 6 percent of all U.S. retail spending.

TIP: Cisco Systems, the dominant Internet router company, is a major beneficiary of the growth of Internet commerce as well as all of the other data and video being delivered over the Internet because 80 percent of the Internet's traffic is routed through Cisco equipment.

One contributor to the growth of online commerce is that more people are connecting to the Internet. This is facilitated by the price of computers falling to as low as $600 in 1998 and the fact that essentially all computers have modems preinstalled. Thus, International Data Corporation projects that the 38 million online users in the United States at the end of 1997 will rise to over 135 million in 2002 and that the nearly 100 million online users worldwide in 1998 will multiply to some 320 million by 2002.

E-Commerce Consumers Feel Secure

The growing multitudes of people connecting to the Internet feel increasingly secure about executing purchases in cyberspace. This is as evidenced by the number of U.S. households that purchased holiday gifts online; the number more than quadrupled from 2 million in the winter of 1997 to 8.5 million in the winter of 1998. And, surveys conducted by Dell Computer Corporation and VISA USA indicated that between 43 and 46 percent of U.S. computer users shopped over the Internet in the fourth quarter of 1998.

Earlier predictions that consumers would be insufficiently secure to submit their credit card information over the Internet have proved to be diametric opposite of reality. First, using credit cards over the Internet is no less secure than giving one's credit card information to a stranger over the phone or at a cash register. Second, because millions of people feel secure enough to transact their stock brokerage and banking activity over the Internet, it is unlikely they will be reluctant to make relatively minor purchases in cyberspace. ("Online Brokerage Forms" in this chapter discusses online brokerage services in detail.)

Third, Internet security continues to improve as more Web sites are undergoing security audits and as encryption becomes more common. (See Chapter 10, "Network Security Providers.") Similar measures have proven sufficient for businesses and banks to rely heavily on electronic commerce for invoice presentment, order placement, and money wiring. Interestingly, the Treasury Department reported that it is 20 times more likely to have a problem with a fraudulently cashed check than with a fraudulently received electronic payment.

Fourth, even if hackers engage in E-commerce fraud or disruption, credit cards afford consumers inviolable protections. Most credit card issuers, for example, limit their customers' exposure to fraud to a $50 deductible, and some Internet commerce facilitators, such as IBM and AT&T, even indemnify these deductibles. Federal law also gives customers the right to dispute charges if merchandise never arrives and to withhold payment while the credit card issuer investigates reported problems.

TRAP: One of the weakest and most overlooked links in electronic commerce revolves around the issue of how items purchased online will be delivered to the customers. Substantial costs are associated with delivering packages to far-flung residential addresses and then returning several times, for 70 percent of online customers are not home when deliveries are made during the day. Alan Graf, Federal Express's chief financial officer, rhetorically asked: "Do we want volume for volume's sake?" His answer: "No." In addition, substantial risks of theft and fraud are inevitable when packages are left on customers' doorsteps. The major package delivery providers are straining to increase their package capacity by 50 percent from 1997 to 2001. Even if they succeed, the rate of capacity expansion will clearly be outpaced by Internet shopping and catalog growth. The result could be higher delivery costs, which might reduce the appeal of electronic retailing.

Additional Drivers of Electronic Commerce

Aside from all of the benefits that electronic commerce offers consumers, electronic retailing will continue to flourish as the result of very high reinvestment rates by retailers, a growing number of merchants making their merchandise available over the Internet, and strong recurring purchases from electronic customers. First, in 1998, online retailers reinvested about 65 percent of their revenue into marketing and ads, compared with a 4 percent reinvestment by traditional stores.

Second, the proliferation of businesses with an online presence offers consumers a greater variety of goods and services. According to the Department of Commerce, there were 1.5 billion registered domain names (e.g., www.dearborn.com) on the Internet as far back as July 1997. More specifically, 100,000 commercial Web sites in the United States conducted sales transactions in 1998, up from virtually none two years earlier.

Finally, existing customers stand to ignite Internet commerce. Research conducted by Boston Consulting Group found that online purchases rise dramatically after a consumer makes his third online purchase. Also, studies show that a satisfied E-commerce shopper talks about favorable experiences and draws six new customers to a merchant's site.

Primary Consumer Attractions for Electronic Commerce

The primary attractions consumers have for engaging in electronic commerce are price and convenience, as noted earlier. Electronic retailers pass on much of their cost savings (derived from the absence of maintaining physical stores) in the form of discounted prices to consumers. Because items purchased through the Internet are almost never taxed, consumers save additional dollars. In addition, the Internet is a nearly perfect medium for bargain hunting—comparing prices from one store to another is only a few mouse clicks away.

TRAP: Although low prices attract shoppers to cyberspace, retailers risk having their profit margins eroded by ceaseless price wars. Thus, some retailers are fighting back against electronic robots by blocking their entry into their Web sites and by disguising the total prices of their merchandise with service and delivery charges.

The introduction of robots—such as Junglee, Inktomi's C2B Technologies' unit, and Bottom Dollar—that search Web sites for the lowest prices on specific items has rendered comparative price shopping essentially effortless. Separately, Juniper Communications' research indicates that even when customers do not find drastic price savings via the Internet, they do not feel like they overpay because they feel empowered by the encyclopedic amount of product information available on the Internet.

In a time-scare era, consumers appreciate the convenience that electronic retailing affords. It is simply easier to shop over the Internet than to drive to a shopping mall, search for a parking space, visit numerous stores, maneuver through crowds, wait in long lines to make purchases, carry items to one's car, and deal with traffic congestion on the way home. The convenience of Internet shopping is especially appealing to the 60 to 70 percent of women who work part-time or full-time and who still do a disproportionate amount of shopping.

The following are among the additional conveniences of electronic shopping:

- Inclement weather does not impede consumers from shopping over the Internet.
- Unlike physical stores with limited hours of operation, Internet retailers are perpetually open for business. Interestingly, America Online indicated that approximately 40 percent of its merchants' 1998 online sales transactions took place during the evening and early morning hours of 10 PM–10 AM. Also, The Gap's online store is one of the company's largest stores. Given that The Gap has stores in close proximity to the preponderance of its consumers, the success of its Web site is a vote for convenience on the part of consumers.
- There are no problems getting waited on in cyberspace.
- Electronic retailing is a superb medium for purchasing such items as furniture or home entertainment systems that require spousal involvement. It is difficult for most couples to find the time to shop together for major household items. Rather than driving from store to store, couples can conveniently view selections over the Internet.

Enhanced Convenience of Internet Shopping

The leading Internet retailers such as Yahoo! and Amazon.com are constantly exploring ways of enhancing the online shopping experience. For instance, because electronic retailers track their customers' buying habits, they can make follow-up offers. If a customer buys one Sheryl Crow CD, it is likely the customer will respond favorably to an E-mail soliciting the purchase of Sheryl Crow's next release. The following are examples of innovative features offered by electronic retailers:

- The design quality of Web pages is improving, reducing the number of pages a user has to click through. The pages are more colorful and boast more pictures than before, not just text. For example, Lands' End allows shoppers to electronically model clothes on a three-dimensional mannequin similar in size and shape to a female buyer's own body.
- Yahoo! offered more than 2 million products from more than 27,000 different stores in late 1998. Such arrangements allow customers to enter their personal details and credit card information just once to make multiple purchases, which also safeguards against credit card abuse.

- Amazon.com features a personalization method called collaborative finger-printing that recommends new books by comparing one user's tastes with those of other book buyers purported to have the same tastes.
- Web sites such as Barnes & Noble's use select customers as marketers, offering customers discounts on products for every sale they refer.
- A wave of Web promotional companies—including Netcentives and FreeRide Media—have developed programs to reward consumers for visiting customer Web sites and clicking on ads there. FreeRide arranges for Web surfers to get points they can redeem for free movie tickets, CDs, books, or other items when they visit their clients' Web sites.

Operating Advantages Enjoyed by Electronic Retailers

Electronic retailers enjoy many of the same advantages that benefit catalog retailers such as Lillian Vernon and Coldwater Creek. Electronic retailers, for instance, do not incur the expense of maintaining physical stores and are not bothered by the logistical requirements that having stores entails. Not only do electronic retailers enjoy tremendous savings by eliminating physical stores, but they can actually go so far as to eliminate their warehouses. Retailers that have implemented drop-ship technology simply arrange to have product manufacturers deliver orders directly to customers. In such situations, drop-ship retailers such as Amazon.com essentially receive interest-free loans: they receive payment before orders are shipped but wait at least 90 days to remit payments to manufacturers.

TRAP: Just because Internet retailers do not maintain physical stores does not mean that virtual real estate is free. On the contrary, electronic retailers realize that they must pay steep rents to companies that can provide them with substantial traffic. For instance, in 1998, N2K signed a three-year, $18 million deal to become a tenant on America Online's shopping channel and Auto-by-Tel signed a three-year, $7 million agreement to be the exclusive automobile shopping site on Excite.

Other operating advantages enjoyed by electronic retailers include the following:

- Electronic retailers can achieve a national or international presence immediately.
- Because they are not space constrained, they can offer a virtually unlimited selection of merchandise.
- Electronic retailers gain clear measurement of item productivity. They know immediately when an item is not selling, which allows electronic

retailers to quickly change the price, change its positioning on the Web site, or eliminate the line entirely.

- There is no recovery (e.g., refolding clothing after shoppers rummage through clothing racks) associated with electronic retailing.
- Customer shoplifting is never a concern in cyberspace.

Investment Opportunities

The online retailers can be bifurcated into portal companies that offer virtual shopping mall atmospheres and pure-play retailers. Companies that are involved in providing a shopping mall atmosphere include Microsoft, America Online, Yahoo!, Excite, and Lycos. The second category—pure-play retailers—consist of names such as Amazon.com, eToys, Barnes & Noble.com, and CDnow. Many of the traditional retailers that are establishing electronic retailing—such as Claire's Stores and The Gap—may spin off their online retail divisions.

Online auctioneers such as eBay and uBid present interesting opportunities. These companies simply provide Web sites that enable sellers to offer their goods to potential buyers who negotiate via E-mail. Essentially everything from the online auctioneers is automated, resulting in minimal capital costs because there are no call center agents to take orders and no warehouses to hold inventory. Interestingly, the public TV program *Chubb's Antiques Roadshow* has helped fuel the boom in auctions. By traveling around the country and inviting the public to bring in items to be valued, this show saw its appraisal requests multiply five times in its first two years on the air. Online auctioneers are well positioned to capture much of the $100 million U.S collectibles market.

TRAP: The fact that online auctioneers are almost completely removed from the auctions that take place among their members presents an attractive economic model. However, a risk lies in the fact that their members have been accused of trafficking in illegal items, such as guns and grenades. Should online auctioneers fail to police their auctions, they could encounter adverse publicity at best and crippling lawsuits at worst.

Finally, another opportunity is business-to-business electronic commerce that International Data Corporation estimates will rise from $21 billion in 1998 to $330.6 billion in 2002. Large corporations and institutions can save up to 20 percent of the cost of products by buying on the Web by receiving discounts for bulk purchases. Another advantage of procuring supplies over the Web is that companies can reduce the headcounts in their purchasing departments. Companies offering software that enables electronic commerce include Sterling Commerce and Harbinger.

Check Printers

Electronic commerce will not render check printers obsolete. In 1998, Americans wrote 65 billion checks, double the number in 1978 and more than eight times as many as the average European and 122 times more than the average Japanese. In mid-1998, American consumers still had $600 billion in checking accounts. According to the Financial Stationers Association, more than 47.4 billion business and personal checks were printed in 1997, up 1.4 percent from the levels achieved in 1996.

Some of the reasons for check printers' staying power include the following:

- Americans like to delay paying their bills as long as possible and also like capturing as much float as possible.
- Americans like paper receipts, especially for tax purposes, because the Internal Revenue Service requires checks—not electronic-payment vouchers—as documentation and verification of transactions, which makes consumers hesitant about not having a check as proof.
- The more than 9,000 banks, savings and loans, and credit unions in the United States have made it difficult to achieve electronic standards, thus encouraging checks.
- Banks wish to continue earning money from checks. According to Deluxe Corporation, banks made $1.7 billion from selling checks in 1997 and earned another $1 billion in fees from service charges related to check presentment without sufficient funds. Another reason that banks like checks is that when people move, one of the first things they do is order new checks from their banks. And, technology is making checks easier and less expensive to process.

Thus, should shares of Deluxe Corporation or John Harland become beaten down to an excessive extent from fears of electronic commerce, they may represent compelling value.

Online Brokerage Firms

Online brokers have been experiencing extraordinary growth in their numbers of accounts, in the size of accounts, and in trading activity. Internet brokers should be able to maintain their rapid growth as they penetrate more of the investment community. Penetration stems from investors feeling increasingly confident about the security of Internet trades and that online brokers continue to offer more robust Web features and research tools.

A 1998 survey by the American Association of Individual Investors found that more than 95 percent of those polled were pleased with the quality of their online trades. Forrester Research predicted that online investing accounts would rise from 3 million and $120 billion in assets at the end of 1997 to 14.4 million accounts, representing $688 billion in assets in 2002. Much of this growth will come at the expense of full-service brokers. Finally, online brokers will be able to derive more revenue and achieve better customer retention by expanding their menu of financial services into areas such as banking, mortgage origination, and insurance.

Growth of Investor Ranks Is a Boon to Online Brokers

The growth of online brokerage is partly a reflection of Americans' becoming stock market junkies; their fixation for up-to-the-minute stock quotes is fed by ticker tapes streaming across monitors in airports, restaurants, and worksites. As investment methodologies have become widely taught and as investment information is easily obtained through television, radio, the Internet, and printed media, tens of millions of Americans have become stock market investors. Another driver of the proliferation of investors is that many companies compensate their workers (at least in part) with stock and stock options. (See also "Money Managers" in this chapter.)

The National Association of Investors Corporation reported that the number of investment clubs nationwide soared from 10,000 in 1993 to more than 37,500 in 1998. According to the Federal Reserve Board, one-half of all American households have some exposure to the stock market through direct ownership of shares, mutual funds, or 401(k) retirement plans. These investments are substantial—more than 28 percent of household assets were in stocks in mid-1998, the highest level since World War II.

Account Openings and Trading Volume Soar

According to Stephen Franco of Piper Jaffray, the ten largest online brokerages alone had more than 5.8 million online brokerage accounts in late 1998, more than double the 2.7 million accounts a year earlier. Many more investors that have full-service brokerage accounts are likely to switch to online trading. A PaineWebber internal study conducted in the fall of 1997, for example, revealed

TRAP: Although accessibility to online brokerage services improved substantially, from the stock market swoons of October 27 and 28, 1997 to the panic the week of August 31, 1998, a risk remains that online brokers will continue growing so fast that their technology will not be deployed quickly enough to ensure that all of their customers have unfettered access. For example, in the fall of 1998, many of Ameritrade's customers were infuriated that they could not retrieve account information.

that while only 8 percent of its full-service clients had an online trading account at another firm, a full 30 percent planned to open one in the next 12 months.

Enormous opportunity exists for online brokers to grow as there were approximately 80 million accounts managed by full-service brokers and traditional discounters in late 1998. Moreover, the approximately 20 million portfolios of those who monitored their accounts electronically represent nearly 15 million more accounts that could easily be brought online, as these account holders have demonstrated they are comfortable with the Internet.

During the third quarter of 1998, online traders were making 264,000 trades a day, up almost 90 percent from the previous year. Piper Jaffray estimated that 27 percent of retail trades were entered via personal computers in 1998, a 59 percent increase over the 17 percent of retail trades that online investors made in 1997. Online trading activity has been soaring as a result not only of more online accounts but larger account sizes. In fact, DLJdirect reported that its average online account in the second quarter of 1998 was 36 percent larger than a year earlier.

Extremely inexpensive commissions induce aggressive trading. It is not difficult to find online brokers that will execute a trade for $8 and some, such as Web Street Securities, do not charge any commission for executing trades of selected stocks. And monitoring stock prices in real time is conducive to making investment decisions. Thus, officials at Quick & Reilly reported that their customers trade four times as much when they go online. According to E*Trade, its customers average 25 trades a year, far more than the typical customer of a full-commission firm, who trades once or twice a year, or customers of traditional discount brokerage firms, who trade four to six times a year. The proliferation of handheld (or maybe even wearable) computers will generate even more electronic trades as investors will be able to remain perpetually connected with their brokerage accounts.

Commissions Are Low But Expenses Are Lower

Some investors are critical of online brokerage firms because they believe that the deeply discounted commission schedules will deprive those businesses of profits. While the preceding section more thoroughly explains the economics of Internet commerce, online brokers are spared many of the expenses that confront traditional discount brokers—they need little office space and few brokers as the customers execute their own trades.

Inexpensive commissions are not the primary factor that attracts investors to an online broker. In fact, the largest electronic brokerage firm, Charles Schwab, charged $29.95 a trade in late 1998, which was twice as much as the second largest electronic broker, E*Trade, which charged $14.95 a trade. And Schwab's 30 percent share of the daily online trading volume equaled roughly that of its next three online competitors combined. Schwab officials attributed their online success to their commission rates being 80 percent to 90 percent below full-service brokers' fees, their offering a broad array of innovative services, and the tight integration of their Web-based research products within their electronic trading environment.

Nevertheless, deeply discounted commissions are a reality in the online world, but their impact is mitigated by the following:

- Soaring numbers of trades compensate for some of the lower prices charged per trade.
- Some of the discounted commissions are available only to active traders; some trades are not executed at the least expensive commission levels; some of the advertised commissions apply only to a limited number of trades; and option trading (favored by many online traders) is often more expensive than trading stocks.
- Online brokers derive income from the interest they charge on their customers' margin accounts, from loaning stock to short sellers, and from deploying their customers' cash balances to their own higher-yielding accounts.
- Online brokers continue to receive payment for order flow, which means that market makers (professional traders on exchange floors who earn money by selling stocks higher than they buy them) rebate part of their spreads to the online firms that direct trades to them.
- Online brokers have established their own electronic communications networks (ECNs) that replace some of the human interaction of trading desks by matching trade orders through a computer. ECNs are giving online brokers an opportunity to take business from established market makers and stock exchanges. In fact, James Marks of Deutsche Bank Securities calcu-

lated that ECNs handled as much as 35 percent of the volume on the Nasdaq in late 1998; and established ECNs allow online brokers to collect fees from selling stock quotes to data vendors.

Online Trading Offers Enhanced Features

Online brokers have achieved the irreducible requirement of ensuring secure trading on their systems. In other words, investors should have confidence to trade online because no security breaches with online trading have been reported. For instance, K. Blake Darcy, CEO of DLJdirect, was quoted as saying: "As far as I know, security breaches have not occurred."* According to Scott Schnell, a vice president at RSA Data Security (an encryption software maker), there has never been an incident of someone intercepting a trading session and gaining access to personal financial data. And in September 1998, William A. Perez, a program coordinator in the Federal Bureau of Investigations' financial crimes section, said he was not aware of any investigations of hackers intercepting Web transactions in online trading.

Securities regulators have also taken initiatives to eradicate the fraudulent promotion of stocks on the Internet. For instance, in July 1998, the Securities and Exchange Commission established its Office of Internet Enforcement. By early November 1998, that office had already filed 23 cases against individuals or companies, alleging that they misled investors or failed to disclose details about pay arrangements with companies for touting their stock in online newsletters, message boards, Web sites, and junk E-mails.

Online brokerage services offer their customers much more than peace of mind and minuscule commissions. Online traders like the excitement of being directly tuned into the beating heart of capitalism. Online Web sites have become more tightly integrated with simultaneous displays of broad market averages, real-time stock quotes, news feeds, stock charts, research reports, and trade confirmations.

Other online customers appreciate being able to join online discussion groups as well as being able to post questions and answers about stocks. Some services gratuitously send pertinent news stories about stocks in their customers' portfolios via E-mail. Moreover, investors aren't embarrassed when closing out losing positions online (as they may be when placing orders through a stockbroker); and rather than installing special software, investors can simply access their brokerage firm from the Internet.

---

*Timothy Hanrahan, "On-Line Trading: Is It Safe?" *Wall Street Journal,* Sept. 8, 1998, p. R18.

Online brokers have proved to be dedicated to delivering innovative and important services to their customers. The following are a few examples:

- Many online brokers have arranged to furnish their customers with institutional research produced from the full-service brokerage firms. For instance, E*Trade provides its customers with research reports from Bank-Boston Robertson Stephens.
- Firms such as Charles Schwab, Fidelity Investments, DLJdirect, E*Trade, and Suretrade provide their customers with access to initial public offerings.
- Charles Schwab has developed an E-mail service that alerts customers to such events as their portfolios not being in balance with their asset-allocation models.
- Ameritrade's Web site allows investors to inform the computer—before making trades—if they are basic, intermediate, or advanced investors, allowing the computer to treat different customers differently. If users choose, they can look up definitions such as calls, puts, and spreads in addition to trading instructions.
- Fidelity Investments can alert customers who carry two-way pagers to breaking news or movements in stock prices. These customers can then respond by placing a buy or sell order over the airwaves.
- Online brokers once charged for real-time quotes, but unlimited up-to-the-minute quotes have been almost universally free since the late 1990s.
- Companies like E*Trade offer tear sheets that allow customers to view a portfolio of quotes on their personal computers while in any application.

Online Brokers Can Compete Effectively with Full-Service Firms

Full-service brokerage firms are burdened with several shackles that impede aggressive competition against online brokers. First, the larger firms are wedded to relying on their sales forces for selling stock to generate commissions and to win investment banking business. For instance, Merrill Lynch has some 15,000 brokers in hundreds of offices throughout the world; even rumors about their replacement by online trading would run the risk of their deserting to competing firms.

Second, online brokerage firms such as E*Trade use object-oriented applets (mini computer codes) that can perform such tasks as checking the status of trades or calculating how much a customer paid in commissions during a given month. On the other hand, the mainframe computers operated by the large brokerage firms are not designed to provide answers on the fly. Instead, they are designed to track huge volumes of trades during the day, process them during the night, and mail out uniform-looking statements at the end of the month. The significance is that many online traders are addicted to the services (such as obtaining account balances at two o'clock in the morning) that they receive from their online brokers but that are not available from the "full-service" firms.

Third, many full-service brokers are reluctant to risk devaluing the brand equity behind their names by making their services available to online investors. Morgan Stanley Dean Witter, for example, labeled the research it made available to its online accounts as Discover Brokerage Equity Research and referred to it as "institutional quality research" so as not to tarnish its reputation among its institutional clients. This is an indication that many of the full-service firms will refrain from capitalizing on the tens of millions of dollars they invest in their corporate identity.

Fourth, there is a strong possibility that the full-service brokerage firms will lose significant investment banking revenues to Internet-based brokers. Some companies, such as Spring Street Brewing Company, took themselves public solely through the Internet, and General Motors completed a $500 million bond offering over the Internet as long ago as 1997. In addition, companies such as StockPower and NetStock Direct help publicly traded companies sell shares directly to the public. Interestingly, companies have incentives to encourage their customers to become shareholders; J. C. Penney discovered that on average its shareholders visited a Penney store twice as often and purchased double the amount in a year as a nonshareholder customer.

Finally, consolidation of the online brokerage firms is inevitable, which will result in the larger online firms more effectively competing against the full-service brokerage firms. In late 1998, more than 100 Web sites offered investors the ability to trade online. This clearly seems excessive. As the better capitalized and more innovative sites offer their customers enhanced services, they should capture market share. In the third quarter of 1998, the six largest online brokers expanded their share of the market's trading volume by 150 basis points compared with a year earlier. Another benefit of consolidation is that the remaining operators will benefit from reduced competition.

Online Brokerage Is a Springboard for Other Electronic Financial Services

Not only will online brokerage firms compete effectively against full-service brokerage firms, but they will continue to take market share from other providers of financial services. Piper Jaffray offers one statistic that must be terrifying to the banks: In late 1998, the ten largest brokerage firms had $300 billion in customer assets, nearly double the year-earlier level. According to the Securities

Industry Association, this $300 billion was almost equal to 10 percent of household assets held in bank deposits and represented about 5 percent of assets held directly in equities by households.

Online brokers enjoy first-mover advantages, technological sophistication, the ability to operate at razor-thin margins, and a young customer base to whom they can market financial products for many years. According to a June 1998 report issued by Credit Suisse First Boston, just 27 of the nation's 100 largest banks and thrifts (as measured by assets) offered banking services over the Internet, and 17 of them did not even have a Web site. Thus, Jupiter Communications' projection—that online trading in households will reach 31 percent of the personal investing market by 2002 compared with on-line banking, which will reach only 19 percent of the banking market in the same year—seems valid.

One product line destined to cause severe hemorrhaging for banks is mortgages. Internet-based mortgage sites, which make it very easy for potential borrowers to compare rates and points, are converting mortgage originations into a commodity. In fact, in the late 1990s, increased competition among mortgage lenders caused points to drop to 1 percent of total mortgage amounts from the traditional 3 percent. Cumulatively, Freddie Mac estimates the widespread adoption of automated underwriting will save borrowers $2 billion in closing costs a year. Although delivering mortgages over the Internet is generally not profitable for banks, online brokers' minimal cost structures allow them to make some profit from online mortgages. How much loan origination business is at stake is indicated by Forrester Research's estimate that Internet-originated loans outstanding will soar from $265 million in 1997 to $25.5 billion in 2001. And according to a survey by Killen & Associates, Internet mortgage originations will reach 30 percent of total mortgage originations by 2005.

Moreover, the young, upscale professionals trading online are likely to be heavy borrowers because they are at a stage in life when they are still acquiring major assets like houses and cars. Online brokers' lending efforts will benefit from the well-established consumer tradition of borrowing from such nonbanks as American Express, Discover, and The Money Store.

Finally, many online brokers are becoming increasingly competitive in electronic bill payments, mutual funds distribution, and insurance and credit card sales. Charles Schwab's vision is to offer its customers unlimited financial information and one-stop shopping for all their financial needs. In pursuit of this goal, Schwab teamed up with search engine Excite and Intuit's quicken.com to share content between Web sites about investing, mortgages, retirement, taxes, and insurance.

Investment Vehicles

The brokerage firms that derive a substantial portion of their revenues from online brokerage include Ameritrade, Charles Schwab, Donaldson Lufkin & Jenrette, E*Trade Group, National Discount Brokers, Southwest Securities, Toronto Dominion's Waterhouse Securities, and Track Data.

Money Managers

Managing money for the superwealthy is a rapidly growing industry. The ranks of truly wealthy Americans is growing much faster than the overall population. Because most people do not believe that their pensions and Social Security will sustain them in their years of retirement, aging baby boomers realize that they must invest wisely. The increasing sophistication of financial products and more demanding time pressures throughout society are convincing wealthy people that they require the services of professional money managers. Companies positioned to benefit from the convergence of these trends include trusts, asset management firms, mutual fund companies, and community banks located in wealthy areas.

Ranks of American Millionaires Skyrocket

While the American population is growing 1 percent a year, the number of millionaires is increasing as much as 13 percent a year, or 13 times as fast as the overall American population. A 1998 *Wall Street Journal*/NBC News poll revealed that 24 percent of Americans believed they would eventually become millionaires. As millionaires have become commonplace, having a net worth of $1 million has become insufficient to be considered truly wealthy. In many people's minds, to be wealthy one has to earn at least $1 million a year or have accumulated a net worth many times the $1 million threshold.

TIP: Although most investment banks benefit by underwriting companies that go public, the most leveraged firm in initial public offerings is Friedman, Billings and Ramsey.

Many people today have shattered the $1 million barrier. In my experiences moderating industry conferences at The New York Society of Security Analysts, I have introduced dozens of executives who earn more than $1 million a year or who are at least decamillionaires. My experiences are not an aberration—the Internal Revenue Service revealed that the number of Americans reporting an annual income of over $1 million surged from 14,834 in 1984 to 111,728 in 1996.

Not only are more people becoming millionaires, but a growing number of millionaires are moving into the ranks of decamillionaires and beyond. Even though individuals' wealth is both difficult to ascertain and a moving target, *The Economist* stated that America boasted 170 billionaires (up from a mere 13 in 1982), 250,000 decamillionaires, and 4.8 million millionaires in mid-1998. An indication that having a net worth of several hundred million dollars is no longer a distinguishing characteristic is that the wealth needed to make *Forbes'* list of the 500 richest Americans roughly doubled from not quite $400 million in 1994 to almost $800 million in 1997.

The number of households with at least $1 million of investable assets doubled from 1993 to 1997 and is projected to continue growing at a 13 percent annual rate through 2008. In addition, the number of millionaire Americans is projected to soar from 4.8 million in mid-1998 to 11.8 million in 2010. A diversity of drivers are responsible for Americans becoming so wealthy. Some of these factors include the strength of the stock market, trends in executive compensation, roll-ups (consolidation) of small businesses, and the exorbitant incomes earned by many entertainers and athletes.

TIP: Investors wishing to play the trend in soaring executive compensation can do so through the shares of Marsh & McLennan Companies, which owns William M. Mercer Companies, a leading compensation consultant. Another interesting vehicle is Clark/Bardes Holdings, a compensation consultant that specializes in helping companies generously compensate their employees while retaining maximum tax advantages. Also, ASI Solutions conducts surveys of executive compensation on which consultants' recommendations are often based.

The Stock Market Contributes to Extreme Wealth

There are four main avenues through which a buoyant stock market contributes to people becoming multimillionaires. First, when entrepreneurs take their companies public, they more often than not become overnight decamillionaires. Some founders become much wealthier. Marc Andreeson of Netscape became worth at least $100 million and Jeff Bezos's shares of Amazon.com have been valued as high as $4.5 billion. Usually, the first wave of employees (even junior-level employees) hired by a company that goes public shares in the prosperity. For instance, the first administrative assistant to Oracle's Larry Ellison received shares eventually valued at $35 million.

TRAP: The wealth effect created by a vibrant stock market can also work in reverse. An anemic stock market would cause the market for initial public offerings to evaporate, stock options would expire worthless, targeted corporations would likely reject stock-financed buyout offers, and investors' portfolios could plunge.

Second, executives who are compensated with shares of the stock of successful companies or are given a generous amount of options can amass exorbitant wealth. Examples include:

- According to a *New York Times* analysis of the compensation of chief executives at 279 of America's 500 biggest publicly held companies, average total pay—consisting mostly of salary, bonuses, and the present value of stock options—was $8.7 million in 1997.
- The value of options granted to CEOs and other executives at 2,000 companies surveyed by Sanford C. Bernstein & Co. quintupled from $8.9 billion in 1992 to $45.6 billion in 1997.
- The CEOs of 180 of the nation's largest public companies held an average of $28.7 million in their company's options at the end of 1997, according to the compensation firm Pearl Meyer & Partners.
- In 1997, roughly 1 in 10 chief executives had pay packages worth at least $20 million, up from only 1 in 40 chief executives in 1996.
- Even as far back as 1996, 59 of the CEOs of the 350 largest companies became centimillionaires from their companies' shares, according to Mercer Management.

Rather than limiting stock and stock options to senior executives, companies have widely disseminated them throughout the nation's rank and file. A growing number of companies—such as Intel, PepsiCo, and Starbucks—offer stock options to all, or essentially all, of their full-time employees. According to William M. Mercer, Inc., the percentage of major companies granting stock options to a broad range of employees rose from 5.7 percent in 1993 to 11.1 percent in 1997; and the National Center for Employee Ownership reported that broad-based stock option plans covered about 5 million workers in mid-1998, up from 1 million in 1990. Also, Pearl Meyer & Partners' research has indicated that the nation's 200 largest companies nearly doubled the number of shares authorized for equity incentive plans from 6.9 percent of common shares outstanding in 1989 to 13.2 percent in 1997.

The value of such employee equity compensation can be substantial. At least one out of every seven Microsoft employees, for example, owns a minimum of $1 million worth of their employer's stock. Some 1,500 Dell Computer employees were said to have held at least $1 million in Dell stock in early 1998.

Third, a vibrant stock market facilitates industry consolidation because public companies can issue highly valued shares of stock to owners of businesses they acquire without diluting their earnings. As dominant publicly traded companies acquire smaller, privately held businesses, owners of the acquired companies typically receive millions of dollars worth of the acquiring company's stock. Roll-ups of small firms by their larger competitors have occurred in sectors as diverse as physician practices,* waste management, automotive dealerships (see Chapter 12), and home security (see Chapter 10).

TRAP: Companies that are growing rapidly by acquiring smaller players in exchange for their stock could experience pressure on their shares because the owners of the businesses that sell to the consolidators have little interest in retaining the consolidator's shares. These owners are typically people who have built their businesses over several decades and view the receipt of a consolidator's shares as a means to enjoying the fruits of their labor.

Acquisitions of private companies reached $84 billion in 1996 and appear to remain on a steep upward trajectory. Moreover, sellers are receiving more consideration as the cost of these acquisitions has been rising. According to JP Morgan research, the earnings multiple paid for private companies rose from 15.5 times earnings in 1995 to 18 times earnings in 1996.

Fourth, an ascending stock market creates substantial wealth for holders of publicly traded shares. Investors with a few hundred thousand dollars invested in the stock market at the beginning of the 1990s could have achieved portfolios worth more than $1 million by the end of the 1990s without much difficulty. In total, investors' stock portfolios soared by $6.7 trillion from 1990 to mid-1998; and assets in stock mutual funds reached $4.5 trillion in 1997, up from $1.1 trillion in 1990.

---

*See David Wanetick, *Bound for Growth* (Burr Ridge, Ill.: Irwin Publishing–McGraw-Hill, 1996).

Tens of millions of Americans participate in the stock market as reported by the Internal Revenue Service—20 percent of American tax returns include Schedule D on which capital gains and losses of stock shares are reported. And there were some 80 million brokerage accounts in 1998 (although there were fewer account holders since individuals frequently hold multiple accounts).

Other Sources of Extreme Wealth

Entire industries are mass producing millionaires. The traditionally lucrative professions of law and medicine are being surpassed by sports and entertainment in the creation of wealthy individuals. In addition, hundreds of financial professionals earn at least $1 million a year while thousands of computer programmers accrue $1 million or more through the receipt of stock options. Finally, inheritance remains a major source of individuals' becoming extremely wealthy.

According to *American Lawyer* magazine's survey of the nation's 100 top-grossing law firms, average profits per partner reached $587,000 in 1997 and all of the "Top 10" firms paid their partners an average of at least $1 million. Although lawyers had long coveted partnerships at top-tier law firms and considered working as corporate counsel a stigma, lawyers have recently reversed their preferred career track. Partners at law firms share their firms' profits, which are effectively valued at one times earnings. However, when corporate counselors receive shares from their employers, the shares can be valued at 30 or 40 times a firm's profits. The leverage on earnings is even greater with options.

TIP: Hundreds of lawyers are becoming multimillionaires from suing the tobacco industry. The lawyers for Florida, Mississippi, and Texas who won a $34.4 billion settlement against the tobacco industry were awarded an $8.2 billion fee. These fees are likely to be only the tip of the iceberg, as the legal fees awarded to lawyers representing the 43 additional states and 5 territories that were suing the tobacco industry for the remainder of the $206 billion national settlement in early 1999 had not yet been determined.

It has become common for many athletes to earn at least $1 million a year, excluding endorsements. Even as far back as in 1995, 246 major league football players, 241 baseball players, and 159 hockey players made $1 million or more. For the 1998 season, the National Football League's average salary was about $850,000, while baseball players averaged almost twice that much. Even hockey players earn $1 million on average. In the 1998 round of baseball free-agent signings, just seven teams lavished $730 million on 29 players. Moreover, a centimillionaire class of athletes is emerging. In 1998, the National Basketball Association had 5 players with $100 million contracts, and in December 1998 Kevin Brown signed a record $105 million seven-year contract with the Los Angeles Dodgers.

TIP: A derivative play on the soaring compensation for athletes is through shares of Nike, which acts as an agent for many top athletes and prospers as Nike-wearing endorsees become popular culture icons. In fact, Nike outfitted 230 National Basketball Association (NBA) players and 10 NBA teams in 1998.

Financial services are minting millionaires. In 1997, for example, more than 400 Goldman Sachs bankers collected over $1 million. As commercial banks are migrating into investment banking, they are poaching successful investment bankers with four-by-four contracts—guaranteeing each banker a minimum of $4 million a year for four years.

The motion picture industry remains another breeding ground for millionaires. According to *Entertainment Weekly,* 133 Hollywood stars received at least $1 million per picture in 1996. Of course, superstars like Sylvester Stallone and Demi Moore typically earn tens of millions of dollars for each film, and they are often cast in several pictures every year.

TIP: Mark Leslie, president of Veritas Software, remarked that the extremely tight market for skilled computer programmers compelled him to take his company public. The lesson: to attract and retain skilled talent requires offering stock options that have the potential to be worth millions of dollars.

Finally, baby boomers will be the beneficiaries of an enormous transfer of wealth. Economists at Cornell University estimated that the baby boomer generation would be bequeathed an estimated $10.4 trillion from 1995 to 2020.

Insecurity about Retirement Drives Investors to Professional Money Management

As baby boomers move closer to retirement age, they are becoming more focused on building their financial portfolios. This focus intersects with growing skepticism about the long-term viability of the Social Security system. Surveys conducted in 1998 indicate that 64 percent of baby boomers believe that Social Security will eventually be scaled back or eliminated. These fears are founded on rational analysis of the problematic state of the Social Security system. Although 3.3 workers paid the benefits of each retiree in 1998, only 2 workers are projected to pay for each beneficiary in 2030. Because tax receipts covered only 75 percent of projected benefits in 1998, many authorities have estimated that the Social Security Trust Fund would be bankrupt by 2032. And according to the Census Bureau, some 40 million Americans will be over 65 by 2010, twice as many as in 1970. By 2050, the number of Americans over 65 is expected to double again to almost 80 million.

In light of these challenges confronting the Social Security system, only 10 percent of male baby boomers and 21 percent of their female peers believe Social Security will be their primary source of retirement income. I believe fears about the future of Social Security, concerns about the viability of pension funds, reverse mortgages vacuuming out homeowners' equity, and heavy borrowing from retirement accounts will result in a surge in people turning to professionals for investment advice.

The realization that professional assistance is needed to manage one's finances is reinforced by tax laws changing frequently and becoming more convoluted. The seemingly instant millionaires that result from stock options, entertainment contracts, inheritances, and litigation victories are often money management amateurs. Regardless of how one attains wealth, having significant assets presents a number of challenges—real estate management, portfolio management, retirement planning, estate planning, and liquidating shares received as compensation.

While there is a growing need for asset management, relatively few wealthy households are availing themselves of such services. In fact, less than 50 percent of the $4 trillion held by affluent individuals is professionally managed; and less than one-third of the families that earn over $200,000 a year have their money professionally managed.

However, this undermanagement of assets is beginning to change. Many large companies have been at the forefront of realizing that their senior executives require money management services. According to a 1998 Hewitt Associates survey of 400 large companies, 66 percent provided financial counseling to their top executives. Johnson Associates reported that large companies will typically spend an average of $25,000 for a one-time fee to analyze a top executive's portfolio, and an additional $10,000 to $15,000 annually to manage those finances. These services are becoming increasingly lucrative. Steven Herrmann, vice president of financial education services for American Express Financial Advisors, stated that executive financial services that would have cost companies about

$500 in 1994 or 1995 have expanded to include a range of services carrying an annual price tag of $2,500 to $15,000.

Investment Vehicles

Investors wishing to capitalize on the trend of large numbers of Americans becoming extremely wealthy should consider investing in the following vehicles:

- *Publicly traded trusts.* Companies such as U.S. Trust Corporation, Northern Trust, and Wilmington Trust provide individual account management for all of their clients' assets. Also, FAC/Equities' banking analyst Kevin Timmons pointed out that several banks such as Mellon derive a large percentage of their income from their trust departments. Specific services range from estate planning to philanthropic consulting to issuing all of their clients' personal checks from discretionary accounts.
- *Investment management companies.* Companies such as Alliance Capital Management, United Asset Management, Lexington Global Asset Managers, Atalanta/Sosnoff Capital Corporation, and PIMCO Advisors manage hundreds of billions of dollars through their affiliated companies for high-net-worth individuals, pensions, endowments, union benefit plans, and professional groups.
- *Mutual fund companies.* Mutual fund providers such as Eaton Vance, Pioneer Group, T. Rowe Price Associates, and Federated Investors are positioned to continue benefiting from Americans becoming more ardent investors and baby boomers saving for their retirement. Derivative plays on mutual fund growth are offered through the shares of SEI Investments and State Street Corporation, which provide back office services (such as securities processing and investment accounting) to mutual fund companies.
- *Community banks.* Community banks that are located in areas where tremendous wealth is being created should prosper from the trends discussed in this chapter. Examples of banks that are favorably located include Chicagoland's Wintrust Financial Corporation, Silicon Valley Bancshares, Connecticut-based Webster Financial, Long Island's Roslyn Bancorp, and Santa Barbara Bancorp.

Derivative Wealth Industries

Savvy investors can leverage their knowledge of trends by investing in multiple industries. For instance, investors can apply their knowledge of the growth drivers underpinning the rising incidence of wealthy Americans by investing in industries that will benefit from the same developments. In particular, investors who concur with my thesis about the appeal of money managers should consider investing in exclusive retailers, executive recruiters, art auctioneers, and golf course operators.

Exclusive Retailers

Exclusive retailers like Tiffany's and Neiman-Marcus are poised to benefit from the rapidly rising number of wealthy Americans. According to Age Wave, a research firm, 8.3 million households had incomes of $100,000 or more in 1997. In addition, the incomes of the top 20 percent of Americans, which start at $75,000 a year and are mostly above $90,000, have been growing faster than the incomes of everyone else.

Alongside the opportunity that individuals of increasing wealth provide such exclusive retailers as Nordstrom and Proffitt's (which acquired Saks Holdings in 1998), a very large number of Americans behave as if they were actually extremely wealthy. Striving to become wealthy is nearly a national goal. For instance, while only 58 percent of college freshman polled in 1997 considered becoming "very well off financially" an important objective, 75 percent believed that achieving wealth was an important goal in 1998.

As the nation becomes increasingly prosperous, satisfying material needs has become inadequate. Consumers now strive to satisfy their psychological needs for the accoutrements of wealth. Juliet Schor, a Harvard economist and renowned expert on the wealthy, has postulated that as Americans barely know their neighbors, as civic activity (a potential substitute for spending) has declined, and as religious and social taboos against excessive consumption have deteriorated, Americans define themselves, not by where they live, their civic activities, or their religious beliefs, but rather by the level of their material possessions.

TRAP: Silicon Valley technology entrepreneurs are a large source of the nouveau riche. Many of these technomillionaires, however, are not at all interested in upscale fashion. Jeans, T-shirts, and shorts are office norms. Interestingly, David Filo, a cofounder of Yahoo!, long refused to wear shoes at the office.

Americans have traditionally tried to maintain living standards comparable to their neighbors. However, the new view of life is not through the kitchen window but through the television screen, in catalogs and advertisements that endlessly promote luxury products, or in office settings where lower-level workers are often in contact with wealthy colleagues. As Juliet Schor said: "Today, a person is more likely to be making comparisons with, or choose as a reference group, people whose incomes are three, four or five times his or her own." Thus, Professor Schor argues that most Americans are trying to mimic the lives of the upper 20 percent on the income ladder by dressing and furnishing their homes similarly. Such competitive consumption is a boon for upscale retailers like Gucci Group N.V.

Executive Recruiters

Executive recruiters are a largely overlooked beneficiary of soaring executive compensation. This is primarily because leading executive recruiters such as LAI Ward Howell and Headway Corporate Resources' The Whitney Group typically earn a percentage—usually in the 33 percent range—of a placed executives' first year cash compensation.

Revenue in the global executive search industry grew at a 17 percent compound annual rate, from approximately $3.5 billion in 1993 to $6.5 billion in 1997. Kennedy Information, the leading research firm for executive recruiting, expects the executive recruiting industry to continue to grow at a 15 percent annual rate, with global revenue projected to reach $10 billion by 2000.

Search firms have become more valuable to their clients by not only simply finding candidates but by becoming more specialized and thus better able to evaluate and identify the top candidates in each field. Executive recruiters such as Heidrick & Struggles and Korn/Ferry International should benefit from the following factors:

- Clients are increasingly willing to outsource the recruitment of senior management to experts because astronomical executive compensation has raised the stakes of hiring the right employees. Senior executives demand massive stock options, insist on being indemnified for forfeiting their incentive pay arrangements at their former employers, expect supplemental pensions, and require their new employers to purchase their house when relocating.
- The increase in executive turnover has intensified the competition for highly qualified executives and forced many companies to recruit executives more frequently. Rapid executive turnover is attributable to faster burnout from punishing workloads, the absence of a need to work after executives cash out, and executives' propensity to form new business ventures.

- Other factors resulting in more business for executive recruiters include increased competition from falling trade barriers, deregulation, and adoption of technology. The need to respond to international opportunities, fierce competition, and diminishing product cycles require searching outside organizations to fill positions traditionally reserved for internal candidates.

Art Auctioneers

In addition to wealth creation, art auctioneers—mainly Sotheby's Holdings and Christie's International plc—operate at the intersection of many developments that I believe will cause the value of art to continue its robust appreciation. Interest in works of art has spread throughout the United States as a result of greater wealth, the proliferation of the Internet, and the realization that investments in art collections can be very financially rewarding. Because rising demand for art cannot be satisfied by new works from deceased masters—and because few collectors liquidate their holdings even when prices reach record levels—prices of works of art are positioned to rise mightily.

TIP: Sotheby's and Christie's should benefit from France's vows to open its art market to foreign auctioneers beginning in early 1999.

The skeptics who opined that the Asian economic meltdown in 1997 and 1998 would cause a depression in the art market could not have been more wrong. For instance, a 1964 Jasper Johns painting that renowned collectors Victor and Sally Ganz bought for $15,000 was sold for $7.9 million in a fall 1997 auction; Andy Warhol's Brillo boxes that sold for $500 in 1964 fetched $33,000 in 1998; and Vincent Van Gogh's *Portrait of the Artist without Beard* sold for a record $70 million in November 1998. Similarly, Christie's reported that its jewelry sales rose 13 percent in the first half of 1998 versus the first half of 1997.

Rising Wealth Leads to Art Collecting

One misperception about art collectors is that they are restricted to a gentrified, old-money genre. Nothing could be further from the truth. Many of the nouveau riche collect art as a seal of their arrival. In fact, many young technical wizards who have become millionaires adorn their homes with expensive art. This art appreciation is confirmed by the success of museums in Seattle and San Jose. To house new donations of art, the three major Seattle art museums added a total of 200,000 square feet of space—or more than 4½ acres—from 1992 to 1996. During these years, the Seattle Art Museum tripled in size, added 2,556 pieces of art, and added 8,000 new members to its rolls over the same period of time. To keep attendance at its May 1998 ball to a manageable level, the Seattle Art Museum had to increase its ante for a pair of tickets from $1,000 to $5,000.

Seven out of 25 of the members of the San Jose Museum of Art's Board of Directors in 1998 were from the high-technology industry, with representation from Hewlett-Packard, Network General, 3Com and Lam Research. According to my conversations with museum officials, the museum's Circuit 2000, a group in which members pay $10,000 annual dues, is represented in large number by people from the high-technology community. Moreover, this museum nearly doubled its square footage from 1991 to 1998, and its membership grew threefold from 1996 to 1998.

As Americans become wealthier, they become more cultured and thus the market for works of art expands. In the words of Allen Tullos, an American studies professor at Emory University, "Taste is mainly class language. If you have got the money, you are going to widen your palette." The following are indications that appreciation for the finer things in life has become prevalent throughout the nation:

- Nearly 27 million people attended theatrical stage shows during the 1997–1998 season—almost 60 percent of them from outside New York—generating a record $1.3 billion in ticket sales, according to the League of American Theaters and Producers. The number of nonprofit, professional theater companies in the United States had grown to more than 800 in 1998 compared with fewer than 60 in 1965, according to Theater Communications Group.
- More than 110 American symphonies have been founded since 1980, according to the American Symphony Orchestra League.
- Opera attendance, spurred by the use of computerized supertitles that translate lyrics, climbed to nearly 7.5 million in the 1996–1997 season, up 34 percent from 1980. In 1998, there were 110 professional opera companies in the United States, 34 of which were founded after 1980.
- The percentage of Americans who listened to classical music on the radio rose from 19 percent in 1982 to 41 percent in 1997.
- The number of cases of red table wine consumed in the United States rose from 23.2 million in 1991 to 58.2 million in 1997.
- The percentage of 614 fine-dining establishments rated by Distinguished Restaurants of North America and located in rural areas increased from 19 percent in 1993 to 27 percent in 1998.

- *Bon Appetit* sells nearly one-third of its 1.1 million copies each month in U.S. heartland states, and more than one-quarter of the 810,000 copies of *The New Yorker* do not go to the East or West Coast.

The Internet Ignites Interest in Art

The Internet is proving to be a highly effective medium in delivering images of artworks to an increasingly receptive audience. This is made possible by the fact that many museums take digital photos of their works and make them available via the World Wide Web. For instance, Paris's Louvre Museum has a Web site with a photo of the *Mona Lisa* as well as other paintings and ancient Oriental, Egyptian, Greek, Etruscan, and Roman sculptures. Dozen of museums—such as The Cleveland Museum of Art, the National Gallery of Art in Washington, the Museum of Modern Art, New York, and the San Francisco Museum of Modern Art—make their collections available to Web users.

The Internet is popularizing art by doing more than bringing the most revered paintings to everyone's desktop computer. Viewing art on Web sites is free and virtual galleries are always open. As the Web sites are continually updated, patrons can preview traveling art exhibitions. Most museums provide extensive supporting information for each work and some sites even include audio interviews with artists. Rather than cannibalizing the number of their visitors, museums actually find that making their collections available over the Internet increases museum traffic. Kenneth Hamma, head of collections information planning for the J. Paul Getty Museum in Los Angeles, has said that "museums used to worry that people would look at art online and then not visit museums. Now we know that the more you show people what you have, the more they want to see the real thing."

TIP: Sotheby's and Christie's International prosper by not having to pay their employees excessive compensation. One reason is that art experts who wish to work for a major auctioneer have no alternative employers. Even though art dealers could seek employment at museums, museums pay much less than the auctioneers. Finally, many of the people that work for Sotheby's and Christie's are so wealthy that annual salaries are largely immaterial.

Sotheby's seized on the opportunities presented by the Internet by launching a Web site detailing the more than 500 auctions in 80 collecting categories that Sotheby's holds every year. Increasing demand for art through electronic distribution is exciting because greater demand is not matched by increasing supply (the great artists are dead and collectors rarely sell just because prices are rising), which causes prices to rise. This is a potent combination as art auctioneers' profits are a function of the commissions (based on the prices of the collectibles they sell) received.

Art Is Being Recognized as a Legitimate Investment

Collecting art has traditionally been more of a demonstration of one's wealth than a means to achieving wealth. However, more collectors should surface as there are more financial imperatives to amassing an art collection. First, after spending more than a decade calculating 280 years' worth of auction prices, Yale School of Management economist William Goetzmann calculated that a diversified portfolio of good art can beat the stock market with an average annual return of 17 percent.

Second, tax laws have been amended to allow fractional ownership, whereby an art owner receives a tax break when donating a portrait to a museum for part of the year but is still allowed to keep the painting in his home for the balance of the year. (Similarly, Nevada's passage of a tax break on valuable art placed on public view resulted in Mirage Resort's Bellagio Gallery of Fine Art displaying $300 million worth of fine art.) Third, some lenders, such as Citibank, lend money against their customers' art collections.

In conclusion, the growing number of Americans interested in art and the new breed of profit-minded art collectors should heighten the bidding battles for artworks, antiques, and jewelry, which will accrue to the benefit of Sotheby's and Christie's International.

Golf Companies

Golf has traditionally been considered a sport reserved for the wealthy. In fact, many of the ultrarich are distinguishing their residences with driving ranges, putting greens, and even complete golf courses. Although millions of wealthy individuals are devoted golfers and the growth in the number of wealthy Americans is positive for the golf industry, younger and less affluent people are taking up the sport. However, a dichotomy has arisen as far as the companies that will benefit from these trends. Golf course operators will enjoy a much more prosperous future than will golf club manufacturers.

Golf Enjoys Broader Appeal

A steadily rising number of Americans are playing more rounds of golf each year. In fact, the number of golfers climbed 7 percent in 1997 to 26.5 million and some 5.6 million Americans are avid golfers, meaning they play 25 or more rounds a year. Other indications of golf's soaring popularity: The Golf Channel has more than 17 million viewers and broadcasts 24 hours a day; U.S. overall spending on golf fees and equipment increased from $7.8 billion in 1986 to $15.1 billion in 1997; and golf courses continue to open at a voracious rate. In 1996, 442 new U.S. golf courses opened and 450 courses opened in 1997; at the beginning of 1998, there were 932 courses under construction and 720 in the planning stages.

Golf is becoming more popular because young people are participating in the sport for the first time and because aging baby boomers are increasing their commitment to the game. Partly as a result of the appeal of Tiger Woods and Michael Jordan, ethnically diverse young people began learning golf in the late 1990s and were a primary reason that, according to the National Golf Foundation, the number of beginning golfers rose 51 percent in 1997 to 3 million. Baby boomers, too, are driving demand for golf higher. The abundance of middle-age people contributed to the total number of golf rounds played growing 15 percent in 1997 to 547 million. This demographic will be even more significant because the Census Bureau reports that the number of Americans over 50 will climb 39 percent between 1996 and 2010. As golfers age, they tend to play more rounds of golf each year. (Disposable time is increasing; golf is a game in which practice yields improvement; and golf is not strenuous or conducive to injury.) Golfers between 30 and 40 years old average 12 rounds of golf a year, but people between 50 and 60 average twice as many rounds, and golfers between 60 and 65 years old manage to play 40 rounds of golf a year.

TIP: Golf apparel designers such as Cutter & Buck are positioned to profit from the growing interest in golf. Because golf is the only sport that allows players to look as fashionable on the course as off, golfers can wear their golf clothes all the time.

Golf Club Operators

Golf course operators, such as Family Golf Centers and Golf Trust of America, are in the enviable position of being able to raise their rates without experiencing any customer attrition. In fact, it is common for golfers to reserve tee-off times weeks (if not months) in advance; and it is no longer unusual for people to arrive at golf courses at 4:00 in the morning to commence playing. Moreover, although heightened demand allows course operators to charge higher fees, the operators experience no corresponding increases in their expenses.

Many golf courses have expanded their offerings by establishing chipping greens for practicing short-game shots, bunkers for sand play, enhanced ranges with precise markings, and videotaping services for assessing a golfer's swing. Some of the better courses have facilities that allow golfers to practice shots in a variety of simulated conditions such as swinging into, or with, the wind. An increasing number of courses provide miniature golf courses, batting cages, and restaurants for family members who do not golf. While all of these expansions provide new sources of revenue, the golf course operators are not exposed to anemic foreign economies as were golf club manufacturers in the late 1990s.

Finally, the dominant golf course chains like Family Golf Centers and Golf Trust of America should be able to increase their fees and achieve cost savings through economies of scale as they continue to consolidate their fragmented industry. According to the Golf Range and Recreational Association of America, 83 percent of the 2,700 stand-alone driving ranges in 1997 were independently operated. Because these small operators usually lack the capital to expand their offerings, they are likely to sell to consolidators or go out of business.

Golf Club Manufacturers

Until the conditions described below reverse, investors would be wise to take a cautious stance towards golf club manufacturers, such as Callaway Golf, Adidas (which owns the TaylorMade line), Fortune Brands (which owns Titleist), and Coastcast. Callaway had been the most vulnerable to the following concerns in the late 1990s, but the points made below represent obstacles for all golf club manufacturers:

- Asia, long considered a lucrative export market for golf clubs because of that region's golf fanaticism, was extremely weak economically in the late 1990s. For example, Japan's economic difficulties resulted in the bankruptcy of more than 100 golf courses.
- Many of the new golf clubs are too expensive for the youngsters that account for a growing proportion of America's golfers. As Robert Marvin, former vice president of The Seidler Companies, said: "I really doubt that a 13-year-old is going to spend $600 on Callaway's Biggest Big Bertha driver."*

---

*Interview with Robert C. Marvin, *The Wall Street Transcript,* May 25, 1998, p. 48.

- Golf club manufacturers that believe they are on technology's cutting edge sometimes find themselves on technology's bleeding edge. Oversize clubs and larger sweet spots have made golf much easier for beginners. For instance, Callaway's Big Bertha woods are made of state-of-the-art lightweight titanium that allows bigger heads, bigger "sweet spots," and longer shafts, all of which lead to longer drives. In fact, the average drive on the pro tour increased from 260.3 yards in 1993 to 269 yards in 1998. The problem with this technological success is that the U.S. Golf Association is concerned that these club heads act with an improper spring-like action and could ban their use on the tours the association sanctions. Thus, Callaway found itself in the uncomfortable position of arguing that its clubs do not help people improve their scores.
- Some golf clubs have such high commercial values that they have become a target of thieves. In fact, the insurance industry reported that $120 million worth of insured golf clubs were stolen in 1998.

Cigar Companies

Many investors believe that cigar producers, distributors, and retailers represent a sound derivative play on the wealth creation theme. Indeed, there seems to be some correlation between the strength of the stock market and the popularity of cigars. From 1991 to 1997, as the Dow Jones Industrial Average climbed threefold, sales of premium cigars rose more than fourfold to roughly 500 million in 1997. However, I would like to offer the following words of caution before investors take positions in companies like Consolidated Cigar, General Cigar, and 800-JR-Cigar:

- Cigar sales have already decelerated. While unit growth for premium cigars was 67 percent in 1996, the Cigar Association of America reported that sales of large cigars increased a paltry 1.2 percent during the first nine months of 1998.
- Because of the loose correlation in the strength of the stock market and cigar sales, a decline in the stock market could adversely impact cigar companies.
- The fad appeal of smoking cigars should decline as each marginal newcomer is somewhat behind the curve, diminishing the activity's hipness and prestige. The trendsetters are likely to move to some other form of social statement.

- Because cigars are more alkaline than cigarettes, tar, nicotine, and other chemical compounds can pass through the lining of the mouth and throat and into the bloodstream more readily. The result is that cigar smokers are four to ten times more likely to die from cancer of the mouth, larynx, and esophagus than nonsmokers, according to the American Lung Association. Secondhand cigar smoke is also a health hazard. Accordingly, in 1998 the Federal Trade Commission was considering requiring cigar advertisements to carry the U.S. surgeon general's health warning.
- There could be political consequences from opponents of cigar smoking deriding the practice of "blunting," or smoking marijuana through hollowed-out cigars.
- It is likely that stipulations under the national tobacco settlement—such as restrictions on the display of tobacco products—will end up applying to cigars as well as cigarettes. The lack of visible display space could hit cigar makers harder than cigarette makers because cigars are often impulse items and shoppers are not as familiar with cigar brands as they are with cigarette brands.
- When cigar volumes rise dramatically, so too do the costs. This is especially true for the tobacco leaf needed for premium cigar wrappers. In the mid-1990s, when cigar sales were feverish, compensation for cigar rollers in major producing countries such as the Dominican Republic and Honduras soared as they were in increasingly short supply. Trained rollers were lured with $1,500 signing bonuses and gifts of mopeds and houses.* Even though premium cigars are more expensive at the retail counter, the costs of labor and the quality of tobacco leaf required for high-end brands are vastly higher than the costs and quality for machine-made versions. Thus, premium cigars have only slightly higher profit margins than mass-market cigars.
- The eventual end of the Cuban embargo will herald fierce competition for American cigar manufacturers.
- Consumers recognize little difference between premium cigars and less expensive ones. According to blind taste tests performed by *Cigar Aficionado* magazine, some $1.30 cigars were more popular with smokers than rival brands selling between $4 and $11.
- Consumers have become less brand loyal than was the case several decades ago. In the 1960s and 1970s, cigar buyers were typically older men who smoked one or two brands of cigars regularly. These smokers often bought a few boxes of their cigars at a time, especially when they were on sale.

---

*Jim Carrier, "Smoke Without the Mirrors," *New York Times,* Dec. 26, 1998, p. C1.

Now, younger buyers typically limit their smoking to special occasions and are more inclined to experiment with a variety of brands.

Although many investors believe that cigar makers offer an opportunity to play the trend of large numbers of Americans becoming extremely wealthy, the industry-specific considerations listed above should temper investors' interest in purchasing shares of companies like Swisher International Group and Holt's Cigar Holdings.

Collection Agencies

Just as there are companies positioned to prosper from the rising number of wealthy Americans, there are companies poised to reap the rewards of collecting remittances from the growing legions of Americans inundated with debt. For example, the Federal Reserve Board reported that the percentage of families carrying an outstanding balance on their credit cards rose from 40 percent in 1989 to 48 percent in 1996, while median balances rose almost 40 percent from $1,100 in 1992 to $1,500 in 1995. According to the Nilson Report, outstanding debt on credit card accounts alone will rise from $321 billion in 1995 to $587 billion by 2000.

Bankruptcy Filings: Once a Scarlet Letter, Now a Badge of Honor

Unprecedented numbers of Americans are assuming excessive amounts of debts because they believe there is no longer a stigma associated with filing for court protection from creditors. The number of Americans seeking bankruptcy soared to 1.4 million in 1997, up from 172,000 in 1978. High rates of personal bankruptcy filings should persist because the record wave of teenagers is coming to the age when credit becomes especially intoxicating. The growing incidence of bankruptcy filings by young people was revealed by a Visa USA survey that found that 8.7 percent of bankruptcy filers in 1996 were under 25 years of age, whereas a few years before the share of such young people was about 1 percent.

TIP: Other ways of playing the trend of indebtedness include investing in the credit bureaus (e.g., Equifax or TRW, Inc.); companies that buy accounts receivable at deep discounts from banks, retailers, and finance companies and then collect on them (e.g. Creditrust); and purveyors of secured cards (which are backed by deposits) such as Providian Financial.

Another driver of personal bankruptcy filings is their lack of social taboo. While filing for bankruptcy protection was once a source of embarrassment, MasterCard International reported that roughly half of the individuals who file for personal bankruptcy protection do so on receiving advice from their friends and family. Movie stars such as Kim Basinger declaring bankruptcy lend an air of celebrity to filing; and books such as *Debt Free! Your Guide to Personal Bankruptcy Without Shame* encourage abuse of the bankruptcy system.

Credit Agencies Are a Viable Solution

A growing number of businesses have become more aggressive in pursuing their receivables. As deregulation in the telecommunications and electric utility industries sparks cutthroat competition, companies are accepting customers with blemished credit records. With the increasing popularity of health maintenance organizations, health care institutions now face the challenge of billing not only large insurance companies but also individuals who are required to make small, one-time copayments. Finally, governments are pursuing everything from child support payments to parking tickets and delinquent taxes with vigor.

Creditors are increasingly turning to collection agencies to reduce their receivables problems. According to the American Collectors Association, receivables referred to third parties for management and recovery in the United States grew from $43.7 billion in 1990 to $116.0 billion in 1996. The following are reasons why many creditors prefer to outsource to collection agencies:

- Agencies' fees are based on results, not on time spent on prolonged negotiations.
- Because collection agencies, acting as independent third parties, are less hampered by buyer-seller relationships, they can effect collection with minimum damage to goodwill, increasing the chances of retaining customers.
- By employing the services of a professional collection agency, a client's staff is free to spend time and effort in other productive areas.

The trends described above will continue to be a boon to the dominant collection agencies like NCO Group and Outsourcing Solutions. These companies also derive benefits from consolidation in the collection industry—such as achieving economies of scale and demanding higher recovery rates—which was fragmented by 6,000 businesses in 1997. Moreover, the collection industry will thrive as a result of falling telecommunications costs, greater efficiency of call centers, and the ease of identifying debtors and collecting information on them.

CHAPTER 5

Water

Investors should seek what is in scarce supply relative to its demand. Nothing will be in more demand and in increasingly scarce supply than clean, potable water. Water accounts for over 86 percent of the body's mass, and people begin to feel thirsty after a loss of only 1 percent of bodily fluids and risk death if fluid loss nears 10 percent. Five days without water and we perish. Because water is vital to life, the growing unavailability of drinkable water will render water the most precious natural resource.

Water Management

On the one hand, demand for freshwater will continue to soar as the world's population grows and water use per person rises with the urbanization and industrialization of underdeveloped nations. Water will face growing demand from the agriculture sector for irrigation and from a wide array of manufacturers. Water is in such demand that Brian Gavin, vice president for Exploration at Minera Andes, remarked that countries such as Argentina and Chile regularly invest more money exploring for water reserves than for gold and silver reserves. Heightened demands for access to potable water sources are already causing military posturing in numerous parts of the world.

On the other hand, the finite supply of freshwater is threatened by pollution. There is no more water on earth now than there was 2,000 years ago, when the population was less than 3 percent of its current size. Today, only 3 percent of the world's water is fresh and nearly 90 percent of this potential supply is locked in the form of ice at the polar regions. As a result, only 0.3 percent of the world's water from surface or groundwater sources is readily available for consumption.

Benjamin Franklin once said: "We will only know the worth of water when the well is dry." In much of the world, the well is already dry and droughts will become increasingly severe in the future. In mid-1998, 31 countries, accounting for roughly 8 percent of the world's population, faced chronic freshwater shortages. By 2025, researchers at Johns Hopkins University expect 48 countries to face shortages, affecting more than 2.8 billion people—35 percent of the world's projected population. The United Nations forecasts that by 2050 the number of countries facing water stress or scarcity will rise to 54, and their combined population of 4 billion people will represent 40 percent of the projected global population of 9.4 billion. In short, the utilities that deliver water as well as the companies that diagnose, decontaminate, filter, desalinate, build the pipelines that deliver water, and bottled water providers are positioned to prosper.

Growing Demands Are Placed on Diminishing Water Supplies

Every person added to the planet places greater demands on the limited supply of freshwater. The nearly 2 billion people added to the planet since 1970 reduced per capita availability of water by one-third in 1998 compared with nearly two decades earlier. As the world's population increases by some 80 million people each year, the demand for freshwater increases about 64 billion cubic meters a year.

In 1996 the world's human population was using an estimated 54 percent of all the accessible freshwater contained in rivers, lakes, and underground aquifers. This percentage of available water usage is conservatively projected to climb to at least 70 percent by 2025, reflecting population growth alone, but will grow to even higher levels if per capita water consumption continues to rise at its current pace.

Many millions of people are already deprived of sufficient water. Population Action International estimates that 430 million people, or about 8 percent of the world's population, live where water reserves are scarce. More than 230 million people live in 26 countries classified as water deficient. This maldistribution of water will be exacerbated by faster population growth rates—and more pronounced seasonality of rainfalls—in the regions of the world that already face the most serious shortages of water. For instance, of the 14 countries in the Middle East, 11 are already facing water scarcity. In 5 of these countries the populations are projected to double within the next two decades.

About two-thirds of the world's population lives in areas receiving only one-quarter of the world's annual rainfall. Misaligned distribution of rainfall is compounded by short bursts of intense rains that cause floods and are followed by many months of drought. For instance, the monsoon in Bangladesh in mid-1998 inundated over half of that country, killed more than 520 people, destroyed much of its rice crop, and, according to the World Bank, will be accountable for 3.5 million Bangladeshis contracting diarrhea. India receives 90 percent of its rainfall during the summer monsoon season, which lasts from June to September. For the other eight months the country gets barely a drop of rain. As a result, India and other developing countries can make use of no more than 20 percent of their potentially available freshwater resources.

Depletion is another threat to the availability of freshwater. In a growing number of places, people are withdrawing water from rivers, lakes, and underground sources faster than these reserves can be replaced. In this century, while world population has tripled, water withdrawals have increased by a factor of six. Contemporary examples of rapid depletion of water reserves include the United States, where overall groundwater is being withdrawn 25 percent faster than its replenishment rate; Israel, whose annual water use exceeds its renewable supply by 15 percent; and Jordan and Yemen, whose withdrawals from groundwater aquifers exceed replenishment by 30 percent every year.

Urbanization Increases Water Use and Leads to Flooding

The majority of people now live in cities. The World Resources Institute estimates that 60 percent of the world's population will live in cities by 2020, and by 2025 more people will live in cities than were present in the entire world in 1985. Increased urbanization in both developed and developing nations places significant pressure on water supply, sanitation, and water resource management.

Urbanization increases water use dramatically. In 1900 the average American household used as little as 10 cubic meters of water per year compared with modern-day usage rates in excess of 200 cubic meters. Much of the 20-fold rise in water use from a century ago is accounted for by the fact that virtually every contemporary American household has running water. The North Carolina Agriculture Extension Service reports that the following are among the reasons that household water flows freely:

- Bathing consumes 30 or more gallons of water, and showers use 5 to 8 gallons of water a minute.
- Faucets leaking only one drop of water a second waste nearly 2,500 gallons a year.
- Automatic clothes washers use 40 to 80 gallons of water a load.
- Washing a full load of dishes requires at least 14 gallons of water.
- Garbage disposal units in kitchens use as much as 4 gallons of water a minute.

Moreover, because water costs households very little money, consumers are largely insensitive to the quantities they use. In contrast, a century ago running water was largely unavailable to households outside of big cities, so most Americans obtained their freshwater from wells or public standpipes.

The inability of many rapidly growing cities to ensure adequate water supplies is contributing to acute sanitary deficiencies. In the 1990s, cities in developing countries have had to cope with about 60 million new arrivals every year. Because many agencies are not equipped to manage growing demands on their water supply, some cities run short of water. When people are deprived of water for bathing, washing their clothes, or toileting they resort to improvising these activities at local rivers. Often, they have no choice but to return to these rivers for collecting drinking water.

Another debilitating result of urbanization is the replacement of natural vegetation with impenetrable surfaces. Natural vegetation such as fields, forests, and farmlands absorbs rainwater, allowing it to soak into the surface. In particular, the root structures of forests act as nature's sponges as they soak up water. In contrast, streets, roofs, parking lots, and manicured lawns all provide impervious surfaces that prohibit rain from soaking into the ground. Because urbanization reduces the amount of rainwater that can soak into the ground, groundwater reserves disappear and floods become more frequent.

Industry Exhibits a Voracious Demand for Pure Water

Industrial demand for water in the United States is estimated at $100 billion and is growing 8 percent annually. While it takes 1,000 gallons of water to grow one pound of food, 40,000 gallons of water are required to produce steel for just one car. The primary reason that factories use such large quantities of water is that very little of this water is absorbed. Rather, most of the water in industrial applications is used to wash waste away and to cool equipment.

TIP: Rod Lache of Deutsche Bank Securities points out that biotech drug manufacturing is between seven and ten times more filtration intensive than is making a drug via the classical process. In classical drug manufacturing, researchers combine relatively clean chemicals and filter them to make the end product. With a biotech drug, scientists start out with a cell—a living mammalian or yeast cell—and manipulate the DNA so that the cell creates a protein, and that protein is the drug. But to synthesize that drug, scientists need to filter away the cell body. Thus, most of the cell body becomes a waste product, which must be discarded with the help of filters from companies like Millipore Corporation and Pall Corporation.

Another driver for industrial water treatment is that companies wish to deliver consistent products to their customers. Coca-Cola's bottlers, Starbucks coffee shops, and McDonald's restaurants employ water treatment systems to achieve consistent products. The semiconductor industry, too, has become increasingly adamant in its demands for the highest purity water because the densely packed circuits on silicon wafers eliminate all tolerance of variability.

Investment Vehicles

The rapidly rising cost of water is driving a diversity of companies into the arms of companies that can manage the recycling of water. In states such as California, the compound annual growth rate for the price of water was 9.1 percent from 1960 to 1996. According to Ernst & Young, the unit price of water has grown on average between 10 percent and 12 percent every two years, well above the rate of inflation. With a view towards controlling their water costs, companies like Dow Chemical and LSI Logic, which once ran their own water treatment systems, are now entrusting those jobs to companies such as U.S. Filter. These arrangements call for customers to pay the water treatment companies by the gallon for water of specified purity.

TIP: A derivative play on the trend toward the outsourcing of water management is to invest in the companies (such as U.S. Filter, Waterlink, and CUNO) that sell equipment to water treatment companies. Interestingly, wastewater treatment plants operate in very corrosive environments, causing them to require a steady stream of replacement parts.

Similarly, municipalities from Buffalo to Milwaukee are attempting to reduce their water costs by turning the management of their water utilities to water management companies, including United Water Resources, Philip Services, and Air & Water Technologies. The exorbitant cost of upgrading municipal water infrastructure systems—$2 billion is the assessment for Atlanta—is driving privatization. The universal appeal of these services is evidenced by an average of one city per week in 1997 having issued requests for proposals on privatizing its water management. Water management companies offer investors a great deal of revenue visibility as they enjoy very long contracts—some lasting as long as 20 years.

Water Delivery

In the emerging nations, there is essentially no water infrastructure. Even in the developed markets, the water infrastructure is woefully inadequate. Some of the water systems in the United States were built during the Lincoln administration, and some water tunnels in New York City have not been inspected since they were built, which in some cases was 1917.

Consequently, in some major U.S. cities, as much as 80 percent of the water intended to be delivered to consumers is lost en route. In fact, Boston loses 80 percent of the water drawn out of its reservoirs for delivery to end users, which explains why New England, one of the wettest parts of the country, faces water shortages every year. And Southern California's Metropolitan Water District determined that its canals were leaking at least $130 million worth of water into the desert annually.

Water losses often threaten municipal dysfunction. While there are hundreds of water main ruptures in New York City each year, one rupture on July 5, 1998, created a crater on the streets of the Upper East Side that was 30 feet wide and more than 8 feet deep. The water gushing from this rupture caused many hospitals to reduce their services. For example, Sloan-Kettering Hospital reduced its surgeries by 70 percent and its doctors kept only 40 percent of their appointments. Years' worth of laboratory research in the basements of these hospitals was compromised. Further health risks were presented when the water break released asbestos surrounding water pipes, which the water subsequently carried throughout the Upper East Side.

The United States is by no means the only developed country to be afflicted with a decrepit water delivery infrastructure. In late July 1998, the municipal government of Sydney, Australia, warned its 3 million residents not to drink the water because of the presence of giardia and cryptosporidium. Sydney's hospitals were required to reduce the number of surgeries because of a lack of clean water to wash wounds. Bars in the city that prides itself as the most livable on earth were ordered to stop serving drinks with ice and supermarkets ran short of bottled water.

Faulty Water Pipes Allow Toxic Chemicals to Invade Water Systems

Not only do leaking pipes result in tremendous water loses, but leaking pipes also allow contaminants to seep into water systems. Consumers in developed nations are drinking such contaminants as lead, copper, and pesticides. Radon, arising from underground uranium deposits, is sometimes inhaled during bathing. The Environmental Protection Agency (EPA) estimated that nearly one-fifth of the U.S. population was exposed to contaminated municipal water in 1995 and that 69 million Americans lived in communities whose water exceeded the recommended levels for lead.

The ubiquity of potential lead contamination was highlighted by the EPA's determining that faucets can be significant sources of lead in drinking water.

Lead contamination in drinking water can occur whenever water comes into contact with lead-bearing materials such as metal alloys, commonly found in faucets. Because water is corrosive, as it passes through a faucet it can cause lead in the metal to leach into drinking water.

The most morbid outbreak of illness in the United States as a result of water-borne pollutants was the 1994 outbreak of cryptosporidium in Milwaukee, causing 400,000 people to become sick and over 100 people to die. The Natural Resources Defense Council reported that over 45 million Americans drink water from plants contaminated with cryptosporidium, so it is not surprising that more recent outbreaks have occurred in Seattle, New York City, and Hoboken. In efforts to preempt water-borne epidemics, the EPA and the Centers for Disease Control have issued directives advising the millions of Americans with HIV and AIDS, and those undergoing treatment for cancer or recipients of organ transplants, to boil their water to avoid further compromising their immune systems.

TIP: Water utilities like American Water Works, California Water Service Group, and Consumers Water are attractive vehicles to play the deployment of capital in water infrastructure, as these companies' profits are a function of their return on investment.

Companies like Nalco Chemical, Cytec, Ciba Specialty Chemicals, and Calgon Corporation are developing heartier disinfectants. Although these disinfectants will be helpful in eradicating many pollutants at treatment plants, water will remain susceptible to contamination as it travels through unreliable pipes en route to end users. Moreover, organisms such as giardia are growing resistant to disinfectants such as chlorine. Therefore, massive investments in new water delivery infrastructures are required.

The World Bank has estimated that by 2007 investments of between $600 billion and $800 billion will be required to meet the total demand for freshwater, including sanitation, irrigation, and power generation. Also, the World Bank estimates that $150 billion in capital investment is required in Europe over the ten-year period ending 2007 to maintain compliance with European Union standards on water usability. The United Kingdom alone must spend close to $60 billion building wastewater treatment plants over the next decade to meet European water quality standards. Even Hungary will need to invest about $3.5 billion over the next two decades to connect all of its citizens to wastewater treatment plants. To ensure a safe water supply in the United States, the EPA estimates $138 billion will have to be expended by 2016 to upgrade or replace infrastructures to comply with standards set by the Safe Drinking Water Act.

Investment Opportunities

The enormous investments in infrastructure present an opportunity for companies—such as Ameron International, Zurn Industries, Walter Industries, U.S. Filter and Waterlink—that manufacture water pipes and complementary equipment.

Water Purification

The inadequate availability of potable water is accentuated by extensive pollution. Many of the diseases with the highest morbidity rates are attributable to the consumption of polluted water. Further exacerbating the lack of clean water is global warming, which causes water to retain higher rates of salinity. The culmination of these factors is becoming so severe that military tensions are resulting. These factors underscore the demand for chemical companies that purify water, filtration companies that remove contaminants from water reservoirs, and companies that desalinate abundant ocean water.

TRAP: One obstacle to deriving adequate returns on water infrastructure investments is that very few people in developing nations are accustomed to paying for water. In fact, an analysis of World Bank–financed projects indicates that consumers pay only about 35 percent of the costs of supplying water in developing countries.

Water Pollution Rages out of Control

Water for human use is threatened all over the world. Citizens in developed countries dispose of pollutants—that range from street litter, fertilizers, pesticides, herbicides, pet waste, motor oil, and paint—in storm drains and ditches. Storm drains carry large amounts of polluted water into local streams, ponds, lakes, rivers, and, ultimately, into water treatment facilities.

The industrial sector is another contributor to polluted water. Industrial pollutants, such as wastes from chemical plants, are often dumped directly into waterways. In other instances, chemicals from waste disposal sites soak through the earth into groundwater. Water running through mines carries pollutants into streams and underground aquifers. Radioactive material finds its way into water basins from leaks at nuclear power plants and radioactive waste dumps. Finally, Royal Caribbean, a leading cruise ship operator, admitted to systematically discarding its ships' waste into the ocean without treatment.

People and factories share the designation of water polluters with animals. Farm animals annually produce 130 times more waste than human beings, but the disposal of animal waste goes virtually unregulated, according to U.S. Representative George Miller.

Water Pollution Fouls Water Basins

The combination of individual, industrial, and animal pollution results in extensive contamination to water supplies throughout the world. Researchers at Johns Hopkins University estimate between 200 and 400 major chemicals contaminate the world's rivers. Agricultural chemicals, eroded sediment, and animal wastes have fouled over 173,000 miles of America's waterways. Each year roughly 450 cubic kilometers of wastewater are discharged into the nation's rivers, streams, and lakes. In the United States alone, more than 700 chemicals have been detected in drinking water, 129 of them considered highly toxic.

TIP: The alarming levels to which America's water has been polluted has sparked a government response. For instance, in September 1998, the Department of Justice, the Department of the Interior, and the EPA announced that they would jointly bring 142 civil and criminal cases against alleged polluters located along the Mississippi River. Such actions will increase sensitivity among the companies that dispose of their wastewater along waterways. This should be a boon to companies like Minnesota Power, Ionics, and Osmonics that sell water diagnostics and monitoring equipment.

Many countries have not enacted standards to adequately control water pollution, and the majority of countries that have promulgated water quality legislation cannot enforce their water quality regulations. The result is that as much as 95 percent of all domestic sewage and 75 percent of all industrial waste in developing countries is discharged into surface waters without any treatment whatsoever. The following are among the horrendous consequences visited on the world's water sources:

- Even though adequate monitoring and notification procedures are still lacking at many of America's most popular beaches, pollution caused at least 4,153 beach closings and advisories in 1997. These closings were prompted by fears that the bacteria-contaminated waters carried microorganisms that would cause a wide range of diseases, including diarrhea, hepatitis, respiratory illnesses, and ear, nose, and throat problems.

- In Thailand and Malaysia, rivers often contain 30 to 100 times more pathogens, heavy metals, and poisons from industry and agriculture than is permitted by government health standards.
- Over three-quarters of China's 50,000 kilometers of major rivers are so polluted that they no longer support fish life.

Once contaminants reach water reserves, wildly disproportionate amounts of water are rendered unsafe for human consumption. For instance, one drop of oil can render up to 25 liters of water unfit for drinking; one gram of 2,4-D (a common household herbicide) can contaminate 10 million liters of drinking water; and one gram of lead makes 20,000 liters of water unsafe for drinking.

Contaminated Water Poses Monumental Health Threats

In view of the growing disequilibrium between supply and demand for water and the degree of pollution that the world's waterways endure, it should not be surprising that much of the world's health problems are attributable to insufficient access to, and the contamination of, water. About 2.3 billion people, or 80 percent of the people that contract diseases in emerging nations, suffer from diseases that are linked to water or the lack thereof.

Examples of the prevalence of water-borne diseases abound. Some 60 percent of all infant mortality is linked to infectious and parasitic diseases, most of them water-related; and 35 percent of all gastrointestinal diseases are attributable to water-borne contaminants. In Bangladesh, three-quarters of all diseases are related to unsafe water and inadequate sanitation facilities; and in Pakistan, one-quarter of all hospital admissions are the result of water-related diseases.

Worldwide, the lack of water for sanitary waste disposal and the paucity of clean water for drinking, cooking, and washing is to blame for over 12 million deaths a year. In fact, billions of lives are at risk of contracting water-related diseases as an estimated 3 billion people lack a sanitary toilet and over 1.2 billion people are in jeopardy because they lack access to safe freshwater.

Millions of people suffer from infections that are transmitted by vectors—insects or other animals capable of transmitting infections, such as mosquitoes and tsetse flies—that thrive and breed in or near polluted water. Such vectors infect humans with malaria, yellow fever, dengue fever, sleeping sickness, and filariasis. Many other diseases—including trachoma, leprosy, tuberculosis, whooping cough, tetanus, and diphtheria—are considered water-scarce in that they thrive in conditions where freshwater is scarce and sanitation is poor.

Other factors are attributable to water-induced health deterioration. Floods, for example, are particularly damaging to water integrity. According to China's

Ministry of Civil Affairs, the floodwaters along China's Yangtze River Basin in the summer of 1998 affected as many as 240 million people and cost at least 2,000 lives. Many people were condemned to drink whatever water they could find even if contaminated by human waste. Outbreaks of skin infections, infectious diarrhea, cholera, and typhoid were the earliest detectable diseases resulting from these floods. In many parts of the world people share their rivers and streams with animals, so animal feces and dead livestock become mixed in the inhabitants' water sources.

Global Warming Contributes to Multiple Water Problems

The earth's atmosphere continues to heat up. Climatologists are confident that over the past century, the global average temperature has increased by about half a degree Celsius each decade. Projecting ahead, scientists at the United Nations Intergovernmental Panel on Climate Change expect a two to six degree increase in global temperature by 2100.

Global warming is a detriment to the availability of drinkable water for several reasons. First, global warming contributes to rising water levels. Most scientists agree that the oceans have been creeping upward by two millimeters a year for at least the past several decades. The United Nations estimates that sea levels could rise by as much as two feet by 2100. One reason for this is that carbon dioxide and other heat-trapping greenhouse gases in the air increase the temperature of the ocean and seawater, and these substances expand when heated. In addition, Antarctica and mountain glaciers in Europe's Alpine valleys continue to melt, and the water released into streams and rivers has been adding to the sea level.

TIP: Warmer weather is conducive to an increase in the rat and mouse population, which is of benefit to rodent trap manufacturers such as Ekco Group.

As mentioned in the beginning of this chapter, the aggregate amount of water on the face of the earth has remained relatively constant for thousands of years. Thus, rising sea levels result in a greater proportion of the world's water being brackish and therefore not fit for consumption. Stephen Kass, a prominent environmental lawyer at Carter, Ledyard and Milburn, has noted that rising sea levels threaten the availability of potable water because tidal waters that flow under the coast lines will invade an increasing number of freshwater aquifers. This is because salt water is denser than freshwater and exerts a constant pressure to permeate the porous aquifers. When freshwater levels in the aquifers fall below sea level, the freshwater pressure fails to keep salt water from moving inland and upward in the aquifers. Additionally, rising water levels can disrupt water treatment plants that are at risk of overflowing as they are typically located at the bottom of declining topographies.

The second major risk of rising temperatures is that more frequent and severe storms will occur because a hotter planet experiences greater rates of evaporation. More intense evaporation leads to greater rainfalls and snowfalls. The increased variability and extremes in precipitation will exacerbate existing problems in water quality and sewage treatment and in erosion and urban storm water routing. The following are among the many examples of devastating floods resulting from the inability to successfully route storm water:

- In September 1998, vast areas and dozens of towns in Chiapas State (Mexico) were flooded. Electricity lines, water pipes, at least 30 bridges, and large parts of highways were ripped out and left 400,000 people stranded. According to the Chiapas state government, 90 people were killed and at least 70 were missing even before many houses covered by mudslides were excavated.
- In August 1998, flooding from tropical storm Charley led to the death of 19 people in south Texas.
- South Korean floods claimed at least 165 lives in August 1998 as two Han River tributaries flooded around Seoul.

TIP: Another way to play the global warming phenomenon is to invest in the companies that manufacture air-conditioning systems (such as Fedders Corporation) or companies that repair air-conditioning systems (such as Pameco Corporation). Companies such as these will be beneficiaries of substantially higher temperatures. For instance, subsequent to temperatures in 11 southern states in the summer of 1998 rising between 16 percent and 26 percent above their averages, President Clinton made homeowners in these 11 states eligible for $100 million in emergency federal aid to purchase fans and air conditioners and to pay electric bills.

Water Shortages Threaten to Spark Wars

Safe drinking water is so scarce and the consequences of being deprived of it are so severe that competition for potable water is likely to be the source of military tension—hardly shocking considering that the Latin origin of the word *rival* means "one using the same stream as another." Not only will the citizenry of many nations be faced with dire thirst and water-related diseases, but their reduced water availability will strain their ability to sustain food production.

All of the countries in North Africa, except Morocco, already import half or more of their grain. By 2000, six out of seven East African countries and all five North African countries bordering the Mediterranean will face acute water shortages. Without progress in securing reliable sources of freshwater, the prospects for improving food production and increasing food security are remote. And if China diverts too much water from agricultural uses, grain production is likely to suffer, which could force China to import more grain. Thus, the Worldwatch Institute has warned that China's water scarcity could soon become the world's grain scarcity.

Another primary reason that a water-deficient world is an inherently unstable world is that river basins and other water bodies do not respect national borders. Nearly 100 countries share just 13 major rivers and lakes, and more than 200 river systems cross international borders. In Africa, about 50 rivers are each shared by two or more countries and virtually all rivers in the Middle East are shared by several nations.

One potential tinderbox stems from Syria's and Iraq's dependence on water from the Tigris and Euphrates rivers for drinking, irrigation, and electricity generation. This dependence is of concern because Syria and Iraq have repeatedly accused Turkey of threatening the already insufficient flow of the Euphrates and Tigris rivers by building dams in violation of the rights of the countries downstream. In fact, the *Al-Zawra* weekly quoted Iraq's Minister of Irrigation Mohamoud Diyab al-Ahmad as saying that "Iraq will sue Turkey if it insists on pursuing its present water policy of building dams that inflict great damage on Iraq and Syria."

Elsewhere, Egypt is building a canal to divert water from the Nile River, which may cause problems with its downstream neighbors. Singapore launched a massive campaign to conserve water after neighboring Malaysia threatened to cut off the water it supplies to Singapore. A Jordanian parliamentary committee blamed water tainted with worms and weeds on corruption from Israel's Lake Tiberias. Separately, the U.S. Central Intelligence Agency was reportedly monitoring the water supply in the Gaza Strip in 1998 for fear that shortages would fuel unrest among young Arabs.

Investment Opportunities

Chemical companies like Nalco Chemical, Cytec, Clarion, and Calgon Corporation offer a range of additive solutions for purifying water. Another strategy for purification is provided by such filtration companies as Millipore and Pall Corporation. Interestingly, the filtration companies tout their products with the promise that filters provide greater consistency in water purification because excessive or insufficient chemicals may be added to treated water.

The growing demands on potable water are gradually forcing people to look to ocean water for solutions. Because less than 1 percent of the total water on the planet is fresh and usable, desalination, the conversion of sea water into freshwater, is beginning to play an increasingly important role in creating new water sources. Four Persian Gulf states—Bahrain, Kuwait, Saudi Arabia, and the United Arab Emirates—have so little freshwater available that they have already resorted to desalinization, without which they would be unable to support anywhere close to their current populations.

While Ionics and Osmonics are two of the leaders in industrial desalinization efforts, Recovery Engineering manufactures portable water-purifying devices that are suitable for the more than 6 million trips that Americans take to developing countries each year and for extended outdoor activities. Without using such desalinating and decontaminating devices, consumers would risk illness when they drink water that they may otherwise assume is free from contamination. Further, portable desalinating devices eliminate the inconvenience associated with carrying freshwater, boiling water from natural sources, or using iodine tablets.

Bottled and Filtered Water

As consumers in even the most developed countries become more aware of the dangers of drinking tap water, they will increase their purchases of bottled water as well as home water-treatment systems. These markets are enormous—U.S. demand for home water-treatment systems and bottled water is worth a combined $5.9 billion—and very underpenetrated as only 20 percent of the American populace consumes bottled water, and a mere 10 percent of U.S. households use drinking water filters. Fears of drinking tap water, which should lead to the increased adoption of bottled water and water filters, are already reaching broad levels; market studies conducted in the late 1990s indicated that 85 percent of the American population is concerned about the quality of their drinking water. This sensitivity will be heightened by:

- The dissemination of EPA reports claiming as many as 12 million Americans drink water that should be filtered but is not
- Consumer water bills itemizing the pollutants in residential water by no later than mid-1999

- The realization that delivery systems that bring tap water from reservoirs to consumers' glasses have been found to contain lead, copper, radon, and a potpourri of other contaminants that can cause everything from severe headaches to cancer

When water arrives at residential taps, it may be loaded with silt, excessive levels of dissolved solids, pesticides, and high levels of chlorine. Julia Child remarked that her Santa Barbara tap water turns her Chinese tea into mud. Because demand for water has largely outgrown municipalities' ability to eradicate nontoxic contaminants, the primary focus of municipal water treatment plants is to ensure that all bacteria is removed from the public water. The primary method for eliminating bacteria is to add chlorine, but the drawbacks are that large quantities of chlorine in water are unhealthy, unpalatable, and malodorous.

Companies (such as PepsiCo's Aquafina, U.S. Filter's Culligan unit, Ionic's Aqua Cool, and Nestle's Perrier division as well as its ten American brands, including Poland Spring and Arrowhead) that sell bottled water are capitalizing on consumers' fears and inadequate remedies. Consumers are comforted that bottled water is at least nominally regulated by the Food and Drug Administration (FDA) as a food product and must meet a variety of applicable food packaging regulations. As a result, the average annual bottled water consumption per capita in the United States rose from 1.5 gallons in 1976 to 11 gallons in 1996, partly as a result of bottled water's capturing more venues, including newsstands and pushcarts. In recent years sales of plastic bottles of water have been growing 28 percent to 30 percent annually and still have potential to grow as the per capita bottled water consumption in Europe is 19 gallons a year.

According to Beverage Marketing Corporation, sales of bottled water soared from $2.65 billion in 1990 to $4 billion in 1998. The demand for bottled water is driven as much by fashion as by fear. Many dieters view drinking large quantities of water as a way to curb appetites. Even though the International Bottled Water Association suggests that a 200-pound person doing moderate activity should drink 88 ounces of water a day, it is almost impossible to drink too much water—a claim that no other beverage category can make. Today's health-conscious consumers are attracted to bottled water's absence of calories, additives, and sugar. Some bottled waters are actually healthy as they contain calcium, magnesium, potassium, and sulfates.

Water may be used for natural medicine or homeopathic healing throughout more of the world. The lineage of bottled water as a healing agent traces back several centuries to Pope Boniface VIII and Michelangelo, who swore to the ability of Fiuggi, a low-mineral water in the volcanic area southeast of Rome, to relieve kidney stones.* To this day, some European pharmacists must be able to match various varieties of water with their reputed medicinal powers to pass their licensing boards, and many European pharmacies stock bottled water for prescriptive purposes.

Taste is another major reason people prefer bottled water to tap water. Chlorine, which is most often used to disinfect tap water, leaves an aftertaste and leads to other problems. The preference for bottled water's taste and a near prohibitionist atmosphere about alcohol has led to some bottled waters achieving celebrity status. For instance, Arthur von Wiesenberger provides a road map to the best-tasting waters through his publication *The Taste of Water* guides for conducting water tastings. Interestingly, Star Kist packages tuna in bottled natural spring water; and water bars can be found in gyms and home-furnishing stores in Boston, New York, and Los Angeles. Markups of bottled water can be as high as 600 percent in the case of S. Pellegrino, and Richard Heckmann, president and CEO of U.S. Filter, has noted that Evian costs $350 a barrel.

Foreign markets are very promising sources of growth for bottled water companies. In 1998, *Reforma,* a major Mexican newspaper, estimated that Mexicans have increased their consumption of bottled and purified water tenfold over the past six years. Data compiled by the Japan Softdrinks Association showed mineral water output surged 32 percent in 1997. Still only one in four people in Japan drank tap water in 1998 as concerns grew over quality, according to the news daily *Asahi Shimbun.* Separately, U.S. immigrants from developing countries drive domestic demand for bottled water as they are used to relying on bottled water to avoid consuming tap water. In fact, Glacier Water Services reported that 60 percent of its sales in its California locations are to Latin or Asian customers.

Home Filtration as a Solution to Water Scarcity and Contamination

Bottled water has traditionally enjoyed major advantages over home filtration solutions. First, bottled water is regulated by the FDA (which regulates all consumables), whereas tap water is regulated by the Environmental Protection Agency and is regarded as a utility. Second, home filtration systems typically cost hundreds of dollars to install plus the added expense of ongoing maintenance and repairs. Third, it had been difficult for consumers to know when to change filters and how to maintain them. Sink-top filters often contained charcoal, which had a tendency to wear out long before it was replaced and could even become a breeding ground for bacterial growth.

---

*Corby Kummer, *The New York Times Magazine,* Aug. 30, 1998, p. 56.

Nevertheless, home filtration systems have some appeal for consumers and investors. Of the water used by a typical household, only 1 percent is used for cooking or direct consumption. Thus, it would be very expensive to filter water to the level of purity that bottled companies provide at the municipal level. Recovery Engineering's PUR Self-Monitoring Water Filter products shut off the water flow when a filter reaches the end of its useful life. These filters also provide an ongoing read of the filters' useful life so that consumers know when to replace their filters. Finally, the fact that customers must regularly replace components of their water treatment equipment—such as membranes, filters, pumps, and valves to maintain necessary purity levels—results in a predictable flow of recurring revenues to the home filtration industry.

CHAPTER 6

Extreme Sports

Extreme, often death-defying, sports—encompassing everything from bungee jumping to wakeboarding and from skateboarding to snowboarding—have become wildly popular. Industry observers have attributed the appeal of extreme sports to the large baby boomer echo scaling their teenage years. Young people are turning to extreme sports for the adrenaline rush that comes from trying to cheat death. (For instance, a record 1,300-plus mountaineers tried to climb Mount McKinley in 1997 even though 118 died trying over the 65 preceding years.)

While teenagers are increasingly disaffected with organized team sports, they are attracted to the egalitarianism of more individualized sports. (No one is cut from the skateboarding team.) Some commentators believe that the attraction to alternative sports is a natural progression of teenagers' attraction to alternative music and film. Separately, the improving functionality of extreme sports equipment allows older people to participate in these activities. Thus, the extreme sports trend presents opportunities for certain sporting goods manufacturers and retailers, safety helmet makers, and companies that host extreme sporting events.

Extreme Sports

Despite the physical intensity, perilous predicaments, and injuries sustained by participants in extreme sports, millions of Americans are avid extreme athletes. In 1998, there were at least 6.5 million skateboarders in the United States (up 35.8 percent from 1997), 4.5 million snowboarders, 1.5 million stunt bikers, and 1 million all-terrain boarders (die-hards who race down ski slopes while lying on contraptions resembling skateboards).

Most industry followers believe that these sports will become increasingly popular. According to *World Sports & Marketing,* skateboard and snowboard enthusiasts will double and wakeboarders will soar sixfold between 1998 and 2000. Jim Fitzpatrick, executive director of the International Association of Skateboard Companies, has stated that the roughly 300 public and quasi-public skateboard parks in 1998 would double by the summer of 1999. (One reason for this projected growth is that states such as California have enacted laws that absolve cities from liability by placing skateboarding in the same category of "at-your-own-risk" sports like surfing.)

Extreme Sports Are Almost Mainstream

Extreme sports are winning large corporate sponsorships and vaunted television time slots because these activities appeal far beyond the ranks of extreme athletes. Blue chip companies like PepsiCo and Kodak sponsor extreme events and incorporate extreme sports imagery into their advertising. Snowboarding was brushed with legitimacy when it became an official sport at the Winter Olympics in Nagano, Japan, in February 1998. The Gap added an extreme sports line in the fall of 1998. ESPN has been producing X Games since the early 1990s and maintains that its coverage reaches more male viewers from ages 12 to 34, per household, than any other sporting event on television. (Interestingly, extreme sports make for good television because they provide fast action with a possibility of death.)

TIP: Far more people prefer to simulate the thrills of participating in extreme sports than taking the actual risks such activities entail. Imax Corporation is positioned to take advantage of these armchair extremists by operating theaters featuring giant screens (up to 99 feet in diameter) that fill viewers' peripheral vision with three-dimensional images. Another investment vehicle in this arena is Iwerks Entertainment, which had exhibited its multisensory, large-format ride simulation features for over 125 million people by 1998.

The following are among the many signs of general public interest in at least viewing extreme sports in the late 1990s:

- A film about Mount Everest set box office records at IMAX theaters and Jon Krakauer's novel *Into Thin Air* spent more than a year on best-seller lists.
- Alfred Lansing's *Endurance* (a book about the 1914 Shackleton expedition that was marooned in the Antarctic) was originally published in 1959 but resurfaced in 1998 on best-seller lists, and Tristar made a big-budget film of the adventure.
- Membership in the Explorers Club in New York reached its all-time high in 1998 and the National Geographic Society created the position of "explorer in residence."

- *Expedition News* estimates that corporations' annual support of expeditions has risen from $10 million in the mid-1980s to more than $200 million in 1998.
- The number of adventure travel outfitters in the United States tripled in the decade ending in 1997 to more than 8,000, and sales of outdoor equipment have quintupled from the mid-1980s to $5 billion a year in the late 1990s.

Equipment Manufacturers and Suppliers

The extreme sports equipment manufacturers and retailers are obvious beneficiaries of the growing popularity of extreme sports. For instance, footwear represents a rapidly expanding opportunity as noted by Gruntal & Co. analyst Michael Conn, who estimated that the U.S. alternative sports footwear market measured $450 million at wholesale in 1996 and continued to grow 25 percent a year from that point.

One vehicle for playing this trend is Vans, which is one of the largest manufacturers of performance footwear for such alternative sports as skateboarding, BMX bicycling, and snowboarding. In addition, companies such as Benetton, Adidas, and Artemis Innovations make shoes with smooth plastic plates that allow wearers to slide along handrails, ledges, and other structures. Such shoes are popular as they can be worn anywhere and do not have to be carried as do skateboards. Separately, alternative shoes and other alternative sporting gear are sold at retailers such as Gadzooks and Pacific Sunwear of California. Included in this paraphernalia is protective gear for the knees, wrists, and elbows. Much of this well-ventilated protective gear is made of lightweight materials and is designed to ensure that wearers do not overheat or feel weighted down.

Another company prospering from extreme sports is Salomon, whose sales grew 40 percent from $543.7 million in 1993 to $762 million in 1997 after introducing mountain bikes, snowboard clothing, snowboards, and its X-Scream line of skis. K2, Inc. offers skis that incorporate piezoelectronic dampening technology, which dissipates vibrations, allowing people to ski down hills without much shake. Outside of skiing equipment, K2's Smart Shock technology electronically stiffens a bike's suspension, depending on the terrain.

Safety Helmets

Because all extreme athletes are advised to wear helmets, safety helmets represent a vehicle for riding the growth of all variations of extreme sports. In addition, managed care providers are trying to reduce the severity of accidents sustained by their enrollees by beseeching them to take such precautionary measures as wearing helmets. For instance, Prudential Insurance was subsidizing the cost of bicycle helmets by selling them to its members for $10; and more states are requiring bicyclists to wear helmets, and similar requirements are being considered for skiers and skaters. Finally, the publicity surrounding the deaths of Sonny Bono and Michael Kennedy has heightened the call for helmet requirements.

Ski Helmets

The market for ski helmets was underpenetrated in 1998, but there are many reasons to believe that a greater percentage of skiers will wear helmets manufactured by companies such as Bell Sports in the future. Less than 10 percent of skiers were wearing helmets in early 1998, but, according to SnowSports Industries of America, sales of ski helmets jumped from 66,143 in 1995 to 80,537 in 1997. Helmets were used in ski schools for the first time in 1997, and the popularity of snowboarding and freestyle moves has increased the use of helmets.

The following are among the additional reasons that more athletes will don helmets:

- The death of U.S. Representatives Sonny Bono and Michael Kennedy from injuries sustained while skiing increases awareness of helmets.
- State Senator Robert Bacon of Colorado was considering including skiing in a 1998 bill that would mandate helmets for in-line skating and bicycling for children.
- The American Medical Association issued a report in December 1997 recommending that adolescents and children be urged to wear ski helmets.
- Many ski resort operators require helmets for mountain biking on their trails during the summer.
- A growing number of ice-skating rinks recommend helmets, especially for children.

Bicycle Helmets

Legislators realize that bicycle helmets can save lives and reduce trauma. According to data from the Department of Transportation, 96 percent of bicyclists killed in 1996 were not wearing helmets. And the Snell Foundation reported that helmets decrease the risk of head injury by 69 percent, brain injury by 65 percent, and severe brain injury by 74 percent.

Despite such grim statistics, only 20 percent of cyclists and in-line skaters wore helmets all or most of the time in 1997, according to the Brain Injury Asso-

Sports Medicine/Tissue Regeneration

As a result of the inherently dangerous nature of extreme sports, more knees are being damaged and more bones broken. This is especially true as older adults are increasingly active in aggressive sports and as more women participate in athletics. First, more than 180,000 people over 40 years of age were admitted to emergency rooms as a result of playing sports in 1996, up nearly threefold from 1986. In particular, 47,143 bicyclists over 40 years old were admitted to emergency rooms in 1996, more than double the 20,149 admitted a decade earlier; and in 1996 more than 43,000 skiers over 40 years old were taken to emergency rooms for treatment, up twelvefold from 1986.

Second, women are playing strenuous sports far later in life than they ever did before. The popularity of the Women's National Basketball Association and the fame achieved by women skiers and soccer players are encouraging women to engage in more competitive sports. Of note is that women are three times more likely than men to sustain tears in their anterior cruciate ligaments (ACLs), the most important ligament controlling and stabilizing the knee and the most difficult to repair. According to the National Collegiate Athletic Association, women soccer players tore their ACLs at least twice as often as their male counterparts, and the rates in basketball were at least three times higher for women; other studies have confirmed similar patterns, often with wider gaps.

Knee Damage

Knee damage is extremely widespread and, heretofore, difficult to treat. Every year some 5 million Americans visit orthopedists and emergency rooms with complaints about their knees—the single most common area treated by orthopedic surgeons. Roughly 375,000 of these visits result in ACL reconstruction procedures. Skiers suffer a very high incidence of ACL damage. Tears of the knee's ACL have replaced the shattered limb as skiing's most common serious injury. Over the 20 years ending in 1997, the rate of reported ACL injuries has tripled, and they now affect about 20,000 skiers each year, according to a Vermont Safety Research study.

A great deal of research is being conducted on knee damage. In fact, of the 60 papers presented at the July 1998 American Orthopedic Society for Sports Medicine convention, 47 addressed some aspect of injury to the knee. Knees are unlike skin or bone in that their cartilage can not repair itself or regenerate naturally; and because cartilage also lacks blood vessels and nerves, patients often do not realize damage has been sustained until well after the fact.

Tissue Regeneration

One of the most promising methods of treating cartilage damage as well as bone damage is tissue regeneration. This procedure entails harvesting cells during arthroscopy, expanding them in culture media, then implanting them into the cavity. According to Dr. Richard D. Coutts, adjunct professor at the University of California, San Diego, articular cartilage is ideal for tissue engineering because it does not have intrinsic repair capacities. Tissue regeneration is attractive in knees because articular cartilage does not need to be vascularized or innervated.

Industry Players

Two of the best vehicles for gaining exposure to developments occurring in cartilage regeneration include Genzyme Tissue Repair and Integra Life-Sciences, which offer a collagen matrix as a scaffolding system on which cells can build. Other companies working on similar products include Reprogenesis and Guilford Pharmaceuticals.

On the bone damage front, Creative Biomolecules has been developing a pastelike substitute for bone grafts, spiked with the protein that normally stimulates human bone growth. Indications are that this product will be a good substitute for bone grafts that require the patient to endure two painful surgical procedures: one to harvest bone chips from elsewhere in the patient's body and a second to implant them. The Genetics Institute unit of American Home Products is developing a similar product.

Companies that offer more traditional methods of treating knee and bone damage (such as arthroscopy) include Biomet, Bionix Implants, Conmed, Exactech, Johnson & Johnson, Stryker, and Tyco.

ciation. However, sales of bicycle helmets should continue to increase as more states and municipalities promulgate helmet use laws. According to the Bicycle Safety Helmet Institute, states with mandatory helmet laws included more than one-third of the U.S. population in 1998. Similar laws at that time had been proposed in a number of additional states, including Arizona, Colorado, Iowa, Kansas, Maine, and Wisconsin. (In comparison, all but three states required some or all motorcyclists to wear helmets in 1998.)

Not only are helmet use laws resulting in more helmet sales, but the growing number of bicycle adherents should likewise spur helmet sales. According to *Bicycling* magazine, the number of people bicycling to work has grown more than 20 percent from 1993 to 1998 to 7 million. Bicycle riders appreciate the exercise, environmental friendliness, and the ability to pass stalled traffic. As a result, more companies are offering lockers, showers, and other bike-friendly facilities. In fact, there is even a national Bike to Work Day, and cities like Madison, Wisconsin, have extended the event to a full week.

TIP: Helmet companies enjoy substantial repeat revenues. First, most authorities recommend the replacement of helmets every five years. This is because outgassing of glues dissolves liner material, general liner deterioration occurs as a function of hair oils, and body fluids and normal wear and tear all contribute to helmet degradation. Second, consumers like to upgrade their helmets as improvements in the protective characteristics of helmets are usually made over five-year periods.

Industry Players

The predominant manufacturer of helmets is Bell Sports. Boeri and Briko are particularly competitive in Europe. Another player in producing helmets is Mine Safety Appliances.

Auto Racing

Auto racing was the fastest-growing spectator sport in the United States in the late 1990s. Revenues generated by auto racing companies—such as International Speedway and Penske Motorsports—are fueled by soaring attendance, the granting of lucrative broadcast rights, marquee sponsorships, and the licensing of racetrack naming rights. I believe this combination will prove to be a high-octane formula for the financial success of racetrack operators like Dover Downs and Speedway Motorsports.

Auto Racing Attendance Soars

Auto racing enthusiasts have been proliferating even though auto racing events are more expensive to attend than traditional spectator sports. Statistics compiled by Goodyear show that almost 17 million fans attended auto races in North America in 1997, a 9.4 percent increase over 1996. Attendance at the National Association for Stock Car Auto Racing's (NASCAR's) main racing series, the Winston Cup, reached more than 5.8 million fans in 1997, up 80 percent since 1990.

The average attendance at each of the NASCAR Winston Cup events in 1997 was 190,355, which was more than 3 times greater than the average attendance at National Football League (NFL) regular season games; close to 7 times larger than average Major League Baseball (MLB) games; and over 11 times greater than average attendance at National Basketball Association (NBA) games. This attendance disparity becomes even more dramatic when placed in conjunction with average ticket prices. Average ticket prices in 1997 for NFL, MLB, and NBA games were approximately $37.00, $11.98, and $34.08, respectively. At Winston Cup events in 1997, the average stadium ticket cost $60.00, while camping on the infield cost $75.00.

TIP: A derivative vehicle through which investors can play the popularity of auto racing is Action Performance Companies, the leader in the marketing of motorsports merchandise such as apparel, souvenirs, and die-cast car replica collectibles.

Attractions of Auto Racing

The fast pace of auto racing, fierce competition among the drivers, and high accident rates contribute to America's fascination with auto racing. As H.A. "Humpy" Wheeler, president of the Charlotte Motor Speedway in North Carolina, once said: "NASCAR sells the greatest drug in the world, and that is adrenaline." The industry tries to keep its fans' adrenaline rushing by imposing restrictive guidelines on car design and engine horsepower to promote fairness. In fact, tracks constructed by NASCAR in the late 1990s came under attack for fostering accidents by having too many tight turns, abrupt bankings, and pavement that narrowed to 50 feet in some places. Separately, increasing television coverage is driving attendance.

TIP: One way of gaining exposure to the auto racing industry while avoiding the risks of racetrack operators' pouring capital into new racetracks is through the shares of Featherlite. Featherlite builds aluminum trailers used to transport racecars and makes trackside marketing trailers that showcase racing memorabilia.

The following are among the other reasons that racing fans are drawn to auto racetracks:

- Because most Americans drive cars every day, fans often relate more to auto racing than other popular sports. This is especially true for the more familiar looking NASCARs.
- NASCAR drivers remain extremely open to fan interaction and rarely suffer from bad publicity.
- The way in which NASCAR allots points (which are tabulated throughout the season to determine the year's champion) rewards consistency and provides an added dimension to the sport.
- Fans in the crowd enhance their racing experiences by utilizing radio scanners to intercept the latest strategies devised by drivers and their crews.
- Another interesting development has been the advent of video cameras inside racecars, which has added to the excitement of the races.

Broadcasting Generates Revenues

One major revenue generator that race track operators enjoy is television contracts. These contracts were worth at least $100 million in 1997 as five major television networks brought NASCAR's Winston Cup series to 160 million viewers, according to A. C. Nielsen. Stockcar racing in 1997 became the second most watched pro sport on U.S. television, behind the National Football League. Taking a longer-term perspective, from 1990 to 1997, auto racing ratings grew by 23 percent on ABC, 22 percent on CBS, 50 percent on ESPN, 44 percent on TBS, and 30 percent on TNN. During the same period, the average number of households watching such events increased 8.3 percent to 3.9 million.

Racecar driving has been appealing to television networks because it's inexpensive compared with broadcasting other spectator sports. In fact, television rights for NASCAR were about $0.35 per household in mid-1998, versus $1.81 for the NFL and $0.95 for the NBA.

Additional Attractions of Racetrack Operators

Racetrack operators such as Champion Auto Racing Teams and Racing Champions are generating substantial revenue from a multitude of sources. First, selling stadium naming rights to corporations had begun in the late 1990s and has proven to be extremely lucrative for other sports. For instance, Staples paid $100 million for naming a sports stadium in Los Angeles, Pepsi spent nearly $68 million for a facility in Denver, and Bank One Ballpark cost Bank One $66 million.

Other sources of supplemental revenue include concessions, corporate hospitality suite rentals, entertainment venues, and race driving schools. Companies like Speedway Motorsports are pursuing ancillary events such as concerts and auto fairs to increase utilization at their facilities.

Second, corporate sponsorships are becoming a more important factor for the industry. More than 79 Fortune 500 companies are involved in NASCAR, and sponsorship involvement grew 9 percent in 1997 to exceed $400 million. In addition, even though auto racing is traditionally a male sport, the fact that more women are viewing auto races is evidenced by makers of such products as Tide, Lipton Tea, and Kellogg's Corn Flakes sponsoring races.

Third, as auto racing branches out from the Southeast to cities like Los Angeles and Detroit, it is gaining a national following. In turn, more national broadcasts are airing races and further broaden the sports' appeal.

Finally, there are many barriers to entry into the industry, which accrues to the benefit of current competitors. New tracks cost in excess of $100 million, and NASCAR and other sanctioning bodies require a track record of successful promotion as a prerequisite for granting a major race date.

Investment Vehicles

The primary publicly traded auto racetrack companies include Champion Auto Racing Teams, Dover Downs, International Speedway, Penske Motorsports, Racing Champions, and Speedway Motorsports.

Paintball and Laser-Tag

Two fast-action combative games—paintball and laser-tag—have drawn wide appeal. They are among the most accessible extreme sports. This is especially true for teenagers who find it difficult to gain frequent access to skydiving, hang gliding, river rafting, or bungee jumping. This accessibility results in repeat business for the paintball and laser-tag companies.

Paintball Makes a Splash

In paintball, teams wage mock war on each other by shooting paint at their opponents. While a predominantly male-oriented sport, paintball is used by companies trying to foster greater camaraderie throughout their ranks. Some of the large companies that have taken their employees through a paintball course include Blue Cross and Blue Shield of Illinois, DJ/Nypro, and Domino's Pizza.

In 1997, industry revenues were about $250 million and were expected to have reached roughly $300 million in 1998. This growth is partly fueled by the 3 million paintballers (that play six to eight times a year) who spend up to $1,000 on their guns. The most competitive of these contestants are members of the National Professional Paintball League. And the most virile warriors compete in the ESPN-televised World Paintball Championships, where they encounter rivals from as far away as Australia and Russia.

Another driver for paintball is the fact that the game becomes increasingly exciting as more combatants participate. Interestingly, there has been a surge in the number of bachelor parties held at paintball fields; these parties enable males to bond without offending soon-to-be brides with traditional bachelor parties. Among those who believe there are solid underlying reasons for men engaging in such behavior is Richard Wrangham, a Harvard University anthropologist, who has said that paintball allows men to display aggressive, coalitionary behavior—an evolutionary necessity for the male of the species, who must learn to hunt and wage war. Such behavior is inherently pleasurable to men, according to Steven Pinker, a psychologist at the Massachusetts Institute of Technology. And paintball's sheer physicality is one of the last refuges of maleness, according to Peter Schwartz, a sociologist at the University of Washington.

Paintball Industry Players

Sales of Brass Eagle, the largest producer of paintball gear, exploded from $2.8 million in 1994 to about $32 million in 1997, much of it from selling guns costing as much as $400 through Kmart and Wal-Mart. Other manufacturers of paintball equipment include Kingman International and Tippmann Pneumatics; and Ivax Corporation encapsulates paint to ensure the projectiles splat appropriately on impact.

Laser-Tag Hits the Right Spots

Laser-tag is similar to "capture the flag." It is played in intricate mazes to pulsating music, flashing strobe lights, and piped-in fog, pitting teams of players against each other as they try to shoot their opponents and destroy their enemy's base. Players fire their laser beams at sensors on their opponents' vests. Each hit is recorded via remote control on a computer that keeps score.

Millions of children were playing laser-tag in the late 1990s. In mid-1998, there were 506 laser-tag centers in the United States, up from only 8 centers in 1992. According to the International Laser-Tag Association (ILTA), 100 more facilities were scheduled to open by the beginning of 1999. Although observers may be concerned that these facilities may encounter community opposition, the ILTA has reported that at least 600 proposals for laser-tag building permits have been granted without any community opposition. Laser-tag is more than just an American phenomenon as evidenced by the more than 1,000 centers throughout the world.

Investment Opportunities

Sales of laser-tag paraphernalia for home use—such as battery-operated guns and vests—reached $100 million in 1998, a tremendous increase from $30 million in 1997. The leader in laser-tag equipment is Toymax International, but Tiger Electronics, a Hasbro unit, makes laser-tag gear as well. Versent Corporation offers the world's premier laser-tag concept, with over 50 owned and operated Laser Quest Centres in North America. Additionally, Sony Entertainment operates laser-tag facilities.

CHAPTER 7

Travel and Tourism

The world travel industry accommodated 6 billion trips annually in the late 1990s and accounted for 10 percent of the world's annual economic growth. By the end of the first decade of the 21st century, the global tourism industry is expected to triple in size to almost 2 billion travelers spending $1.83 trillion a year, or $5 billion a day. Some of the drivers behind this growth include the fall of repressive regimes, the proliferation of trading blocks, the expansion of multinational businesses, and localities promoting themselves as travel destinations. A few of the industries positioned to benefit from this growth include airport and airline service contractors, corporate jet manufacturers, rental car companies and computerized reservation systems operators.

The Travel Industry

International travel is a growing phenomenon. According to the World Tourism Organization, in 1978, when the world's population was 4.4 billion, 287 million people took international trips. By 1996, when the global population stood at 5.7 billion, 595 million tourists traveled internationally. In 2020, the World Tourism Organization predicts 1.6 billion of the world's 7.8 billion people will take a foreign trip.

TIP: Bombardier is analogous to a transportation equipment mutual fund in that it manufacturers everything from airplanes to railroad locomotives and from subway cars to snowmobiles.

Travel is booming in part as a result of the end of the Cold War as there are now more countries for foreigners to visit. Also, there is tremendous unbridled demand for travel from formerly suppressed nations: one of the political freedoms most cherished by citizens of former communist countries is the unrestricted ability to travel abroad. In fact, Boeing has estimated that passenger miles in the former Soviet Union will grow 7.1 percent annually between 1996 and 2006.

Other factors contributing to the growth in world travel include:

- *The ascendancy of regional trading blocks.* Neighboring countries are forming integrated trading pacts from North America (i.e., the North American Free Trade Agreement) to South America (i.e., Mercosur) and from Europe (e.g., the European Union) to Asia (e.g., the Association of Southeast Asian Nations). The relaxation of border controls among the countries participating in trading blocks is a boon to regional travel. A common currency—the euro throughout 11 European nations—is especially conducive to tourism by relieving travelers of currency conversions and comparisons.
- *Reduced airfares.* Airfare reductions are largely the result of international airline deregulation and privatizations that have invigorated competition among the airlines. In addition, greater seating capacity on new aircraft enables increased air travel.
- *International companies are becoming more multinational.* In 1998 there were some 3.2 million American expatriates. Relocation consultant Windham International reported that 81 percent of the firms they surveyed in 1997 predicted that their overall expatriate population would grow by the year 2000. International travel is boosted by expatriate executives visiting their companies' headquarters and their families.
- *The proliferation of remote computer networks, satellite telecommunications, and videoconferencing.* This proliferation spurs business travel because executives can be nearly as productive when they are halfway around the world as they are in their home offices.
- *The realization by nations that increasing tourism is the fastest way to fuel development.* Attracting tourists to a country's natural allurements brings in foreign currency without requiring capital expenditures on developing tourist attractions. Similarly, state travel offices in the United States spent more than $478 million on tourism development in fiscal year 1997–98, about 6.5 percent more than in fiscal year 1996–97. Local authorities have learned that they can easily derive substantial revenue by raising taxes on hotel rooms and rental cars. Because tourists leave in short order and do not participate in local political processes, they raise no objections.

Americans Are Habitual Travelers

According to the Travel Industry Association of America (TIAA), American travelers spent more than $470 billion on travel in the United States in 1996 and more than $3.2 trillion worldwide. Also, U.S. travelers embarked on a record 251 million vacation person-trips in the summer of 1998, up from 244 million person-trips in the summer of 1997.

Americans show no signs of moderating their travel. David Bradley, a managing director at JP Morgan, pointed out that only 12 percent of all Americans had been on a commercial airliner in 1970. By 1995 that percentage had grown to 58 percent and is expected to reach at least 70 percent by 2008. According to industry research from BACK Associates, U.S. citizens flew 52.1 million international flights in 1997, up from 14.3 million in 1975. The State Department revealed that Americans were issued a record 6 million passports in 1997 and had more than 45 million passports in circulation. Interestingly, some Americans travel so extensively that the State Department has begun issuing citizens, whose itineraries will fill up their passports before they return to the United States, two passports simultaneously.

Business travel, which accounts for 60 percent of all travel in the U.S., has been rising as a result of growing corporate prosperity, the removal of trade barriers, and the pursuit of foreign markets. According to the TIAA, there were more than 43 million business travelers in the United States in 1997, up 12 percent from 1994. Some 14 percent of these travelers, or about 6 million people, were considered frequent business travelers—that is, those who take ten or more trips a year. And family members were nearly three times more likely to be included on business trips in 1998 than in 1990.

TIP: Chauffeured vehicle service providers—such as Carey International and SuperShuttle International—that focus on air travelers provide additional avenues for playing the growth in travel.

The following are among the other trends causing Americans to increase their travel: The overwhelming majority of immigrants are now free from worries of persecution, so they frequently visit their native lands. The United States had a higher proportion of foreign-born individuals (9.7 percent) in 1998 than at any time in the previous six decades. This percentage could rise in view of reports by the Immigration and Naturalization Service that an unprecedented 2 million immigrants were awaiting citizenship in mid-1998. Similarly, the growing number of people with dual citizenship find fewer hurdles in their travels. The travel industry also stands to benefit from aging baby boomers, who find travel an enjoyable outlet for their disposable time and discretionary dollars. In fact, research from the TIAA indicates that travelers 65 and over plan the longest trips of any age group, with an average of 13 nights per trip.

Investment Opportunities

The following industries are positioned to prosper from the confluence of rising demand for travel and tourism in the United States and around the world: travel services providers, airport and airline services contractors, corporate jet manufacturers, rental car companies, extended-stay lodging concepts, the vacation ownership industry, ski resort operators and cruise lines.*

Airport and Airline Services Contractors

The Travel Industry Association indicated that Americans took 1.2 billion person-trips in 1998, up 4.8 percent from 1997. Also, the number of international visitors to the United States increased to over 50 million for the first time ever, rising 5.4 percent to 51.1 million visitors in 1998.

TIP: Another company positioned to benefit from increased traffic through airports is American Locker, which designs airport baggage-cart vending systems as well as electronic lockers for airports.

Aviation and airline security and staffing firms like AHL Services and International Total Services benefit from being situated at the epicenter of soaring airport traffic and the growing incidence of outsourcing by airports. The inundation of airports by weary travelers presents major security and logistical challenges for airport authorities as well as pushing the airlines' ability to serve their passengers to the limit (in terms of ticket issuing and baggage handling, for example). In response to these challenges, airports are realizing that outsourcing to third-party providers results in a more efficient delivery of their responsibilities and relieves them of such labor management issues as recruiting, retention, workers' compensation, and whimsical labor regulations.

Services traditionally offered by companies like Ogden Corporation that participate in this $50 billion market opportunity include passenger profiling, luggage scanning, baggage claims, sky caps, aircraft cleanup and searches, frequent flyer lounge operations, and shuttle buses. More recent services provided by contractors include providing employee parking lot security, checking employee

---

*See David Wanetick, *Bound for Growth*, for a discussion on other industries exposed to travel and tourism.

Travel Services Providers

During 1996, commercial airlines carried 500 million passengers, a 7 percent increase over 1995. Domestic travelers and international visitors to the United States spent $523.8 billion in 1998, up 7 percent from 1997. According to Airlines Reporting Corporation, airline ticket sales will soar from $70 billion in 1997 to $110 billion in 2003.

Companies that provide travel accommodations—book the flights, reserve the hotel rooms, and arrange for rental cars—stand at the vortex of the surging growth of travel and tourism. Moreover, the travel services industry—which generated $115 billion in sales in 1997—is ripe for consolidation; it remains highly fragmented with roughly 30,000 travel agencies in the United States in 1999. Thus, Travel Services International's revenues soared throughout the late 1990s as this publicly traded, leisure travel services company had been growing both internally and through acquisitions. Another investment vehicle is Navigant International, which is a leading provider of corporate travel management services

An overlooked beneficiary of the blistering volume of travel is the computerized reservation system (CRS) industry. CRSs such as Galileo International and Sabre Group Holdings electronically link travel agencies to airlines, hotels, car rental firms and other travel services providers. In addition to monthly connection charges, CRSs receive payment based on the number of reservations made through their systems. As a purely volume-driven business (CRSs are not adversely impacted by discounting), CRSs stand to benefit from the growth of online reservations.

Another source of investment opportunity in travel services is online reservation agents like Preview Travel and Microsoft's Expedia unit. The Travel Industry Association of America found the number of Americans who booked trips online soared from 6 million in 1997 to 18 million in 1998. Jupiter Communications believes that online travel-related sales in the United States will soar from $923 million in 1997 to $12 billion in 2002 and that the percentage of airline tickets purchased online will rise from 2.5 percent in 1997 to 8.4 percent in 2002.

Some of the drivers behind the success of online reservation agents such as Pegasus Systems include the following:

- Although approximately 80 percent of the airline bookings in the United States are transacted through travel agents, there is very little consumer loyalty among individuals and small-office travelers.

- In September 1997, the commission rate for airline tickets to traditional travel agencies was reduced from 10 percent to 8 percent. This led many agencies to reduce their service levels to lower their costs, institute service fees to make up for the lost commissions, or sometimes do both, providing an opportunity for low-cost travel providers to excel.
- The Internet drives demand for travel by offering virtual tours of cities, landmark sites, hotels, and resorts. Full-service travel sites offer perks like weather updates, aircraft seat maps, and gate information for departing flights. Also, some hotels offer special discounts for Internet shoppers.

identification cards, and providing wheelchair operators to transport disabled or elderly passengers.

Future Market Opportunities

According to Mercer Management, only about 2 percent of the world's commercial airports were privately managed in early 1998. This is changing. The European Union mandated that airport authority licensing be opened to increased competition for providing a range of ground services beginning January 1999. Also, newly privatized airlines typically focus on improving their operating performance by outsourcing functions beyond their core competency. In fact, British Airways wants to outsource everything from spare parts and routine maintenance to flight training.

Additional opportunities for airport and airline services contractors are likely to present themselves as the White House Commission on Aviation Safety and Security has endorsed X-raying and matching all checked baggage (see Chapter 10, "Bomb Detection Companies"); implementing a passenger profiling system; and requiring under-the-wing security guards for parked aircraft. Finally, many small and regional carriers were still providing their own ground handling and cleaning services in mid-1998.

Corporate Jet Manufacturers

Demand for corporate jets is being propelled by the soaring demand for travel as well as the perception of corporate jets as a time-saving solution for itinerant executives and a status symbol for the growing masses of extremely wealthy people referred to in a previous section. Businesses legitimately justify the purchase of corporate jets from companies such as Boeing and Raytheon as an efficiency-enhancing tool; and fractional ownership programs make corporate jet ownership more economical for the wealthy. Moreover, the investment merits of this $6 billion-a-year industry were validated by Warren Buffett's mid-1998 acquisition of Executive Jet.

Corporate Attraction to Private Jets

Rising prosperity throughout corporate America during much of the 1990s fueled record purchases of corporate aircraft. The CIT Group's Third Annual Corporate Aircraft Outlook reported that new jet and turboprop business aircraft sales in the United States during 1997 soared 27 percent over sales in 1996. In 1997, 439 business jets worth $5.5 billion were delivered, up from 352 jets worth $3.7 billion delivered in 1996. According to the Teal Group, about 4,100 jets valued at $53 billion will be produced over the ten-year period ending in 2006, which compares favorably to the 3,076 jets worth $37 billion delivered during the previous ten-year period.

TIP: Corporate jet manufacturers offer investors lucid revenue visibility because their backlogs are both substantial and secure because buyers are typically required to make a $2 million nonrefundable deposit for each order they place.

Although difficult to quantify, companies earn real returns on their investments in aircraft. Jack Olcott, president of the National Business Aviation Association, said: "A business aircraft provides the ability to be more successful by extending overall market reach." Corporate jets allow executives to save time, travel more comfortably, enhance on-board productivity, and impress clients. These advantages over commercial flights are so great that Warren Buffett changed the name of his corporate jet from "Indefensible" to "Indispensable."

Corporate Jets Save Executives Time

More important than the panache of flying in corporate jets is the time that can be saved. Corporate aircraft manufactured by companies like Gulfstream Aerospace are faster, more reliable, and responsive to executives' demands while offering greater route flexibility than commercial alternatives. First, Bombardier's Global Express can fly more than 6,500 miles nonstop at speeds nearing

670 miles per hour compared with the typical 747 commercial plane that flies at 638 miles per hour. Second, according to statistics released by the Department of Transportation, only 70 percent of the nation's commercial flights operated on a timely basis in mid-1998 in contrast with the typical dispatch reliability of corporate jets that exceeds 97 percent.

Third, instead of waiting for scheduled departures, corporate jets depart at an executive's convenience. Thus, business aircraft are particularly appropriate when executives have to travel on short notice. Corporate passengers do not waste time going through security or waiting in lines for tickets. And business aircraft depart the moment their passengers board. Because there is no waiting for baggage or transportation on landing, passengers can be on their way to their destinations within moments of arrival.

Fourth, private jets are extremely practical for flying routes that airlines do not serve, serve infrequently, or serve only through connecting flights. Corporate jet passengers have access to 5,500 airports across the United States, 4,950 more than commercial flights reach. And most of the destinations served by the major airlines are routed through hubs that subject travelers to layovers, risk of delayed connecting flights, and greater incidence of lost luggage. Remote foreign destinations are even more difficult to reach on commercial airlines. Gary Fitch, director of Enron Corporation's flight operations, noted that "some of the places that we go to in South America are nearly impossible to reach via commercial means. If you tried to, it would take days just getting in and out."

The time savings and economies associated with an executive's flying on a corporate jet are compelling and virtually necessitate private jet travel when several executives require the same travel arrangements.

No Plane, No Gain

Skyrocketing executive compensation (discussed in Chapter 4, "Money Managers") is evidence that corporations regard their senior managers as key strategic assets. Because executives already work marathon hours, and because there are a limited number of hours in a day, companies are striving to squeeze more productivity out of their workers (see Chapter 8). The time-saving facets of corporate jets are just one way in which executives' productivity can be enhanced. Other reasons that business aircraft engender productivity include:

- Private flights avoid distractions common on commercial flights, such as crying babies and movies.
- Business planes commonly offer satellite phones and data/fax communications, real-time news, weather, and live financial feeds.

- The flexibility of having private planes at their disposal helps executives beat rivals to fleeting opportunities. Also, business travel allows executives crucial hours to collect their thoughts before their next meetings.
- Negotiations can be successfully concluded because of the flexibility of company airplanes. Michael Mondavi, president and cofounder of Robert Mondavi Winery, once remarked: "We found that we could finish our meetings without the concerns about catching a scheduled flight."
- Traveling with clients on corporate jets often impresses clients—important for building relationships. Critical negotiations and discussions about sensitive issues aboard private aircraft do not occur on regularly scheduled airline flights. Moreover, business jets allow executives to keep their clients captive.

Not only do executive jets offer unparalleled comfort, but they also improve executives' family lives by eliminating unnecessary overnight trips. According to one survey conducted by *The Wall Street Journal,* senior executives average 49 business trips involving air travel every year. One poll of top executives' use of their company's airplanes indicated they could avoid 17 nights away each year by using business aircraft rather than the airlines.

Corporate Jet Manufacturers Accommodate Customers

Despite the utility of private jets, owning and operating them is extremely expensive, even for profitable companies and wealthy individuals. For instance, the planes are idle for the vast majority of the time, and their depreciation and maintenance expenses are horrendous. Realizing this, jet manufacturers have devised financing arrangements that reduce the financial burdens typically associated with owning private jets.

TRAP: Mandatory retirement of pilots at the age of 65 and reduced recruitment by the military will decrease the availability of pilots. For instance, the 12 largest airlines lost 1,000 pilots to retirement in 1996, and that number is expected to peak at 2,300 in 2007. As the pool of pilots shrinks, their remuneration will rise and could stunt the growth of corporate

First, fractional ownership allows companies and individuals to pay a fraction (usually one-fourth or one-sixth) of a jet's cost to secure a specified number of flight hours each month. When someone purchases a share in a corporate jet, his or her preferred type of aircraft is guaranteed within four to ten hours of submitting a request. These fractional arrangements have become popular because they eliminate enormous capital outlays, crew-staffing headaches, and onerous maintenance schedules. Furthermore, fractional programs are profitable for the manufacturers because they can sell more planes and better leverage their fixed production costs as well as more adroitly manage such operating costs as pilots, insurance, crew training, hangars, and administrative services.

Second, companies like Gulfstream have embarked on short-term operating lease programs. These programs are well suited for companies that have short-term, full-time needs for air travel but wish to avoid the ongoing responsibilities associated with owning aircraft.

Industry Participants

The major manufacturers of corporate jets include Boeing, Bombardier, Gulfstream Aerospace, Raytheon, and Textron's Cessna Aircraft division. Derivative plays include aircraft suppliers such as Moog, Precision Castparts, Sundstrand, and Wyman-Gordon.

Rental Car Companies

Rental car companies like Hertz and Avis Rent A Car are becoming increasingly compelling investment opportunities. Not only do their revenues typically grow faster than air travel overall, but these newly independent companies are determined to generate robust profits.

According to *Auto Rental News,* the U.S. rental car industry grew an average of 8 to 10 percent a year during the 1990s and generated $16.4 billion in revenue in 1997, up 12.3 percent from 1996. During the same period, U.S. passenger miles increased only about 4 percent per year. In light of airport rental car transactions growing at 1.5 times the rate of air travel since 1970 (in part because more travelers need to rent cars to drive to suburban offices as discussed in Chapter 10, "Highway Safety") and the Federal Aviation Administration projecting that U.S. air travel will grow at a 4.5 percent annual rate through 2002, rental car companies should be able to increase their revenues some 7 percent a year. However, efforts by rental car companies to increase their presence in the insurance replacement, corporate relocation, and resort time-share markets may prove this growth estimate conservative.

Driving toward Profitability

Until the late 1990s, the major rental car companies were owned by the large automobile manufacturers. The rental car units were viewed as dumping grounds for cars that failed to appeal to consumers. As a result, rental car lots were typically overstocked with vehicles that kept rental car rates from rising more than 1 percent a year between 1986 and 1996. Also, managers of the rental car divisions were not performing optimally because they did not report to shareholders.

TIP: Because much of the demand in the rental car industry is derived from airlines, raising prices does not reduce demand. Because renting cars represents less than 10 percent of the cost of a typical business trip, higher rental rates are easily absorbed by business travelers' budgets.

In the 1996–1997 time frame, the major car companies began spinning off their rental car units into independent companies. Driven by shareholders demanding profitability and wishing to maximize their stock incentive grants, management teams have been increasing prices by roughly 7 percent a year, or seven times the annual rate just a few years previously. Further, these companies quickly employed yield-management technology, which entails analyzing historical data about demand patterns and changing prices as frequently as every 15 minutes in an effort to rent each car for the highest possible price.

Among the numerous measures rental car companies have taken to enhance customer satisfaction are implemented flight notification systems that alert rental offices that flights have arrived so paperwork can be prepared by the time a customer approaches the rental counter. Another measure aimed at customer satisfaction was taken by Hertz when it rolled out its weather-protected Hertz Return Centers. As Hertz Executive Vice President Joseph R. Nothwang explained, "We've got the customer covered during the return process all the way from the car to the terminal."

Rental Car Firms Buy Low and Rent High

Rental car companies such as Budget and Republic Industries (through its ownership of National and Alamo) are able to obtain their fleet of vehicles at steeply discounted prices from the automakers. The reason is that auto manufacturers have a deal with the rental industry whereby they will repurchase almost all of the cars they sell to the rental car industry at predetermined prices. (Nevertheless, the buyback prices are usually considerably higher than the actual value of the cars at the time of the repurchase.) Through these repurchase agreements, the auto manufacturers effectively subsidize the rental industry.

And rental car operators like Thrifty and Dollar have been managing their costs more aggressively. For instance, beginning in mid-1998, rental car companies began paying airline frequent flyer miles based on dollar costs of the rentals (e.g., 100 miles per $100) versus a flat 500 miles per rental, resulting in an average cost of $2.50 per transaction, a 60 percent savings. Furthermore, in early 1999, more than 30 states allowed airport concession fees to be passed onto customers. Thus, frequent flyer savings and concession fee pass-throughs are estimated to save several million dollars for Avis and Hertz alone in 1999 versus 1998.*

TRAP: Customers of the rental car agencies have probably noticed innocuous-sounding charges on their bills such as "occ chg" (for "other charges and credits") or "ex serv" (for "for extra services"). However, not all of the money collected by rental car companies can be included in their reported revenues. Cities impose high taxes on out-of-towners to cover the cost of projects that locals would balk at financing. Boston imposed a $10 surcharge on auto rentals to help pay for a convention center. Newark International Airport added 75¢ to rentals to pay for its airport monorail. And renters in Florida find a "FLA Surcharge" at the bottom of their bills, a tax that covers tires and battery disposal fees.

Other Attractions of the Rental Car Industry

The following are among additional investor attractions of the rental car industry:

- Plummeting gasoline prices. Rental car companies benefit from low gas prices for two reasons. First, low gas prices make the total cost of renting a car less expensive for the consumer. Second, customers are less likely to fill the gas tank when returning the vehicle, which results in their being charged a large premium by the rental car agency to refill the tank.
- Low interest rates are important for the rental car industry because they have large fleets heavily financed with debt.
- There are significant barriers to entry into the rental car business. First, the auto companies are reluctant to sell cars to anyone other than the major fleets because of the unattractive economics associated with selling to fleets. Second, airport space is limited and the best counter space is already rented to the major rental companies. Third, large investments, on the order of tens or hundreds of millions of dollars, are needed in computerized systems to track and optimize fleets.

---

*Jordan Hymowitz, BankBoston Robertson Stephens, "Auto Rental Update: Hail to the Victors Valiant," November 11, 1998, p. 4.

• The rental companies are less cyclical than the airlines. First, when airline travel starts to slow, the airline industry reflexively reduces prices to entice customers. These reduced prices hurt airline earnings but keep the airplanes full, and airline passengers still rent cars. Second, the prices rental car firms pay for their fleets tend to vary depending on the business cycle. Car manufacturers sell cars at retail first, and then dispose of what is left to rental fleet operators, often at heavily discounted prices. When retail demand for cars falls, which is what typically happens in a recession, the automakers discount more heavily to the rental car fleets, thereby reducing the rental car companies' costs. Thus, it is not surprising that Avis's domestic revenues increased every year from 1978 to 1998 while Hertz's domestic revenues increased every year but one over the same period.

Extended-Stay Lodging Operators

Extended-stay lodging operators—such as Extended Stay America, Suburban Lodge, and Homestead Village—accommodate guests who require lodging facilities for several weeks or several months. While extended-stay facilities are similar to hotels in offering maid service and tourist information, their units are designed to give customers a sense of being at home. Large kitchens and outdoor barbecues are examples of efforts to engender greater comfort.

Revenues in the extended-stay sector grew 43 percent to $1.7 billion in the ten months that ended October 31, 1998—far in excess of the 4.8 percent rise for the U.S. lodging industry as a whole. The extended-stay sector's rapid growth is a reflection of societal changes. The trend towards outsourcing is resulting in more contractors receiving temporary assignments: computer programmers are retained to integrate new software; environmental engineers need to spend a few weeks reviewing their clients' disposal processes; and lawyers may spend many months away from home when they conduct due diligence. Also, extended-stay facilities serve as homes-away-from-home for people going though life changes, such as a relocation, job loss, career transition, or divorce. Finally, corporate clients often use interim housing to meet seasonal, temporary, or start-up needs.

In return for accommodating customers for longer durations, extended-stay operators such as Marriott International's Residence Inn and Prime Hospitality's HomeGate charge more modest nightly room rates than do traditional hotel operators. Employers and clients appreciate this as the average hotel room cost $75 a night nationally (and $150 a night in the top 32 markets) in 1998. Thus, extended-stay providers are positioned to prosper from a continuing trend among companies to save money on travel expenses. In fact, research conducted by American

Express indicates that between 1994 and 1998 the percentage of companies permitting employees to stay in deluxe or first-class rooms dropped 33 percent—from 28 percent to 19 percent.

TIP: Of all the extended-stay operators, Execustay demonstrates a particularly interesting business model. Because Execustay does not own its own facilities, it locates and furnishes a residence within 24 hours of receiving a request. By not investing in real estate, Execustay is better prepared to contend with a recession or industry overbuilding than its rivals.

Its history of rapid growth notwithstanding, the extended-stay industry enjoys a bright growth horizon because it remained underpenetrated in early 1999. Out of 3.6 million hotel rooms in the United States, only 100,000 were of the extended-stay variety. Cristina Ampil of PricewaterhouseCoopers said there was a need for about 300,000 such rooms.* Concurring sentiments are echoed by Harry Venezia of Raymond James, who opined that although less than 3 percent of hotel rooms conformed to the extended-stay concept in mid-1998, demand was between 8 and 10 percent.

The Time-Share Industry

Ownership of vacation lodging (or time-sharing) has been one of the fastest-growing segments of the leisure sector. Domestic time-share sales grew from $1.5 billion in 1992 to $2.7 billion in 1997. According to Bryan Maher of BT Alex Brown, global industry sales will grow 25 percent to $6 billion in 1999.

Providers of time-share resorts—such as Fairfield Communities, Silverleaf Resorts, and Sunterra Corporation—have clearly hit on a popular concept. More than 4,000 vacation ownership resorts have been developed and over 3.1 million American households owned a time-share in 1998. Vacation ownership resorts are located in more than 82 countries and owners reside in 174 countries.

The following are among the factors contributing to the widespread popularity of time-shares:

- Time-shares feel more like second homes than hotels because they typically offer full kitchens and laundry facilities. Interestingly, having a full kitchen

---

*Robyn Taylor Parets, "Making Room: Corporate Trends Fuel Demand for New Extended-Stay Hotels," *Investor's Business Daily,* Dec. 18, 1998, p. A4.

allows the owner to reduce his or her expenditures on food, which is a substantial travel-related cost.

- Time-shares are far less expensive than outright ownership of a vacation residence, although they offer the same tax advantages of second-home ownership. This is because most deeded time-share intervals are financed with mortgages. In the absence of a definition of an existing second home, financing a vacation lodging creates a tax-deductible interest expense that can be written off similarly to mortgage interest on a primary home.
- Many time-share owners can swap their time-share intervals for time at any of several thousand resort locations worldwide. Also, a growing number of vacation ownership resort operators are enhancing the flexibility of their product offerings through such innovations as floating weeks, split or carryover weeks, credit/point systems, cruise or yacht vacation alternatives, and upgrade options.
- Time-share customers are protected from escalating vacation costs in future years by prepaying their vacation costs through the purchase of time-share intervals.

In addition to these attractions, time-share providers like Trendwest Resorts and Vistana will benefit from demographics. Two-thirds of time-share owners are between the ages of 35 and 59. The median age of a time-share buyer is 50, and 10,000 Americans were turning 50 every day in 1998. Also, the average income of a time-share buyer was over $70,000 in 1998, nearly double the average income of all U.S. households, and 54 percent of buyers have a college degree. Only a very small portion of these favorable demographics owned time-shares: penetration was 3 percent of all qualifying households of the U.S. market, less than 2 percent in Europe, and less than 1 percent in Asia in 1998.

Ski Resort Operators

I believe that ski resort operators—especially those with resorts that appeal to foreign skiers, such as Vail Resorts, American Skiing, and Intrawest—will benefit from demographics, the rising popularity of extreme winter sports (see Chapter 6), and the absence of a new supply of suitable ski mountains coming onstream.

Demographics Drive Demand

Demographics are helping the skiing industry as a result of the magnitude of the echo boom generation (see Chapter 3, "Teenage Apparel Retailers"). According to Leslie Otten, president and CEO of American Skiing Company, "approximately 60 percent of all participants take up skiing and snowboarding before reaching the age of 23, and demographic analysis shows that there are now more Americans in this age bracket than at any time in history."

Aside from the number of teenagers, the popularity of snowboarding is attracting younger people to ski slopes. In fact, snowboarders accounted for nearly 21 percent of the 54.1 million skier days recorded in the United States for the 1997–1998 season, an 81 percent increase over the 1994–1995 season. As for older skiers, the emergence of parabolic-shaped skis is making it easier to ski down the slopes.

Other Investor Attractions

Foreigners are increasingly attracted to American ski venues. From the winter of 1995–1996 to the winter of 1997–1998, the number of foreign skiers as a percentage of total skiers at Colorado resorts increased from 6 percent to 9 percent. More Britons skied in North America (primarily in Colorado) than in Switzerland in 1998. Such trends should continue as British Airways initiated direct daily service between London and Denver, and Lufthansa has direct flights between Frankfurt and Denver.

TRAP: Radical environmentalists could cause additional problems for ski resort operators. In protesting the expansion of ski and resort facilities on scenic forest lands, the Earth Liberation Front claimed responsibility for starting seven fires that cost Vail Resorts $12 million in damages in late 1998.

Foreigners are lucrative guests for American ski resort operators. Foreigners generally not only spend more money, they generally stay for at least a week, whereas the average out-of-state visitor skis for four days. Also, a Latin American tradition of turning overseas trips into shopping sprees is heightened by the radical change in climate that is especially beneficial to companies like Vail Resorts that own many retail outlets.

Separately, companies that control popular ski runs enjoy tremendous barriers to entry because potential competitors cannot build more mountains. Also, there is little room at the tops of the best mountains outside of avalanche paths, no-growth initiatives, while also being the recipients of good and reliable weather.

Cruise Line Operators

Cruise line operators like Carnival Cruises and Royal Caribbean represent interesting prospects. The number of North American cruise passengers increased from 1.4 million in 1980 to 5.1 million in 1997, representing an 8.4 percent compound growth rate. In 1998 seven large vessels were introduced and drove a 10 percent weighted average increase in capacity. Industry analysts forecast an 8 percent compound annual growth rate in new supply over the five-year period ending in 2003. This supply is likely to be filled as the cruise market is largely untapped—only 8 percent of North Americans have ever taken a cruise as of late 1998.

Among the reasons that cruises are popular with vacationers and travel agents is the predictability of the costs, 85 percent of which are paid upfront. And travel agents like to book cruises because they receive commissions on both the plane and cruise portion of the excursion.

TRAP: A derivative play on the cruise line industry can be found in the shares of Steiner Leisure Limited, which provides spa services, massages, and hair styling and sells more than 160 personal care products on cruise lines.

CHAPTER 8

Health Care

Over $1 trillion is spent on the health care industry annually in the United States alone. Managed care's focus on reducing the total costs of health care delivery is a boon to the pharmaceutical industry because taking medicine often preempts doctor visits and hospitalizations. In fact, drug sales in the United States rose a healthy 16.6 percent in 1998, which benefits the alternative drug delivery companies as well as the clinical research organizations. Also, the aging population represents long-term sustainable growth for the assisted living facility providers. Finally, greater attention to appearance is fueling the growth of contact lens manufacturers, liposuction device companies, and purveyors of laser surgery.

Assisted Living Facilities

It is often said that money is made by those companies that offer solutions to seemingly intractable problems. One of the most pervasive problems facing the nation is the issue of caring for the country's senior seniors, or people that are at least 85 years old. The magnitude of this problem is illuminated by the fact that some 60 percent of this population requires assistance with at least one activity of daily living, which includes walking, eating, bathing, dressing, and toileting. More specifically, the Agency for Health Policy and Research reported that 26.9 percent of the over-85 population needs help going outside; 25.9 percent with walking; 17.3 percent with bathing; and 11.7 percent with dressing. Demand for providing care for the elderly will soar in lockstep with demographics and rising life expectancy and will be aggravated by the inadequacy of traditional care providers.

The most promising solution to these intersecting factors lies in the assisted living facility (ALF) industry. Assisted living centers offer a combination of hospitality (e.g., housekeeping and meal service) and 24-hour nonacute health care services, such as ensuring compliance with medication and monitoring vital signs. As Kevin M. Hunter, the New York regional coordinator for Sunrise Assisted Living, described his company's services: "We are like a big bed-and-breakfast, with the difference being that we care for frail seniors who cannot, or should not, live independently any longer."

Unlike nursing homes, assisted living facilities allow their residents the dignity of maintaining private living quarters. Moreover, these facilities provide assistance with activities of daily living and foster group activities that help reduce the rate of the elderly's physical and cognitive degeneration. Victor A. Regnier, a professor of architecture and gerontology at the University of Southern California in Los Angeles, stated: "The biggest advantage of not staying alone in your own home is the social and behavioral contact that you have with other human beings. We know from studies that have been conducted that social contact is the most important marker for successful aging."

Demographics Drive Demand

Assisted living facilities like Assisted Living Concepts and Alternative Living Services enjoy a solid source of demand because people unquestionably need greater assistance during their later years. Assisted living facility providers are positioned to benefit from the post-85-year-old age group growing faster than any other. In fact, the U.S. Census Bureau projects that the number of people aged 85 and beyond will double from 3.5 million in 1997 to 7 million by 2020. The Census Bureau predicts that the percentage of people over 85 years will reach 4.8 percent of the U.S. population, or 18.9 million by 2050, up from 1.3 percent of the overall population in 1994. This explosive growth is attributable to baby boomers reaching their sunset years and to advances in health care. Accordingly, the Census Bureau predicts that by the year 2050, 42 percent of people 65 and over will survive to age 90, an increase in the survival rate of 65-year-olds from 25 percent in 1980.

Traditional Arrangements Prove Inadequate

Although the elderly have traditionally relied on spouses and children for assistance with their daily living regimens, the following are among the reasons that familial dependence will clearly become less common in the future:

- Roughly half of the people 85 years old and beyond are single. The Census Bureau indicates that the number of elderly individuals living alone has increased to 30.3 percent in 1998 from 7.3 percent in 1960. Statistics based on 1993 data found that for women the likelihood of living alone increases to 57 percent for those aged 85 and over from 32 percent of 65 to 74-year-olds. With the growing number of baby boomers either choosing not to marry or divorcing, these projections will trend higher.

- Until only recently, the oldest daughter or daughter-in-law usually assumed responsibility for assisting her (or her husband's) parents. As a result of the continuing increase in the number of working women, fewer daughters will be able to find adequate time to devote to their parents.
- The continuing high divorce rate is resulting in fewer former daughters-in-law willing to care for their ex-husband's parents.
- Looking further into the future, I expect the decline of the nuclear family and the easing of the notion of familial duty will make children less attentive to their parents. Many young women freely admit they will not take as good care of their parents as their middle-aged parents take care of their grandparents.
- The growing incidence of children spending less time with their parents—because of abandonment, divorce, or displacement as parents form multiple families—is likely to cause parent-child bonds to attenuate.
- These societal shifts will be further aggravated by the parent-support ratio—the ratio of individuals over 85 to those between the ages of 50 and 64—increasing from 3:1 in 1950 to 10:1 in 1993, and to a projected 29:1 by the year 2050. This expected jump is partly due to the fact that by 1990 approximately 26 percent of the baby boom generation was childless.
- People are living so long that a large portion of the children willing to help their parents are too old or too frail themselves to assist their parents with walking, bathing, and toileting.

Although family members' inability to care for the elderly largely precludes the elderly from remaining at home, managed care payers often disallow non-acute seniors from living in nursing homes, long the default option for seniors in need of assistance with daily living. Even if managed care payers were amenable to paying for nursing home care, with the number of nursing home beds for every 1,000 people over 85 years of age projected to plunge from 690 in 1976 to 350 in 2000, these traditional warehouses for the elderly clearly lack sufficient capacity. This capacity constraint is unlikely to be relieved as new construction of nursing homes is restricted by 37 of the 50 states having instituted Certificate of Need regulations that require state approval for additional nursing home beds. As surprising as it may seem, hospices (facilities designed to comfort moribund patients) are a less welcoming destination for the elderly, as the U.S. government has sued several hospices for unacceptably high incidences of residents living more than six months past the date of admission.

On the other hand, health maintenance organizations and government medical payers are attracted to ALFs because they realize that assisted living facilities cost 35 percent less than nursing homes and nearly 15 percent less than home health care, which in most cases is not provided on a daily basis. Consequently, health care payers are more aggressively referring to ALFs the 25 percent or more of the nursing home patients that the Department of Health and Human Services estimates could be treated in less acute settings.

Managed care companies cite studies, such as one from the National Institute on Aging that found that chronic disability rates dropped 14.5 percent between 1982 and 1994 among those aged 65 to 95 years, to rationalize restricting access to nursing homes. Such studies are noteworthy because chronic disabilities and associated limitations of physical activities are primary risk factors for diseases such as stroke, coronary heart disease, diabetes, and cancer—conditions among the elderly that often lead to nursing home care.

Another source of referrals to ALFs are long-term insurers, which provide guaranteed renewable insurance contracts that pay for nonacute, long-term nursing and personal care services. In fact, long-term insurers have begun to offer assisted living as a policy option.

Assisted Living Facilities to the Rescue

Profits in the ALF industry will be fueled by growth in the number of residents served and by opportunities for margin expansion. With about 1 million Americans residing in assisted living projects in mid-1998, according to the Assisted Living Federation of America, revenues collected by providers of assisted living facilities have been growing by between 15 percent and 20 percent annually in the late 1990s. However, there are tremendous opportunities for growth in residents as Census Bureau figures have shown that 6.5 million older Americans need some help with their daily living activities, and that number is expected to double by 2020. Also, pricing should remain healthy as only about 900,000 ALF beds are expected to be available in 2000, while the number of elderly requiring assistance with activities of daily living (ADLs) is expected to grow to more than 8 million. The publicly traded ALFs have a great deal of market share to capture as they only accounted for 10 percent of ALF services in 1998.

Many seniors will easily be able to afford to live in an assisted living facility. According to a study completed by the National Data Planning Corporation, the percentage of those over 85 who earn above $25,000 a year increased to approximately 36 percent in 1998 from 25 percent in 1990. Because few senior seniors remain in the workforce, a large portion of this income is generated from interest-earning assets. Assuming a 5 percent return on investment, these people could have some $500,000 in interest-earning assets. If need be, this principal (and the principal from non-interest-earning assets) and contributions from family members could be used to pay for living in ALFs. Because 51 percent of these facilities charge an annual rent of $18,000 or less, ALFs are within the reach of many seniors even without resorting to tapping principal or seeking help from family members.

Some of the other investment attractions of the ALF industry include:

- *Opportunities for margin expansion.* As assisted living companies extend their networks, they will experience dramatic reductions in their cost structures (e.g,. administration, marketing, procurement of supplies), which will generate operating leverage. By offering such ancillary services as adult day care, home health care, and Alzheimer's and hospice care, providers can attract seniors to the continuum of care earlier as well as enable them to age "in place" longer as their acuity needs increase. Little additional capital needs to be expended to serve longer-term residents, thus reducing turnover and consequently reducing sales and marketing costs.
- *Little reimbursement risk.* Roughly 90 percent of the revenues collected by ALFs are privately paid, thereby removing price limits, payment delays, and regulatory oversight that accompanies reimbursement.
- *Limited government regulation.* Because the industry does not have to comply with many government regulations, operators are relatively free to design their buildings, staff their facilities, and provide the potpourri of services they believe will maximize their profits.
- *Increasing credibility.* The industry gains legitimacy as brand-name hospitality players like Hyatt and Marriott offer assisted living services.

Despite the numerous attractions that ALFs offer investors, the following are among the risks you should be aware of:

- Easy financing may result in the overbuilding of assisted living facility providers. However, some of this risk is offset by building moratoria placed on ALFs in states such as North Carolina.
- Hotel companies like Extended Stay America that specialize in offering suites for extended periods of time are purposely designing their facilities to be converted into ALFs should the extended-stay lodging concept fail to deliver expected returns (see Chapter 7, "The Travel Industry").
- Rising government regulation of the industry is likely to coincide with ALFs receiving a declining percentage of their revenue from private payers.
- Due to the communal nature of ALFs (e.g., residents spend many of their waking hours in group activities and dining together) and the attenuated immune systems of their residents, communicable diseases can reduce an ALF's occupancy rate relatively quickly. As Peter Martin, a leading ALF

analyst with Jeffries & Company, noted: "One flu can reduce an ALF's occupancy by four residents in short order."

Investment Vehicles

The following are among the publicly traded assisted living facility providers: Alternative Living Services, American Retirement Corporation, ARV Assisted Living, Assisted Living Concepts, Balanced Care Corporation, Brookdale Living Communities, Capital Senior Living, CareMatrix Corporation, Diversified Senior Services, EdenCare Senior Living Services, Emeritus Corporation, Grand Court Lifestyles, Karrington Health, Regent Assisted Living, and Sunrise Assisted Living.

Contact Lenses

It is estimated that approximately 50 percent of the world's population, including 130 million Americans, are in need of some form of vision correction. One of the brightest investment opportunities for remedying these vision deficiencies lies squarely on the eyeballs of the more than 26 million Americans wearing contact lenses.

Contact lenses have been available for several decades, but the advent of soft lenses has stimulated significant penetration of the eyeglass market by dramatically reducing the discomfort of earlier rigid lenses. Over the next few years, the growth of the contact lens industry will be attributable to the transition to disposable lenses, demographics, product innovation, and international opportunities.

Perhaps the most exciting growth driver is the continuing shift to disposable lenses, which offer users the convenience of avoiding a daily cleaning regimen and heightened safety by reducing the risk of infection. The transition from annual replacement lenses to daily disposable lenses is a boon to contact lens manufacturers as the revenue they receive soars more than sixfold. This is not all bad for disposable users, however, because they offset much of their expenditures on disposable lenses by eliminating costly cleaning and disinfecting supplies.

Because the number of soft contact lenses sold in the United States has grown at a 28 percent compound annual rate from 1987 to 1997, manufacturers can now produce lenses with great economies of scale that, together with less expensive packaging materials, reduce unit prices and expand the market. Daily disposables, the segment of the disposable market that offers the most repeat revenues, have a great deal of room to grow as these lenses only accounted for 2 percent of the total contact lens market in mid-1998.

New Products Are Positioned for Demographic Shifts

Looking ahead, demographics should cause the $2.7 billion worldwide contact lens market to grow as much as 15 percent annually. In the United States, most people begin wearing contact lenses when they are between 14 and 24 years old, smack dab in the middle of the baby boomlet the nation is experiencing. Middle-aged people also offer promise for the contact lens industry. Some analysts have estimated that bifocal contact lenses could become a $1 billion market opportunity by offering baby boomers, who would otherwise wear reading glasses on top of their contacts, a more aesthetic alternative. Appearance-enhancing bifocals will be an important factor since 66 percent of all American adults believe that people look more attractive in contacts than glasses. Since people typically are in their forties whey they begin to require bifocals, disposable bifocal lens manufacturers will enjoy many decades of recurring revenue due to the roll-out of this value-added product.

TIP: Direct marketers of contact lenses, such as 1-800 Contacts, offer their customers convenience and time savings while enjoying high levels of recurring revenues, especially when filling orders for disposables. When customers call that company's easily remembered eponymous phone number, over 80 percent of the calls are answered within 20 seconds. New orders for lenses manufactured by companies such as Johnson & Johnson and Bausch & Lomb are processed in 4 minutes and reorders in less than 1 minute.

Interestingly, disposable contact lenses are particularly well suited for mail-order delivery because of their size and weight and because they lack the fashion risk common in other retail segments. In addition, the predictive nature of disposable contact prescription refills lends itself to sound inventory practices and the avoidance of price markdowns.

The downside to direct marketers of contact lenses is that 27 states currently do not mandate the release of contact lens prescriptions to patients—essential for placing orders. According to the American Optometric Association, optometrists in such populous states as California, Illinois, and Pennsylvania can refuse to provide patients with their prescriptions.

Bifocals are not the only recent product innovation in the industry. Contact lens companies such as CooperVision and Ocular Sciences offer specialty lenses, including the daily-wear toric lenses for people with astigmatism (who were traditionally unable to wear contacts) as well as eye-color-enhancing tinted lenses. Wesley Jessen has gone a step further with the introduction of its Wild Eyes line of contact lenses that cover the wearers' irises with stars, spiral designs, and other features. Wild Eyes were initially targeted to teenagers prone to tattoos and body-piercings but are attracting more of a mainstream audience. In early 1998, Con-TEX received Food and Drug Administration clearance to sell its OK rigid gas-permeable contact lenses that allow wearers to remove the lenses after only a few hours of use and still see clearly the rest of the day. Also, several companies are introducing lenses with protection against ultraviolet rays.

Foreign markets present another frontier of opportunity. While 20 percent of Americans in need of optical care wear contact lenses, the penetration rates are much lower abroad. In mid-1998, the penetration rates of contact lens wearers was 7.1 percent in Europe and 15 percent in Japan. As the penetration rates in foreign markets approach those of the United States, another 50 million contact lens customers could be served.

Cosmetic Medicine

Americans, particularly men, are increasingly appearance conscious. For example, the circulation of *Men's Health* magazine soared from 100,000 in 1988 to 1.6 million in mid-1998. Indications that women are concerned about their appearances include magazines like *Cosmopolitan, Glamour, Mademoiselle,* and *Vogue* that had circulations of 2.7 million, 2.1 million, 1.2 million, and 1.1 million, respectively, in 1998. Beneficiaries of heightened appearance consciousness include liposuction providers, companies that provide the medical devices necessary to perform cosmetic surgery, and laser device companies whose instruments resurface skin and remove tattoos.

TIP: According to the *Journal of Dental Research,* the most destructive form of gum disease, periodontitis, afflicts about 67 million Americans. Periodontitis develops when plaque builds up under the gums, creating toxins that destroy the tissues that anchor teeth to bone. In advanced cases, a tooth can become loose and fall out as bone is destroyed. CollaGenex Pharmaceuticals is developing Periostat, which is a pill that could stop the advance of that decay and thus help people retain their teeth and maintain their appearance. CollaGenex estimates that 13 million people seek help for periodontal disease each year, with $6 billion spent on such treatments.

Weight Loss Solutions

The U.S. Census Bureau of the estimates there were more than 58 million obese Americans (26 million men and 32 million women) in 1998. According to the American Dietetic Association, as many as 9.3 million adults were morbidly obese and 300,000 were dying every year in the late 1990s because they were too fat. The number of obese Americans is expected to double by 2030, and some authorities have warned that essentially all Americans will be overweight in a few generations.

There are many reasons why Americans are becoming increasingly overweight. Only 20 percent of Americans exercise for the recommended minimum 30 minutes a day. The media's stories of bulimia and eating disorders stress the problems associated with insufficient eating. And as the media constantly report on different diets, they often describe why various diets do not work. Thus, people become disillusioned and believe that diets do not work at all.

The following are additional reasons that Americans are becoming fatter:

- In a 1997 survey of 21,500 Americans, the Agriculture Department found that only 3 percent eat healthy, balanced diets. And not one got 100 percent of the recommended daily allowances for the ten most essential nutrients.
- There is very little advertising for healthy foods such as fruits and vegetables. On the other hand, there is a tremendous amount of advertising for such junk food as ice cream, candy, cakes, and fast food.
- People are consuming more take-out food, which tends to be high in fat, carbohydrates, sodium, and calories. Also, take-out food is usually eaten quickly, which means that more of it is usually consumed.
- The media (and society at large) have over-glorified attractive bodies. Thus, the bar for weight loss is too high for almost everyone to achieve. For instance, overweight people try to exercise for a few weeks. Then they realize they still do not look like Claudia Schiffer or Arnold Schwarzenegger. Thus, they become discouraged and stop working out.
- Many people who stop smoking overeat.
- There are movements to accept fat people. For instance, tabloid talk shows lambaste people for not being tolerant toward overweight people. The National Association to Advance Fat Acceptance (NAAFA) is lobbying for laws against discrimination of fat people by holding events such as its Million Pound March in Santa Monica in August 1998. Macy's featured the Delta Burke Collection, which advertises, "Eve wasn't a size 6 and neither am I."

- Labor-saving devices are too integrated into daily life. For instance, people used to open garage doors manually; now they have electric garage door openers. The result is that physical exertion is no longer a part of daily life, so people must make a concerted effort to exercise.
- Many people who work at home do not feel compelled to conform to any office protocol. According to a 1996 survey of home-business owners conducted by *Income Opportunities* magazine, 36 percent reported eating and drinking more since working from home. Almost one-quarter admitted to using eating and drinking as an excuse to take a break; and one-third reported gaining weight.
- Twenty-five percent of children are fatter than is healthy and they are becoming overweight at younger ages. One reason is they spend more time in sedentary activities such as playing video games as opposed to playing outside. This is problematic because once people gain weight, it is very difficult to lose it.

Obesity Is Spreading Internationally

According to Arnaud Basdevant, a lead speaker at the Eighth International Congress on Obesity in Paris in 1998: "We used to consider obesity a problem of industrialized, rich countries. But now it has become a world pandemic." The World Health Organization (WHO) estimates that the number of obese people will soar from 50 million in 1998 to 300 million by 2025. For instance, in Mauritius, the WHO estimates that the percentage of obese people will rise from 7 percent in 1987 to 32 percent of the population by 2025. Some 7.4 million Europeans are morbidly obese and one in five Brazilians are expected to be obese in 2025, more than double the number in 1989.

Investment Opportunities

One way that investors can play the trend of people consistently gaining weight is to invest in companies—such as Mentor Corporation, Medical Alliance, and Zevex International—that manufacture devices used to perform liposuction. Liposuction was the most commonly performed cosmetic procedure in the late 1990s, according to the American Society of Aesthetic Plastic Surgery. More than 200,000 people had liposuction in 1997, more than tripling the number of liposuction patients in 1992, according to the American Society of Plastic and Reconstructive Surgeons. Incidentally, one of the attractions of liposuction is that the marks from the incisions usually heal to the point of being undetectable.

Pharmaceuticals offer another avenue for gaining exposure to the growing incidence of heavyset people. For instance, GelTex Pharmaceuticals is developing a polymer that can latch onto fat and remove it from the body; and companies like Interneuron Pharmaceuticals produce drugs that prevent the brain from sending hunger signals.

TIP: Over the ten-year period ending in 1997, the average American woman added one and one-quarter inches of padding around her hips and one inch in her stomach. In 1998 one-half of all U.S. women wore size 14 or larger and 10 percent of American men wear size 2XL or larger. According to the NPD Group, spending on special-size clothing outpaced spending on regular apparel by almost 2 percent a year.

One of several vehicles for taking advantage of the trend of Americans' increasing weight is Bylane's, a catalog concern focusing on large sizes, whose sales exceeded $1.3 billion in 1997; the company had more than 2 million names for its catalogs. Heavyset people may be more inclined to buy from catalogs than from stores. In addition, more women may need to shop at such stores as Catherine Stores and United Retail Group, and more men may have to shop at such stores as J. Baker's Casual Male Big & Tall stores.

Cosmetic Surgery

According to the American Society of Plastic and Reconstructive Surgeons (ASPRS), the number of cosmetic procedures nationwide increased by 50 percent to nearly 700,000 from 1992 to 1997. Another sign of the nation's rising interest in maintaining youthful appearances is that membership in the American Academy of Anti-Aging Medicine rose from 12 doctors in 1993 to more than 4,300 doctors in April 1998.

Breast Implants and Reconstruction

Comprehensive studies from esteemed scholars at Harvard University, among other institutions, indicating that breast implants do not adversely impact a woman's health have resulted in a resurgence of breast augmentation procedures. In fact, the number of cosmetic breast implant procedures (90 percent of which were saline based) in the United States soared from 32,000 in 1992 to 122,285 in 1997.

TRAP: Investors should be wary of investing in fitness centers. For instance, Bally Total Fitness Holding reported in its 1997 10-K that more than one-half of its customers do not renew their memberships. At least 85 percent of those memberships are financed, and the company does not do credit checks. In 1997, the Securities and Exchange Commission ordered Bally to stop recognizing membership payments before they are received. The SEC also ruled that, against installment payments owed, Bally has to keep reserves for uncollectible accounts. In such situations, investors should make sure that reserves for uncollectible accounts are not allowances for people who cancel their memberships.

In addition, the high incidence of breast cancer is resulting in a greater number of reconstructive breast procedures. According to a study by the ASPRS, there were 50,000 reconstructive breast procedures performed in 1997 compared with 29,000 in 1992.

TIP: Other advantages associated with investing in companies that are exposed to cosmetic medicine include the absence of government reimbursement issues and insignificant compliance with Medicare/Medicaid.

The aging population and increased awareness among middle-aged women in the United States of the dangers and incidence of breast cancer should lead to increased numbers of mastectomies and corresponding increased opportunities for reconstructive breast implants. Excluding skin cancers, breast cancer is the most common type of cancer among women in the United States, accounting for one out of three (or 180,000) cases of cancer diagnosed each year. Separately, at least 26 states had legislation in 1998 requiring insurance carriers that reimburse female policyholders for part or all of the cost of radical mastectomies to offer partial or full reimbursement for reconstructive breast implant surgery as well.

The primary companies positioned to benefit from breast and penile augmentation as well as breast reconstruction are Inamed, Collagen, and Mentor Corporation.

Collagen Implantation

The aging population is increasingly turning to collagen injections for removing small lines of aging such as those found in the forehead and around the lips. Also, many depressed scars respond nicely to Collagen.

The use of collagen has two major advantages. First, it is very safe with only rare allergic reactions to the material. Second, collagen can be implanted as an office procedure. Although there is some initial swelling around the implantation site, within a day this disappears and the treatment area returns to normal. And the improvement that is gained is almost immediately apparent.

One of the primary investor attractions associated with collagen implantation is that the material's effects are not permanent because collagen is slowly absorbed by the body. Within a period of three months to two years, the effect of the collagen completely disappears unless reinjections are carried out. Thus, plastic surgeons are receptive to performing collagen implant procedures, since these procedures present recurring revenue opportunities.

Interestingly, men are big advocates of collagen implants. At least 10,000 penile enlargements had been performed in the United States by 1998; and a growing number of men are receiving pectoral and calf implants.

The two primary players in collagen implantation are Mentor Corporation and Collagen.

Laser Surgical Procedures

Cosmetic applications with lasers include skin resurfacing, wrinkle removal, hair transplantation, hair removal, and tattoo removal. Patients' vanity may be driving the demand for surgical procedures, but so too does physicians' desire for extra income. For instance, doctors performing wrinkle removal charge roughly $3,000 for an entire face, which takes an hour on average, and $750 for a specific area of the face, such as the eyes, which require about 15 minutes.

One of the most interesting applications of laser surgery is tattoo removal, which will piggyback on the tattooing trend. In a 1997 study of more than 2,100 adolescents from schools in eight states, a report by the Texas Tech University School of Nursing found that one in ten had a tattoo and that over half were interested in getting tattooed. One attraction of getting tattooed, according to Dr. Charles Shuster, a former director of the National Institute on Drug Abuse, is that it may be addictive, as the brain releases chemicals that work much like morphine or heroin when the body is in pain.

Many of the people who are getting tattooed will later want to have their tattoos removed. According to one Manhattan tattoo artist, "people used to get tattooed to mark significant people, places and occasions in their lives, and they knew it was permanent. Now they are doing it just to get tattooed, and you wonder what they will think of the thing 20 years from now." Communities in West Texas and Illinois, for example, bear all of the cost of removing gang-related tattoos for delinquents who foreswear gang activity. Finally, the advantages of using lasers for tattoo removal are that each session is fairly short, no anesthetic (or at most a local anesthetic) is needed, and damage to the skin heals quickly.

A separate promising application of laser technology is hair transplantation. The market for this application consists of an estimated 40 million bald men in the United States. Pharmacia & Upjohn (maker of Rogaine) has estimated that American men spend over $67 million a year on minoxidil (the hair-growing ingredient in Rogaine) and $400 million a year on wigs and toupees.

The primary beneficiaries of the growing use of laser surgical applications include Candela, ESC Medical Systems, Palomar Medical Technologies, ThermoLase, and Laserscope.

Automated External Defibrillators

There is a good chance that automated external defibrillators (AEDs) will become as ubiquitous as fire extinguishers by 2010. AEDs resuscitate people experiencing ventricular defibrillation by providing electrical shocks through paddles placed on the victims' chests. According to the American Heart Association, roughly 350,000 Americans are struck with sudden cardiac arrest each year. As of the late 1990s, victims had only a 5 percent chance of surviving sudden cardiac arrest.

The key to saving the lives of those undergoing sudden cardiac arrest is to deliver electric shock immediately. It is often said that one's chances of dying increase 10 percent every minute when the heart's electrical system malfunctions, but this is actually an understatement of how quickly sudden cardiac arrest can claim lives. Most people do not survive more than five or six minutes of sudden cardiac arrest, and substantially no one lives more than ten minutes after the onset of ventricular defibrillation.

Because rapid application of AEDs is of paramount importance in saving lives, health care payers cannot legitimately argue in favor of centralizing the availability of AEDs. (This is in contrast with health care payers that attempt to reduce medical costs by centralizing the delivery of health care to achieve economies of scale.) Although it may be cost-effective to place all of a city's magnetic resonance imaging machines in one hospital, the same cannot be said for AEDs. On the contrary, AEDs must be dispersed as widely as possible so that heart attack victims will have the speediest access to them. When quickly and properly applied, studies show that sudden cardiac arrest survivors have a good long-term prognosis—nearly 80 percent are alive one year later and nearly 57 percent are alive five years later.

First-Responders Are a Ripe Market for AEDs

Defibrillators have traditionally been sold primarily to hospitals. Even though this market offers some potential for replacing older, manual defibrillators with AEDs (and placing more AEDs throughout hospitals), the real excitement for AED sales lies outside the hospital setting. AED manufacturers have tremendous potential to sell to traditional emergency medical technicians because no more than 50 percent of ambulances, 15 percent of fire department vehicles, and 1 percent of police vehicles carried automatic external defibrillators in mid-1998. It is extremely important for these first-responders—especially the police as they are the most mobile—to be prepared to apply AEDs as patients are unlikely to survive a trip to the hospital.

TIP: Companies through which investors can gain exposure to AEDs include Medtronic, Hewlett-Packard, SurViVaLink, and Laerdal. Also, companies such as Bergen Brunswig and Marquette Medical Systems are involved in distributing AEDs.

First-responders began to purchase AEDs in the late 1990s. For instance, Medtronic's Physio-Control unit sold its AEDs to the Cincinnati police force, and Salt Lake City's fire departments rely on Hewlett-Packard's AEDs. Also, the International Association of Fire Chiefs has called for all fire suppression vehicles in the United States to be equipped with AEDs and for all fire personnel to be trained in their operation.

A Variety of Locales Are Receptive to AEDs

The American Heart Association estimates that 100,000 American lives could be saved every year if AEDs were placed where large groups of people congregate. Despite more first-responders purchasing AEDs, the risk for a sudden cardiac arrest victim waiting until an emergency medical technician arrives to receive a shock is just too great. In Chicago, for example, the average wait for an ambulance is 6 minutes, 34 seconds and it takes an average of 4 minutes, 50 seconds for a fire truck to arrive. In New York City it takes more than 12 minutes for an emergency vehicle to get to a scene and fewer than 2 out of 100 sudden cardiac arrest victims survive.

In light of such information and in view of the very favorable publicity that results when lives are saved as a result of the availability of AEDs, many locales are receptive to placing AEDs on their premises. Accordingly, Medtronic sold its portable LifePak AEDs to Boyd Gaming's seven casinos in Las Vegas, the Rose Garden and Coliseum in Portland, Oregon, and the Silver Dollar City theme park in Branson, Missouri. Similarly, Hewlett-Packard's Heartstream unit sold its Forerunner AEDs to American Airlines, New York City's Grand Central Station, and the San Francisco 49ers. Both the White House and the Kremlin have AEDs as does the New York Stock Exchange.

While many large companies—such as Michelin North America, Raytheon, State Farm Insurance, and Bankers Trust—have AEDs, they are far from the only entities increasingly attracted to AEDs. State troopers assigned to protect their governors carry AEDs in their vehicles in the event they need to provide immediate assistance. Gated communities and golf courses often equip their security vehicles with AEDs; and AEDs are growing in popularity with rural residents whose remote locations preclude being reached by paramedics. Also, AEDs are becoming so inexpensive (at $3,000 or less) and easy to use that individuals are beginning to buy them.

Most National Football League teams as well as many college teams have AEDs at every game and practice. Interestingly, sports stadiums are a very fertile market for AEDs—these venues generate a great deal of excitement and are very difficult for emergency medical technicians to reach. According to Dr. Mary Ann Peberdy, assistant professor at the Medical College of Virginia Hospital, purchasing AEDs would add only an extra 1¢ to the cost of a ticket sold in the National Hockey League, 2¢ in the National Football League and National Basketball Association, and 4¢ in major league baseball. On average, each major sports facility would need to purchase 25 defibrillators to cover its patrons sufficiently.

Legislation and Litigation Drive Sales of AEDs

One driver of pervasive deployment of AEDs is legislation. The Cardiac Survival Act, reintroduced in Congress in 1997, would require states to develop training programs for first-responders. Further, this act would extend "Good Samaritan" protection to those using AEDs, meaning that if a well-intentioned person used an AED and the victim still died, the rescuer would be insulated from liability. As of mid-1998, 35 states beat the federal government by enacting legislation that protected lay people using defibrillators in rescues, and another four states had similar legislation pending.

Another boon for AED manufacturers would be the passage of the Airline Passenger Safety Act. Realizing that there is no chance to save someone from sudden cardiac arrest when they are airborne without an AED, U.S. Congresswoman Barbara Kennelly introduced this act in Congress in 1997. The Airline Passenger Safety Act calls for deployment of AEDs on all commercial aircraft and requires each member of flight crews to be trained in the use of AEDs. The act also extends a Good Samaritan provision by exempting from liability both the airlines and passengers who offer assistance during an in-flight medical emergency. The act resulted in AED sales even before it became enacted; American Airlines placed AEDs aboard all of its flights by the end of 1998.

TRAP: In many states, insurers threaten to discontinue liability coverage if AEDs would be in the hands of someone who is not a medical technician.

Litigation is another driver of potential AED ubiquity—several venues have been found liable for not having AEDs available to revive their patrons struck with sudden cardiac arrest. Cases in point include Busch Gardens and Lufthansa Airlines—both of whom have been successfully sued for failing to apply defibrillators on a timely basis.

Ease of Use Spurs Demand for AEDs

AEDs are becoming an increasingly acceptable medical device as a result of their declining costs, ease of use, and enhanced functionality. While it was not uncommon for manual defibrillators to cost close to $10,000, AEDs cost as little as $3,000 in 1998. As volumes continue to rise, prices should fall even further.

In the past the application of manual defibrillators was limited to trained doctors, paramedics, and nurses. In contrast, AEDs are intuitively easy for lay people to operate. The ease of use of AEDs is largely due to automation and quick analysis of rhythm by the defibrillator without requiring the operator to interpret the rhythm. Some AEDs do not even have a rhythm screen, thereby eliminating the anxiety of rhythm interpretation and chance for error by nonmedical personnel. In advanced AEDs, computerized analysis of the victim's heart condition is communicated by automated voice prompts that direct the rescuer with commands such as "apply pads," "do not touch patient," and "deliver shock now." With some AEDs, placement of adhesive defibrillator pads is all that is required of the operator and permits hands-off remote defibrillation. Many AEDs feature safeguards for both the shocker and the recipient, and some AEDs' technology is based on biphasic waveforms that reduce the risk of damaging the heart by optimizing the electric jolts for individuals based on their size and weight.

The Red Cross already offers instruction in the administration of electric shock with AEDs and the American Heart Association is lobbying for the integration of defibrillator and CPR training. According to some trainers, course participants almost always learn how to operate AEDs within 15 to 30 minutes.

The following are among the additional advantages associated with state-of-the-art AEDs:

- AEDs are as light as four pounds and about the size of a hardcover book, which makes them easy for gated community security guards to store in their scooters as well as fire and police to store in their vehicles, where space is at a premium, and makes them easy for rescuers to whisk up staircases.
- Defibrillators are durable enough to withstand the chronic hard use that is common in the prehospital emergency environment.
- Many AEDs automatically self-test themselves daily, which increases reliability and reduces maintenance. Alarms sound when the self-test detects a malfunction, thereby notifying building managers of a problem.

Personal Emergency Response Systems

Companies manufacturing products that allow elderly and infirm people to conveniently retain their independence and dignity at reasonable rates will experience growing demand for their products. Personal emergency response systems (PERS)—help buttons that connect subscribers to emergency responders at the press of a button—are increasing their subscriber count at roughly a 20 percent annual rate. Because only a very small part of the potential user base had subscribed to a personal emergency response system in mid-1998, PERS suppliers should be able to maintain their heady growth rates for many years. For instance, Lifeline Systems, one of the largest PERS vendors, had only 216,000 subscribers in mid-1998 (but this was 22 percent more than in mid-1997) and many of these were Canadians.

PERS consist of small help buttons that are worn like a watch or a necklace and a console connected to a subscriber's phone. When pressed, the button transmits a radio signal to the console, which automatically dials a response center where operators answer calls and send help. The hands-free devices provide for two-way communications, allowing the subscriber and operator to discuss the former's problem. In the event the subscriber cannot communicate the nature of the trauma, the operator is guided by computerized information given by the subscriber about whom to contact depending on the situation. In emergencies, ambulances are dispatched. However, sometimes all that is required is to request that a friend or neighbor assist the caller confronted with a less threatening situation—such as finding the subscriber's medication or helping him up after a fall.

The following are additional advantages associated with a PERS:

- Subscribers can use their PERS to answer incoming phone calls by using the console unit as a speaker phone. This feature is well suited for subscribers who have limited mobility and may at times be unable to reach the phone to answer a call.
- PERS can be easily integrated with a wireless smoke detector to further protect subscribers. When activated, the smoke detector sends a signal to the console unit, which immediately calls the monitoring center to alert operators of a smoke or fire condition in the home.
- In the event of a home intrusion, silent panic activators can transmit a silent signal to the monitoring center that will allow the operator to listen into the home. If the operator hears a suspicious noise, local authorities will immediately be notified.
- Most systems are completely waterproof, which allows subscribers to wear their lifelines in the shower or bath, where many falls occur.
- Most systems dial even when the phone is in use or off the hook.
- The console generally does not require rewiring to connect the subscriber with the operator.

PERS Benefit from Demographics and Interest from Medical Payers

PERS are gaining increasing popularity among single senior citizens as well as with persons afflicted with physical disabilities, heart problems, histories of strokes, or diabetes. These are attractive demographics to serve. For instance, the number of Americans over 75 years of age is expected to rise from 13 million in 1990 to 21 million in 2020 (see "Assisted Living Facilities" in this chapter). PERS are often procured by users' children to give them peace of mind. This is especially true for the 12 percent of the nation's workforce that is responsible for the care of an elderly parent. The percentage of working children responsible for their parents' well-being is expected to rise as high as 33 percent by 2020.

Managed care payers are beginning to advocate the use of PERS as they realize that PERS save costs by allowing hospital patients to return to their homes faster. Indeed, there has been a push for reducing the time patients spend in hospitals; in fact, the American Hospital Association reports that the average hospital stay has declined from 7.1 days in 1986 to 6.2 days in 1996. PERS' costs are further reduced as some hospitals and social agencies subsidize electronic monitoring fees for low-income users. It is increasingly common for hospitals to use these systems to monitor the elderly in their neighborhoods so as to avert emergencies.

Similarly, some insurance companies are paying for PERS when doctors' recommendations are submitted. These medical payers believe that the rapid response that PERS allow increases survival rates and reduces treatment costs. Such contentions are supported by a multitude of studies, one of which was published in the *New England Journal of Medicine* and reported that people found within 1 hour of a fall are five times more likely to survive than those who remain helpless for over 72 hours.

TIP: Companies that serve the $3 billion home health aids industry with devices that make it easier for older and disabled Americans to live independently are positioned to prosper. Companies like Invacare and Sunrise Medical manufacture products such as plastic finger loops that fasten to keys to help turn keys in doors. Rods with small suction cups attached at the end enable people to pick up a variety of objects without having to bend or stretch. Other items help people turn lights on and off, pull up their socks, thread needles, and turn pages of books. The growth of this industry is evident from the growth of its suppliers' consortium, the VGM Group, whose membership soared from 11 firms in 1986 to about 1,300 companies in

PERS Allow Subscribers to Remain in Their Homes

PERS provide investors with a vehicle to play older Americans' reluctance to leave their homes. In fact, a 1997 clinical study proved that users of PERS from Lifeline Systems were ten times less likely to need a long-term care facility, such as a nursing home, than people who did not use such PERS. The aged's aversion to leaving their homes is partly attributable to fear over the care they believe they will receive in hospitals and nursing homes. Even a survey conducted by the American Hospital Association in 1997 revealed that patients sense diminished respect and detect a decline in the caring nature of hospitals.

Older Americans' fear of mistreatment and neglect in nursing homes is not unfounded. The U.S. Department of Health and Human Services' Office of Inspector General received 1,613 reports of abuse allegations in 1997, 14 percent more than the average from the previous three years. The Office of the Inspector General took disciplinary actions related to nursing home abuse in 382 cases in 1997, more than double the number in 1996. According to studies conducted by sociologists at the University of Tennessee, 4 percent of nursing home workers acknowledged they stole money, jewelry, and other items from residents. Ten percent of these respondents reported that they witnessed other staff stealing. A surprisingly large number of nursing home caregivers have criminal records. In fact, about 5 percent of the applicants seeking positions as nurse's aides were found to have disqualifying criminal records in Illinois's screening program in 1996 through 1997.

TIP: PERS companies offer investors very good revenue visibility because they collect a reliable stream of monthly subscription fees.

Senior citizens who believe they can live independently with only the occasional assistance of a home health care professional will find that the government is reducing payment for traditional home health care services. The Balanced Budget Act of 1997 included well over $16 billion in reductions in home care outlays over five years, resulting in home health care agencies reducing home care visits. Also, the fact that the Health Care Financing Administration (HCFA) is requiring home health care agencies to undergo periodic recertification processes to determine if they meet more stringent government regulations will result in more agency disqualifications. Fewer home health care services will be delivered as HCFA is nearly doubling the number of comprehensive audits of home health care agencies it performs each year, from 900 to 1,800, and is increasing the number of claims it reviews by 25 percent. The net result is that less supervision by home health care professionals will increase the need for the elderly to immediately summon assistance through the use of PERS provided by companies such as Lifeline Systems, American Medical Alert, and Response USA when experiencing emergencies.

Infectious Diseases

Nearly universal resistance to today's most potent antibiotics threatens to lead to the uncontrollable spread of infectious diseases. Over the past 20 years more than 30 new pathogens—including HIV, Ebola, Marburg virus, Lassa fever, and Legionnaire's disease—have claimed tens of thousands of lives. Similarly, the potential destruction that common viruses can cause is made evident when considering that in recent times influenza has been killing up to 20,000 Americans a year. However, during the winter of 1918–1919, the Spanish flu caused 20 million deaths worldwide.

The prospect of a repeat of such carnage resulted in a 1998 White House initiative that classified infectious diseases as a major national security threat. A Clinton administration directive called for heightened surveillance of global epidemics and $25 million to monitor and fight the spread of "superbug" bacteria that resist current drugs. Actions such as these should be a boon to the pharmaceutical companies developing enhanced antibiotics.

The Next Pandemic Looms

Experts are virtually unanimous in believing that another pandemic will occur. The chief of the Centers for Disease Control and Prevention's Influenza Branch, Dr. Nancy Cox, said: "We can say with certainty that there will be another pandemic. We just don't know when." Some disease control planners are so certain that another pandemic will occur that they refer to the present period of time as the "interpandemic period." Other epidemiologists are said to have developed contingency plans for infectious diseases that could claim the life of the president as well as masses of American citizens.

Although the arrival date of the next pandemic may be indeterminable, the prevalence of infectious diseases has already reached alarming proportions. The death rate in the United States from infectious diseases soared nearly 58 percent between 1980 and 1992, largely from the spread of AIDS and a greater incidence of older people, who are highly susceptible to germs. By the late 1990s, microbes were causing one-third of the world's 50 million-plus deaths each year. U.S. Surgeon General David Satcher warned Congress on March 3, 1998, of the threat of infectious diseases: "We are seeing a global resurgence of infectious diseases." Recent evidence of such resurgence includes the following:

- Dozens of infectious diseases previously believed to have been vanquished—malaria, cholera, yellow fever (which alone claimed 15 percent of Philadelphians in 1793), and tuberculosis, which currently plagues 30 million people worldwide—are returning.
- Some 25,000 new cases of tuberculosis are diagnosed in the United States each year and 3 million tuberculosis patients die worldwide every year. In 1998, the World Health Organization warned that tuberculosis could infect 1 billion more people in the next twenty years.
- In 1980, diphtheria was virtually unknown in Europe. By the late 1990s, an epidemic that accounted for 90 percent of the world's diphtheria cases spread from Russia and the Ukraine to Eastern Europe, Germany, and Norway.
- Warm wet winters in New Mexico and Colorado caused the population of hantavirus-carrying rodents to explode in 1997 and 1998. Hantaviruses have since caused gruesome deaths—marked by capillary rupture, severe shock, and renal failure—in the western United States. This outbreak was of particular concern because most of its victims died in the prime of their

lives, with strong resistance to infection, and since permutations of hanta-virus provoke 200,000 hospitalizations for hemorrhagic kidney disease in Europe and Asia each year.

Infectious Diseases Threaten to Spread with Historic Alacrity

Most health experts believe that the next pandemic will be sparked by the flu. Over the past two-and-a-half centuries, 10 to 20 human influenza pandemics have swept the globe. The most devastating of these was the Spanish flu, which occurred during the winter of 1918–1919, caused more than 20 million deaths (of which 500,000 were Americans), and affected more than 200 million people worldwide. More recent pandemics included the Asian flu of 1957–1958, which claimed 70,000 lives, and the Hong Kong flu of 1968–1969, which caused 34,000 deaths. Most pandemics originate from aquatic birds, and the two most recent had their genesis in China.

Even though a much feared 1997 Hong Kong flu failed to explode into a pandemic, pigs remain very fertile intermediary hosts of avian and human viruses. (When pigs catch a bird flu and a human flu at the same time, the two species' viral genes mix, creating a potentially dangerous new strain.) Both pigs and poultry are commonly raised on the same commercial farms, which facilitates inter-species transmission of influenza viruses. After new strains of the flu are incubated in pigs and relayed to humans, influenza spreads extremely quickly as the method of transmission is mainly respiratory.

A separate concern about the ease with which infectious diseases can spread is illuminated by the transmission of mad cow disease, the deadly brain infection that results in Creutzfeldt-Jakob disease. This slow-developing brain infection manifests itself in humans as mental deterioration, slurred speech, and difficulty in walking that worsens until death. Many thousands of Britons who ate hamburgers and steaks that derived from cows that harbored mad cow disease might be harboring this disease for many more years before related symptoms surface. Of even more concern is that vegetarians contracted mad cow disease as a result of using products, such as cosmetics, derived from infected cows. Contracting mad cow disease from cow byproducts poses a considerable threat of a pervasive spread of the disease for several reasons. Many animals' parts are mixed together, so one infected animal can contaminate enormous supplies of meat, cosmetics, and leather accessories. The animals' end products are distributed over many geographic regions; and end users, not aware of the risks of such products, take no precautions.

Travel Contributes to the Spread of Infectious Diseases

The speed and volume of international travel are cited by the Institute of Medicine as principal factors contributing to the global emergence of infectious diseases. Over the last century and a half, the time required to circumnavigate the globe has decreased from 365 days to fewer than 3. As Nobel Laureate Dr. Joshua Lederberg has stated, "The microbe that felled one child in a distant continent yesterday can reach your child today and seed a global pandemic tomorrow."

Microorganisms adapt to changing environments and are carried to every corner of the globe by travelers, whose numbers are growing rapidly (see Chapter 7, "The Travel Industry"). By the late 1990s, more than 1.4 million people were traveling internationally by air every day. Also, more than 15 million people seek political asylum or become refugees in various parts of the world each year. Most of these displaced persons are from developing countries, where infectious diseases are prevalent. Additionally, mass migrations of refugees, workers, and displaced persons lead to a steady growth of urban centers, whose health and sanitation infrastructures are often unable to cope with such influxes. Thus, population movements have been ideal conduits for the global spread of new and reemerging infectious diseases.

Examples from the mid-1990s to the late 1990s of the ease with which infectious diseases travel include:

- Virtually all 309 measles cases reported in the United States were traced to infected persons who had acquired the virus abroad.
- Troops returning from the Persian Gulf War brought with them a potentially new form of the parasitic blood and bone marrow infection called leishmaniasis.
- A report in the *Journal of the American Medical Association* warned that yellow fever, on the rise in Africa and South America, could invade parts of the southeastern United States, where it has not been seen since 1905.

Public Health Infrastructure Is Responsible for the Resurgence of Infectious Diseases

The lack of a public health infrastructure, inadequate sanitation, and poor hygiene are other factors that contribute to the rise of infectious diseases. In Russia, not only are surgical instruments seldom sterilized between procedures, but some bloodied instruments are simply run under water for a few seconds before being inserted into another patient. Also, in Russia and elsewhere, it is common for drug users to inject themselves with needles found in the garbage and discarded by others. As discussed in the chapter on the water industry, the unavailability of clean running water often results in people using the same water basins for depositing human waste as for drinking. Thus, it is no surprise that diphtheria is spreading rapidly in Russia and that cholera is spreading unimpeded in Latin America.

Poor sanitary conditions are not confined to the developing world. Even American hospitals are partly to blame for the spread of infectious diseases. Some 2 million Americans acquire infections in hospitals every year and nearly 90,000 patients in the United States die of hospital-acquired infections annually. Researchers estimate that hospital-acquired infections are responsible for $4.5 billion in annual health care costs.

The rate of nosocomial (i.e., hospital-borne) infections per 1,000 patient days has increased 36 percent, from 7.2 in 1975 to 9.8 in 1995. One reason that hospitals are breeding grounds for the transmission of infectious diseases is simply because hospitals are where many sick people and their communicable diseases reside. Failing to properly dispose of medical devices, patients' gowns, and eating utensils can cause diseases to spread. Also, when surgeons cauterize patients' organs, plumes of smoke rise. When the organs being cauterized are infected, the infection rises and spreads throughout the operating room, even though vacuums capture most of the plumes of smoke.

Routine procedures, such as blood transfusions and dialysis, often result in the transmission of infectious diseases. For example, the costs of infectious diseases could soar because 4 million Americans who had hepatitis C were involved in blood transfusions at hospitals and blood banks before blood purity screening began in 1992. In fact, hepatitis is America's biggest blood-borne epidemic, with an infected population four times the size of the AIDS epidemic.

Additional Vectors Contribute to the Spread of Infectious Diseases

The spread of infectious diseases is particularly serious for the many people who are plagued with compromised immune systems. Those infected with HIV, recovering from burns, or receiving medications for cancer or organ transplantation are likely to have attenuated immune systems. Many scientists believe that animal-to-human organ transplants are especially dangerous because many animals harbor dormant retroviruses such as HIV. While these retroviruses remain inactivated in their hosts, the risk of transmission soars as they become activated when the organ is transplanted into another species. Others at high risk include the elderly, people in nursing homes, and people with little access to health care, such as the homeless, migrant farm workers, and the poor.

The assemblage of children whose immune systems are underdeveloped and the aggregation of elderly people whose immune systems are deteriorating are both conducive to the spread of infectious disease. The more than 11 million children deposited into child care facilities are at great risk for intestinal infections, respiratory illnesses, and middle-ear infections because of their deficiently developed immune systems, close proximity to one another, and tendency to engage in unhygienic activity (see Chapter 1). The fact that doctor visits for childhood ear infections, the leading cause of visits to pediatricians, increased 150 percent between 1975 and 1990 to approximately 24 million a year, seems to indicate at least some loose correlation between the growth of child care facilities and the spread of infectious diseases among children.

Similarly, the growth of assisted living facilities presents increased risks of the spread of infectious diseases because seniors have a high degree of illnesses, their immune systems are usually compromised, and they live in close proximity to each other (see "Assisted Living Facilities" in this chapter). Whether hosted by children or the elderly, many infections are spread to other family members and the community at large.

A separate contributor to the spread of infectious disease is dirty currency. *Discover* magazine inspected randomly collected currency circulating in New York City in 1998. Its study revealed five identifiable bacteria: spherical coagulase-negative staphylococci and micrococci; diphtheroids; propionibacteria and various species of bacilli. The proliferation of these bacteria can extend to several people each day for each contaminated piece of currency that changes hands.

Resistance to Traditional Antibiotics Soars

Viruses and infectious diseases continue to evolve by mutating into superstrains to which most humans have no immunity and which lie far beyond the reach of many existing treatments. These protean strains appear suddenly, and the resulting pandemics vary from serious to catastrophic. Speaking about humanity's vulnerability to mutating microbes, Rockefeller University's Joshua Lederberg said, "We have never been more vulnerable. When I go through all the adaptations made by the microbial world to make a living at our expense, I sometimes wonder how we are still here."

The real risk of having insufficient defenses against mutating microbes is that millions of people could die of once routine and traditionally easily controllable infections. For instance, ear infections in children could range into potentially brain-damaging meningitis. Professor Lederberg remarked that "the odds of Ebola breaking out are quite low, but the stakes are very high. With antibiotic resistance, the odds are certain and the stakes are just as high."

Antibiotic resistance is not a potential threat, but a very real threat whose manifestations are becoming increasingly costly in terms of lost lives. Every antibiotic has lost its effectiveness against at least one form of infection that it used to combat and nearly every strain of bacteria is at least partially resistant to today's arsenal of antibiotics. Many germs are becoming resistant to as many as six or seven drugs at a time. When doctors prescribe antibiotics for even minor infections, they often prescribe several antibiotics that are to be administered together because no single antibiotic is effective against even common strains of infections. The following are among the threats that resistance to antibiotics pose:

- According to the Centers for Disease Control (CDC), resistance by pneumococcus infections to penicillin soared sevenfold, from 5 percent in the mid-1980s to 35 percent in the mid-1990s.
- In the course of a two-year study completed in 1995 at Cornell University Medical School, researchers found a 14-fold increase in the number of patients infected by bacteria impervious to all commonly used antibiotics, including Vancomycin, which was traditionally considered the last line of defense against infectious diseases.
- From the beginning of 1997 to mid-1998, the CDC documented the first four cases ever of Vancomycin Intermediate-Resistant Staphylococcus Aureas (VISA), the world's most potent counterattack against antibiotics. Dr. Stuart B. Levy, director of the Center for Adaptation Genetics and Drug Resistance at Tufts University, calls this "the worst thing that could happen in clinical infectious disease." Staph is a common and robust organism; it innocuously lies on the skin and in the nostrils of healthy people. However, if it gains access to the body through scrapes, cuts, or surgical incisions, it can cause lethal infection of the bloodstream. Should VISA strains become common, simple cuts and scrapes could become mortal wounds.
- According to the Institute of Medicine, more than 90 percent of the 9 million cases of staphylococcus aureas (which kills in hours by destroying heart valves) are now resistant to penicillin and a wide variety of other antibiotics, including methicillin, the drug that is next to last in the line of defense before Vancomycin. In New York City alone, methicillin-resistant staph killed 1,409 people in 1995.
- Roughly 20 percent of tuberculosis patients in the United States are affected with strains that are resistant to at least one of the antituberculosis drugs on the market.
- Salmonella DT 104 is resistant to most major antibiotics, including ampicillin, streptomycin, and tetracycline. In England, this disease killed 40 percent of infected cattle and hospitalized 36 percent of the people stricken by it. DT 104 has swept through food, animals, and people across Europe and threatens to become an epidemic in the United States. According to a report

in the May 1998 issue of the *New England Journal of Medicine,* 34 percent of salmonella cultures sampled in 1996 turned out to be DT 104, compared with just 0.6 percent in 1979–80.

Contributors to Antibiotic Resistance

The increasing prevalence of antibiotic drug resistance is a natural outcome of the use and overuse of antibiotics. Despite public education campaigns to persuade doctors not to prescribe unnecessary drugs, 20 to 50 percent of the 145 million prescriptions given each year to outpatients are unnecessary as are 25 to 45 percent of the 190 million annual doses of antibiotics delivered in the nation's hospitals. When bacteria or fungi are exposed to an antibiotic, the drug kills, or attenuates the growth of, the susceptible pathogen. However, any variant in the bacterial population that has spontaneously undergone a genetic change that confers drug resistance will have a selective growth advantage. In other words, many strains of bacteria have become resistant to antibiotics because each time an antibiotic is administered, a few bacteria mutate to avoid the drug.

Although antibiotics do not technically cause the resistance, they create situations in which the resistant pathogen can multiply in the presence of the drug, increasing the population approximately a millionfold in a day and quickly becoming the predominant microorganism. Resistance to overprescribed antibiotics develops so quickly that Dr. John D. Siegfried of the Pharmaceutical Research & Manufacturers of America commented: "If we released ten new lifesaving antibiotics tomorrow, in ten years we would have resistance problems with them too unless we changed our practices."

Another problem associated with excessive antibiotic prescriptions is that liberal prescriptions to children will deprive their immune systems of the opportunity to fully develop by fighting off common infections. Similarly, excessive sugar consumption weakens immune systems, rendering them less formidable defenders against microbes. Separately, much of the $26 billion spent on antibiotics each year is wasted because these superstrains have learned how to avoid almost all of the 160 variations of the mere 16 basic compounds from which most antibiotics prescribed in the late 1990s were constructed.

Not only do resistant bacteria spread rapidly from infected patients to healthy individuals, but there are also fears that antibiotic resistance in animals could spread to antibiotic resistance in humans. In fact, for more than three decades, European farmers fed avoparcin to livestock to keep them healthy so that they would grow faster. But in the late 1990s, Denmark and Germany banned the drug, claiming that if resistance to avoparcin developed in the farmyard, it might spread to bacteria in hospitals.

Investment Vehicles

The number of pounds of antibiotics produced each year in the United States has soared from 2 million in 1954 to more than 50 million in 1998. Most of the major pharmaceutical companies—Merck, Pfizer, Johnson & Johnson, Bristol-Myers Squibb, and Schering-Plough—are pursuing the development of new antibiotics. However, I believe the greatest beneficiaries of the more than $2.8 billion annually directed towards antibiotic research in the late 1990s will be companies that develop drugs that will overcome resistance to infectious diseases. As discussed above, so many different germs have figured out ways to avoid so many different drugs that a whole new class of pharmaceutical agent is needed.

Drug discovery tools enable companies to develop a self-renewing pipeline of truly innovative antibiotics that have a good chance of staying ahead of resistant bacteria. Robotics and high-speed equipment allow researchers to test thousands of compounds against a disease target every day (see "Clinical Research Organizations" in this chapter). And the gene-sleuthing revolution has made it possible to learn where to attack selected diseases at their weakest points. For instance, Cubist Pharmaceuticals uses robotics and sophisticated data management software to determine which of thousands of chemicals will effectively destroy various microbes. Microcide Pharmaceuticals utilizes bacterial genetics to uncover functionally important genes for use as targets in the discovery of entirely new classes of antibiotics. And, Genome Therapeutics has sequenced the genetic blueprint of bacteria and then compares libraries of candidate drugs to use as weapons against these targets.

Another attraction of drug discovery companies is their collaboration with major pharmaceutical players. Cubist Pharmaceuticals has relationships with Bristol-Myers Squibb and Merck, whereas Microcide Pharmaceuticals collaborates with Johnson & Johnson, Daiichi Pharmaceutical Company, and Pfizer. Genome Therapeutics works closely with Astra and Schering-Plough.

Collaborations with large drug manufacturers effectively underwrite the smaller companies' research and development efforts as well as relieve them of manufacturing expenses. However, drug discovery companies usually retain the rights to internally develop and commercialize certain proprietary products. It is also important to realize that companies engaged in developing antibiotics enjoy abbreviated clinical and regulatory review processes because:

- The results of laboratory and animal tests are highly correlated to the effect in humans.
- It is easy to find subjects for human clinical trials because most people have a resistance to the antibiotics available and people afflicted with infections are willing to undergo experiments that may prevent their infection from spreading.

- Results from human clinical tests are unambiguous as the infection is either eradicated or it is not. In contrast, drugs for depression yield ambiguous results.
- Companies that produce antibiotics benefit from their discoveries being reviewed under the Food and Drug Administration's fast-track approval process, which leads to faster commercialization and greater returns on investment.

Alternative Drug Delivery

Even the most potent drugs lose their effectiveness if not administered properly. Substantial limitations are associated with delivering most chemical-based drugs orally and with administering substantially all biotechnology remedies by injection. Thus, companies such as Alkermes, DepoTech, and SuperGen that discover alternative methods for delivering drugs will face enormous markets.

Even though most alternative drug delivery companies were in their research stages, alternative drug delivery technologies generated $11.5 billion in sales in 1997, an 18 percent increase from 1996, and accounted for over 12 percent of total pharmaceutical sales. SG Cowen estimated that between 170 and 180 new drug delivery products could be launched from 1997 to 2002 by the 34 companies its analysts cover versus the 121 products on the market as of late 1998.

When novel mechanisms for delivering drugs are discovered, the relevant companies are usually awarded full patent protection. Not only are potential sales enormous but the costs of conducting clinical studies and submitting new drug applications to the Food and Drug Administration (FDA) are only a fraction as time consuming and expensive as is the case for traditional ethical drugs.

Downside of Oral and Injection Drug Delivery

Most drugs are designed to be administered orally. However, the digestive tract is not always the best route to deliver drugs to targeted sites. First, the high acid content and enzyme activity of the digestive tract can degrade drugs well before they reach the site of absorption into the bloodstream. In other words, the digestive tract would digest protein-based macromolecule drugs—which are what most biotech drugs are composed of—as if they were protein-based foods such as hamburgers.

Second, many macromolecules are too large to effectively traverse the cells of the epithelium in the small intestine to reach the bloodstream. Third, many drugs become insoluble at the low pH levels encountered in the digestive tract. Because only the soluble form of the drug can be absorbed into the bloodstream, the transition of the drug to the insoluble form can significantly reduce the amount of compound absorbed. The small percentage of chemicals delivered by drugs results in drug manufacturers overloading capsules with chemicals, which is not only costly but results in unpredictable bioavailability (the amount of the drug administered that is ultimately absorbed into the bloodstream).

TIP: According to David Robinson, president of Specialized Health Products International, needlestick injuries cost the U.S. health care community $3 billion a year.* Legislation requiring the use of safety needle devices manufactured by companies such as Specialized Health Products International, Bio-Plexus, and Retractable Technologies was implemented in California in 1999, and 28 U.S. senators were backing similar requirements on a national level in early 1999.

Separately, the vast majority of the 250 biotech drugs that were being reviewed by the FDA in late 1998 were designed to be administered by injection. However, the following are among the limitations associated with injectable drug delivery platforms:

- Needles present the risk of needlestick injuries that occur when a needle that has been exposed to a patient's blood accidentally penetrates a health care worker's skin. Contaminated needles can transmit deadly bloodborne pathogens, including HIV and hepatitis B. The Occupational Health and Safety Administration has required controls on the handling and disposal of contaminated needles as well as mandated follow-up testing for victims of needlestick injuries. These regulations have significantly increased the cost of using needle syringes.
- Using needles to administer medicine presents the risk of penetrating a patient's vein.
- Injections risk triggering infections because the body's natural defense barriers are breached.
- Because patients are averse to needles, compliance with injectable prescriptions is low.

The Wall Street Transcript, CEO Interview, David A. Robinson of Specialized Health Products International, Dec. 14, 1998, p. 41.

Advantages of Alternative Drug Delivery Platforms

Companies that are researching alternative drug delivery technologies—such as Elan Corporation, Alza Corporation, and Emisphere Technologies—believe that new methods of drug delivery will not only circumvent the shortcomings of oral and injectable delivery but will offer many enhancements over such methods. First, because the alternative methods more accurately target the intended delivery sites, more exact dosages can be administered as less of a compound is absorbed along the routes to selected organs. This allows drug companies to reduce their expenditures on chemicals and reduces the risk of patients enduring side effects, because chemicals are not misdirected.

Second, such mechanisms as sustained-release drugs (in which compounds are released slowly over a multihour period) yield more consistent dosages throughout the day. These consistent dosages are easier for the body to absorb than traditional pharmaceuticals that delivered shocks to the body as high levels of chemicals are released at once, resulting in the body often experiencing miniwithdrawal symptoms as it was deprived of needed chemicals for many hours. Thus, alternative delivery platforms often reduce side effects—such as withdrawal, nausea, and headaches—associated with traditional drug delivery.

Third, both sustained-release drugs and patches reduce the frequency of administering drugs, resulting in easier compliance for patients. Once patients take a sustained-release drug or don a patch, they do not have to remember to take a regimen of pills throughout the day. Because the new technologies improve compliance, they also improve efficacy. Finally, side effects are easier to resolve with some forms of alternative drug delivery mechanisms. If patients believe their patch is causing them to feel nauseated, they can simply remove the patch. There are no corollaries when one has digested an ethical drug or an injection of a biotech remedy.

Alternative Drug Delivery Offers Substantial Financial Rewards

Companies that are commercializing new techniques for delivering drugs—such as Fuisz Technologies, SEQUUS Pharmaceuticals, and Penederm—should enjoy lucrative futures. Partly as a result of health care payers' attraction to the efficacy of alternative drug delivery, SBC Warburg Dillon Read projected that sales of these drugs would soar from $11.5 billion in 1997 to $25 billion in 2006.

Alternative drug delivery companies benefit from a reduced risk of discovery. One reason is that they focus on applying their innovative delivery technologies to drug compounds that have proven to be effective but have lost their patent protection. (The fact that $20 billion worth of blockbuster drugs will lose their patent protection between 1999 and 2005 presents a massive opportunity for alternative drug deliverers.) Because a great deal of scientific data about prescribed compounds is available, the commercialization times for reformulating these compounds into novel delivery vehicles are as much as 50 percent shorter than is the case for compounds delivered orally or intravenously.

Generic Drug Manufacturers

Many investors believe that the $20 billion branded pharmaceutical manufacturers will lose in patent expirations between 1999 and 2005 will be a boon for generic drug manufacturers like Mylan Laboratories, Teva Pharmaceuticals, and Barr Laboratories. However, the following are only a few of the reasons an expected boon for generic drug makers may not hold true:*

- Managed care providers are willing to allow their enrollees access to branded drugs because: (1) they often have arrangements to purchase a nearly unlimited array of drugs from the pharmaceutical industry for fixed, predetermined prices; (2) they wish to avoid negative publicity associated with depriving their enrollees of branded drugs; and (3) challenging every prescription written for their enrollees is prohibitively expensive.
- Branded drug companies generate demand for their products by (1) spending heavily—at least $10.8 billion in 1998—on direct-to-consumer advertising; (2) dispatching salespeople to visit doctors, hosting medical seminars, and paying well-known professors to laud their products; and (3) generously distributing free samples of chronic remedies to doctors—on which patients often end up for the remainder of their lives. It is unheard of for generic drug manufacturers to engage in such activities.
- Branded drug manufacturers engage in aggressive litigation. Once a branded drug company sues a generic company over patent infringement, the FDA must place a 30-month freeze on a generic drug application. Even if the generic company wins FDA approval once the 30-month delay expires, most will not risk going to market until the patent litigation is resolved because if a generic drug maker is found guilty of patent infringement, it can be held liable for damages based on the branded drug maker's lost profits.**

---

*For more discussion on this issue, see David Wanetick, *Bound for Growth.*
**Amy Barrett, "New Teeth for Old Patents," *Business Week,* Nov. 30, 1998, p. 92.

In addition, drug delivery companies are often successful in licensing the rights to patented compounds owned by the major pharmaceutical companies but abandoned because of the side effects they induced. In many instances, redesigning a drug for alternative delivery is all that is needed to eliminate side effects. These licensing rights spare the licensors the enormous costs associated with discovering formulas in the laboratory.

TIP: Clinical trials for alternative methods of delivering established drugs like morphine and insulin need only focus on whether such methods are safe and effective. Thus, commercialization costs can be as little as $25 million, just a fraction of the $500 million that the Congressional Budget Office reported is the average cost to bring a traditional pharmaceutical to market.

Finally, drug delivery companies that introduce unique therapies to the market can be awarded full patent protection. This is crucial because patents bar generic competition—which commonly causes prices of branded drugs to fall by more than 90 percent—for 20 years.

Exciting Applications of Alternative Drug Delivery

The most promising developments occurring in the alternative drug delivery industry are discussed below.

Needle-free injections. Companies such as Bioject and PowerJect Pharmaceuticals have already commercialized jet injection technologies that enable health care professionals to reliably deliver medication through the skin without a needle. These devices use compressed gas to deliver medication into patients' body tissue at up to three times the speed of sound. These needle-free syringes have a huge potential market as there are roughly 1.4 million syringes sold in the United States annually. Moreover, Bioject and PowerJect should experience growing popularity on the part of needle-fearing patients and health care payers who are eager to avoid costs associated with the spread of needle-induced infections.

Pulmonary delivery. The market for pulmonary (i.e., lung) drug delivery was $1.7 billion in 1997 and is expected to grow to $9 billion by 2000. Lungs are a prime route for difficult-to-deliver compounds because they are highly vascularized (i.e., contain many blood vessels) and are therefore very absorptive. Major drivers of pulmonary delivery include improved medicine for respiratory illnesses such as asthma, cystic fibrosis, and chronic obstructive pulmonary disease. Pulmonary delivery is the preferred route for treating most lung diseases because much smaller amounts of drugs are needed than for systemic administration, and the drug can be applied directly to the site of action. The rapid delivery that the pulmonary route offers is especially important for treating indications—such as diabetes and pain—in which speed can dramatically improve therapy.

Companies like Aradigm Corporation, Inhale Therapeutic Systems, and Dura Pharmaceuticals are marketing medicine-bearing canisters that users put into their mouths. By pressing a button, medicines are shot into the back of their throats, through their bronchial tubes and into their lungs.

Vaginal drug delivery.   Infertility is one of the largest markets that vaginally delivered drugs are targeting. Although the infertility market is large, it has not been well served. There were an estimated 16 million infertile couples in western countries in 1998. Of the estimated 1.2 million American couples who visited fertility clinics in the United States, the average bill ranged between $3,000 and $8,000 for one to two years of treatment.

Until the late 1990s, one of the best hopes for infertile women was daily progesterone injections for 3 weeks before pregnancy and then another 12 weeks afterward, or about 100 needles in all, with only 25 percent effectiveness. This unpleasant experience was often complemented by such side effects as perpetual nausea, vomiting, breast pain, headaches, and bleeding. In response, companies like Columbia Laboratories are developing promising vaginally delivered infertility remedies. This alternative delivery strategy may solve a fundamental physiologic problem associated with delivering progesterone: Natural progesterone cannot be taken orally as it is metabolized and therefore rendered pharmaceutically inactive, and synthetic progestins can cause birth defects and therefore are not suitable for women of reproductive age.

Passive transdermal delivery.   Passive transdermal systems deliver drugs through the skin via passive diffusion. This technology allows a steady delivery of medicine at low dosages over long periods of time and is best suited for drugs that are inherently permeable, such as nicotine, nitroglycerin, and hormones. In late 1998, Elan had 15 transdermal patches under development, including ones targeting smoking cessation, anxiety, motion sickness, and attention deficit disorder. Alza developed the Testoderm patch, which is a transdermal system for once-a-day testosterone replacement therapy, and TheraTech has been pursuing patches for diabetes and angina.

Industry Players

The following are among the publicly traded companies involved with alternative drug delivery: Alkermes, Alza, Aradigm, Bioject, Columbia Laboratories, DepoTech, Dura Pharmaceuticals, Elan, Emisphere Technologies, Fuisz Technologies, Inhale Therapeutics, NeXstar, Penederm, PowerJect Pharmaceuticals, SEQUU Pharmaceuticals, SuperGen, and TheraTech.

Clinical Research Organizations

As providers of clinical and marketing services to pharmaceutical, biotechnology, and medical device companies, clinical research organizations (CROs) are ideally situated to prosper from a multitude of crosscurrents. Drug discovery is accelerating as a result of drug companies aggressively ratcheting up their research budgets and the widespread adoption of genomics, high throughput screening, combinatorial chemistry, and bioinformatics. Attracted to the opportunities for cost savings that CROs represent, drug and device companies are outsourcing more of their developmental and marketing tasks to CROs like Kendle International. As CROs' revenues swell, their expenses will plunge as a result of the efficiencies yielded by document management software companies.

TRAP: Employees of CROs can easily run afoul of securities laws because they are immersed in the daily developments of experimental drugs. Positive feedback from an academician or a nod from the FDA can cause the shares of a research stage company to explode. Thus, it is imperative that CROs establish strict policies governing their employees' stock trading.

Benefits of Outsourcing to Clinical Research Organizations

Clinical research organizations such as Covance and Quintiles Transnational engage in activities such as locating volunteers for clinical studies, monitoring drug and device trials, writing reports of studies, submitting all pertinent data about a drug or device to the Food and Drug Administration (FDA), shepherding candidate drugs through the FDA's approval process, and preparing outcomes studies. CROs like PAREXEL International market their clients' products through pamphlets, press releases, phone calls, and visits to doctors' offices.

CROs like Boron LePore & Associates even go so far as offering contract sales services, in which they actually sell drugs for their clients.

There are numerous reasons why large drug companies are increasingly receptive to outsourcing activities. First, drug discoveries have no commercial worth if FDA approval is not obtained; and General Accounting Office studies show that experienced submitters to the FDA (e.g., CROs) are three times more likely than nonexperienced submitters to get drugs approved.

Second, research indicates that CROs' expertise in conducting clinical studies and preparing new-drug applications for FDA review results in faster approval times.* Every month that is shaved off the time until commercialization is extremely important because some patent-protected blockbuster drugs such as Eli Lilly's Prozac and Merck's Vasotec generate sales of more than $200 million a month. Third, outsourcing to CROs allows drug and device companies to operate with fewer clinicians and salespeople. These reduced labor requirements are especially important for companies whose discovery of promising compounds and readiness to commercialize new products is episodic.

TRAP: CROs' contracts are usually terminable on only 60 to 90 days' notice by their clients. Clients can terminate or delay contracts for a variety of reasons, including the failure of products being tested to satisfy requirements, undesirable clinical results of the product, insufficient patient enrollment or investigator recruitment, or production problems resulting in shortages of the drug.

Growth Drivers for CROs

Revenues generated by CROs will continue to rise rapidly as their clients increase their spending on research and outsource more of their clinical and marketing responsibilities. According to the Pharmaceutical Research and Manufacturers of America, American drug makers boosted research and development expenditures by nearly 11 percent in 1998 to $20.6 billion, or more than three times the $6.5 billion invested in research and development in 1988. Worldwide research and development expenditures were more than $35 billion in 1998 and were projected by a consensus of securities analysts to reach $50 billion by 2002. Also, according to James Patricelli of Dain Rauscher Wessels, pharmaceu-

---

*For more on the FDA approval process, see David Wanetick, *Bound for Growth*.

tical and biotechnology products will redeploy $12 billion generated from spinning off noncore assets on research in 1998. As a result of a greater commitment to research, the drug industry had 6,200 molecules in the drug development pipeline in 1997, up 50 percent from 1993.

Of the roughly $18.3 billion spent on pharmaceutical research in 1997, CROs captured only $3.3 billion. Of the $16.3 billion in worldwide clinical development spending—the primary target of CROs—CROs accounted for about $2.7 billion. Although CROs have captured only a minority portion of their markets (and they still have plenty of room to grow), their revenues grew twice as fast as spending on overall pharmaceutical research from the mid-1990s to the late 1990s. Thus, analysts at SBC Warburg Dillon Read estimate that the amount of clinical development business outsourced to CROs would nearly double, from $2.7 billion in 1997 to $5.5 billion in 2000.

The following are among the underlying drivers of CROs' revenue growth:

- The rate of pharmaceutical development is about to soar as a result of genomics, high throughput screening, combinatorial chemistry, and bioinformatics. First, genomics companies like Human Genome Sciences can sequence 11 million DNA letters a day. This sequencing determines which genes trigger specific physiological functions. Once specific genes are identified, the discovery of proteins that can deactivate a mutation in that gene can cure a disease. Second, high throughput-screening devices from companies such as Molecular Dynamics and Perkins-Elmer are used to test the actions of thousands of proteins against a molecular disease target (itself identified by genomics). Third, combinatorial chemistry is an automated process by which a successful compound is turned into related offshoots for different drugs. Fourth, bioinformatics uses software to digest torrents of data generated by the other three tools. CROs will benefit from accelerated drug development as they will have more drug candidates on which to administer clinical studies and to shepherd through the FDA's approval process.
- Inasmuch as history is a guide, the wave of consolidation sweeping through the pharmaceutical (e.g., Astra and Zeneca) and medical device industries (e.g., Johnson & Johnson and Depuy) throughout the late 1990s will result in the loss of clinicians who are key to particular trials and approvals. It is more expedient to retain a CRO than to replace many mutinous workers. Also, consolidation often triggers a review of the combined company's practices and procedures, in which a strong case for outsourcing to CROs often becomes evident. Finally, as companies combine they tend to focus on drugs that can serve the largest markets because serving smaller markets

will not noticeably boost a large company's earnings. Thus, the large companies have a proclivity to license drugs (that are targeted to smaller markets) to smaller pharmaceutical firms that are likely to lack the clinical personnel necessary to commercialize the drug.

- Regulatory requirements for drug and device approvals are increasingly rigorous. In return for the FDA reducing its average review time from 29.2 months in 1992 to 13.7 months in 1996, the FDA demands more meticulously prepared new-drug applications.

- The number of drug trials has exploded far beyond the dictates of the FDA. One reason that trials often continue after FDA approval has been granted is to enable the drug company to market its drugs for more consumer-friendly indications. For instance, Bristol-Myers Squibb spent $50 million after Pravachol was approved in order to be able to market that anticholesterol drug as a compound that could also reduce the risk of first-time heart attacks. Thus, the typical new medication underwent almost 70 clinical trials in the late 1990s compared with just 30 trials in the 1970s. As a result, DataEdge LLC reported that the testing bill for each new drug submitted to the FDA was rising 12 percent a year in the late 1990s.

- As a result of drug makers' unfamiliarity with foreign markets, CROs have traditionally played a critical role in getting foreign pharmaceutical companies' drugs approved in the United States as well as getting American drugs on foreign markets. Global regulatory expertise is becoming increasingly important as evidenced by more than 25 percent of all Phase III trials being simultaneously conducted in more than one country. Drug and device companies appreciate the fact that outsourcing to CROs allows the inventing company to pursue marketing approvals in several countries simultaneously. This is conducive to building a sales base for companies' products faster than if they were pursuing approvals in one country at a time.

- Essentially, all of the biotechnology companies are exclusively engaged in research. As a result of not having anyone on staff to prepare new-drug applications, they have little choice but to outsource such responsibilities; and this will be a major driver for CROs. Although roughly 65 biotech drugs were on the market in late 1998, nearly 300 more biotechnology drug products and vaccines were in human clinical trials, and hundreds more were in preclinical development.

- Managed care is a boon to CROs for three primary reasons. First, the cost pressures that managed care exerts reinforce the necessity for pharmaceutical companies to reduce their expenses. Second, HMOs and other payers are requesting more therapeutic outcomes data, which requires the collection of more detailed clinical data. Third, managed care is steering enrollees away from costly inpatient settings such as hospitals. Patient privacy laws are making it more challenging to locate suitable volunteers, and experienced doctors are difficult to find—only about 4 percent of doctors in the U.S have been involved in clinical trials since 1990. As subjects of clinical trials become more dispersed, they become more difficult for the drug and device companies to locate, thereby making CROs' services more valued.

- Testing new drugs requires thousands of patients to take part in dozens of clinical tests, and the more inconvenient it becomes to monitor them, the more inclined drug companies are to outsource to CROs.

- Because it costs roughly $500 million to bring a drug to market and because the drugs' effective patents only last about eight years, drug companies want their drugs to be used for as many indications as possible. Thus, after the drugs have been approved, the producers want CROs to conduct further studies to determine their efficacy for other indications. For example, after Eli Lilly's Evista was approved for osteoporosis, it was learned that Evista can also battle breast cancer.

Finally, as one of the biggest paper shufflers, CROs are positioned to benefit from rapidly declining costs associated with processing Himalayan heaps of data, documents, and images. As more thoroughly discussed in the chapter on document management, great strides are being made in processing, retrieving, and manipulating data, documents, and images. CROs will also benefit from advances in fax resolution that allow faxes to be scanned into computers, scanning equipment, voice recognition systems, and remote data entry technology (see Chapter 12, "Voice Recognition").

TIP: LanVision Systems is particularly well suited to help CROs manage their paper flow.

The results of aggressive revenue growth and declining costs were already being realized in 1998. For the first nine months of 1998, Quintile's net profit margins rose to 6.9 percent from 6.6 percent a year earlier. And Pharmaceutical Product Development's net profit margins soared from 3.5 percent in the first nine months of 1997 to 6.2 percent in the first nine months of 1998.

Industry Players

The publicly traded CROs include ClinTrials, Quintiles Transnational, PAR-EXEL International, Boron LePore & Associates, Covance, Icon plc, Ilex Oncology, Kendle International, and Pharmaceutical Product Development.

Vaccines

Vaccination is a cost-effective means of disease prevention that has already prevented millions of deaths and has virtually eradicated many diseases that once afflicted mankind. The worldwide market for vaccinations should soar as substantially everyone in the world is a candidate for vaccinations and as more price-sensitive payers of medical care realize the tremendous cost savings that vaccines represent. Vaccine manufacturers also benefit from limited liability, minimal marketing costs, and subsidization from international humanitarian organizations.

Revolutionary methods of designing vaccines—such as DNA vaccines—offer the promise of retarding diseases as destructive as cancer and AIDS. These enhanced vaccines offer the prospect of solving the problems brought about by resistance to the contemporary arsenal of drugs (see "Infectious Diseases" in this chapter). Moreover, DNA vaccines will be less expensive to administer and will achieve higher compliance than traditional vaccines as well as eliminate the risk of triggering the diseases that inoculations were designed to prevent.

TRAP: By their very nature, vaccines offer their manufacturers little opportunity to capture repeat revenues.

Everybody on the Planet Is a Candidate for Vaccinations

The vaccine market is beginning to blast off as vaccines are expected to achieve revenues of $8 billion by 2000, up from $1 billion in 1989. In 1997, 200 years after the discovery of vaccines, only 16 vaccines were in common use. However, in 1998 more than 100 potential new vaccines were in clinical trials throughout the world—more than any other form of medication. Although vaccinations are typically directed toward narrowly targeted markets, they often reach much larger segments of the population. Hepatitis vaccines originally went to doctors, nurses and children at high risk, but 2 million to 3 million people in France alone were receiving these treatments annually by the late 1990s after France began administering them to all of its adolescents.

The volume of vaccines administered will soar as the result of severe under-penetration. Even though there are roughly 200 million vaccine injections in the United States each year, millions of Americans have not been inoculated for vaccine-preventable diseases. In fact, less than one-half of the children under age two in the United States are fully vaccinated, and 70,000 Americans die each year from vaccine-preventable diseases like measles and hepatitis B. In addition, many adults may have to be revaccinated as some of the vaccines they received as children were designed to be effective for only 20 years. The growing risk of biological attack, particularly from smallpox, could be a driver that prompts tens of millions of adults to be reimmunized (see Chapter 10, "Combating Biological Weapons of Mass Destruction").

Another driver of vaccinations is the attraction medical payers in developed countries find in the reduction in expenditures that vaccines make possible. Since the advent of widespread vaccinations, the incidence of many diseases—such as measles, mumps, diphtheria, pertussis, poliomyelitis, and rubella—has plunged precipitously. Also, ineffective vaccines tend to fail earlier than drugs, providing physicians with earlier warning as to the advance of disease. In sum, the Centers for Disease Control and Prevention have reported that for every dollar spent on a vaccine, $16 is saved in ongoing treatment costs.

TIP AND TRAP: One of the benefits from the promotion of vaccination by international relief agencies is that vaccine manufacturers enjoy much smaller marketing costs than manufacturers of other pharmaceuticals. However, investors must scrutinize vaccine manufacturers that sell a sizable portion of their products to Third World nations. Since these vaccines can be quite expensive and the developing world is so poor, the drug companies may be pressured to provide the vaccines at or below cost, even when taking into account subsidization by international relief agencies.

The underrepresentation of vaccines is much more pronounced in developing countries, and even the most xenophobic nations have been receptive to Western and international agencies immunizing their citizens. Officials from such organizations as the Red Cross held national vaccination days in 110 countries from 1988 to 1998. More than 450 million children under age five were vaccinated in 1997 alone; in one day in 1998, 2 million volunteers immunized 134 million Indian children. (Interestingly, even the fiercest combatants have suspended war to allow health care officials to immunize civilians. Fighting ceased in Afghanistan in 1997 on an immunization day and tanks were requisitioned to transport vaccine, and Sri Lanka called a one-day truce to factional fighting in 1998—the

"Day of Tranquillity"—so children could be immunized.) More vaccinations will be given as a result of such philanthropic contributions as those from Microsoft's Bill Gates, who announced in early December 1998 that he would donate $100 million for immunizing children in developing countries.

The vaccination rate for the major childhood diseases has grown from 5 percent of the world's children in 1974 to nearly 80 percent in 1998. The World Health Organization's vaccination effort, while targeting only six diseases, saved the lives of about 3 million children in 1997 alone. I believe the success vaccinations have demonstrated in preventing death will encourage support for vaccinating more people. This is especially true as medical directors in developing countries realize that diseases such as polio could be wiped out permanently by inoculating every person on the planet.

Vaccine Manufacturers Enjoy Limited Liability

Vaccine manufacturers are substantially immune to product liability suits because a 1986 federal law shields vaccine products from all liability not related to manufacturing error. This law established the Vaccine Injury Compensation Trust Fund (the Trust Fund), which provides funding for vaccine-related injuries and deaths from vaccines administered after October 1, 1988. Thus, any judgments against vaccine manufacturers are paid out of the Trust Fund or by the federal government (if the vaccination causing the death or injury was administered before October 1988)—not by the vaccine manufacturers.

The Trust Fund is funded by a flat-rate tax on each dose of vaccine purchased. In 1998, this tax was 75¢ per dose for all approved vaccines. However, industry authorities with whom I conferred indicated that the fact that the Trust Fund is overfunded and that more vaccines are about to be sold should result in a reduction of the tax rate. One reason that the Trust Fund is overfunded is that damages are limited to compensatory awards and exclude punitive awards.

New Vaccines Are Entering the Market

The following are some of the vaccines (and their intended uses) that have a good chance of becoming commercially available early in the first decade of the 21st century:

- Aviron's influenza vaccine—FluMist—reduced the incidence of flu among children by 93 percent and cut the rate of flu-related ear infections with fever by 98 percent, in a large-scale study conducted by the National Institutes of Health. Since FluMist is delivered in a nasal spray rather than an injection, children should be less resistant to having it administered. Government statistics indicate that 35 million to 50 million Americans contract the flu each year and that some 20,000 die from the virus.

- SmithKline Beecham's LYMErix vaccine was found to be about 79 percent effective in preventing Lyme disease, which is inflicted by ticks, and infected about 16,000 people in 1996. Advanced Lyme infections can lead to neurological damage, heart problems, and arthritis. Three LYMErix shots can be administered over six months instead of the typical one-year period. The condensed inoculation period is helpful as these shots reduce the time a person is vulnerable to Lyme disease, helps ensure that more people finish the three-shot regimen, and enables physicians to keep better track of their vaccinated patients.

- American Home Products' Wyeth Lederle Vaccines Unit was developing a vaccine in late 1998 that provides protection for newborns against a germ that is the most common cause of childhood maladies ranging from deadly meningitis and severe blood poisoning to ear infections. The same bacteria are also the leading causes of pneumonia, which kills more than 1 million children under five years old each year in the developing world, and otitis media (or middle ear infections), which leads to 30 million visits a year to pediatricians in the United States. Bacterial meningitis is an especially dire childhood disease, killing more than 20 percent of its victims with daunting speed and leaving many survivors with brain damage, paralysis, and deafness. This vaccine could be a real breakthrough because vaccines usually do not work in children under age two as their immune systems are insufficiently developed to respond to vaccines.

- North American Vaccine's CERTIVA is a combined diphtheria, tetanus, and acellular pertussis vaccine.

- ImmuLogic Pharmaceutical is developing a cocaine vaccine that would spark creation of antibodies to bind cocaine in the bloodstream, reducing the amount entering the brain and discouraging relapse.

- Companies such as Aquila Biopharmaceuticals, Vical, and SmithKline Beecham are developing vaccines for malaria. Many public health experts call malaria the world's most grievous disease. The parasite slays an estimated 2.7 million people a year and infects some 500 million worldwide. While nearly all of malaria's victims are citizens of developing countries, malaria was the top cause of casualties among U.S. troops in Somalia (despite the military's extensive use of malaria medications), and it has surfaced in New York and Virginia. Realizing that mosquito control efforts are faltering and that malaria is developing resistance to drugs, Gro Harlem Brundtland, the director general of the World Health Organization, launched a $20 million plan in May 1998 for cutting malaria-induced deaths in half by 2010.

Vaccines Will Soon Enjoin the Battle with Cancer

Vaccines have traditionally been used to embolden the human immune system to mount an attack on foreign and harmful pathogens. Researchers typically design their vaccines to target antigens that serve as markers on cells to alert the immune system that certain seemingly benign cells are really cancerous cells and must be destroyed. Because cancerous tumors result from the uncontrollable division of formerly healthy cells, the scientific community long believed that administering vaccines would cause the immune system to search and destroy healthy cells. A corollary to this problem is that the antigens on tumor cells do not reliably attract the vaccine's attention.

Scientists are pursuing two methods to overcome these problems. The process of developing tailored vaccines begins when a surgeon removes tumors from a patient, places them on dry ice, and sends them overnight to an antigenics laboratory, where heat shock proteins are extracted, multiplied, and returned to the surgeon. Some 15 days later, after recovering from the operation, the patient receives a shot of the vaccine. Then the enhanced antigens spark an immune assault on the tumor. The generic approach entails administering a vaccine consisting of three or four cancer cell lines that are shared by most patients with a given type of cancer.

Unlike most vaccines that are only designed to prevent a malady, cancer vaccines will be used to eliminate, prevent, and treat cancer. Also, aging baby boomers in remission from cancer will be suitable candidates for receiving injections to avoid relapse. There are several advantages of combating cancer with vaccines. Because immunotherapy uses biological substances to strengthen the body's own immune system, vaccines promise to be a more natural and better targeted means of treating cancer than radiation, surgery, and chemotherapy by offering decreased toxicity compared with radiation or chemotherapy. Immunological approaches, using the exquisite recognition capacity of the immune system, should allow physicians to detect cancer earlier, which is an important advantage in controlling the disease. Initial trials have been extremely encouraging. Some of the vaccines have prevented tumors from returning in humans and other vaccines have cured cancer in animals. Virtually all vaccines appear to be very safe with no side effects such as nausea or hair loss.

In 1998 there were more than 90 trials of cancer vaccines around the world. Among the biotech companies trying to identify tumor-specific antigens are ImClone Systems (targeting lung cancer antigens); Genzyme (which had isolated melanoma antigens); Dendreon (targeting prostate antigens); PerImmune (pursuing colon cancer); GeneMedicine (taking aim at head and neck cancers); and

Corixa and Biomira (both of which were pursuing the development of breast cancer vaccines).

HIV-AIDS Vaccines

AIDS presents an enormous opportunity for companies that can develop appropriate vaccines. Although the AIDS-related death rate has declined in the United States, the number of new infections (40,000 annually as of 1998) has not dropped. HIV infections more than doubled between 1994 and 1998 in many parts of Asia and Africa, where 90 percent of the world's 30.6 million HIV-infected individuals live.* As a result, there is a great deal of political support for research into HIV vaccines. In fact, in early December 1998 President Clinton announced that the National Institutes of Health would increase funding by 31 percent to $200 million to find a vaccine against AIDS.

Obstacles to developing a vaccine for AIDS are as high as the market is large. First, introducing live pathogens into the body to prompt an immune response (the common method for diseases such as polio and influenza) is unacceptable for AIDS because a fatal reaction could be ignited. Second, the AIDS virus has proved remarkably resistant to conventional vaccination approaches, in part because the virus attacks the immune system itself, and in part because it is capable of "hiding" from the body's antibodies. Indeed, even people who produce antibodies cannot rid their bodies of HIV. And, finally, HIV vaccine trials have an inherent conflict. For ethical reasons, researchers must continuously educate participants to refrain from unsafe sex practices and other measures that can spark infection without a vaccine. All participants in these trials also receive a written warning not to expect any protection from the injections because they may have received a placebo. However, if participants refrain from risky behavior such as unsafe sex and sharing needles, the chances of measuring a vaccine's effectiveness are vastly reduced.

Despite these challenges, researchers believe that a strategy of reducing the infectiousness of AIDS patients will bear some fruit. During the two to three months immediately after infection, a person is extraordinarily contagious—maybe 1,000 times more so than during the entire rest of their infection period. Scientists believe that this primary phase is directly or indirectly responsible for up to 80 percent of all HIV infections. In other words, most people are being infected with HIV by people who themselves have only very recently been infected. Thus, companies such as Chiron and VaxGen are designing vaccines to

---

*Joannie M. Schraf, "Miracle Vaccines," *U.S. News & World Report,* Nov. 23, 1998, p. 64.

reduce AIDS patients' infectiousness. Although people may still contract the AIDS virus, the promise of these vaccines is that victims will never get very infectious and will not be able to infect anyone else.

This strategy of reducing the infectiousness of AIDS patients is referred to as vaccine efficacy for infectiousness (VEI) and entails the injection of proteins that are expected to prompt the immune system to make antibodies against HIV. Although the body may take two to three months to develop antibodies in response to a natural infection—too slow to fight off the virus before it gains a foothold in the body—someone who has been given a viral preview via vaccination would immediately begin introducing antibodies when the real invaders arrive.

Thus, VEI might break the AIDS epidemic if it can just stifle the explosion of the virus during the superinfectious primary phase. There is historical precedent for the VEI tactic. In the 1950s, when the Salk polio vaccine was introduced, it actually prevented very few people from contracting the polio virus. Instead, it severely reduced the sickness (the symptoms like paralysis) of an infected person and reduced how infectious people were.

TRAP: If the VEI vaccination approach proves scientifically successful, it will run into a serious problem. It will be extremely difficult to persuade people to get vaccinated. Twentieth-century public health officials have vaccinated millions of people against everything from measles to the flu with the logic that recommended shots will save one's life or stop a person from getting sick. On the contrary, with VEI vaccines, people must be persuaded to take shots that will only save other people's lives.

DNA Vaccines Offer Tremendous Potential

The birth of DNA vaccines can be traced to the difficulties associated with mass-producing the classic varieties of vaccines from plasma. There are often shortages of serum from infected patients and the production costs of plasma-based vaccines are high and time consuming. Also, the advent of AIDS heightened public resistance to the use of vaccines derived from human plasma.

In the late 1990s, companies like SmithKine Beecham, Merck, Vical, and American Home Products were producing DNA vaccines that entailed inserting DNA fragments into the body. After DNA vaccines are absorbed directly into cells, these cells produce antigens that prompt a strong immune response against invading pathogens. In this sense, DNA vaccination resembles a viral infection because the biosynthetic machinery of the host is used for protein synthesis.

DNA vaccination is administered by needle injection or by particle bombardment into host organism tissues. An example of the latter method is helium dry powder sprays shot through gene guns that push pieces of viral DNA into skin cells at three times the speed of sound.

Development of DNA vaccines should be spurred by advances in genetics. By the early part of the first decade of the 21st century, researchers will likely have uncovered the sequences of the genomes of most, if not all, of the world's pathogens. Thus, DNA vaccines can soon be designed to target most of the diseases that plague mankind.

TIP: Despite the appeal of DNA vaccines, the heightened interest in producing traditional vaccines should be a boon to companies that collect plasma for use in vaccines as well as blood-testing kits. In addition, antibodies harvested from plasma remain the only preventive treatment for diseases like rabies and hemolytic disease of newborns. According to the Marketing Research Bureau, the worldwide market for finished products made from plasma-based products grew from $1.5 billion in 1984 to $5.4 billion in 1996. More stringent regulations—covering investigations into a donor's background, tests to detect the presence of disease-causing organisms, and the length of time required for donor centers to be granted regulatory licenses—act as barriers to entry that should accrue to the benefit of the dominant plasma-collection companies such as Serologicals, NABI, and Sera-Tec Biologicals.

One of the primary advantages of DNA vaccines is that, because they evoke a cell-based immune response, they eliminate the risk that dead or weakened whole viruses present—namely, the vaccine will spark the disease that it is intended to prevent. This is not a hypothetical concern—all of the polio cases in the United States are the result of the viruses in the administered vaccines overwhelming the recipients' immune systems.

A purified DNA vaccine may also generate fewer side effects as well as present minimal risk of an allergic reaction compared with traditional vaccines. For example, the influenza virus for vaccination is grown in chicken eggs. Thus, people with egg allergies can have serious allergic reactions to these vaccines because some egg proteins are carried along into the current influenza vaccines.*

---

*Peter S. Freudenthal, "Vical Inc.: Using 'Genes in a Bottle' to Fight Infectious Diseases and Cancer," BankBoston Robertson Stephens, May 12, 1998, p. 11.

DNA vaccines can be manufactured much faster than traditional vaccines. This is a very important improvement over traditional vaccines that require as long as nine months to be brought into widespread use. Common pathogens such as influenza and pneumococcal bacteria mutate so rapidly that by the time traditional vaccines become available, the targeted pathogen has already mutated into a more virulent strain. Thus, DNA vaccines should overcome one of the perennial frustrations of traditional flu vaccines: they have to be continually reformulated to fight new or long-dormant strains of influenza virus that sweep across the country each season.

The following are among the other advantages associated with DNA vaccines:

- DNA vaccines are patentable, whereas the same is not always true for traditional vaccines. Of course, having a patent-protected monopoly on a vaccine allows the producer to earn attractive profit margins.
- Because recipients' bodies serve as the factories for protein production, there is no limitation on the quantities of vaccine that can be produced, which reduces production and delivery costs for the companies that develop DNA vaccines.
- All DNA vaccines can be produced using similar techniques. The ability to use generic production methods greatly simplifies the development and production process.
- Reduced production and distribution costs allow DNA vaccine manufacturers to sell their vaccines at prices far below those of traditional vaccines. Already, scientists at the National Institute of Allergy and Infectious Diseases have developed a DNA vaccine at a fraction of the cost of a similar vaccine produced by traditional methods. These reduced prices are especially important when many of the vaccines are administered in the developing world.
- DNA vaccination provides long-lived immune responses, unlike many component vaccines that require multiple inoculations to maintain immunity. An ancillary benefit is a reduction in the risk of blood-transmitted viruses.
- DNA vaccines for multiple diseases can be given in a single inoculation— important because it reduces the costs of administration and improves compliance. In the United States, the full course of childhood immunizations requires 18 visits to a doctor or clinic.
- DNA vaccines are extremely stable. Unlike many conventional vaccines that must be held at a constant temperature, DNA vaccines can be stored under a vast array of conditions, either dried or in a solution. This eliminates the need for the cold chain—the series of refrigerators required to maintain

a vaccine during distribution—and will greatly improve the ability to deliver vaccines to remote areas in developing countries.

Vaccine Developers

Among the companies developing vaccines are American Home Products, Aquila Biopharmaceuticals, Aviron, ImmuLogic Pharmaceutical, North American Vaccine, SmithKline Beecham, and Vical.

CHAPTER 9

Dental Care

Dental practice management companies—essentially incorporated groups of dentists—are the source of some of the most promising investments within the health care industry. The provision of dental care is growing rapidly, and dentists receive a higher percentage of their revenue from private-paying patients than do doctors and are less exposed to government reimbursement and managed care dictates than physicians.

Dental Care Providers

The annual aggregate domestic market for dental services was estimated by the Health Care Financing Administration to be approximately $42.9 billion for 1995 and is projected to reach $79.1 billion by 2005. The dental services market has grown at a compound annual growth rate of approximately 8.1 percent from 1980 to 1995, and is projected to grow at a compound annual growth rate of approximately 6.3 percent through the year 2005. Dental care expenditures per capita have soared from $50 per person in 1983 to $175 per person in 1998 and are estimated to be as much as $350 per person by 2010. As a result of advances in technology and aggressive preventive treatments, Peter Frechette, CEO of Patterson Dental, said that by 2010 there will be another 1 billion teeth for American dentists to work on.

Although only one-half of Americans visit a dentist on a regular basis, the following are among the factors that will result in dental care providers capturing more of their market.

Dental care providers can serve more people with dental problems that are currently not receiving treatment. Unlike indications of medical problems, many people with dental problems simply ignore them. Rob Mains, managing director at Advest, makes the contrast clear:

Chest or joint pain is rarely ignored; tooth or gum pain often is. Examples are the large number of adolescents whose crooked teeth are not straightened versus the small number whose crooked backs are untreated; or the large number of adults who develop unchecked gum disease, leading to tooth loss, versus the small number who develop unchecked diabetes, leading to limb loss. There is certainly a difference in the severity between dental and medical symptoms, but the conclusion is still valid: the dental services industry has a long way to go to capture the business that it should be realizing.

Even though dental practice management companies are building demand for their affiliated dentists through advertising, the underserved market is large enough to ensure that cannibalization will not run rampant.

There is increased availability and permutations of dental insurance. The American Dental Association (ADA) reports that the key factor keeping individuals with a dental condition away from the dentist is cost. A variety of dental plans are removing this barrier by providing benefits at lower premiums. The percentage of the American population with dental benefits has risen from 23 percent in 1994 to 55 percent in 1998. Traditional indemnity plans have captured 91 million members while newer dental referral networks (which provide access to dental care at guaranteed costs) count 5.5 million members. The 27 million Americans enrolled in dental health maintenance organizations are attracted to the predictable out-of-pocket expenses, and the 25 million enrollees in dental preferred provider organizations appreciate being able to choose from wider networks.

The aging population will demand more dental services. More than 64 million Americans are 50 years or older and between 10,000 and 12,500 baby boomers will turn 50 every day until 2014. The aging population is largely able to afford dental care as evidenced by the ADA's report that 65 percent of seniors believe their teeth are healthier than their parents, while 77 percent of seniors believe their children have better oral health than they did at the same age.

Modern technology is making dental care less traumatic. Fear of pain has traditionally been another major inhibitor of dentist visits. Lasers often lead to less bleeding, pain (as lasers can pinpoint a much more precise area on the tooth than a standard drill and do not vibrate), and postoperative discomfort than traditional drilling and are increasingly used for soft-tissue work, such as gum surgery. Air abrasion systems, which remove the surface of teeth (for fillings and to cut away tooth decay) with a high-pressure spray of tiny pieces of metal, are replacing needles and drills.

Separately, a new method of pain relief is electronic anesthesia and consists of placing electrode patches on the face or gums. The patient, instead of the dentist, controls the level of the current with a hand-held unit.* Another method of delivering anesthesia involves Milestone Scientific's The Wand, which is a pencil-thin instrument that looks far less threatening than the traditional needle and allows dentists to electronically anesthetize small sections of the jaw or even one tooth instead of half of the patient's mouth.

Heightened concern with appearance is a boon for cosmetic dentistry. Consumers spent $383 million in 1997 on over-the-counter tooth whiteners, up 185 percent from 1995. Patients are paying up to $600 to bleach their teeth (whitening teeth that coffee, smoking, or age have yellowed) and similar laser treatments can cost up to $1,500.

Greater retention of teeth presents opportunity.   The increased focus on preventive dentistry is yielding results. The nearly one-in-eight American homes that have at least one electronic dental care device collectively spent over $184 million on these products in 1997. These devices include electronic toothbrushes, flossing guns, oral irrigators, and ionic brushes that repel plaque. Consequently, the majority of children now in elementary school will graduate from high school without ever having had even one cavity. Larry Neibor, managing director at Robert W. Baird, explains that just as fluoridation preserves teeth by strengthening the enamel, newer dental advances will result in teeth being repaired rather than removed. As people retain their teeth longer, more dental work is required as opposed to replacing teeth with dentures.

The rising tide of immigrants should fuel demand for dental services. Access to dental care is a privilege only reserved for the elite in many formerly communist and developing countries. (During the days of communist rule, it was said that the Soviet Union offered its citizenry self-service dental care. The state gave its comrades a hammer and a sickle and the rest was up to them.) It is not uncommon for even extremely wealthy Europeans to leave their dental problems uncorrected. Foreigners universally admire Americans for retaining straight white teeth, and immigrants are likely to try to emulate their new countrymen.

---

*Melba Newsom, "The Latest Remedies for Dental Chickens," *Investors' Business Daily,* July 7, 1998, p. A1.

People will discover new ways to damage their teeth. Both the ADA and the Food and Drug Administration have challenged the safety of store-bought tooth-whitening kits. Their primary concerns are the use of bleaching agents, such as hydrogen peroxide and carbamide peroxide, which contain acids that can corrode enamel. Also, the bottled water obsession is detrimental to teeth because almost no bottled water is fluoridated (see Chapter 5, "Bottled and Filtered Water"). Finally, dentists have already reported a surge in chipped teeth as a result of the growing popularity of tongue studs.

Dental Practice Management Companies

Dental practice management companies (DPMs) are similar to physician practice management groups (PPMs) in providing management and administrative services to affiliated dental practices. Publicly traded DPMs—such as Castle Dental Centers, Coast Dental Services, Interdent, and Monarch Dental Companies—are building integrated dental networks by entering into exclusive management service agreements with dentists. These arrangements consist of a DPM purchasing the assets of practices for a combination of cash and stock and then compensating the dentists based on revenue growth and profit margin expansion.

Since the DPMs own the practitioners' assets and are obligated to pay their dentists a salary, they have a vested interest in increasing the dentists' profitability. DPMs help their dentists achieve enhanced financial results by using their greater size to negotiate more favorable contracts with dental HMOs (DHMOs), malpractice insurers, and dental suppliers. The 23 percent annual growth experienced by DHMOs is boosting patient count at DPMs. In return for a high volume of patients, the DHMO pays the dentist a flat per member, per month fee, and the dentist is at risk for providing services to the DHMO's members (a.k.a. capitation). Although capitated rates appear low at first glance, the services most heavily used under most DHMO contracts are routine: two cleanings and exams and a set of X-rays each year. These arrangements usually result in dentists' reducing their costs of delivering dental care, which, together with enhanced patient counts, boosts profitability. Profits can be enhanced further by offering services like whitening that are not covered by DHMOs.

DPMs provide the capital necessary to expand the number of operatories and procure equipment. Having state-of-the-art equipment boosts office efficiency and attracts patients because much of the new equipment reduces procedure time and makes for less traumatic patient visits. The availability of modern technology encourages dentists to join DPMs so they can perform specialty work such as endodontics (root canal), periodontics (gum care), pediatric orthodontics, prosthodontics, cosmetic dentistry, and maxillofacial surgery.

The declining number of dental graduates, together with the appeal of DPMs, means that few young dentists will be looking to acquire practices from retiring dentists. Therefore, independent dentists are increasingly reluctant to invest in expensive equipment which will accrue to the benefit of DPMs.

DPMs relieve dentists of much of the back-office work, including filling out insurance forms, collecting remittances, maintaining bank records, preparing tax returns, hiring hygienists and other office staff, and complying with labor laws. The benefit of belonging to a DPM network is highlighted in the case of hiring and career opportunities. DPMs allow individual dental offices greater reach when seeking hygienists as they can advertise an open position throughout their entire DPM network. Similarly, dentists and hygienists affiliated with a DPM find it easier to practice dentistry when they relocate to an area served by their DPM.

DPMs help dentists by turning disparate dental offices into branded franchises, and they are marketing these brands aggressively. DPMs can afford to market their brands regionally or nationally, even through television. Individual dentists cannot afford to advertise through expensive media, and most dentists feel that marketing their own services is less than professional. DPMs further promote their dentist partners by applying marketing techniques and traditional retail principles of business to the practice of dentistry, including locating practices in high-profile locations, offering extended office hours, devising more affordable fee arrangements and payment plans for patients, and expanding the range of services offered.

Joining a DPM allows dentists to spend more time practicing dentistry as opposed to running their businesses. Affiliating with a large dental group gives dentists more time to spend away from the office as dental partners can cover one another's emergencies. Dentists have other reasons to join DPMs. Many are attracted to the upfront payment, and others look forward to receiving consistent paychecks and employer-sponsored benefits, such as paid vacations, participation in 401(k) plans, and stock options. DPMs are also a viable option for dentists who wish to develop their managerial skills because DPMs require regional managers and business development professionals.

In addition to these benefits, DPMs provide a logical solution to one of dentists' greatest concerns: losing one's entire practice from personal illness or broken fingers. If a soloist cannot perform his dental procedures, few patients will delay their visits until his return. By joining a DPM, patients can seamlessly be directed to affiliated dentists until their own dentist recovers.

DPMs Hold More Investment Promise Than PPMs

Although similar to PPMs I believe DPMs have more investment appeal.*
DPMs enjoy a more fertile market, will be able to consolidate their market more
efficiently than PPMs, and are better suited to accepting capitation from managed
care companies. In contrast to the delivery of medical services, dental services
are primarily paid by the patient. Because consumer out-of-pocket expenditures
account for 45 percent of the payment for dental services compared with no more
than 19 percent for medical services, less of dentists' revenue is subject to the
scrutiny, limitations, and payment delays associated with managed care and government programs.

While there is a glut of physicians, a shortage of dentists is developing. The
ranks of physicians more than doubled from 334,028 in 1970 to 737,764 in 1996.
In contrast, the American Association of Dental Schools has reported that 7 of
the 62 dental schools open in 1986 closed by 1998 and that first-year enrollments
fell from 6,301 in 1978 to 4,255 in 1996. No significant expansion of class sizes
or establishment of dental schools was budgeted for 1999.

Because the dental market is underserved, more dental offices can be established without taking patients away from colleagues. (Fewer dentists can open
more offices as most dentists work only two or three days a week.) The same cannot be said for physicians. Virtually every cancer sufferer is already an oncologist's patient, so when an oncologist opens a new office, his new patients will
most likely come at the expense of another oncologist's practice. The appeal of
the dental industry is that greater accessibility of practitioners converts dormant
demand into appointments.

DPMs Are Positioned to Grow through Consolidation

Dental practices are riper for consolidation by DPMs than physicians' practices
are for aggregation by PPMs. In view of the fact that only 1,000 out of the nation's
150,000 dentists were affiliated with DPMs in mid-1998, DPMs have barely
begun to penetrate dental practices. Most of this market could be captured by the
DPMs because a full 91 percent of dentists are private practitioners as opposed to
clinical practitioners, who are unlikely to become DPM dental affiliates.

Eighty-eight percent of the country's dentists are either solo practitioners or
practice with one other dentist, whereas 50 percent of physicians will practice in
groups of three doctors or more by 2000. Advest's Rob Mains has noted that even
for large dental groups, DPMs have to negotiate with only a few founders,

---

*See David Wanetick, *Bound for Growth.*

whereas PPM consolidators have to negotiate with all of the doctors involved. The fewer decision makers a consolidator has to negotiate with, the faster mergers and acquisitions become consummated. Another aspect of the dental industry that is conducive to consolidation is that 79 percent of dentists are generalists, whereas 80 percent of physicians are specialists. Consolidators find it much easier to analyze general practices than a diversity of specialized fields.

TIP: Like many other professionals, medical professionals cherish their independence and wish to be treated with respect. Sometimes PPMs and DPMs are so eager to wring profits out of their doctors' offices that they fail to exercise the requisite professional courtesy. OrthAlliance has avoided this problem by sharing in its affiliated orthodontists' revenues rather than its profits so that it will not be tempted to micromanage its orthodontists.

As several panelists at The New York Society of Security Analysts' Dental Industry Conference held in June 1998 opined, ego often impedes consolidation, and dentists are less egotistical than physicians. One reason is that they earn less money. *Modern Healthcare* reported that doctors in family practice earned $137,805 in 1997, whereas specialists earned $230,000—much more than the ADA's reports of general dentists earning $117,610 and dental specialists $177,590. Physicians' egos are also a reflection of American society's glamorization of their profession. While virtually all TV soap operas and a growing number of evening programs, such as *Chicago Hope* and *E.R.,* feature successful physicians in enviable settings, movie and TV stars seldom portray dentists.

DPMs Will Prosper under Capitation

Capitation—providing complete care for predetermined fees regardless of services rendered—has been problematic for PPMs. However, because dentists are more focused on prevention than doctors and because there are almost no catastrophic physical conditions in dentistry, DPMs will perform better under capitated arrangements. Dentists make concerted efforts to examine their patients every six months. Once in the chair, patients' dental health can be determined relatively inexpensively and quickly. Scheduling subsequent dental appointments helps dentists maintain more predictable patient flows.

On the contrary, physicians' batteries of patient examinations usually begin when patients report symptoms. For PPMs operating under capitation, performing such diagnoses is like playing Russian roulette—the patient could require a procedure or implant costing in excess of $100,000. DPMs are not nearly so anxious when their dentists review X-rays because the costs of performing even the most expensive dental procedure is much lower than delivering other forms of health care.

TIP: Savvy investors can often take advantage of the stock market mistakenly classifying DPMs and PPMs together. When many PPMs' shares plunged due to earnings disappointments and the unraveling of the PhyCor-MedPartners merger in late 1997, shares of many DPMs fell in sympathy even though their fundamentals were in no way impacted by such events.

Investment Opportunities

The primary DPMs include Castle Dental Centers, Coast Dental Services, Interdent, Monarch Dental Companies, and Pentegra Dental Group.

Dental Health Maintenance Organizations

Dental HMOs should experience a more lucrative future than medical HMOs. Similar to HMOs, DHMO enrollees' premiums are paid to the dental care provider directly, through payroll deductions, or by the enrollees' employers. Members covered under DHMO plans obtain basic dental procedures (such as exams, X-rays, cleanings, and certain fillings) at no additional charge beyond premium payments (other than, in some cases, a small per visit copayment). DHMOs establish copayments for more complicated services such as root canals and crowns. Managed dental care plans also cover services provided by specialists participating in the dental panel, including oral surgery, endodontics, periodontics, and pediatric dentistry. DHMO members typically receive a reduction from the specialist's customary fees for the specialist services performed.

Enrollees select a dentist from their DHMO's panels to provide dental services in return for a portion of the premium paid to the DHMO. Thus, the dentist receives steady monthly capitated payments from the DHMO based on the number of enrollees who have selected the dentist. DHMOs can substantially eliminate the risk of incurring a high incidence of expensive dental procedures among their enrollees. Because DHMO payments to the dentists are fixed, the incentive to control costs and manage the risk of overutilization of dental services is shifted to the dentists.

Concerns over the rising cost of dental care have resulted in the growth of managed care in the dental industry. According to the National Association of Dental Plans (NADP), enrollment in managed dental care plans grew from 7.8 million patients in 1990 to 26.5 million patients in 1997. NADP estimates that DHMOs' penetration of the population with dental benefits will increase from 18 percent in 1997 to 35 percent in 2000.

Several key reasons account for the growth of such DHMOs as First Commonwealth, CompDent, and Safeguard Health. Enrollees are attracted to lower premiums and predictable out-of-pocket expenses resulting from published schedules of co-payments. Data from the NADP show that DHMOs provide a 40 to 50 percent cost savings over other types of dental benefits. Because the monthly premiums are very low—roughly $15—DHMO coverage is a highly valued, yet inexpensive, benefit for employers to offer their employees. Even when employers choose not to pay for their workers' dental benefits, the premiums are reasonable enough for employees to purchase DHMO coverage themselves. Employers are willing to facilitate employee purchases of DHMO coverage because doing so creates the appearance of the employer's subsidizing dental benefits. Moreover, DHMOs provide the added value of quality assessment mechanisms, such as credentialing, peer reviews, site visits, and the establishment of dental care standards.

Investment Opportunities

The major DHMOs include First Commonwealth, CompDent, Pentegra, and Safeguard Health.

Orthodontic Services

I believe that the providers of orthodontic care are the most promising niche within the dental industry. Orthodontist practice management groups (OPMs) offer their affiliated orthodontists the same benefits DPMs offer their affiliated dentists: negotiating power, back-office support, and marketing support. Similar to general dentistry, the orthodontic chains have barely begun to penetrate their market: less than 5 percent of the nation's orthodontists were affiliated with publicly traded orthodontist chains in mid-1998.

A distinguishing characteristic of OPMs is that orthodontists are the dental providers most insulated from the reimbursement pressures that managed care organizations exert on other practitioners. As a result of the elective nature of orthodontia, a full 70 percent of orthodontic services are performed on a private-pay, fee-for-service basis, while 25 percent of such services are covered by traditional dental insurance and less than 5 percent of these services are reimbursed from managed care payer or government reimbursement sources.

Contrary to medical specialists, patients do not need a general dentist's referral to begin orthodontic treatment. Not only does this expand OPMs' markets, but the large orthodontic chains have been able to leverage their having the first point of contact with patients. Local dentists feel compelled to refer patients to the orthodontic chains (rather than independent orthodontists) in anticipation of reciprocity. Orthodontists stand to gain much more than dentists for reciprocating referrals because their numbers stand at slightly more than 9,000 compared with over 150,000 general dentists.

TRAP: As with any hot industry, investors must be cautious about an excessive supply of stock choking the life out of an industry. Seven dental services companies went public and three secondary offerings were completed in 1997. This flurry of supply caused these stocks to underperform the broad market in the first half of 1998.

A favorable payer mix and referrals are two reasons orthodontic practitioners enjoy the most lucrative dental practices. According to a 1997 study from the *Journal of Clinical Orthodontics,* the median annual revenues for orthodontics in 1996 was $513,000—over $100,000 more than average general dentists' fees. Mike Harlan, CFO of Apple Orthodontix, calculated that orthodontia is the most profitable segment of the dental industry with operating margins averaging 40 to 45 percent.

Another reason for orthodontists' profitability is that—after the initial examinations, preparation of molds, consultations, and application of braces—orthodontists spend very little time with their patients. Follow-up visits usually consist of assistants performing most of the preparatory work for orthodontists, who spend no more than about two minutes tightening braces. The minuscule time orthodontists spend treating their patients allows for high volumes of patients. Some of the publicly traded orthodontic chains have conducted time-motion and workflow studies to determine the optimum office layouts for facilitating the maximum level of traffic and to increase capacity utilization rates above the 50 percent that Mike Harlan believes is typical for unaffiliated practitioners. Thus, it is no surprise that orthodontists affiliated with industry leader Orthodontics Centers of America treat 75 patients a day versus the industry average of 42 patients and start 500 new patients a year versus the industry average of 170 new cases.

Demographics Boost Demand for Scarce Orthodontists

The $3.9 billion orthodontics industry has been growing more than 7 percent a year and should be able to maintain this rate of growth from a combination of attracting more (appearance-conscious) patients and raising prices. New patients are coming from several age groups: The American Association of Orthodontists is urging parents to have their children screened around age seven, and an increasing number of children undergo "early treatment" starting as young as two or three. Many orthodontists are doubling as facial orthopedists and are using early treatment more to modify their patients' malleable jaws than to straighten teeth.

The baby boom echo generation offers greater numbers of potential adolescent patients than even the baby boom generation. (See the chapter on Teenage Retailers for relevant statistics.) Moreover, this market is lightly penetrated as revealed by a landmark University of Florida study showing that only one of every five children born in the United States who could benefit from orthodontic services receives treatment. In addition, adults now comprise nearly 30 percent of the market and people within that demographic segment who get braces are growing 20 percent annually, the fastest growing segment of the orthodontics market.

Orthodontists are realizing more demand for their services as the result of Americans' increasing concern about their appearance, and the orthodontists are capturing patients with accommodative financing. Not only do braces enhance one's smile but lingual braces (which reside on the tongue side of one's teeth) eliminate the stigma associated with undergoing a corrective orthodontic course.

Orthodontist chains are attracting patients by offering flexible financing— including very modest down payments—without incurring worrisome levels of uncollectible receivables. Once braces are applied, patients have a strong incentive to continue their treatments (that last some 26 months) if they wish to have their braces eventually removed. The long-term, predictable nature of an orthodontic treatment course provides analysts with good visibility into OPM companies' revenue streams.

Orthodontists should be able to increase their fees simply by application of the law of supply and demand. Their market is growing some 7 percent a year, but the number of net new orthodontists is negative as there is a lack of young orthodontists. It is difficult to become an orthodontist; only the top 2 to 3 percent of dentists are admitted to accredited programs, according to Samuel Westover, CEO of OrthAlliance. Most programs last two to three years after dental school, and availability has been reduced as a consequence of one-third of these programs having become defunct over the past 10 years. On average, only 250 new professionals graduate each year.

The average age of today's orthodontist is 50, and Robert Schulhof, CEO of Omega Orthodontics, predicts that 4,500 orthodontists will want to sell their practice within the next ten years. This means that an average of 450 orthodontists will wish to retire each year and thus the 250 graduates are insufficient to take over these forfeited practices. This dearth of demand will result in consolidators raising their fees as the result of a lack of competition as well as buying practices of retiring orthodontists for reasonable multiples because the older orthodontists have few alternative exit strategies.

Investment Opportunities

The primary publicly traded players in rendering orthodontic services include Orthodontic Centers of America, Omega Orthodontists, OrthAlliance, and Apple Orthodontix.

CHAPTER 10

Security and Safety

Crime has been on a long-term downtrend. In 1998, the U.S. homicide rate dropped 27 percent from 1997 and there were just over 600 murders in New York City in 1997, down dramatically from 2,262 in 1990.* Violent crimes declined 7 percent and property crimes fell 5 percent in the first half of 1998 versus the same period in 1997, according to the Federal Bureau of Investigation (FBI). The Justice Department's National Crime Victimization Survey revealed that Americans suffered less at the hands of criminals in 1997 than they had at any time since the poll was first taken in 1973.

TIP: Military and law enforcement agencies across the world are turning to dynamic simulation-based firearms training. Companies such as Firearms Training Systems reduce live fire costs related to ammunition, range maintenance, trainee transport, weaponry wear, and environmental remediation. Moreover, these systems offer real-time feedback and evaluation of accuracy, reaction time, and situational judgment.

Security Services

In view of such statistics, investors may believe that the reduced incidence of crime bodes ill for security companies. However, it is because security companies are successful in selling their various security devices and systems that security providers represent attractive investment opportunities. Also, even though national crime rates are falling, 52 percent of Americans polled in mid-1998

---

*James Morrow, "The Incredible Shrinking Crime Rate," *U.S. News & World Report,* Jan. 11, 1999, p. 25.

responded they were more worried about personal safety than a year earlier. Interestingly, it is said that the security industry benefits from a barrage of free advertising: much of the news focuses on crime. Of particular interest are the investigative and personal protection services providers, bomb detection companies, drug-testing companies, surveillance camera companies, antipiracy solutions providers, computer network security providers and prison management companies.

Investigative and Personal Protection Services Providers

Over 3.2 million Americans lived overseas and 50 million Americans traveled abroad in 1998. (See Chapter 7, "The Travel Industry.") Many of these Americans are subject to the high rates of kidnappings and other violent crimes in developing countries. For instance, some 20,000 to 30,000 people are taken hostage each year. Mexico City reported 2,000 kidnappings in 1997 (although many kidnappings go unreported), and there were reported to be 7,500 murders in Sao Paulo, Brazil. Even the most well-guarded senior executives are no match for determined terrorists: The 30-man security force of Deutsche Bank's chairman, Alfred Herrhausen, failed to save him.

Separately, as the American economy becomes increasingly dependent on intellectual property for competitive advantage, this property becomes a more valuable target for thieves. The proliferation of computers, scanners, and fax machines renders corporate espionage nearly effortless. Because of the computer's power to copy and transmit information, intangible assets can be expropriated more easily than ever, often without arousing immediate suspicion. Quite often nothing is missing, and the original remains in place. People leave no evidence and there are no fingerprints.

These trends increase the demand for companies that provide personal protection and investigative services. Companies positioned to profit from these trends include Kroll-O'Gara, Pinkerton's, and Wackenhut.

Personal Protection Services

According to the U.S. State Department, U.S. executives were the victims of more reported violent attacks in 1997 than diplomats and noncombat military personnel combined. Corporate executives are targeted because their net worth is widely known, their travel activity is relatively public, and the chances of large payouts are higher than for noncorporate travelers. In the past, kidnapping and extortion were the biggest fears for corporate executives, but companies are increasingly wary of potential threats from disgruntled employees, hostile bidders, strikers, and political activists. In fact, an animal rights activist pleaded no contest to planting a sophisticated pipe bomb near the company parking space of U.S. Surgical founder, chairman, and chief executive Leon Hirsch.

Other incidents from the 1990s include Sidney J. Reso, president of Exxon International, who was abducted and killed in 1992 by a husband-and-wife kidnapping team demanding a ransom of $18.5 million. Adobe Systems' president and cofounder Charles Geschke was abducted at gunpoint from the parking lot of his company's California headquarters in 1992. And while the ramifications of Microsoft's Bill Gates's and Proctor & Gamble's John Pepper's being hit with pies in their faces in 1998 were relatively innocuous, their assailants could have inflicted much more serious injuries. As a result of fears of similar events, at least 25 American CEOs had round-the-clock protection in the United States in 1998, and thousands of American expatriates enjoy such services. In addition, thousands of celebrities and wealthy individuals avail themselves of personal protective services.

Companies that provide personal protection include Pinkerton's, Wackenhut, and Kroll-O'Gara. These companies train security personnel in antiterrorist tactics and provide risk assessments of various countries and crisis management services. Kroll-O'Gara also manufactures armored vehicles, some of which can retard fire from high-powered machine guns and come equipped with fire extinguishers and tear gas launchers. Interestingly, some armored vehicles can be equipped with one-way bulletproof windows (which stop bullets from entering but allow bodyguards to shoot out) as well as armoring that can withstand running over land mines.

Similarly, Armor Holdings provides a variety of bulletproof apparel and other projectile resistant products. As the awareness of kidnapping grows, so too does the demand for kidnapping and ransom insurance, which is written by companies such as Marsh & McLennan and CNA Financial Corporation.

Investigative Services

The extent of corporate espionage reached alarming proportions in the late 1990s. Consider:

- The FBI reported that 23 foreign governments were systematically vacuuming U.S. corporations for their intellectual assets.
- The White House Office of Science and Technology estimated that business espionage is costing U.S. companies an estimated $100 billion a year in lost sales.

- According to FBI reports, 1 of every 14 notebook computers sold in 1996 in the United States was reported missing—the majority of them stolen.
- In the United States, more than 1,100 incidents of illegal industrial espionage hit some 1,300 companies in 1996, up from 589 incidents and 246 companies in 1992, according to the American Society for Industrial Security.
- Membership in the American Society for Industrial Security, the main association for security chiefs, grew by 20 percent to 30,000 from 1996 to 1998. Membership in the Society of Competitive Intelligence Professionals has more than doubled, to 6,400 members in the three years ending in 1998.

There are numerous reasons for the growth in corporate espionage and the leakage of intellectual property. First, rapid product cycles render it more expedient for companies that are behind in the product introduction curve to steal trade secrets than to accelerate their product development. Second, increased research and development budgets throughout corporate America enhance the value of intellectual property. Third, the obsession with empowering workers avails more employees with access to their company's proprietary information. Similarly, technical people in companies often clamor for open systems that are linked to the Internet, vendors, and customers: such open systems expand the number of people with access to competitive information.

Fifth, the trend of relying on temporary workers, who are less loyal, aggravates the risk of theft of intellectual property. Sixth, divorces are resulting in disgruntled former spouses obtaining access to proprietary information. Seventh, former employees are more likely to leak trade secrets when noncompete agreements are unenforceable, as is the case in several states, including California. Finally, the end of the Cold War has freed up many spies who make their services available.

Companies such as Kroll-O'Gara, Wackenhut, and Pinkerton's stand to prosper from the surge in corporate espionage because they are retained to prevent such infiltration. These companies also perform background checks on prospective foreign partners, which will prove to be increasingly important as businesses conduct more of their affairs abroad.

Antipiracy Solutions Providers

The International Chamber of Commerce estimated that counterfeiting represented a $250 billion global industry in 1998. Everything from currencies to pharmaceuticals and from videotapes to branded apparel are being pirated all over the world. Companies that can ensure manufacturers their merchandise will not be pirated should experience dynamic growth.

Holograms

Holograms—which derive from the Greek words *holos,* meaning "whole," and *gramma,* meaning "message"—are laser-generated, three-dimensional reproductions of objects produced on two-dimensional surfaces. Holograms control the diffraction of light at predetermined angles to create specific visual imagery. When holograms are viewed from different angles, the viewer can see features such as depth and movement, unseen in normal two-dimensional photographs.

Holograms are used primarily for security and authentication purposes. However, embossed holograms are used in the publishing and advertising industries. Holograms are also applied to such consumer products as toothpaste and beer. According to a study by the University of Colorado, sales for the holographic industry grew at a compounded annual rate of 32 percent, from $90 million in 1990 to $617 million in 1997. This study projected a 25 percent compounded annual growth rate for the five-year period from 1998 to 2002.

Safety Applications for Holograms

Holograms are an ideal security solution for many applications. They are extremely difficult to counterfeit and are very easy to understand because no equipment other than the human eye is needed to tell whether or not a hologram has been applied to a product. Holograms are easy to apply to merchandise. Also, holograms for security and authentication purposes usually cost only a few cents apiece.

Enhanced security is especially needed for paper-based products because laser printers are capable of printing nearly indistinguishable replicas of authentic documents. The Secret Service reported that the total value of counterfeit banknotes produced by color copiers and printers has more than doubled every year: fake banknotes amounted to $1 million in 1990 and could reach $2 billion in 2000. Thus, holograms are frequently applied to traveler's checks, gift certificates, prepaid telephone cards, trading cards, passports, and driver's licenses. The following are among the additional security applications of holograms:

- *Currency.* Holograms were placed on at least 12 national currencies—Saudi Arabia's, for example—as of mid-1998. Also, the top four denominations of the euro are using holograms as their main visual security feature.

- *Credit cards.* Merchants can easily spot legitimate credit cards by the appearance of a hologram. This is a growing market for companies such as American Bank Note Holographics because the number of credit cards and debit cards in the United States alone reached 584.4 million in 1997, up 42.5 million from 1996.
- *Pharmaceuticals.* Pharmaceutical manufacturers like Merck, Eli Lilly, and Schering-Plough rely on holograms to ensure patients that they are not consuming pirated drugs. Interestingly, a 1998 rash of fraudulent birth control pills in Brazil forced that country's drug regulatory body to require that all drugs sold must have holographic labels.
- *Apparel.* Clothing designers reduce pirating by shipping their manufacturing licensees the same number of holograms as the number of apparel pieces they are entitled to produce. Under these arrangements, any overruns do not have a hologram, and the retailers that receive the product know that it has been illegally produced.
- *Semiconductors.* Holograms are placed on every Intel Pentium II chip that is manufactured. This prevents others from counterfeiting the product, because even if they are running a computer chip factory in Korea and have figured out how to make chips, they probably will not be able to figure out how to make the hologram.*
- *Intellectual property.* Holograms are placed on videocassettes and digital videodisks and on all recorded music in Latin America.

Holographic Industry Players

The primary makers of holograms are Advanced Deposition Technologies, American Bank Note Holographics, Applied Holographics, CFC International, and Holographic Industries.

Video Copy Protection

It is estimated that consumer video piracy costs the entertainment industry $370 million a year. Paul Kagan Associates estimates that nearly 43 percent of U.S. households with VCRs possessed multiple VCRs in 1998 and were therefore capable of copying videocassettes. This is a grave threat to the motion picture industry as sales from the home video market exceeded box office receipts

---

The Wall Street Transcript, Analyst Interview: Electronic Security—Chris Quilty, Raymond James & Associates, Nov. 23, 1998, p. 72.

by over 50 percent in 1998. With the escalating costs for motion picture production, the motion picture industry is concerned about protecting its valuable video revenue generator.

The introduction of digital versatile disks (DVDs)—one of the most readily adapted consumer electronic products ever—presents serious concerns to the motion picture studios. Any one of the 425 million VCRs in use in 1998, when combined with a DVD player, can make unlimited videocassette copies of a non-copy-protected DVD that are nearly equal in quality to a professionally prerecorded videocassette. The need for reliable copy protection is being heightened by the rollout of inexpensive digital DVD recorders.

TIP: There are a rising number of opportunities for companies such as Pinkerton's that are involved in transporting cash. The proliferation of ATMs—from 80,000 in the U.S. in 1980 to 200,000 in 1998—requires cash to be delivered to more locations and the rollout of the euro will require a massive delivery effort. Companies like Borg Warner Security Corporation are finding new markets in the transportation of credit cards and the results of medical and legal licensing board exams.

This scenario presents a tremendous opportunity for video copy protection companies such as Macrovision. Macrovision helps the motion picture industry guard against the unlawful consumer duplication of its movies by installing its technology on original cassettes.

Surveillance Cameras

The surveillance society is upon us. Chances are you are being watched shopping in retail stores and gambling in casinos and riding on elevators and buses. Anecdotal evidence of the proliferation of surveillance cameras can be seen by the many hours of weekly television devoted to *Hard Copy* and its imitators that revolve on hidden-camera footage. Interestingly, Kenneth Cole billboards tease, "You are on a video camera an average of 10 times a day. Are you dressed for it?" The constant surveillance under which Americans and others live their lives should continue to be a gushing revenue generator for the surveillance camera manufacturers—one study estimates that sales of security cameras alone will total $5.7 billion by 2002.

Security and Crime Prevention Applications

Hidden cameras are widely used for policing. Law enforcement officials from Baltimore to Tacoma have revealed that the use of surveillance cameras in their cars reduces crime, mainly because the pictures allow judges and juries to see exactly what the police see.

New York City's police force is a major advocate of surveillance cameras; they are used to monitor parks, public pools, buses, and subway platforms. The Big Apple's Housing Authority placed bulletproof cameras in corridors throughout city projects, while more of its schoolyards are coming under the watch of electronic surveillance. In two New York state jails—Valhalla and Dutchess County—cameras have been inserted into guards' helmets to complement the ones in the visiting rooms and some cells. And in San Francisco, tiny cameras have been purchased for every car of the subway system.

Hidden cameras manufactured by companies such as Vicon have long been used by grocery stores, department stores, and convenience stores to deter shoplifting and as shields against liability. In fact, since the devices began being deployed in the early 1980s, the percentage of retail businesses with closed-circuit television security systems soared to 73 percent in 1997.

Gambling casinos are often under regulatory mandate to maintain video surveillance equipment, and the Chicago Bulls and the Washington Redskins are among at least 20 professional sports franchises that have installed surveillance cameras in their stadiums to ferret out unruly fans. Many governmental authorities require that ATM machines be monitored with surveillance cameras from the likes of Silent Witness. Fast-food chains like McDonald's protect themselves from litigious customers' product tampering with hidden cameras. Another benefit of using surveillance cameras is that managers can track workers' productivity.

Other Venues of Surveillance Cameras

One sign that surveillance cameras from companies such as Ultrak are becoming ubiquitous is that the Port Authority of New York and New Jersey—just that one agency—had more than 1,200 cameras throughout its airports, bridges, tunnels, and terminals in 1998. Also, cameras have become an integral part of new building and factory construction, along with sprinklers and smoke detectors. According to one study of workplace monitoring, at least 40 million American workers will be subject to reconnaissance in 2000.

In the United States, surveillance cameras are used for monitoring traffic violators in cities such as New York, Los Angeles, San Francisco, and Tucson. Many foreign locales—including Australia, Austria, Belgium, Canada, Germany,

Israel, the Netherlands, Singapore, South Africa, Switzerland, Taiwan, and the United Kingdom—use cameras for traffic control. Television stations are installing cameras on rooftops to monitor traffic jams, record sunsets, and capture images of breaking news events. Broadcasters say their camera networks vastly improve traffic and weather coverage.

Some surveillance cameras capture events inside school buses while also recording brake, stop, warning light indicators and bus speed. Not only do the cameras record incidents such as fights and vandalism, they can also help determine if a bus driver is at fault in the event of an accident. Finally, the use of surveillance cameras for voyeurism is fueled by the ease of disseminating luring pictures and videos over the Internet.

Industry Participants

The purest plays as far as surveillance camera manufacturers are concerned include Sentry Technologies, Silent Witness, Ultrak, and Vicon. Larger competitors include Matsushita, Panasonic, and Philips Electronics.

Bomb Detection Companies

Despite the fanfare surrounding peace agreements in Israel and Ireland, the world remains vulnerable to terrorism. Although much celebration was made out of the Irish peace agreement reached on Easter Sunday, April 12, 1998, I received a press release from Vivid Technologies the following day disclosing that that company received orders for checked luggage inspection systems from Belfast International Airport. The cost of procuring the ingredients to produce powerful explosives has been plummeting, and the availability of these components has been expanding. Bombings at the Atlanta Olympics, The World Trade Center, and the Murrah Building in Oklahoma City are only a few of the results.

TIP: In the fall of 1998, President Clinton directed $1.8 billion under emergency spending for tighter security at the nation's embassies. Federal Signal Corporation should be a beneficiary of such policies as it is a leading manufacturer of concrete barriers as well as access control systems for parking.

Drivers for Bomb Detection Systems

While bomb detection companies have occasionally served as theme plays—blasting ahead when acts of terrorism occur only to implode a short time later—there are reasons why the fundamental outlook for the $3 billion market for explosive detection systems used for checked luggage at airports will remain bright. First, as a result of the explosion of TWA Flight 800 in the summer of 1996, Congress acknowledged the importance of bomb detection systems by enacting legislation that allocated $144 million for the purchase of explosive detection systems and other advanced security equipment for air carriers and airport authorities. More recently, the Clinton administration allocated $100 million for bomb detection in its fiscal 1999 budget. Third, the 36 countries that form the European Civil Aviation Council have vowed to reach their target of 100 percent loaded baggage scanning by 2002.

The following are additional attractions of bomb detection companies:

- Bomb detection technology has become sufficiently sophisticated to detect explosives at high throughput rates, which is important to air carriers wishing to minimize their passengers' check-in delays.
- Higher order rates should allow bomb detection companies to achieve economies of scale in manufacturing and to negotiate reduced costs of materials. Lower manufacturing costs should also result in detection devices being deployed in nonaviation venues, such as government buildings, corporate headquarters, and border crossings.
- Bomb detection companies are major beneficiaries of government-subsidized research grants that accelerate product development and lend a sense of legitimacy to the resulting products without impacting the companies' expense lines.

Land Mine Detection

Much of the same technology that is used to detect bombs is being used to detect land mines, which opens up a very large opportunity to companies such as InVision Technologies. The United Nations projected it would require $33 billion and 1,100 years to remove all land mines with the removal methods used in the late 1990s. The United Nations estimated that there were roughly 110 million active mines scattered in 68 countries (with an equal number stockpiled around the world waiting to be planted) in 1997 and that for every mine cleared, 20 new ones are laid because land mines are an extremely cost-effective weapon.

Companies like InVision Technologies that are positioned to remove land mines should benefit from the attention to the damage that the mines cause. Every month more than 2,000 people are killed or maimed by mine explosions. Anti-personnel mines are priced at $3 to $30 but inflict damage a thousandfold (the cost of fitting amputees with orthopedics is $3,000 in developing countries) without the perpetrator risking direct confrontation. The devastation that land mines inflict received visibility from the efforts of the late Princess Diana of Wales and continue to be an important cause for Jordan's American-born Queen Noor. And Jody Williams won the Nobel Peace Prize in 1997 for her efforts to advance the detection and removal of land mines.

TIP: OSI Systems manufactures personnel screening systems that detect weapons or valuables concealed under a person's clothing. The systems are used for screening in correctional facilities and for asset protection in industrial facilities such as precious metals and computer component companies.

Industry Players

Barringer Technologies was the worldwide leader in trace explosive detection equipment with more than 500 units sold in 39 countries in 1998. In late 1998, InVision Technologies had more than 100 explosive detection units installed in civilian airports worldwide. In addition, InVision's equipment is used to detect mail bombs. Thermedics Detection makes substance and vapor detection and measurement systems for a variety of industrial, laboratory, and security applications. As of 1998, Vivid Technologies had sold some 235 automated explosives detection systems for airport baggage inspection to 29 airports in 14 countries. Vivid's detection systems are capable of inspecting at least 1,500 pieces of luggage per hour.

Drug-Testing Companies

Illegal drug use is pervasive. The National Institute on Drug Abuse estimated there were 4 million drug addicts in the United States, 2 million to 3 million of whom were addicted to cocaine in 1998. Another 800,000 individuals were believed to be heroin addicts. Millions more Americans, though not addicted, use illegal drugs.

Illegal drug use is a devastating problem as it contributes to a tremendous amount of crime. Also, drug abuse costs businesses $100 billion annually in lost productivity, increased accidents, absenteeism, and employee theft. In light of the scope and ramifications of illegal drug use, lawmakers from around the United States are promulgating legislation that is aimed at drug testing.

Damage Caused by Drugs

A disproportionate number of crimes are committed by people under the influence of drugs, trafficking in drugs, or desperate to purchase drugs. According to the Justice Department's Bureau of Justice Statistics:

- A full 57 percent of state prisoners and 45 percent of federal prisoners surveyed in 1997 said they had used drugs in the month before their offense.
- In 1997, 33 percent of state and 22 percent of federal prisoners said they committed their current offense while under the influence of drugs and about one in six of both state and federal inmates said they committed their offense to obtain money for drugs.
- Half of the people who commit a new crime while on parole or probation were under the influence of drugs or alcohol.

Drug Testing

In view of the crimes committed and other hazards that can result when people are driving and operating machinery while under the influence of drugs, the wave of mandatory drug testing has become increasingly broad. From 1983 to 1991, the percentage of the nation's 200 largest corporations instituting screening for applicants and employees rose from 2 percent to 98 percent. In 1986 President Reagan signed an executive order mandating drug testing for many key federal employees, which has turned into comprehensive mandatory testing in many federal agencies.

In 1995 the Department of Transportation passed legislation that expanded mandatory drug testing to over 7.5 million workers a year from 3.5 million. More recently, the fiscal 1999 federal budget included $85 million for a Drug Testing and Intervention Program, which provided state and local governments with funding to develop and implement comprehensive systems of drug testing, drug treatment, and graduated sanctions.

In the late 1990s, in order to reduce prison overcrowding and incarceration costs, lawmakers favored paroling prisoners who were not addicted to drugs. Although it cost about $25,000 a year to keep an inmate behind bars in the late

1990s, drug-testing programs cost $3,000 per person per year plus probation costs. Thus, a flurry of legislation was passed aimed at being especially vigilant of prisoners' use of drugs. For instance, President Clinton announced that his 2000 budget would include $215 million to test and treat prisoners for drug use; Maryland and Connecticut passed laws that reduce prison time for nonviolent offenders who undergo frequent testing for drug use; and in 1999, the federal government began requiring states to have a plan for regularly testing prisoners and parolees to qualify for federal funds to build new prisons.

Industry Players

Two of the leading operators of laboratories for providing drug-testing services to employers are Laboratory Specialists of America and LabOne. Psychemedics also has a drug-testing method that analyzes hair samples, which that company maintains is more accurate in many respects than the widely used urinalysis test. Finally, American Science and Engineering is a leader in designing drug detection systems for interdiction efforts.

Network Security Providers

Traffic on the Internet was doubling as rapidly as every 90 days in 1998. Not only is the volume of traffic soaring but the traffic traversing the Internet is critical to its users. Physicians practicing telemedicine must be able to download the appropriate X-rays, and businesses and consumers must feel confident that their electronic transactions will remain secure.

Network Vulnerability

Saboteurs can inflict mortal damage to businesses and governments because the interconnected nature of networks means that a disruption in one system can have a cascading impact on all other connected systems. According to FBI statistics, theft of data and intellectual property stored on inadequately protected computer networks costs corporate America $63 billion a year. Moreover, the FBI reported that 60 percent of the federal government's computer security systems experienced intrusions by unauthorized users in 1998.

The opportunity for network security providers such as Check Point Software and Security Dynamics stems from the thousands of computer hackers who are constantly trying to break into electronic networks. Far too often they succeed. Peter Watkins, Network Associates' general manager of network security, said that there were some 30,000 software viruses that threatened the wired world in 1998. Other attack weapons range from high-energy radio frequency weapons to interception equipment.

Among the indications and consequences of corporate vulnerability to network infiltration is that 47 percent of the 563 U.S. organizations surveyed by the Computer Security Institute (CSI) and the FBI in a 1997 report had been attacked through the Internet. A full 72 percent of these respondents acknowledged suffering financial losses from such security breaches.

Although most organizations that have had their networks violated are unwilling to confirm their vulnerabilities, notable examples of such occurrences have included the computer network of MCI Worldcom, which, in December 1998, was struck by a virus called Remote Explorer that was particularly dangerous because it spread throughout networks on its own. In September 1998, hackers broke into the *New York Times'* computers and defaced the newspaper's Web page; and in the mid-1990s, Russian hackers illegally transferred $10 million from Citibank into separate accounts around the world.

Year 2000 Vulnerabilities

The fact that companies and government agencies have been rapidly hiring computer programmers throughout the late 1990s to remediate their Year 2000 (Y2K) issues presents many risks to the sanctity of computer networks. In the summer of 1998, Howard Rubin of Hunter College projected that the United States alone would need 500,000 to 700,000 additional programmers to deal with the Year 2000 problem. To fill these slots, many organizations are recalling senior workers who were laid off a few years earlier because their Cobol and Fortran skills seemed obsolete.

Other organizations have been outsourcing Y2K work to the developing world, where the older computer languages are still widely used. With American businesses hiring as many technicians as they can find, U.S. adversaries could use Y2K to infiltrate agents into our utilities, transportation services, and financial institutions. It would take only a few disgruntled programmers to cause mayhem because technicians who fix Y2K problems often have carte blanche access to all areas of an organization's information systems; and this access provides them with a unique opportunity to compromise the systems. They could cause immediate damage and plant viruses, logic bombs, or trapdoors—programming devices to be triggered later and designed to destroy data or allow a hacker access.

Recognition of Risk

The FBI, in response to an expanding number of instances in which criminals have targeted major components of information and economic infrastructure systems, established the International Computer Crime Squads in selected offices throughout the United States. The mission of these squads is to investigate intrusions to public telephone networks and major computer network intrusions. Also, President Clinton issued the Critical Infrastructure Protection directive, which calls for a national effort to assure the security of the increasingly vulnerable and interconnected infrastructures of telecommunications, banking and finance, energy, transportation, and essential government services.

Industry Players

In view of the importance of the information carried over computer networks (which are merging into telecommunications networks) and their vulnerability to attack, companies and government organizations are spending huge sums of money on their network security. According to International Data Corporation, revenue from Internet security services will rise from $4.6 billion in 1998 to $11.6 billion in 2002.

The major players in providing firewalls (which restrict users' access to predetermined parameters within intranets and the Internet) include Secure Computing, Axent Technology, Network Associates, and Check Point Software Technology. Second, companies like Network Associates prevent and destroy network viruses. Third, companies like Entrust Technologies and Verisign offer a technology called public-key infrastructure (PKI) that allows companies to manage the digital certificates and codes their customers or employees use to encrypt data. A digital certificate is a digitally signed statement from a trusted source, such as a bank or company, that is attached to the electronic message and attests to the identity of the business performing the transaction over the Internet. Analysts expect the market for PKI to soar from roughly $50 million in 1997 to $925 million in 2001 and to $1.6 billion in 2002. Fourth, companies such as American International Group and Cigna provide insurance against lawsuits caused by computer network problems.

Prison Management Services

Providers of prison management services like Cornell Corrections and Wackenhut Corrections should continue to benefit from a double growth driver. First, the prison population continues to expand as a result of demographics, stricter sentencing policies, and longer terms served. Second, the expense reductions that private prison management companies offer is compelling to many communities.

Prison management companies have an enormous market opportunity. Correctional authorities at the federal, state, and local level spent over $40 billion annually in the late 1990s, three times as much as they spent in 1985. The number of adult secure beds under contract for private management is forecast to grow at a compound annual growth rate of 26.5 percent through the five-year period ending 2001. Very little of this opportunity has been seized as only about 5 percent of the nation's prison population was under the control of private operators in the late 1990s. Charles W. Thomas, director of the Private Corrections Project at the University of Florida's Center for Studies in Criminology, estimated an average annual growth in private prisons of 25 percent over the five years ending in 2002.

Prison Population Rises Steadily

The imprisonment boom has developed a built-in growth dynamic independent of the crime rate. According to the Justice Department, the U.S. adult prison population in local jails and in state and federal prisons grew 5.2 percent to 1.7 million in 1997 (the largest number in any country in the world), up from 1.1 million in 1990. During that period the incarceration rate in state and federal prisons rose from 445 per 100,000 Americans in 1997, up from 292 per 100,000 citizens in 1990. The Justice Department estimated that 5.1 percent of all persons in the United States will be confined in a state or federal prison during their lifetime if the growth in incarceration rates remains on the same trajectory until 2010.

Reasons for the rising incarceration rate during a period in which overall crime rates have declined include the following:

- *Demographics.* The number of juveniles arrested for committing violent crimes in the United States soared 50 percent from 1988 to 1994; this is the fastest-growing segment of the prison population. The FBI predicted that violent crimes committed by juveniles will more than double by 2010, partly because some 53 million children (or 21 percent of the population) were under the age of 13 in 1998.
- *Tougher sentencing laws.* Mandatory minimum sentences, trying juveniles as adults, truth-in-sentencing laws, and "three strikes and you're out" programs increased average prison stays from 48 percent of original sentences in 1990 to 85 percent in 1997. For similar reasons, the average length of prison stay increased by five months from 1982 to 1995.
- *Reduced use of parole.* Adverse publicity related to crimes committed by parolees and the political pressure against reducing prison sentences for

convicted felons have resulted in the complete abolishment of parole in some states. In many other states parole boards have much less discretion than they used to, which has lengthened the time prisoners serve. In fact, in 1990 decisions by parole boards accounted for 39.4 percent of all prisoners released, down sharply from 55 percent in 1980.

- *Increased arrests of parole violators.* About 30 percent of prisoners in 1998 were incarcerated for parole violations compared with 15 percent in 1980.

Private Prisons Are a Solution for Overcrowding

Overcrowding in prisons resulting from the factors discussed above is a primary driver for the growth of private prison operators such as Correctional Services Corporation. Based on 1995 statistics from the Criminal Justice Institute, the federal prison system was operating at an estimated 125 percent of rated capacity, and state prisons were operating at an average of 108 percent of rated capacity. In the late 1990s, overcrowding was much worse in some states. For instance, California prisons have operated at as much as 188 percent of their rated capacity, and it was expected that California would run out of prison space to house additional inmates by June 2000.

TRAP: Many investors may be intrigued by electronic ankle bracelet manufacturers such as BI Inc., but the success of these companies has been hampered by many factors. First, new prison construction has been absorbing many prisoners. Second, the public is realizing that these devices are not secure because they only record whether a wearer is at home; they do not prevent a convict from leaving his home. Third, most people feel much more secure when prisoners are incarcerated in nearby prisons than they do when they are left alone in their neighborhood. Thus, California's corrections system uses bracelets sparingly, and New York State's prison system has rejected them completely.

Overcrowding has become so extensive that court orders to reduce overcrowding have been handed down in some states—California, for example. Communities are receptive to building new prisons because it creates hundreds of jobs. Communities also know that overcrowding has reached the point in many places that prisoners will have to be released if additional capacity is not built.

Another driver for the construction of new prisons is that many of the nation's prisons have become inadequate with age. According to a Bureau of Justice Statistics study in 1992, there were 293 prisons holding inmates in the United States that were 20 to 49 years old, 289 prisons that were 50 to 99 years old, and 52 prisons that were over 100 years old. Many of these facilities will have to be replaced early in the next decade.

Benefits of Contracting with Private Prison Operators

At least 32 states, Puerto Rico, the District of Columbia, and the three federal agencies with prisoner-custody responsibilities (the Federal Bureau of Prisons, the U.S. Marshals Service, and the Immigration and Naturalization Service) have turned to the private sector to design, build, manage, and operate correctional facilities as have Great Britain, Australia, Canada, and South Africa.

TRAP: A number of challenges obstruct the growth of private prison management companies. First, opposition from unions is strident. For instance, the California Correction Peace Officers Association actively campaigned for an amendment to the California Constitution that would prohibit all state and local governments from contracting with private prison operators; and Illinois has legislation that categorically prohibits prison privatization. Second, in June 1997, the Supreme Court ruled that guards at private prisons are not entitled to the qualified immunity that protects federal corrections employees from prisoner lawsuits.

The following are among the reasons that prison authorities find outsourcing to private operators appealing:

- *Reduced construction costs.* Private prison operators offer upfront reductions in construction and capital costs, and faster response times in being able to build and begin operating facilities. These cost savings have been estimated to range from 10 to 20 percent. Also, private companies eliminate the need for a governmental authority to issue bonds or access taxes to fund prisons.
- *Reduced operating costs.* According to a report of prison operating costs in Wisconsin prepared by the Policy Research Institute, private management produced annual operating costs savings of 11 to 14 percent. Over the life of a 20-year prison construction bond, these savings could pay for most or all of the interest costs of the borrowing. Lower operating costs are achieved as the result of private contractors being able to buy goods and services at the best prices as well as by eliminating government procurement procedures.
- *Reduced bureaucracy.* Private prison operators relieve contracting agencies from having to create additional bureaucracy that is responsible for day-to-day staffing and management of a facility.

- *Better facilities management.* Private prison operators are more aggressive in pursuing contracts to incarcerate prisoners from other jurisdictions that have reached their maximum numbers of inmates.

Industry Players

The primary private prison management companies are Cornell Corrections, Correctional Services Corporation, and Wackenhut Corrections. Some state governments would rather privatize their prisons and retain management in the public sector's hands. This is especially true with a disproportionate number of highly publicized breakouts from privately run prisons. The best way to play the privatization of prisons without management contracts is Correction Properties Trust, the only pure play real estate investment trust in the corrections industry.

Derivative ways of playing the growth in prison populations include the following:

- America Services Group is a leading provider of managed health care services to inmates of correctional institutions—the only Americans that have a constitutional right to health care.
- Mark Solutions manufactures modular steel cells for housing general prison populations as well as for infectious disease isolation units for correctional institutions and health care facilities.
- T-Netix provides specialized telephone call processing and fraud control services to phone companies that supplied over 90 million inmate collect calls in over 1,000 correctional institutions in the late 1990s.
- U.S. Technologies provides labor-intensive outsourced contract manufacturing services with prison inmates who are employed under the federal government's Prison Industry Enhancement Program. Prison operators and some community activists are receptive to allowing their inmates to work because up to 80 percent of inmates' wages are used to pay room and board as well as victims' restitution, child support, alimony, and court fees.

Combating Biological Weapons of Mass Destruction

The chances of Americans experiencing an attack from biological weapons of mass destruction is rising in lockstep with the plunging level of difficulty and expense of producing and delivering such weapons. Only minuscule amounts of smallpox, anthrax, or sarin are necessary to cause thousands of deaths. And these minute quantities of biologics are much harder to detect than nuclear weapons of mass destruction. The federal government is now aware of these threats and has begun to fund programs aimed at preventing and responding to such eventualities. The beneficiaries of these programs will include manufacturers of vaccines and antibiotics (see "Vaccines" and "Infectious Diseases" in Chapter 8) and developers of detection equipment and suppliers of protective clothing (see "Bomb Detection Companies" and "Protective Clothing" in this chapter).

Rising Availability of Biologics Increases Probability of Attack

The growing availability and ease of producing biological weapons increases the probability that they will be deployed—otherwise, they would not likely be produced. According to Russian and Western experts, germ scientists at scores of sites studied some 50 agents and prepared at least a dozen for war. Bombers and intercontinental missiles were ready to disseminate hundreds of tons of smallpox, plague, and anthrax, enough to wipe out entire nations.*

A great deal of evidence has arisen from United Nations weapons inspectors indicating that Iraq has long stockpiled biological weapons. Other rogue nations such as North Korea and Syria are also believed to be developing bioweapons. In mid-1998, it was widely held that at least a dozen nations were involved in biological weapons experimentation.

The porousness of many of the facilities that produce biologics presents another significant risk of these weapons falling into the hands of those who have no reluctance to use them. Biological warfare research facilities are not as well guarded as nuclear facilities. Terrorists could penetrate one of these facilities and, unlike in a nuclear facility, quickly steal a biological agent or simply release an agent into the atmosphere and then leave.

Consider how lax security has become around one of Russia's largest and most sophisticated (but now emaciated) military bioweapons facilities, called Vector, in Koltsovo, Novosibirsk. Through the early 1990s, this was a 4,000-person, 30-building facility with ample biosafety Level 4 laboratories. The building that housed the smallpox, Ebola, Marburg, and hemorrhagic fever viruses was surrounded by electric fences and protected by an elite guard. However, American scientists visiting this facility in the autumn of 1997 found a half-empty building protected by a handful of guards who had not been paid for months. Civilian research facilities are even less secure.

---

*Judith Miller, "Bio-Weapons in Mind, Iranians Lure Needy Ex-Soviet Scientists," *New York Times,* Dec. 8, 1998, p. A12.

It is likely that many of the unpaid scientists who leave facilities like Vector will be employed by rogue nations willing to pay handsomely for their services. Iran has already been scouring the former Soviet Union to hire some of the 70,000 scientists who once worked in laboratories tied to Moscow's vast germ warfare program and has succeeded in recruiting some of them to Tehran.* Terrorist groups are well aware of Russians' desire for hard currency. For instance, the Japanese terrorist group Aum Shinrikyo received training from Russian special forces in the assembly and use of rifles and rocket launchers, and it also purchased a helicopter equipped to spray deadly chemicals from Russia's arms bazaar.

Bioweapons Are Easy to Produce and Deliver

Bioweapons from rogue nations are only a small part of the almost unlimited access that terrorists have to biological agents. Not only can terrorists purchase or steal such weapons from producing nations (Iraq's Education Ministry ordered 70 packages of microbes, toxins, and anthrax spores from the nonprofit American Type Culture Collection in the mid-1980s), but they can hire defecting scientists. In other instances, it is likely that rogue nations will pay freelance terrorists to deploy their bioweapons. Moreover, the fact that bioweapons are increasingly easy and inexpensive to produce increases the number of terrorist organizations that will be able to manufacture them.

Neither the supply requirements nor the technical expertise necessary to produce bioweapons presents high hurdles to overcome. Raymond Zilinskas, a biologist at the University of Maryland, declared that the fermenters and centrifuges used every day in dairies, wineries, and pharmaceutical firms can be quickly converted to churning out lethal bioweapons. Also, the agents producing anthrax, the plague, brucellosis, tularemia, and smallpox can be isolated from natural sources. For instance, tricothecene mycotoxins are derived from corn, and aflatoxin comes from peanuts. As for producing ricin, all that is needed is someone able to follow a well-documented two-step procedure to extract the protein albuminoid toxin from castor beans.

According to the Pentagon, bioweapons can be produced using a recipe found on the Internet, a beer fermenter, a culture, and a gas mask, with a total investment of about $10,000. A Pentagon official was once quoted as saying, "If you buy commercial equipment and put it in a very small room, you can be producing kilogram quantities of anthrax within a month and each kilogram has thousands of

---

*Judith Miller, "Bio-Weapons in Mind, Iranians Lure Needy Ex-Soviet Scientists," *New York Times,* Dec. 8, 1998, p. A1.

potential deaths in it." In fact, a study by the U.S. Office of Technology Assessment estimated that 100 kilograms of anthrax could cause 2 million deaths.

Interdiction of those intending to use biological weapons is next to impossible as bioweapons are extremely difficult to detect by traditional antiterrorist sensor systems. Biological weapons can not be revealed by metal detectors, X-ray machines, trained dogs, or neutron bombardment, as can guns, grenades, and plastic explosives.

In view of the depravity of the World Trade Center and the Oklahoma City Federal Building bombers, it is not difficult to believe that terrorists will strike with biological weapons. It is estimated that 40 percent of terrorist attacks around the globe are directed, in some form, at American interests. In fact, in the late 1990s, some members of Congress reported that classified studies suggest such an attack on American civilians would occur within a decade. Some of the nation's most senior law enforcement officials have publicly stated that attacks with weapons of mass destruction are an eventuality. When Attorney General Janet Reno announced the Justice Department's award of $12 million to 41 cities to buy protective clothing, chemical and biological sensors, and decontamination equipment to protect against terrorists, she avoided conditional verbs by saying, "The first hours of a terrorist attack *are* critical. This equipment *will* help local emergency personnel save lives."*

There Is Precedent for Using Bioweapons

My concerns should not be construed as paranoid hysteria. Bioterrorism has already occurred. The most cited assault was when the Japanese-based Aum Shinrikyo cult killed 12 people and injured thousands more by puncturing plastic bags of sarin in a Tokyo subway station in March 1995. Although the cult later considered this attack an unsuccessful mission, Aum Shinrikyo has shown no interest in revoking its pledge to carry out similar missions.

Before the attack, members of Aum Shinrikyo traveled to Zaire to obtain samples of the Ebola virus for weapons development. Shortly after the attack, police found enough sarin in the sect's possession to kill millions of people. In 1995, Aum Shinrikyo had a net worth estimated at as much as $1 billion. Even by the fall of 1998, Aum Shinrikyo had 5,000 followers in Japan, Russia, Ukraine, Belarus, and Kazakhstan.

---

*Alex Williams, "Fear of Terror," *New York,* Nov. 16, 1998, p. 30.

The following are additional examples of biological weapons deployments:

- In July 1998, four people were killed when they ate Korean rice laced with sarin.
- In 1995, Iraq confirmed that it had produced, filled, and deployed bombs, rockets, and aircraft spray tanks containing bacillus anthracis and botulinum toxin. Iraq also admitted brewing more than 2,000 gallons of anthrax, but American experts think the true amount was three times as much. Also, just before the Gulf War an elite American team penetrated deep into Iraq and kidnapped several Iraqi soldiers. From blood samples of the captured Iraqi troops, it was determined they had built up an immunity to anthrax, meaning that the Iraqis were prepared to deploy anthrax weapons.
- On a similar note, the World Trade Center bombers packed cyanide into the charge that rocked the building, but the chemical apparently evaporated in the explosion.*
- In the early 1990s, the UK Animal Liberation Front mailed several postal devices containing fragments of hypodermic needles that it claimed had been infected with the HIV virus.
- In 1984 the Rajneeshee religious cult contaminated salad bars at ten restaurants in Antelope, Oregon, with S. Typhimurium, which resulted in an outbreak of at least 751 cases of salmonellosis.
- In 1979 an outbreak of human anthrax occurred in Ekaterinburg, Russia, as a result of an accidental release of aerosolized anthrax from a Russian bioweapons facility.

The future is likely to provide further examples of bioattacks. The Federal Bureau of Investigation has reported that the number of credible bioweapons threats has soared from a handful in 1995 to 40 in 1997.

The Most Lethal Weapons of Mass Destruction

Biologics are more threatening than most other forms of weapons of mass destruction because they are highly lethal, spread quickly, are difficult to diagnose, and currently are very hard to treat. To compare, a chemical release or a major explosion is far more manageable than the biological challenges posed by smallpox or anthrax. After an explosion or a chemical attack, the worst effects are quickly over, the dimensions of the catastrophe can be defined, and efforts can be directed at stabilization and recovery.

---

*David E. Kaplan, "Everyone Gets into the Terrorist Game," *U.S. News & World Report,* Nov. 17, 1997, p. 33.

In contrast, victims of smallpox or anthrax may not experience symptoms of a bioattack for several days and will continue their normal interactions with others, thus accelerating the spread of the biological agents. However, biological agents multiply very quickly on their own. For instance, a single disease-producing bacterium can divide every 20 minutes, meaning that an aspirin bottle of bacteria could yield a huge arsenal in one week.

Because no emergency room physicians or infectious disease specialists have ever seen cases of biological attack such as inhalation anthrax, medical laboratories have had virtually no experience in such diagnosis. A bioterrorist attack may be difficult to distinguish from a naturally occurring infectious disease outbreak. Thus, at least three to five days could elapse before a definitive diagnosis could be made, making it very difficult to mount an emergency response and to cope with the mass hysteria among those who fear contamination.

Agents such as anthrax, plague, and smallpox are appealing to terrorists because they can be aerosolized and distributed over large geographic areas. Because biological pathogens reproduce in the host, infectious doses are independent of victim body weight, making the quantity of biological material needed for mass attack very small. Finally, some bioweapons such as anthrax remain lethal for prolonged periods of time.

The Government Responds to the Biological Threat

Realizing that biological weapons represent real and present dangers to Americans, President Clinton requested that Congress add $300 million to the 1999 federal budget to better protect Americans from germ and biological attack. And the Pentagon is so concerned about biowarfare that its budget request for fiscal 1999 included roughly $1 billion in spending through fiscal year 2003 "to bolster U.S. capabilities to counter chemical and biological threats."

TRAP: Obstacles to producing vaccines as antidotes to biological attack include inadequate efficacy testing (there is no disease-endemic area) and high production costs (there is no target population).

One concrete initiative upon which the government embarked was the inoculation of military personnel against anthrax. Before the Gulf War was underway in 1990–1991, about 150,000 U.S. troops were given anthrax vaccinations. In March 1998, the Defense Department inaugurated its five-year program of inoculating all of the nation's 2.5 million men and women in uniform against anthrax by vaccinating Defense Secretary William S. Cohen and General Henry H. Shelton, chairman of the Joint Chiefs of Staff.

The Defense Department policy will benefit manufacturers of vaccines (such as Bioport Corporation, Siga Pharmaceuticals, Cortecs International, SmithKline Beecham, and Pasteur Merieux Connaught) that can be used as antidotes to chemical or biological warfare because of the following:

- The market is enormous because the 2.5 million American troops undergoing inoculation will be complemented by inoculations administered to British and Canadian troops. Other nations (e.g., Israel, South Korea, and Saudi Arabia) that have troops exposed to leaders inclined to deploy bioweapons may adopt such policies.
- Substantial opportunity exists for repeat sales as each soldier will receive six shots spread over 18 months, followed by annual booster shots.
- Although the military represents a tremendous opportunity for antidote manufacturers, the civilian market could be an exponentially larger market. In fact, President Clinton issued Presidential Decision Directive 39 in May 1998 that calls for creating a civilian stockpile of anthrax vaccine and antibiotics to counter biological weapons. The resulting presidential panel recommended spending $420 million over five years for stockpiles of vaccinations and antibiotics.
- The discovery of antidotes to other biological agents, such as sarin and ricin, will dramatically expand the market for vaccines.
- Political support exists for subsidizing companies that can rapidly produce large volumes of vaccines. For instance, the U.S. House Armed Services Committee proposed government subsidies to indemnify pharmaceutical corporations that are willing to establish facilities to produce vaccines at extremely fast rates.

Other Solutions Loom in the Wings

Antidote manufacturers will not be the only beneficiaries of nations preparing for the threat of germ warfare. Antibiotics producers like Cubist Pharmaceuticals, Microcide, Genome Therapeutics, Merck, and Pfizer stand to realize more business because some lives could be saved if a great amount of antibiotics were taken immediately after a biological attack. Manufacturers of protective clothing, such as Lakeland Industries and Bacou USA, should witness more sales of their gear to emergency response agencies. And traditional bomb detection companies like Vivid Industries and InVision Technologies could develop equipment to detect the presence of chemical and biological agents.

Another vehicle for investors to play the threat of germ warfare can be found in the shares of Meridian Medical Technologies. Meridian Medical's Multi-Chambered Nerve Agent Antidote Kits are prefilled, spring-loaded, penlike devices that, when activated and pressed against the body, automatically inject precise dosages of nerve agent antidotes in quick succession.

The following discussion presents examples of other devices being developed in late 1998 to detect and protect against bioweapons. (Even though much of the development of such programs is classified, I suspect that companies like Hewlett-Packard and Texas Instruments are developing similar products.)

The U.S. Department of Defense was working on a handheld sensor capable of scanning the atmosphere for harmful germs and viruses. According to Lawrence DuBois, director of the Defense Science Office, this "canary on a chip" device can detect many toxic chemicals or biological toxins that affect the central nervous system. Mildred Donlon, who heads the sensor device project, noted: "The biosensor contains an immortalized nerve cell, living and growing on an electrically conducting silicon chip. The nerve cell continuously fires nerve impulses. When a toxic substance is present, the interruption of that electrical signal triggers an alarm."

Another research project in development was an injectable bloodscrubber to destroy microorganisms in the bloodstream. Researchers at the University of Virginia developed special heteropolymers that attach to Velcro-like hooks on red blood cells on one end and bind to the targeted viruses with the other. The virus is rendered harmless and removed from the bloodstream after passing through the liver and spleen. The polymers are not expected to affect the normal functioning of the blood cells. The ultimate result of this project could be that soldiers injected with the heteropolymer could engage in combat without having to don a protective suit.

Oak Ridge National Laboratory was developing its Chemical-Biological Mass Spectrometer, a device about the size of a desktop computer that will be capable of detecting a very wide range of lethal chemical and biological weapons, including bacteria, toxins, and viruses as well as such hazardous chemical agents as nerve gas and blister agents. The unit was being designed to work by collecting an air sample, classifying it according to size, then heating it to break down its molecules. Then its mass-to-charge ratio and its chemical signatures would be compared against an extensive onboard library of known toxic agents, such as anthrax and VX gas.

Fingerprinting

Fingerprinting has been used by law enforcement authorities for roughly 100 years. It will continue to be an intrinsic part of the law enforcement information systems industry that G2 Research estimates will generate $1.6 billion in revenue in 2000, up from $700 million in 1995. Law enforcement authorities have built up tremendous repositories of fingerprints because courts around the world have upheld the validity of identifying people based on their unique fingerprint patterns and because fingerprints are easy to retrieve from crime scenes. In 1998 the Federal Bureau of Investigation (FBI) had enough fingerprint cards on file that, if piled on top of each other, would equal 133 stacks the size of the Empire State Building.

Fingerprinting is extremely reliable because each individual's fingerprints contain a unique pattern, distinguishable from the fingerprint patterns of the rest of the population. Not even identical twins share the same fingerprint patterns. Fingerprints (and hand scanners) register qualities like skin temperature, pulse, turgidity, and electric charge, so neither fake digits nor amputated fingers can be improvised. Also, latent fingerprints—those left at crime scenes—may be collected from almost any surface, sometimes even from human skin. Detectives have refined numerous techniques—including the use of lasers (from companies such as Spectra-Physics and Coherent), powders, and alternate light sources—to make latent prints visible.

Fingerprinting is used for much more than keeping track of criminals. For instance, in the late 1990s, the FBI was requiring fingerprints for background checks before immigration applicants could be interviewed and sit for the citizenship test. Similarly, the Immigration and Naturalization Service was relying on fingerprinting to prevent illegal entry. It is due to these uses, and applications outlined below, that Allen & Caron recently estimated that revenues for the fingerprinting industry will surge from $145 million in 1997 to $1 billion in 2002.

Fingerprinting Fares Well against Other Biometric Technology

Although other permutations of biometrics (the identification of individuals based on their unique physical characteristics such as fingerprints, hand shape, or facial appearance) are appropriate for niche applications, I believe that fingerprinting will be the most widely accepted form of identifying people. One competing biometric application—retinal scanning, which involves beaming light into the eye and recording the pattern of blood vessels on the retina—is very secure because such systems cannot be breached by false eyes, contact lenses, or eye transplants. However, I don't believe that retinal scanning is suitable for widespread application as the general public will undoubtedly refuse to have their eyes scanned frequently. Also, voice recognition from companies such as T-NETIX is suitable for telephone-related recognition applications, but static phrases are very easy to swindle with a tape recorder (see Chapter 12, "Voice

Recognition"). Although longer phrases can be used, reliability declines and authorization times expand.

On the other hand, people are much less reluctant to have their fingers scanned compared with their eyes, and although passwords can be forgotten or given to others, the same is not true for fingerprints. Fingerprint data can easily be delivered to, or retrieved from, central databases simply by placing fingerprints on electronic pads, and the false acceptance rate for fingerprints is virtually zero. Finally, fingerprinting is fast and tolerates a fair amount of dirt and small injuries.

Employers Fingerprint to Detect and Deter

Traditionally used primarily for law enforcement, fingerprinting services are enjoying soaring demand as employers attempt to avert both workplace violence and growing legal liability for employing workers with a checkered past. More than 1 million violent workplace incidents occur each year, and the National Council on Compensation Insurance reports that murder accounts for 16 percent of all job fatalities. According to the Workplace Violence Research Institute, the cost of workplace violence in the United States in terms of liability, legal expenses, and lost work time is more than $36 billion annually.

TIP: Iris scanners have several advantages over retinal scanners. As a biometric marker, irises are more distinctive than retinas. Iris detection systems can read the color and unique markings of the iris from several feet away without shining a bright light into the eye. According to IriScan, a leading player in iris recognition, "finding two identical irises at random is approximately 10^{50} times less likely than finding two identical fingerprints."

Furthermore, a landmark ruling holding employers liable for the violence their employees commit was handed down by the Nevada Supreme Court in the late 1990s. This decision ruled that the family of a person killed by a security guard at an apartment complex could sue the guard's employer for failing to look into his criminal background. As a result of such precedent, employers are realizing they must make concerted efforts to screen prospective employees for troubled pasts.

Not only does fingerprinting help employers avoid hiring applicants who have criminal records, but the existence of a fingerprinting policy deters criminals from such businesses altogether. Craig Emanuel, investigations supervisor for the Arizona Department of Education, commented that "you steer more people away than you catch in your net." In addition, employees who have their fingerprints on file are less likely to commit crimes knowing their apprehension is likely to be more certain and swift.

TIP: In light of courts having found that companies bear a responsibility for thoroughly evaluating the trustworthiness of their hires, research from Aon Consulting reveals that about 95 percent of U.S. corporations conduct thorough background checks that include a prospect's driving record, criminal charges or convictions, creditworthiness, and disputes with the IRS. It is not uncommon for prospective employers to query an applicant's coworkers and neighbors about the subject's reputation. These extensive background checks are necessary: The Society for Human Resource Management found that 53 percent of job candidates lied about how long they had held previous jobs, and salary information was inaccurate in 51 percent of the cases reviewed. The difficulty for hiring companies is that previous employers try to avoid defamation-related lawsuits by disclosing very little about former employees to other companies.

Several companies offer solutions to an employer's dilemma of seeking background checks on prospective employees while recognizing former employers' reticence about revealing information. Companies such as Equifax, Trans Union, and Experian prepare and archive consumer reports and compile interviews with potential employees' coworkers, neighbors, and others that sketch a profile of an applicant's character and reputation. Avert, Inc., is a pure play on the verification of job applicants' backgrounds through examinations of company-maintained databases and information gathered by a nationwide network of independently contracted investigators. *The Work Number* from a company by the name of TALX supplies employment and salary verification data through an interactive voice response system. Human resources professionals from the state of Florida, Rockwell International, and Warner Lambert, for example, simply make pertinent employment information available for prospective employers to retrieve over the phone. Former employers achieve cost and time savings, prospective employers obtain rapid information, and TALX receives a transaction fee for each inquiry.

New Employer Groups Require Fingerprinting

Because of concerns and industry regulations, many groups of employees have long been required to submit to fingerprinting before and/or during their employment. These groups have included government workers, employees of banks and brokerage firms, and anyone involved in handling the U.S. mail. Even though these industries will remain sources of demand for fingerprinting as new hires continue to go through their screening processes, the fact that the following are among the many new industries that are just beginning to require fingerprinting will be a long-term boon to the providers of such services:

- States such as California and New Jersey require elder care providers to be fingerprinted.
- States such as Nebraska and Arizona require their public school teachers to have their fingerprints taken, and some school districts even require noncertified personnel such as janitors to be fingerprinted.
- Many of the better child care providers distinguish themselves by advertising that all of their employees have been fingerprinted.
- A growing number of employment agencies and tenant-screening services fingerprint their applicants.
- In an industrywide effort to enhance their image and legitimacy (not to mention to conform to regulations), gambling venues from casinos and riverboats to racetracks rely on fingerprinting to screen all prospective employees.
- Real estate regulatory bodies from California to Missouri require real estate agents to submit to fingerprinting. The regulators believe real estate brokers should have their fingerprints on file because they are entrusted with the responsibilities of frequently chauffeuring their prospects and maintaining keys to their clients' homes.
- In an effort to prevent collaboration with terrorists, airports and airlines are requiring all workers—from air traffic controllers to janitors—to be fingerprinted.

Governments Initiate Fingerprinting Campaigns

Many examples can be found of governmental bodies mandating or encouraging fingerprinting. First, many social service agencies require prospective foster parents to have their fingerprints taken. Second, legislation is in effect in states such as Louisiana to fingerprint children to more quickly locate abducted youngsters.

Third, in states ranging from Georgia to Colorado to West Virginia, fingerprints are a condition for receiving driver's licenses. States are eager to grant contracts for such services to companies such as Polaroid as the states profit substantially from the information they collect from their drivers and resell to insurance and credit-reporting agencies. Fourth, entire countries, such as Argentina and Costa Rica, are developing national identification programs designed to prevent the issuance of multiple identity documents to people attempting to use aliases. Such initiatives are huge sources of revenues for such companies as Printrak International, which was fingerprinting as many as 35,000 Argentineans a day in 1998 and developing a database of more than 50 million Argentineans.

TIP: In efforts to prevent both accidental switches and kidnappings, a growing number of maternity wards are strapping miniature antitheft tags on babies' ankles, wrists, or even umbilical chords. Tags from companies like Checkpoint and Sensormatic are programmed to trigger alarms and surveillance cameras when they get too close to hospital exits, and they can also cause doors and elevators to lock tight. The market for these tags is fertile as more media attention on baby switchings and kidnappings heightens parental demand and as only about 10 percent of the nation's 4,000 maternity units were using these tags in mid-1998.

Fingerprinting Is Well Suited for Access Control

Fingerprinting is used to control access to restricted or sensitive areas ranging from the Pentagon to amusement parks. Identix, one of the leading manufacturers of fingerprinting devices, has placed its access control products in the White House and the Supreme Court. At the 1996 Summer Olympics in Atlanta, hand scanners restricted admission to sensitive areas. Even Disney World pass holders are required to raise a finger to the biometric guardians on their way into the Magic Kingdom.

Finger recognition products do more than merely grant individuals who have preregistered their fingerprints access to particular gateways at specified times. In addition, these products provide an audit trail to monitor access at each location. In fact, Identix sold its Touchlock II single-finger biometric verification readers to all 33 of the state prisons overseen by the California Department of Corrections. The readers provide an exact record of each entry and exit to secure areas and alert the security staff if correctional officers or authorized visitors do not biometrically check out of the secured areas when expected to. Similarly, biometric systems have been installed for monitoring the movement of authorized staff and volunteers into and out of the secured facilities of 11 California Youth Authority sites.

Other Applications of Fingerprinting

Fingerprinting is an attractive fraud fighter. Cities and states across the nation are relying on biometrics to ensure that recipients of government disbursements do not double-dip by filing for benefits under more than one name. Also, employers are installing fingerprint-activated time-stamping machines to prevent their employees from fraudulently time-stamping work records on behalf of absent or tardy coworkers.

Partly to reduce fraud and partly to speed transactions, a growing number of merchants are implementing finger-scanning technology. Kroger's grocery stores (the nation's largest grocery chain) have already credited fingerprint technology with eliminating check fraud. Customers wishing to cash their paychecks at select Kroger's stores place their fingers on an optical scanner at the service desk, and the images are relayed to a personal computer. There, the fingerprint is compared with fingerprints stored in a database—and the system flashes a yes or no decision within a few seconds.

Signature Verification

An interesting niche of opportunity lies in signature verification. Because a signed document is so important in many business cycles, it is imperative that signatures are authentic. Companies such as PenOp have designed electronic systems that can verify whether a signature is authentic and can transmit documents with the signatures from one computer network user to others. A PenOp signature is bound to a particular document at the time of signing and cannot be lifted and attached to something else. These applications should become very popular with traveling salesmen and the life insurance industry, and for electronic commerce. Police forces, too, are interested in signature technology as it will speed the turnaround time for securing judges' signatures on arrest warrants. In June 1998, the Internal Revenue Service announced a pilot program for accepting electronic signatures. An added bonus is that the cost of digitizers has fallen from around $500 in the early 1990s to $40 in 1998.

The following are among the 90 different pieces of biometric data that PenOp software measures at the pen-screen interface: angle of the pen to writing surface; acceleration and deceleration during strokes; horizontal and vertical velocity of signing; number of times pen is picked up and put down; actual placement of lifting and lowering the pen; order in which strokes are made; time taken to complete signature; visible curvature of strokes; and the relative pressure applied throughout signing.

Similarly, manufacturers of automated teller machines (ATMs) such as Diebold and NCR are rolling out ATMs that are activated simply by touching an optical scanner. These biometric ATMs are especially well received in nations where there is a high incidence of illiteracy—users do not have to read prompts for keying in their personal identification numbers or other instructions.

Among the well educated, fingerprinting promises to relieve computer users of being inundated with excessive numbers of passwords, PINs, and log-on authorizations. Instead of a computer user having to memorize a host of log-on routines, it is much easier for him to simply place a finger on a touch authorization system offered by companies like Compaq Computer, Mytec Technologies, American Biometric Company, Key Tronic, and I/O Software. Such biometric computer systems will prove more secure than traditional access authorization procedures because many offices compromise passwords by implementing such policies as requiring everyone to use his or her first name or by eliminating passwords entirely. Although commonplace, such policies provide as much security as leaving the key to a safe in the safe's lock.

Fingerprinting could substantially reduce the billions of dollars that computer companies commit to their customer-support call centers. In fact, Compaq Computer has reported that half the calls its call centers receive from network users are from workers seeking lost or forgotten password information. By most estimates, each of these calls costs between $25 and $50 to facilitate.

Electronic Fingerprint Capture

Another driver of fingerprinting lies in the replacement of the traditional ink-and-roll method with electronic fingerprint capture. Ink-based fingerprinting was inefficient because the cards on which fingerprints were taken had to be scanned before the newly submitted fingerprint could be compared with the database. Also, smudged ink prints easily became unintelligible and a lack of cooperation on the part of the person being fingerprinted complicated the process. Thus, it is not surprising that the FBI rejected up to 60 percent of ink prints submitted by some fingerprinting offices.

When prints were rejected, the local agency was often required to locate the individual, if possible, and have another set of fingerprints taken. As a result, a mid-1990s FBI survey found the average time between taking a set of fingerprints and receiving the results of the search for a match took 151 days. In some cases, employers found themselves with such a backlog of applicants awaiting fingerprinting or results of their background checks that they allowed applicants to begin working without the background check being completed, placing themselves at risk if any of those applicants had a criminal record. More frightening is that in the first half of 1998, police around the United States unwittingly released more than 5,000 fugitives because fingerprint IDs did not come back in time.*

In the late 1990s, the FBI established its Integrated Automated Fingerprint Identification System (IAFIS), under which electronic national fingerprint checks are facilitated without the use of fingerprint cards. Now when fingerprints are captured electronically, the digitized images boomerang to the FBI and back to the local authorities within minutes or hours. Not only does this automatic digitization reduce the number of steps necessary to compare fingerprints (and therefore reduce the risk of error), but multiple cards can be printed from one set of images, eliminating the need to roll the fingerprint numerous times. These electronic databases are making it easier for law enforcement officials to sort and retrieve files. Moreover, these systems can combine fingerprints with a suspect's description and arrest information and transmit these data to central bureaus for later use by law enforcement officials. Because of these and other efficiencies, the FBI announced a goal of receiving the vast majority of fingerprints electronically by the end of the century.

Investment Vehicles

Pure-play fingerprint companies such as Identix, Digital Biometrics, National Registry, SAC Technologies, and Printrak International offer a menu of electronic fingerprint capture devices and are well positioned to prosper from the transition from ink-and-roll to electronic fingerprinting. Other companies involved in processing fingerprinting information include Polaroid, Electronic Data Systems, Hewlett-Packard, Computer Associates, Oracle, and Informix. Atmel manufactures some of the metal oxide semiconductors that keep electronic fingerprint capture systems running, and Verdicom specializes in microchips that authenticate fingerprints.

Food Inspection

Although food contamination is more severe abroad, the incidence of foodborne illnesses and the need for greater food inspection are rising to truly alarming levels in the United States. According to the Centers for Disease Control, about 80 million Americans are sickened by food ailments annually and 9,000 die

---

*Eric Scigliano, "The Tide of Prints," *Technology Review,* January/February 1999, p. 64.

each year. Moreover, foodborne illnesses cost the United States $23 billion a year in health costs and lost production.

Foodborne illnesses are occurring all over the country and are originating at sites ranging from food processors to restaurants. The proliferation of contamination occurring at the nation's food-processing facilities was made evident by the Agriculture Department's temporarily shutting down some or all of the operations at 34 meat and poultry plants during the first three months of 1998 after inspectors found the food contaminated by feces or the plants operating in dirty or unsafe conditions. In contrast, only one plant was shut down in 1997 for similar reasons. A few examples of recent outbreaks of food-related illnesses include:

- In 1993, hamburgers served at Jack in the Box restaurants in the Northwest were believed responsible for the deaths of four children and 600 people becoming ill.
- In August 1997, 17 people in Colorado became sick after eating hamburgers from beef processed by a Hudson Foods plant, leading Hudson Foods to recall 25 million pounds of its ground beef.
- In April 1998, IBP Inc. recalled 282,129 pounds of ground beef that had been distributed to about 50 retail and food service customers after potentially deadly E. coli bacteria were detected in tests conducted by the U.S. Department of Agriculture.
- In early June 1998, Malt-O-Meal Inc. recalled an estimated 3 million pounds of cereal after several government agencies linked one of Malt-O-Meal's store brands to agona, an uncommon strain of salmonella poisoning. The recall was notable for revealing one of the rare instances when a grain-based product carried such a bacterium.
- In June 1998, some 5,000 people attending graduation parties around suburban Chicago became ill from food contaminated with enterotoxigenic E. coli, a strain of gastrointestinal bacteria more commonly associated with traveler's diarrhea than domestic distress.
- On June 23, 1998, 29 people were rushed to hospitals after falling ill from eating tuna steak at New York's Drake Hotel. Dr. Neal Flomenbaum, chief emergency physician at New York Hospital-Cornell Medical Center, attributed these illnesses to scombroid poisoning and said that no amount of cooking would have eliminated the toxin once it formed on the fish.

The many factors contributing to the rise in food contamination and the unlikelihood that these root causes will significantly reverse course in the near future lead me to believe that the food inspection industry will be the recipient of a torrent of regulatory attention and industry expenditures. Among the many causes for soaring foodborne diseases are the following:

- U.S. food imports have doubled to more than 33 billion tons over the past five years, in part as a result of free trade agreements. An estimated 3 million shipments landed on American shores in 1998, and food imports are expected to increase 33 percent by 2003.* This is problematic for the following reasons:
  —Much of this imported food originates in countries that lack high standards for food preparation.
  —Problems abound even when our trading partners have high food safety standards because the farther food travels and the more hands it passes through, the greater the risks of contamination.
  —Congress's General Accounting Office reported that the system of inspection and testing designed to prevent entry of diseased or contaminated food is unreliable and easily subverted. As a result, importers have been found to use chemicals to cover the smell of decomposing fish; to misclassify imports to avoid testing; and to submit already inspected food samples instead of the food represented under the relevant bills of lading.
- American consumers' demand for fresh fruits and vegetables (which have the greatest incidence of microbes) year-round reinforces the country's reliance on imports from the Southern Hemisphere, where the growing seasons are the reverse of ours. In 1997, a full 38 percent of the fruit and 12 percent of the vegetables consumed by Americans were imported.
- Americans are dining out more often, making it is increasingly difficult to control how food is processed, handled, and prepared. The National Restaurant Association reports that the typical American consumes 213 meals away from home each year and more than 44 percent of the food dollar was spent away from home in 1995, up from 25 percent in 1955.
- Lifestyle changes and increases in the number of working mothers have brought greater demand for convenience foods, which are often purchased ready-to-eat or served by warming in a microwave but seldom cooked.

    A prime illustration of how convenience foods contribute to foodborne illnesses is provided by outdoor vendors. Studies have revealed that 40 percent of New York City's outdoor vendors handle foods that can be hazardous. Many stainless steel carts arrive in the morning with tubs of raw meat and poultry, which can carry disease-causing bacteria. The food is often left

---

*Amanda Spake, "Sick of Mean Cuisine," *U.S. News & World Report,* Sept. 14, 1998, p. 28.

unchilled and unheated—ideal for the growth of E. coli, salmonella, and other germs. Some vendors wash their hands so seldom that they use their sinks for storage space. Tests arranged by the *New York Times* of a random sampling of chicken, burgers, and kebabs from vendors' carts showed significant undercooking in 39 of the 51 cases they reviewed, meaning that bacteria would not be eliminated. The combination of risky fare, poor facilities, and unsafe handling is potentially very dangerous.*

- According to Dr. Michael Doyle, the director of the University of Georgia's Center for Food Safety and Quality Enforcement, as many as 1.5 to 5 percent of dairy cows carry the E. coli O157:H7 organism, which can cause diseases from standard diarrhea to kidney failure and death. In modern meat plants, a single contaminated carcass may be ground up with scores of other cows to produce hamburgers. Because farmers often fertilize crops with cow manure, the E.coli organism from one animal can invade vegetables consumed by many.

- Food processed at higher speeds at the nation's slaughterhouses is more difficult to inspect. In fact, chicken processing plants now process ten times as many birds an hour as they had two decades ago.

- Food inspections are very lax. Although the Food and Drug Administration (FDA) is responsible for the safety of all foods (except meat, poultry, and eggs), it must also regulate pharmaceuticals and medical devices. Thus, food inspection is not the FDA's utmost priority. At the FDA, roughly 700 investigators are responsible for overseeing some 53,000 U.S. factories and 30 billion tons of imported food. FDA officials inspect just 1 to 2 percent of the food imports under their jurisdiction, and in 1997 sampled only 0.2 percent of imported produce, a leading source of serious foodborne illnesses. Each U.S. food-processing plant is inspected on average once every ten years by the FDA. Similarly, the Agriculture Department (charged with making meat and poultry safe) has only 8,000 inspectors to patrol 6,500 slaughterhouses and food processors.

Although more than 250 different diseases have been linked to contaminated food or drink in the United States, epidemiologists are highly concerned about the rising virility of some of the more recent strains of bacteria, namely E. coli O157:H7. Most bacteria cannot survive in acidic environments, such as those of apple cider and commercial mayonnaise, but E. coli O157:H7 can. According to Dr. Marguerite Neill, chief of the division of infectious diseases at Brown Uni-

---

*"Street Vendors Serve Up Dangerous Foods," *New York Times,* May 17, 1998, p. 1.

versity School of Medicine, "most bacteria do not produce disease unless a person is exposed to millions of them. But as few as 10 or so E. coli O157:H7 can produce illness—far too few to see or smell." This is regrettable as infections induced by E. coli O157:H7 are now the leading contributor of kidney failure in children, with at least 1,000 youngsters developing kidney failure from these infections each year causing 3 to 5 percent of them to die.

Government Responds to Food Threat

Politicians and regulators have begun to take notice of the spread of foodborne illnesses. Under new regulations, processors are required to implement inspection processes throughout their food preparation regimens instead of regulators bearing all the responsibility when they merely spot-check food before it leaves the processing plants.

For its fiscal year beginning October 1, 1998, the federal government allocated $609 million for the Food and Inspection Service, an increase of $20.5 million over the previous fiscal year; and the Clinton administration proposed spending an additional $101 million on more vigorous food inspection, surveillance, and early-warning systems. President Clinton also called for the creation of a national institute for food safety research to coordinate public and private research.

These are not huge sums of money. As Dr. Michael Osterholm, an epidemiologist at the Department of Public Health in Minnesota said: "If you gave me all the money in the world, I'm not sure I could keep these bacteria out of the food supply." (And securing a safe food supply will be made more difficult because of the Year 2000—Y2K—problem. In 1998 the General Accounting Office warned that the U.S. Agriculture Department was having a great deal of difficulty rectifying its Y2K computer problem and its failure could have serious implications for public health and safety.)

However, the funds allocated to food inspection have a multiplier effect in that they result in the food-processing and handling industries purchasing more inspection and irradiation equipment. Another factor that should motivate the purchase of such equipment is that in the summer of 1998, the Clinton administration asked Congress to give the Department of Agriculture "new authority to impose tough fines on businesses that violate food safety standards."

Companies Offer Food Contamination Solutions

Companies are taking a three-pronged approach—detection, purification and vaccination (see Chapter 8, "Vaccines")—in their fight against foodborne illnesses. One company involved in detecting bacteria-contaminated food is Texas Instruments, which is developing a handheld biological sensor for the household market. A purer play on food contamination detection is Neogen Corporation, which develops and markets over 140 diagnostic test kits for detecting toxins in meat, seafood, grains, nuts, and spices. Similarly, Molecular Chemistry develops instruments to detect harmful bacteria in meat, poultry, and dairy foods.

Irradiation is a leading method of food remediation. When subjecting food to radiation from radioactive or machine sources, irradiation irreparably damages bacterial DNA and consequently prevents harmful cells from reproducing. Not only does irradiation fail to make food radioactive (nor does it noticeably change taste, texture, or appearance), but irradiation delays spoilage. Testimony about the safety of irradiation comes from endorsements by the United Nations World Health Organization and the American Medical Association. Already, to protect those most susceptible to bacterial attack, hospitals and nursing homes serve irradiated chicken and pork to patients who have AIDS or cancer or have received organ transplants. More than 50 percent of all disposable medical equipment and 8 percent of all spices are irradiated in the United States each year. Also, the Hawaii Department of Agriculture approved $2 million to promote irradiation on tropical fruits in 1998.

TIP: According to Van Negris of Kehoe, White & Van Negris, EPL Technologies offers solutions for maintaining the integrity and shelf life of fruits and vegetables with its proprietary processing and packaging technologies.

It is no surprise that two of the leading irradiation companies—Sterigenics International and Steris Corporation—have considerable experience in the sterilization of medical devices. Food processors are likely to support companies like SatCon Technology that detect and irradiate food. Because meat and other foods can be irradiated after they are packaged—but before they are transported to a supermarket or a restaurant—food processors would have a strong defense in any possible liability cases.

Another method of purifying foods is the use of ozone. Companies like Cyclopss Corporation design equipment that manufactures ozone, which electricity can deliver to food surfaces for disinfection. Ozone is one of the most powerful oxidants known and can kill E. coli 0157:H7, salmonella, listeria, giardia, and cryptosporidium when applied in controlled environments.

Finally, researchers at Boyce Thompson Institute for Plant Research in Ithaca, New York, have developed a genetically engineered potato. When eaten, the potato provokes an immune response to some strains of E. coli. These researchers anticipate that their potatoes will be the forerunner of many edible vaccines that will protect against a wide range of diseases, including cholera and hepatitis B.

Protective Clothing

Manufacturers of protective clothing are positioned to benefit from rising regulations covering worker safety and the willingness of employers to furnish their workers with protective clothing to achieve attractive returns from fostering better worker safety. Companies such as Lakeland Industries and Bacou USA are likely to experience sales growth resulting from the government's preparations for responding to chemical and biological assaults (see "Combating Biological Weapons of Mass Destruction" in this chapter). Another revenue driver for this $4 billion industry is heightened environmental remediation.

Employers Realize Benefits of Protective Clothing

Protective clothing is needed to reduce the incidence and severity of workplace injuries and fatalities. Each year more than 55,000 Americans die because of workplace hazards, while 7 million more sustain injuries that result in lost work time, medical treatment costs, work restrictions, or job transfers. The economic costs associated with work-related accidents amount to roughly $121 billion a year. As a result, more industries are falling under the Occupational Safety and Health Administration's purview, with fines for violating a growing array of regulations quite severe at up to $70,000 per violation.

Even in instances when employers are not required to furnish their workers with protective clothing, such garments offer high payback in terms of reduced employee turnover and more effective recruiting, fewer medical liabilities, more moderate insurance premiums, and lower levels of litigation. Litigation can be extremely expensive as Cargill's Excel unit learned when it reached a $9.05 million settlement in 1998 with one of its employees. The settlement arose from Cargill failing to provide the plaintiff with protective gear that resulted in his suffering second-degree and third-degree burns over 65 percent of his body when he was showered with a solution of scalding water and acid.

Protective Clothing Is a Suitable Response to Biowarfare

I believe that the protective clothing industry is positioned to benefit from the government's beginning to prepare for attacks from chemical and biological weapons of mass destruction. Under long-standing authorities, such as the

National Oil and Hazardous Substances Pollution Contingency Plan, the Environmental Protection Agency (EPA) is required to prepare for and respond to any release of oil, hazardous substances, pollutants, or contaminants that may present an imminent and substantial threat to public health. Also, Presidential Decision Directives 39, 62, and 63 issued in 1998 mandate that the EPA participate in a federal response program specifically aimed at preparing for, and responding to, terrorist incidents such as chemical or biological attack.

Under the Defense against Weapons of Mass Destruction Act, the EPA began working to train local first-responders (e.g., local fire, police, and emergency medical personnel) in 120 of the nation's largest cities in 1998. Also, the Defense Department budgeted almost $50 million in its 1999 fiscal year to train and equip Army Reserves and the National Guard to respond to the effects of weapons of mass destruction. According to Reserve Affairs Brigadier General Roger C. Schultz, a sum of $50 million would be requested annually for such training and equipment.

Because the EPA is one of the agencies heavily involved in preparing for bio-attacks, it is likely to prefer buying from vendors with which it is familiar. Companies positioned to benefit from the convergence of these factors include the following:

- Lakeland Industries manufactures heavy-duty, fully encapsulated chemical suits made of Viton, butyl rubber, and Teflon. These suits have traditionally been used to protect wearers from exposure to hazardous chemicals for toxic cleanups and chemical spills, or in industrial and electronic plants.
- Bacou USA makes Survivair face masks that protect workers from toxic vapors, chemicals, or particles in the workplace. In addition, Bacou's bio-systems atmospheric monitors alert workers to the presence of toxins or gases and chemicals that can explode or cause a fire.
- Vallen Corporation sells and rents a series of portable digital electronic instruments used to detect the presence and levels of toxic and combustible gases.
- Aramsco is one of the world's largest distributors of safety-related gear, including germ and chemical suits, respirators, and portable, inflatable decontamination facilities that can be flown by helicopter to the site of a bioattack.

Additional Uses of Protective Clothing

Protective clothing manufacturers develop and sell protective garments for every part of the body and for a wide array of industrial applications. The following are examples of applications served by protective gear.

Environmental remediation. Two specific developments should spur demand for protective clothing used by companies remediating the environment. First, pursuant to legislation passed in 1997, $2 billion in federal tax incentives has been made available to companies wishing to revitalize brownfields. (Brownfields are tracts of land left undeveloped because of the costs associated with the correction of their environmental safety deficiencies.) Lakeland Industries will be a prime beneficiary of such legislation, as disposable protective clothing is required for many of the tasks involved in remediating brownfields.

Second, the eventual passage of the Superfund Reform Act should accelerate the cleanup of over 500 toxic waste sites in the United States. In fact, the property and casualty insurance industry had reserved up to $10 billion for such purposes by 1998. According to Christopher Ryan, Lakeland Industries' CFO, the average cost of cleaning up these sites is $270 million, and sales of Lakeland's protective clothing could consume as much as 7 percent of these dollars.

Eye injuries. An estimated 1,000 eye injuries occur in American workplaces each day at a cost of more than $300 million a year in lost production time, medical expenses, and workers' compensation. The typical industrial worker goes through six pairs of protective glasses a year. Bacou USA is the market share leader in nonprescription protective eyewear, frames for prescription protective eyewear, laser protective eyewear, and safety goggles. Vallen Corporation also manufactures eye protection devices, including emergency eyewash products.

Hearing impairment. Occupational hearing loss is the most common occupational disease in the United States (see Chapter 12, "Noise Pollution"). More than 30 million workers are exposed to hazardous noise and an additional 9 million are at risk from other ototraumatic agents. Not only is hearing loss pervasive but once hearing loss occurs, it is irreversible. There are great repeat revenue opportunities for earplug makers, as disposable earplugs are discarded after a day's work and reusable earplugs are replaced every week. Companies that manufacture protective hearing devices include Vallen and Bacou USA.

Heat protection. According to Secretary of Labor Alexis Herman, some 500 workplace deaths result from exposure to excessive heat each year. Lakeland

Industries' solutions to this problem include Kevlar gloves, which can withstand temperatures of up to 400 degrees Fahrenheit while allowing industrial workers to safely handle sharp unfinished sheet metal. Some of Lakeland's fire suits are designed for industries dealing with volatile and highly flammable products. Lakeland also manufactures protective clothing for firefighters in domestic and foreign fire departments as well as for fire brigades at its client companies.

Highway Safety

The nation's highways are in need of great repair and expansion. They are dilapidated and inadequate to handle the surging number of miles American motorists drive each year. Moreover, the decay of U.S. highways—together with a host of factors such as the repeal of speed limits and a rising incidence of older people and teenagers driving—has made intercity driving hazardous. These hazardous conditions present tremendous opportunities for companies that offer highway safety solutions as well as for the businesses that will participate in expanding and rebuilding the country's interstate highway system.

TIP: Parking operators such as Central Parking and Holberg Industries are growing rapidly by acquiring small operators in the highly fragmented $26 billion U.S. parking-space market. In fact, most of the more than 1,000 companies that operated roughly 5 million nongovernment parking spaces in 1998 generated less than $5 million a year in revenue. Other growth drivers for this industry include outsourcing by property management companies that wish to be relieved of parking management, privatization of government parking facilities as has already happened in the United States and the United Kingdom, and foreign expansion as Central Parking has extended its reach to Canada, Chile, Germany, Malaysia, Mexico, Puerto Rico, Ireland, and Spain.

U.S. Highways Are Unsafe at Any Speed

America's highways have deteriorated because of overuse and underinvestment. First, there were more than 200 million automobiles in the United States alone in the mid-1990s (compared with the 200,000 cars and trucks in the entire world in 1905), and the Department of Transportation expected 50 percent more cars on the road by 2008. Another contributor to the stress placed on U.S. highways is a truck fleet that has become heavier and travels farther. Between 1982 and 1992, the number of trucks with operating weights above 80,000 pounds increased by 180 percent from 18,000 to 50,000, and the total number of vehicle miles traveled by this weight class rose by 193 percent. Also, the number of heavy-duty Class 8 trucks sold in the United States rose from 185,000 in 1996 to about 220,000 in 1998.

As for underinvestment, the Road Information Program reported that capital investment in highways per 1,000 vehicle miles of travel (adjusted for inflation) decreased by 17 percent between 1985 and 1995. Thus, it is not surprising that the Department of Transportation's 1995 report to Congress stated that nearly one-third of the most heavily traveled major U.S. roads are in poor or mediocre condition.

Among the ramifications of the plight of America's highways are the increase in highway accidents and deaths. Highway fatalities are the number one cause of death for people between the ages of 1 and 37, and the number three cause of death for people of all ages. According to the Labor Department, job-related highway fatalities, the biggest cause of work fatalities, rose to a record 1,387 in 1997; and the Department of Transportation reported that the total societal cost of automobile crashes exceeds $150 billion annually.

The nation's degenerating highways are not the only culprit in these tragedies: inept driving plays a large role as well. Congress's revocation of the national 55-miles-per-hour (mph) speed limit in late 1995 resulted in nearly every state's lifting some of its posted speed limits to between 65 and 75 mph. Emboldened by plunging gasoline prices, the improved power of new trucks, sport utility vehicles, and minivans, and an enhanced sense of security as a result of air bags and antilock brakes, Americans often exceed even those limits. For instance, a study from the Texas Transportation Institute shows that the proportion of vehicles exceeding 70 mph on rural freeways increased by 65 percent after Texas raised its speed limits. And the California Highway Patrol revealed that the number of motorists ticketed for exceeding 100 mph in Los Angeles County reached 791 in 1997, up from 556 in 1992.

Faster speeds on highways, reduced reaction times associated with faster speeds, and greater variability in the range of speeds traveled have resulted in more dangerous driving conditions. In fact, 41,907 people died in motor vehicle crashes in 1996, the fourth consecutive year of such increases.

Demographics Could Not Be Worse

With record numbers of fearless teenagers hitting the roads at the same time that the baby boomers' eyesight begins to plunge into opacity, demographics could not loom any more threatening for road safety. As an approximation of the growth in the number of young drivers, the number of people between the ages of 13 and 19 will increase from 25 million in 1997 to over 30 million by 2010. Reflecting the actuarial fact that young drivers are more accident prone than older drivers, insurers have traditionally levied higher premiums on young drivers. Young drivers could be even more accident prone as the American Automobile Association reports that while in the 1960s and 1970s virtually all high schools had some form of driver's education, driver's education has been eliminated in about half the schools.

Of more concern than the numbers of young drivers is the kinds of vehicles they prefer to drive. Surveys by automakers have found that up to 90 percent of the nation's teenagers prefer sport utility vehicles (SUVs) to cars. While high-ticket prices on new SUVs had largely kept SUVs beyond teenagers' reach throughout the 1990s, used SUVs will be more affordable for teenagers. This is problematic from the standpoint of highway safety for a number of reasons. Used vehicles are inherently less safe because, for example, brakes wear with age. Drivers tend to operate their vehicles more recklessly because they feel invincible in large vehicles. The incidence of fatal accidents involving pickup trucks and utility vehicles increased 95 percent from 1975 to 1995. Also, teenagers are more likely to show off with their friends than exercise caution because they are driving with children. The severity of accidents involving large vehicles is much greater than accidents involving smaller vehicles. According to the Insurance Institute for Highway Safety, car passengers were 27 times more likely to die after being hit broadside by a light truck or SUV as were drivers of the larger vehicles.

In addition, the number of Americans over 65 years old will rise from 31.6 million in 1990 to 39.7 million by 2010. This demographic trend is of concern because the lens of the eye becomes three times more opaque as a person matures from 20 to 60. Also, Harvard University research shows that the time it takes to recover sight after an adjustment from light to dark or dark to light is directly proportional to the driver's age.

Highways Experience Uncontrollable Congestion

Americans are driving more miles than ever. Between 1973 and 1995, there were 24 percent more people in the United States, 45 percent more licensed drivers, and 60 percent more registered vehicles driving 84 percent more miles. Yet the number of highway miles only increased by 4 percent during that period.

Some of the reasons for increased travel include the following:

- *A growing workforce.* From 1970 to 1995, the civilian labor force increased by 59 percent, from 83 million to 132 million. More working Americans translates into more people commuting. The 1990 National Personal Transportation Survey found that employed persons with a license drove 15,280 miles compared with 8,048 miles for those unemployed.

- *More women in the workforce.* The number of women working outside the home nearly doubled, from approximately 32 million in 1970 to about 61 million in 1995.

- *Growth in households.* From 1970 to 1995, the number of households increased by 56 percent, nearly twice as much as the increase in population would suggest. More households results in more trips for shopping, procuring medical attention, and other daily errands.

- *Reduced densification.* The farther away people live from cities, the more they drive. This is because cities are so compact that their residents can either walk or take public transportation to their routine destinations. When people live in, or telecommute from, the suburbs, they must drive everywhere they want to go. Between 1980 and 1990, the central cities lost 500,000 people, whereas the suburbs gained 17.5 million. At the same time, the suburban share of jobs rose from 37 percent to 42 percent. The number of telecommuters in the United States is expected to grow from 6.4 million in 1995 to 10.7 million in 1999.

- *Reduced carpooling and use of mass transit.* Census data from 1980 and 1990 show that overwhelming numbers of American workers are abandoning car pools and mass transit to drive to work alone. The percentage of the workforce that carpooled declined from 20 percent in 1980 to 13 percent in 1990. During the same period, the percentage of the workforce that took mass transit to work fell from 6.4 percent in 1980 to only 5 percent in 1990.

Congestion Results in Road Rage

Because of congestion resulting from more miles driven, a higher incidence of accidents, and inadequate highway capacity, motorists have become more aggressive, which in turn leads to even more traffic incidents. According to the American Automobile Association, the number of aggressive driving incidents—defined as incidents in which an angry driver or passenger attempts or succeeds in killing or injuring another driver, passenger, or pedestrian in response to a traffic dispute—grew 7 percent a year throughout the late 1990s, resulting in 12,610 injuries between January 1990 and September 1996. And some 1,500 motorists are killed or wounded each year as a result of highway shootings.

Solutions to Highway Congestion

Congested roadways in 50 of the nation's major urban areas cost almost $1 billion a week in lost travel time and wasted fuel. A study by the Texas Transportation Institute found that motorists in those areas lose the equivalent of a full workweek, or 40 hours, stuck in traffic every month.

TRAP: A substantial portion of public sector funding for road improvement derives from fuel taxes based on the volume of gasoline sold. As vehicles continue to achieve greater fuel efficiency, funding for highway investment could be threatened.

Congress and President Clinton have recognized the need for highway expansion and improvement. In January 1999, the Clinton administration proposed an increase in spending on public transportation of $341 million to control traffic congestion. More important, in the spring of 1998, the Transportation Equity Act for the Twenty-First Century (TEA-21) was enacted. According to the American Road & Transportation Builders Association (ARTBA), TEA-21 will result in a jump of federal funding for highway programs from $23 billion in 1998 to more than $28 billion annually over the five-year period ending 2003.

The ARTBA stated that TEA-21 is a $217 billion highway bill that will boost federal highway spending by 44 percent through 2003 compared with the previous six years and will be responsible for reconstructing an estimated 150,000 miles of roads. The following are among the additional reasons that TEA-21 will result in the expedient expansion and repair of the country's surface transportation system:

- Under provisions of TEA-21, firewalls have been placed around highway investment in the federal government's budget process. This guarantees that all incoming revenue to the Highway Trust Fund will only be used for transportation investment, not general governmental purposes.
- TEA-21 provides expanded authority to leverage public monies to attract private funds for financing transportation infrastructure projects. Specifically, TEA-21 makes available $500 million in Highway Trust Fund revenue over six years to support credit assistance up to $10 billion.
- TEA-21 will speed transportation project delivery by requiring a coordinated environmental review process between federal and state agencies.

Companies Positioned to Benefit from TEA-21

The companies that are best positioned to benefit from the $217 billion that will be disbursed under TEA-21 can be classified into four primary categories: engineering firms, contractors, suppliers, and traffic management companies. Engineering firms (collectively slated to receive 8 percent of the $217 billion TEA-21 commitment) that are likely to reap some of the rewards from TEA-21 include Flour Corporation, Jacobs Engineering Group, URS Corporation, CDI Engineering, Aztec Industries, and Tetra Tech. Favorably disposed contractors include Granite Construction, Perini Corporation, Brown & Root, and Parsons Corporation.

Perhaps the most interesting group of suppliers consists of the cement companies—namely, CalMat Company, Dravo Corporation, Florida Rock Industries, Lafarge Corporation, Southdown, Texas Industries, and Vulcan Materials. Also, companies like Caterpillar, Ingersoll-Rand, Manitowac, Terex, and United Dominion should benefit from TEA-21 as they should be able to sell and lease more tractors, graders, compactors, and loaders to the contractors.

TIP: The cement industry is a sector worthy of investor consideration. First, cement companies are highly leveraged to TEA-21; in fact, public works projects accounted for over one-half of the total cement consumption in 1998. Second, domestic consumption has been well above capacity, leading to rising prices. In fact, in 1997 U.S. plants produced 86 million tons of cement, although cement consumption was 102 million tons. (We had to import the difference.) Third, stringent environmental regulations ensure that supply will remain constrained as it takes at least two years to build even a modest-sized cement kiln.

TEA-21 notwithstanding, it is extremely expensive to expand the nation's physical highway capacity. In fact, adding one lane of interstate highway can cost $30 million per mile in an urban area and $10 million in rural locales. In view of such expenses, an already well-received method of improving the flow of traffic on existing roads is the use of highway advisory radio systems. Quixote Corporation led the development of smart highways in 1998 by commanding 60 percent of the U.S. market for highway advisory radio systems. These systems use flashing lights and message signs to warn motorists of traffic problems and instruct them about the radio stations providing more information and alternative routes. Also, traffic reporting services such as Metro Networks alert wearers of Seiko pager watches about traffic problems.

Another method of facilitating more traffic through existing highway capacity is the use of prepass systems. For instance, Lockheed-Martin deployed its E-ZPass system in the New York City area, which allows motorists who have prepaid their tolls to drive past toll booths. These systems speed the flow of traffic because drivers do not have to decelerate, fumble for change, or roll their windows down. In the early .2000s, electronic collection systems will better manage traffic by varying the tolls collected. For instance, the highest fees will be charged during times of peak traffic to discourage driving.

TIP: Similar to prepass systems, Cubic Corporation deploys automatic fare collection (AFC) systems for mass transit authorities. AFC systems save passengers time and relieve mass transit patrons of the necessity of carrying exact change. Cubic's advanced contact-free AFC systems will allow commuters to pass turnstiles and board buses without even swiping their transit

Companies like Scientific Atlanta are developing more futuristic methods of traffic management. Some of these methods will eventually consist of a network of traffic sensors around a metropolitan area that communicate with a central traffic computer. Electronic information from on-the-road sensors will be supplemented with information on what traffic is usually like at a particular time of day and instantaneous updates from drivers calling in on wireless phones. Vehicles will be equipped with on-board navigators from companies like Hughes Electronics that will garner up-to-the minute traffic information from the central traffic computer on alternative routes, the time a certain route is likely to take, and forecasts of expected traffic conditions. Congress has supported such intelligent transportation efforts by appropriating $95 million a year through 2004.

The final method for accommodating more commuters through existing infrastructures is to encourage people to rely on bus service from operators such as Coach USA. Environmentalists support extending incentives to bus operators because decreasing the number of automobiles on the road reduces pollution; employers of low-income workers rely on buses to deliver their employees on a timely basis; Atlantic City casinos alone depend on nearly 1,200 buses each day to bring gamblers to their venues; and buses are needed to shuttle tourists throughout America's cities. Interestingly, another driver for the bus operators is privatization by municipalities, which increased from $200 million in 1987 to $1 billion in 1997.

Solutions to Highway Hazards

I believe the conditions causing increasing highway danger will evoke a consensus among legislators that resources should be committed to improving highway safety. However, specific funds will be released as a result of the May 1998 enactment of TEA-21. TEA-21 will be a boon to the makers of highway safety products for two primary reasons. First, TEA-21 sets aside $80 million for the purchase of such safety devices as signage, railings, and crash cushions. Second, the 44 percent increase in funding for highway rebuilding and expansion over the six years ending in 2003 will result in the aggressive purchase of equipment such as work zone markers to protect construction crews.

The following are intriguing vehicles for profiting from the growing demand for highway safety products:

Quixote Corporation. Quixote is by far the leading producer of crash-cushion systems and other barriers that absorb the force of impact in vehicle collisions. Other promising products include truck-mounted impact attenuators designed to reduce the severity of rear-end collisions with work vehicles; BarrierGate, an automatic sliding gate that enables emergency vehicles, by operation of a wireless remote system, to pass through concrete median barriers; and Odin Anti-Icing System, which uses advanced microprocessor technology to activate liquid anti-icers on roadways before freezing occurs. Quixote has also introduced a truck-weighing station that does not require trucks to stop.

Stimsonite Corporation. Stimsonite accounted for 80 percent of the retroflective pavement markers (the lights dividing the lanes of highways) installed on the world's highways in 1998. Also, Stimsonite's optical films are used on essentially every variety of road sign, improving the brightness by as much as four times more than ordinary sheeting material. Such brightness can be the difference between life and death. With Stimsonite's films, motorists driving 55 mph receive a crucial additional seven seconds to read, decide, and maneuver their vehicles based on what such signs indicate.

Trinity Industries. Trinity Industries is a leading manufacturer of guardrails. These guardrails are designed to be sufficiently strong to prevent vehicles from breaking them, and they are also designed to absorb maximum impact, thereby cushioning automobile occupants as much as possible. This is important as the Insurance Institute for Highway Safety found that more than one in four deaths on U.S. roads are a result of collisions with roadside objects like guardrails.

Remote Electronic Monitoring

Prepass systems are only one permutation of remote electronic monitoring. Applications for this emerging industry include monitoring residential electric utility meters, vending machines, home security systems, office copiers, traffic lights, and personal safety devices such as pacemakers. Benefits of such enabling technology include reduced energy consumption as homeowners can turn off lights when away from home; self-diagnostics of office products as copier companies can dispatch repairmen before customers place a service call; and reduced out-of-stock inventory as vending machine concessionaires can replenish their machines before the most popular items sell out.

Examples of particularly exciting applications of remote monitoring are discussed below.

Remote modulation. Whirlpool's chief financial officer, Ralph F. Hake, noted that his company spends $50 on each warranty service call. Thus, Whirlpool planned to install electronics in its refrigerators and washing machines that will alert its service centers to malfunctions. Forward-looking companies like Whirlpool are developing technologies to correct product glitches over the Internet. Also, Johnson Controls has built-in Internet options in the systems it sells for controlling heat, air-conditioning, and other services in office buildings. That way, a building maintenance chief can run these systems from any computer via the Internet, and a facilities manager can monitor the building's energy consumption.

TRAP: Remote meter reading could be hampered by the fact that many

companies keep their Internet-based networks carefully cordoned off from the global Internet by a series of security barriers that scrutinize the flow of information in and out of their offices. (Philip Morris forbids its employees to disseminate their E-mail addresses to anyone outside the company.) Reasons for such monitoring include fears of hackers and computer viruses. Another restraint on the proliferation of remote electronic monitoring is that the data collected could be used for marketing that is excessively invasive. For instance, even though Whirlpool could sell information to a packaged foods company about how many times people open their refrigerators, the resulting marketing pitches would likely be viewed as inappropriate.

▶**Revenue enhancement.** In collecting fines for parking violations, smart meters send out signals that automatically notify parking enforcers the moment someone is guilty of overtime parking. According to CellNet Data Systems, these meters should enable parking enforcers to write three more tickets an hour. At an average of $25 per ticket (60 percent of which is profit), CellNet estimates that a parking enforcer might generate $360 additional revenue in an eight-hour shift. Interestingly, the next generation of smart traffic meters may do away with parking enforcers altogether. Instead, smart meters will simply relay information about cars to a central computer, which will then automatically write a ticket and mail it to the violator.

Customer convenience. Gasoline giant Mobil Corporation has made buying gasoline as simple as the wave of a wand. Mobil's Speedpass payment system allows consumers to use a small wand on their key chains or transmitters in their cars to pay for gas. The wand and transmitter use radio waves to communicate information to the gas station that allows the company to charge a customer's credit card.

Among the companies best positioned to facilitate remote electronic monitoring are American Mobile Satellite Corporation, CellNet Data Systems, and Checkpoint Systems. In addition, the gallium arsenide semiconductor companies such as Anadigics, TriQuint Semiconductor, and Vitesse Semiconductor produce the semiconductors that drive remote metering technology.

Raytheon Systems. Raytheon's Night Vision headlights extend driver visibility 500 percent by searching for infrared heat that signals a human, a deer, or another obstacle. John Smith, general manager of General Motors' Cadillac division, explains the importance of such equipment: "The risk of dying in a traffic accident almost doubles during nighttime hours, even though only about one-quarter of driving occurs after dark."* In fact, nearly two out of three pedestrian deaths occur after dark.

Control Devices. Control Devices makes sensors that detect moisture on either side of an automobile's glass and activate the wipers or defrosters before drivers notice any change in visibility. Control Devices also has devices that sense the onset of twilight and automatically switch on the headlights.

---

*Paul A. Eisenstein, "Seeing Ahead," *Investors' Business Daily,* Aug. 24, 1998, p. A4.

Texas Instruments, Ultrak, Cubic Corporation, and Sentry Technology Corporation. Companies such as these manufacture and install surveillance cameras for monitoring traffic violators (see "Security Services" in this chapter). These cameras typically help communities enforce traffic laws by automatically photographing vehicles whose drivers run red lights. Tickets are mailed to owners of violating vehicles after police review the photographic evidence. The cameras reduce the incidence of automobile accidents as drivers who run red lights cause a quarter-million traffic crashes a year. In fact, during the first six months after traffic cameras were mounted at four San Francisco intersections, the number of drivers who ran the red lights there dropped by 42 percent.

Brite Voice Communications. According to International Data Corporation/ Link, some 6.1 million people in the United States were working in their cars in mid-1998. Csaba Csere, editor in chief of *Car and Driver* magazine, has commented: "There are plenty of people who are not capable of safe driving if they devote 100 percent of their faculties to the task. The last thing they need are cell phones, navigation systems, and high-powered stereo systems to distract them." Dialing phone numbers is one of the activities that distracts drivers and makes driving more dangerous for everyone.* Companies like Brite Voice Communications produce voice-activated telephone dialing systems that relieve drivers of the necessity to look up numbers and then dial. (A similar solution is telephone headsets discussed in "Telephone Headsets" in Chapter 11).

TIP: Photographic detection devices are used extensively in many locales, including Australia, Austria, Belgium, Canada, Germany, Israel, the Netherlands, Singapore, South Africa, Switzerland, Taiwan, and the United Kingdom. Red-light cameras are used for law enforcement in New York City, Los Angeles, San Francisco, and Tucson. More cities should deploy these devices because a May 1998 Harris poll found that Americans favor cameras by two to one. One reason for their popularity is that their start-up costs are usually offset by fines paid by violators, savings from crashes prevented, and by freeing police to focus on other enforcement efforts.

---

*Robert L. Simison, "Car Toys for Grown-ups," *The Wall Street Journal*, Dec. 11, 1998, p. W1.

CHAPTER 11

Telecommunications

Deregulation of the worldwide telecommunications industry continues to result in steadily declining rates, which in turn boost usage of telephone services. While fierce competition often erodes profits among telephone service providers, there are safer vehicles for investors to gain exposure to the dynamic telecommunications industry. First, the telephone billing service providers provide an essential service for the multitudes of new industry entrants. Second, wireless phone carriers are realizing that prepaid calling enhances earnings by reducing uncollectible revenues. Finally, telephone headsets are proving to be an ergonomic as well as efficiency-enhancing solution for the millions of people that spend substantial time talking on the phone.

Telephone-Billing Providers

Many industries will benefit from increased outsourcing by their customers. For telecommunications-billing providers (TBPs), outsourcing is just one revenue driver. The diversity of entities offering telephone service will expand the client base for companies such as Billing Concepts and USCS International that prepare telephone invoices. The continuing launch of enhanced services like call return and voice-activated dialing is another demand driver for TBPs. So, too, is the trend of convergent billing brought about by phone companies' offering one-stop shopping and providing local, long-distance, and wireless phone service together with cable, paging, and Internet access.

Deregulation Creates Customers and Complicates Invoice Generation

Deregulation in the United States as well as throughout the world stands to take much of the credit for driving direct billing revenue from $2.8 billion in 1997 to as much as $8 billion in 2000. Deregulation in the telecommunications services industry is resulting in the proliferation of upstart service providers taking market share from the heretofore entrenched local phone monopolies. Competitive access providers, long-distance carriers, wireless players, cable companies, and electric utilities are all vying for a piece of the $110 billion in revenue spent on local phone service in the United States each year.

Few of the newly created phone companies (or even the reincarnated telephony vendors) have the time to develop their own billing systems. Because sending out invoices, tracking receivables, and depositing remittances are critical activities for any business, these phone service challengers prefer to outsource these responsibilities to established autonomous direct-billing firms rather than hastily develop internal billing systems that cost millions of dollars and quickly become obsolete. In fact, there has been virtually no internal direct-billing development throughout the late 1990s.

The utility of transferring the billing responsibility onto third-party providers is reinforced by the billing process becoming increasingly complicated by the convergence of basic telecommunications services. Both the wireline and wireless phone companies are responding to their competition by offering a wider selection of basic services, such as Internet access, paging, and cable television. The strategy is to entwine customers with a bundle of services that are collectively cheaper than each service would be on a stand-alone basis. Because discontinuing any one service will cause the entire package of services to unravel, the hope is that customers will continue to receive all of their telecommunications services from their existing carriers. Most phone companies believe that the successful execution of this strategy will result in greater customer loyalty and reduced customer switching.

TIP: Some advanced intelligent network services are particularly attractive to phone companies. For instance, voice mail systems manufactured by companies such as Centigram Communications not only generate subscription revenue for the phone company but voice mail ensures that more calls placed get answered. This is crucial because calls that are placed but not answered tax the phone company's infrastructure without producing any revenue. Thus, voice mail allows the phone company to charge for all of the calls placed to the corresponding numbers. Moreover, voice mail generates many more calls as voice mail subscribers place incremental calls to retrieve their messages.

Billing complexity rises in proportion to the number of enhanced services customers receive. The phone companies are trying to extend their strategy of locking customers in by offering a wide array of enhanced features—everything from voice-activated dialing to three-way calling and from call return to voice mail. Once people learn how to use three-way calling and set passwords necessary for retrieving their voice mail, they will be reluctant to change carriers because they would have to relearn these tasks. More of these services will be introduced because they effectively wring more profit from existing customers. Whether customers pay a monthly subscription fee or are on a pay-per-use basis, the profit margins are robust because little human intervention is required.

According to Susan Passoni of SG Cowen & Company, once customers subscribe to enhanced services, they usually take five or six service options with their basic service. As more professionals work away from their offices, whether from home or on the road, they need sophisticated calling features to improvise office capability. Roughly 70 percent of all business transactions are conducted over the telephone, and as corporations seek to improve productivity and customer service, enhanced services become a compelling option.

Customization Complicates Billing

The replacement of monopolies with fierce competition is forcing phone providers to be more responsive to their customers in offering customized pricing. Thus, it is no surprise that wireless carriers often have as many as 100 different pricing plans that seem to change all the time. The movement to a plethora of call-rating scenarios is further complicated for the TBPs as the wireless providers often break down the cost of a call by minute, with the first one to two minutes charged differently than other parts of the same call.

Another challenge to preparing accurate invoices is due to the popularity of alternative payment methods such as debit cards, prepaid arrangements, and dial-around calling (in which callers circumvent their carriers of record by dialing a code before dialing their intended number). Billing systems also have to accommodate threshold billing, under which customers are granted discounts on certain services when they spend a predetermined amount on that service or other services. TBPs must be prepared to accommodate customers who want multilingual billing or billing-date flexibility. In the future, the most successful billing systems will handle multiple billing formats such as those that offer flat rates and postal pricing and those that have time and distance sensitivity. In addition, TBPs will have to devise invoices that can itemize the amount of data that customers send and receive, as companies like Sprint have announced plans to charge their customers according to their data consumption.

Interconnection and Consolidation Spur Demand

TBPs are positioned to prosper from deregulation allowing long-distance companies to offer local service by leasing local carriers' infrastructure. The resale of elements of local exchange networks, as mandated by the Telecommunications Act of 1996, should prompt most local exchange operators to lease their local infrastructure on a wholesale basis. As a result, wholesale billing will create a new billing submarket called interconnect billing, under which billing between the originating and terminating carrier is reconciled. Each carrier involved must have data readily available to keep track of network usage. Such usage data then needs to be settled between operators, compared with invoices, and held for review. The systems must also be flexible enough to keep track of each carrier's terms and to add new services and rates over time. In addition, billing cycles have to be reconciled as they are likely to be different among the retail and wholesale carriers. Finally, the billers will have to account for the interexchange carriers' contributions to universal funds.

Investors should realize that mergers of phone carriers do not reduce demand for billing services. Rather, mergers of phone companies require more concerted billing efforts. Phone company mergers require the uniformity of two disparate billing systems, mailing dates, and invoice designs. Many companies would rather avoid the difficulties of merging incompatible billing platforms, and the associated turf battles, by retaining TBPs.

Outsourcing: Winners Take All

Harry Blount, senior telecommunications analyst at CIBC Oppenheimer, has noted that the cost of bandwidth plunged 100-fold from 1990 to 1998 and could plunge another 100-fold by 2008. As the cost of transmitting phone calls and data for the phone companies falls precipitously, the phone companies' other costs—such as those for preparing invoices—appear relatively more onerous. Thus, the motivation is to delegate these services to outsourcers that can use their economies of scale to deliver the services more cost efficiently.

Accurate and reliable billing can account for a phone company's success or failure. TBPs must ensure that all billable traffic has been captured while even inadvertent overbilling will result in punitive fines from regulators. TBPs must collect all taxes levied on phone service—no small undertaking considering that long-distance phone calls can result in the imposition of as many as nine taxes. Billing is also important for maintaining good customer relations as about 99 percent of a telecommunications company's customer interaction occurs through monthly bills.

If you ever have the opportunity, look at your company's telephone bill. You will see that the bill is meticulously itemized, with each call delineated by the phone from which the call was placed, the number and destination called, the date and time of the call, the duration of the call, and the cost of the call with discounts deducted from that cost. Even if your company only subscribes to the phone company's long-distance offering, the invoice is just short of a miracle. Tens of thousands of pieces of data are presented without any mistakes and delivered on time every month. Because the traditional phone companies have done a superb job of timely delivering meticulously itemized phone bills, customers have been conditioned to refuse to tolerate the slightest inaccuracy in their telephone invoices. This is an especially high hurdle to overcome in an era of rampant slamming (deceptively changing a customer's long-distance carrier), cramming (charging for enhanced services without the customer's permission), and fraud.

Thus, the phone companies are likely to limit the outsourcing of their billing to TBPs that have a stable of referenceable accounts. Some TBPs are further securing their place as preferred vendors by offering accounting services and handling customer inquiries. One innovative service offering comes from Billing Concepts, which offers its customers advanced funding, under which qualified participants are advanced up to 80 percent of their receivables within five days of submitting their call records—a very valuable program for customers who cannot afford to wait for the typical 60-day billing cycle to receive payment.

Cost Reduction Opportunities

While industry revenues are rising at a 59 percent compound annual growth rate, TBPs' costs stand to drop as a result of economies of scale, Internet invoice presentment, and electronic remittance collection. Print and mail-related costs such as paper and postage, remittance processing, late notices, and handling of exceptions are all costs the biller will be able to reduce or eliminate. TBPs could also realize a reduction in billing-cycle float, which includes such things as mailing and processing time, delivery time, and time delay before which funds become available. In the summer of 1998, there were more than 50 million Internet users and more than 6 million Americans had made purchases over the Internet. In a survey conducted by BellSouth of its business and residential users, a full 79 percent of those polled indicated they were interested in using online billing. TBPs can also save (their clients) money by redesigning invoices that are easier to read, as 60 percent of all customer service calls are generated by confusing statements.

In addition to reducing costs, TBPs can harness electronic bill presentment as a means of charging for premium services. For instance, carriers can analyze a customer's profile or their click stream to determine what products or services that customer needs. Billing also yields a myriad of such information as market segmentation data, including patterns of local, national, and international calls, time of use, and seasonal distribution. The data collected from these billing systems help identify the profitability of products and markets. Also, such segmented data allow carriers to target markets with customized pricing plans.

TIP: Some invoice preparation companies are designing invoices to increase their clients' corporate identity. And by using high-speed spot color printing systems from companies like Accent Color Sciences, invoice preparation companies are increasing their revenues by obtaining advertising from sponsors that place ads or their logos on the invoices.

Billing data can also be used for analysis of past promotional or marketing campaigns or how past competitors' campaigns affected a carrier's existing customer base. Billing systems permit retention analysis for identifying users likely to disconnect their service. These tools make a carrier a better service provider by developing loyalty, which ultimately reduces switching and increases profitability.

Other Investor Attractions

The following are among the additional attractions TBPs offer investors:

- The growing complexity of billing not only persuades more phone providers to outsource, but it allows TBPs such as Convergys to increase their rates.
- The dominant TBPs, such as LHS Group and Saville Systems, are largely insulated from competition by new entrants. Along with high barriers to entry comes prohibitive switching costs. Because the phone companies are reluctant to change their billing providers, TBPs enjoy large recurring revenue streams, and investors benefit from a high degree of revenue visibility.
- Deregulation of the electric and gas utility industries is beginning to open up vast possibilities for TBPs. These industries are beginning to experience the advent of competition, bundling of services, and interindustry mergers in much the same way that telephone providers already have.

Investment Vehicles

The following are among the publicly traded billing service providers: Billing Concepts, Convergys, LHS Group, Saville Systems, and USCS International.

Prepaid Calling Cards

Sales of prepaid calling cards are growing faster than even the International Telecard Association (ITA), the prepaid industry's trade association, projected. The ITA estimates that $2.4 billion worth of prepaid telephone calling cards were sold in 1997, 200 times the $12 million sold in 1992 and more than double the $1 billion level previously estimated. The ITA forecasts that prepaid sales will soar to between $4 billion and $5 billion by 2001. An industry that was nonexistent in the United States at the beginning of the decade now has several monthly trade magazines and has even spawned an annual convention.

Initially introduced in Portugal and Italy in the 1970s as a coinless way of making phone calls, prepaid cards allow users to purchase a fixed amount of phone time before calls are placed. To redeem stored time, users simply dial the access and prompt numbers on the back of the card before dialing the number of the intended party. I believe this nascent industry's growth will maintain its torrential trajectory as prepaid calling cards are popular with every affected constituency— callers, service providers, and retailers and corporate sponsors that sell and distribute them.

TRAP: Even though long-distance carriers such as AT&T, MCI World-com, and Sprint offer their own prepaid calling cards, prepaid calling cards present two serious problems for long-distance carriers. First, many people that have a long-distance carrier place their long-distance calls by way of pre-paid calling cards, thereby circumventing their carriers of record. Second, not only are long-distance carriers losing a significant portion of their high-margin long-distance traffic, but they cannot take any preventive measures aimed at reducing call loss as they cannot determine which of their customers are bypassing their services.

Callers Appreciate Prepaid Cards' Convenience, Limited Costs, and Enhanced Services

Before prepaid calling cards, Americans had to rely on conventional telephone credit cards, pay phones, collect calls, or long-distance cellular services. Each of these methods carries per-call surcharges and often inordinately high rates.

According to Ron Contrado, CEO of Homisco, prepaid calling can be as much as 64¢ less expensive per minute than credit card calling, but the average savings yielded by prepaid services is 15¢ per minute. One reason is that prepaid calls are delivered at a fixed-rate charge per minute regardless of the time of day and, in the case of domestic calls, regardless of the distance of the call.

Prepaid calling cards provide for a single point of access to the telecommunications network and eliminate the need for callers to fumble around for change or memorize credit card numbers. With prepaid cards, callers can leave messages for the recipients, whereas they are unable to do this when placing collect calls. Moreover, prepaid cards are safer than phone company cards because if a prepaid card is lost, a customer only loses the card's face value. However, with a phone company card, a thief can incur unlimited charges using the consumer's PIN number.

The following are among the enhanced services that prepaid calling card providers offer:

- Online recharging allows purchasing additional minutes easily by phone with a credit card when the initial prepaid minutes expire. In some cases, prepaid cards can be recharged through automatic teller machines.
- Conference calls can be facilitated by connecting multiple parties.
- Callers can establish personal speed-dial directories that consist of preprogrammed frequently called numbers that can be activated at the touch of one number.
- Users can arrange to listen to news, weather, and sports by calling into dedicated numbers set aside by prepaid card providers.
- Sequential calling allows users to make additional calls without the need to exit and re-enter the platform.
- Message delivery allows users to leave messages for later delivery for parties who do not answer the phone or whose lines are busy.
- Access to personalized voice and fax mailboxes allows users to receive, retrieve, save, and delete voice mail messages and facsimile transmissions as well as forward faxed information to any facsimile machine or personal computer.
- Multilingual prompting allows users a choice of languages for voice prompts that guide them through the call flow process.
- Whispered reminders interjected during phone conversations—audible only to the user—inform users how much prepaid time remains in their accounts.

Prepayment Appeals to a Wide Array of Demographics

Prepaid cards are witnessing growing demand by people with few alternatives as well as from well-heeled business users. Many low-income residents and immigrants can neither afford wireline installation costs nor have the references necessary to establish accounts with local phone providers. Thus, prepaid cards are a communications solution for the 25 million American households that the pawn shop industry claims do not have checking accounts. Prepaid cards are especially popular with the more than 22 million people in the United States without a home phone and the 38 million American adults without credit cards necessary to place credit card calls.

A growing number of companies (as well as other organizations such as the military) are issuing prepaid cards rather than traditional long-distance calling cards to their employees who travel. Expense managers are finding that these cards add more predictability than allowing employees to submit open-ended expense reports at the end of the month. (For similar reasons, parents buy prepaid cards for their children.) In addition, prepaid cards reduce companies' costly surcharges at hotels and provide an efficient means of tracking communications expenses. As more business executives use prepaid cards, the stigma of prepaid calling recedes.

Wireless Communications Spurs Growth for Prepaid Cards

Prepaid calling is one of the biggest beneficiaries of the intense competition in the wireless phone industry driving the number of American wireless subscribers from 54 million in 1998 to 108 million in 2002. As wireless duopolies in each region have yielded to competition from as many as nine wireless providers, companies have resorted to giving away handsets. Because approximately one-third (or 15 million people) of all applicants for traditional cellular phone service are rejected for credit reasons, a very large number of people given free handsets represent grave credit risks for phone operators. Thus, activating wireless phones on receipt of prepayment is a solution for avoiding invoice collection problems.

Wireless users appreciate being free from long-term contracts and monthly bills. Prepayment is a viable option for wireless users who want to limit their airtime exposure and for parents who want to provide their children the security of a wireless phone but in a way that limits the cost of airtime. While only about 2 percent of America's 54 million wireless subscribers used prepaid service in 1998, Donaldson, Lufkin & Jenrette estimated that prepaid service accounted for 25 percent of all new wireless customers in 1998. The Yankee Group predicts that by 2002, about 20 percent of cell phone users, or 22 million subscribers, could opt for prepaid arrangements. This seems like a reasonable projection since Salomon Smith Barney reported that the number of prepaid callers in Europe was 22 million (or 25 percent of the total European market) in 1998.

TRAP: The absence of paper trails (there are neither contracts nor bills) is making prepaid wireless phone service attractive to criminals and tax evaders. Additional regulations imposed on carriers because of these concerns would represent another cost of doing business.

Prepaid Calling Cards Are a Lucrative Line for Phone Companies

Phone companies earn very attractive margins on their prepaid calling cards because the users are unaware of, or insensitive to, the implied rates they are paying. People purchase a stipulated dollar amount of calling time when they buy prepaid cards, and it is not always clear how many minutes of phone time they can expect. Because of this price insensitivity, phone companies can charge rates that are as much as 27¢ per minute higher to prepaid users than they can charge to traditional billed customers. Many of the users who realize that prepaid service is costing them more money have no alternative because their credit ratings and inability to make deposits disqualify them from receiving regular telephone service.

Prepaid service is virtually essential in emerging markets as the absence of credit bureaus makes it impossible to determine the creditworthiness of applicants, and unreliable mail delivery renders the process of remitting payments on a timely basis impractical. Also, hyperinflation in many developing countries would result in the real value of money collected being notably less than the sums invoiced.

Regardless of whether prepaid service is provided in developed or emerging countries, the following are additional advantages associated with prepaid services that accrue to the carriers:

- An increased customer base at no risk
- A broadened market reach and the ability to capture younger users
- Receipt of payment in advance, which translates into higher predictability of revenues, eliminates billing and collection efforts, improves cash flow, and lowers switching
- Greater use of network capacity because prepaid users generate an average of about 40 calls a month at an average length of 2 minutes, yielding 80 minutes of use per month

- Collection of revenues for minutes that are not redeemed as users who retain prepaid cards past their expiration dates forfeit their remaining minutes (Ron Contrado of Homisco estimates that such breakage represents 5 percent of all prepaid minutes sold, a percentage likely to rise because it is increasingly common for prepaid issuers to set firmer expiration terms.)

Distribution Channels Are Receptive to Prepaid Cards

While retailers appreciate the healthy profit margins associated with selling prepaid calling cards, much of the industry's growth is attributable to businesses and other organizations buying prepaid cards in bulk. These entities buy prepaid telephone calling cards designed with their own products, services, or corporate logos on the front of the cards as giveaways to promote brand recognition or introduce a new product or as a way of rewarding or providing an incentive to their customers. For instance, thousands of companies are using these cards as rewards for responding to surveys, test driving new cars, or opening bank accounts.

Most corporations and organizations that purchase prepaid cards for promotions find that the high perceived value of free phone time resonates with users much more than other giveaways that are quickly discarded. Moreover, prepaid phone cards act as miniature billboards for the distributing organizations in that customers see the organizations' logos and printed messages before they dial. Prepaid cards that double as business cards, key chains, or luggage tags are especially effective in reinforcing such images. (In fact, prepaid cards have become so popular, and promotions so individualized, that many people collect and trade them in much the same way that children trade baseball cards.) A further impression is made on users when they hear prerecorded audio messages before they dial a number.

Businesses, charities, and trade associations are attracted to the ability to generate and manage valuable databases by using prepaid cards. By determining which area codes and recipients the dialers called, these organizations can build more robust customer profiles. Further, prepaid sponsors can track and reward specific favorable customer behavior by reverse-matching the customer to the personal identification number associated with his card.

Investment Opportunities and Risks

Investors can participate in the burgeoning prepaid calling-card industry through two vehicles. First, they can invest in companies that supply the actual prepaid calling cards to retailers and promoters. These companies include PICK Communications, SmarTalk Teleservices, and SecurFone America. Second, investors can gain exposure to the industry through companies that manufacture the telecommunications systems that make prepaid calling possible. The leading publicly traded companies in this area include Brite Voice Communications, Boston Communications Group, and Comverse Technology.

Nevertheless, investors should be aware of the potential for greater scrutiny over the prepaid industry that could lead to heightened regulation. First, regulators are aware of the ease with which fraud can be visited on the industry. All a fraudulent operator has to do is sell a piece of plastic with the promise (but without actually having access to the telecommunications infrastructure) to process calls. In view of these concerns, the Florida Public Service Commission, which has long required card issuers to be certified, has held hearings at which its staff has recommended an aggressive consumer education program and fines of no less than $1,000 for renegade companies operating without certification. That staff has also recommended that the commission urge underlying long-distance carriers to obtain payment in advance from prepaid card companies in order to avoid billing disputes and ultimately card shutoffs.

Second, Congress is concerned that few carriers are paying a 3 percent excise tax on prepaid calls delivered to their networks as was mandated by a revision in the Internal Revenue Code in 1997. Greater enforcement efforts in this area would result in the carriers passing their higher costs onto the prepaid card providers. Similarly, several states, such as Texas and Wisconsin, and over 150 cities in California have already imposed their own point-of-sale taxes on the industry.

Telephone Headsets

The $500 million market for telephone headsets is ripe for aggressive growth. The proliferation of wireless telecommunications and the rapidly declining costs of placing calls throughout the world is resulting in people spending much more time talking on the phone. Telephone headsets are achieving heightened popularity because these devices allow their users greater comfort and efficiency. Also, the rising wave of legislation prohibiting automobile drivers from using cellular phones without headsets will prove to be a boon to headset manufacturers such as Plantronics.

Market Opportunities

While everyone who uses a telephone could benefit from telephone headsets, people whose jobs revolve around placing or receiving calls are the biggest users of headsets. It is standard procedure for call center agents—such as telemarketing personnel, reservation agents, telephone operators, and air traffic controllers—to use headsets. According to *Call Center* magazine, there were approximately 100,000 call centers in the United States in 1997; and Herb Tinger, senior vice president at FAC/Equities, estimates that additional call-center seats are being added at a rate of 15 to 20 percent annually. This estimate is corroborated by the approximately 134 billion minutes of 800/888 phone traffic in 1997 growing 15 percent a year.

TIP: Telephone headset makers are not the only beneficiaries of call center growth. Manufacturers of hardware and software that run call centers, such as GeoTel Communications and Aspect Telecommunications, are beneficiaries of call center growth as well.

Call centers will remain a steady driver of telephone headset sales because call centers are becoming an increasingly preferred form of direct marketing as a result of steadily declining telecommunications costs—whereas postage costs for direct mailers have been consistently rising. Call centers are growing as deregulation in the telecommunications and electric utilities industries unleashes fierce competition for customers. The proliferation of technology is creating mass confusion as evidenced by the computer industry's receiving at least 200 million customer calls each year. The 20 billion catalogs mailed by direct marketers each year keep call center phones ringing. Not only are headset manufacturers prospering from the growth in call centers, but the heavy utilization of headsets within call centers results in headset companies receiving 30 to 40 percent of their call center revenues from replacement sales, which represent a substantial annuity.

TIP: In addition to headsets, investors can gain exposure to the growth in call centers by purchasing shares of publicly traded telemarketers such as Sitel, APAC TeleServices, and West TeleServices.

The market for intensive phone users is much larger and much less penetrated than the call center market. Although U.S. call centers have 4 million agents, some 40 million corporate employees—business executives, insurance and real estate agents, stockbrokers, lawyers, accountants, and home office businesspeople—use their phones at least three hours a day. Because the vast majority of these office workers use computers, they find it cumbersome to hold a handset while talking and typing.

As Americans are increasingly pressured to engage in multitasking, they will turn to telephone headsets that allow them to carry on phone conversations while taking notes, using a calculator, or performing other tasks. Headsets also provide users the mobility to walk around their offices, allowing them to locate files, retrieve printouts, or make photocopies. Even though speaker phones offer similar mobility, they are not as well suited for business use because the other party feels they are not receiving full attention.

TIP: Another way to play the growing importance of call centers is to invest in companies that consult the centers—that is, monitor the effectiveness of agents and recommend better methods of handling calls. The leading company here is ASI Solutions.

The retail market is another large source of opportunity for such manufacturers of headsets as GN Netcom. First, in 1998 about 30 percent of American homes contained offices and *Barron's* reported that that percentage would rise to the 50 percent level by 2001. As home office users purchase headsets for their businesses, they are likely to use the headsets in other parts of their home. Second, as retail consumers have already largely adopted cordless phones, headsets that allow greater comfort along with movement should be a natural progression.

Further, in the next several years millions of pedestrians could replace their handheld phones with hands-free headsets. It is simply unwieldy to walk while talking on a phone, especially while carrying packages or navigating through crowded city streets. Pedestrian use of headsets should be facilitated by mobile phones incorporating headset ports. Although about 40 percent of the 200 million mobile telephones sold in 1998 incorporated headset ports, the industry is nearly unanimous in believing that these ports will soon be a standard feature in wireless handsets.

Headsets Yield Users Greater Productivity and Comfort

Adding hands-free headsets to conventional office telephones substantially improves productivity and overall call volume while reducing phone-related employee downtime and physical discomfort. The following are results from a late 1990s study on headset use conducted by H. B. Maynard & Co.:

- Workers equipped with headsets had an overall productivity increase of up to 43 percent over the control group, and time spent on telephone-related work activities was reduced substantially.

- Repeat calls were made without interruption, and ordinarily time-intensive tasks (such as typing or checking reference materials while on the phone) were performed far more quickly and efficiently with headsets.
- Not only was a reduced error rate and improved service record noted, but workers on the phone full-time with headsets placed an average of 16 more calls a day than those using traditional handsets.
- Perhaps most telling of all, workers equipped with headsets reported higher morale, lower fatigue levels, and fewer phone-related physical complaints.

Telephone headsets are ergonomically correct. Using a headset prevents spinal damage, which occurs when one holds a conventional receiver with his or her face. According to Susan Duckworth Handy, a physical therapist, "Unlike corded headsets, cordless versions allow users to get up from their chairs and move around, which helps relieve stress on the spine."* Also, results from a study conducted at Santa Clara Valley Medical Center in San Jose, California, revealed that headset users experience 35 percent less muscle tension than handset users.

Telephone Headsets Reduce Drivers' Distractions

Although the chapter on highway safety more fully discusses the growing dangers of driving, wireless telecommunications are certainly a major contributor to driver distraction. A study released in 1997 by the *New England Journal of Medicine* found that drivers are four times as likely to get into an accident if they use a cellular phone in the car. A survey by *Prevention* magazine indicated that 18 percent of respondents believed that their use of cellular telephones was distracting while they were driving. Also, the National Highway Traffic Safety Administration (NTSA) has stated that people driving a car while using a cellular phone are as dangerous as drunken drivers.

Talking on handheld cellular phones while driving is both a potentially deadly combination and a pervasive problem; there were some 50 million cellular phones on the road nationwide in the late 1990s, and this number was projected to reach 80 million by 2000. More than 85 percent of cellular telephone owners use their phones at least occasionally while driving and more than 27 percent use their phones during half or more of their trips.

As a result of concerns about driving safety, legislators throughout the world are promulgating laws that prohibit drivers from using handheld electronic

---

*Laura Lipton, "Working Without Using Your Hands," *The Wall Street Journal,* Dec. 11, 1998, p. W13C.

devices. Countries that have banned people from using handheld cellular phones while driving include the United Kingdom, Germany, Switzerland, Italy, Brazil, Israel, Portugal, Chile, and Australia. Also, local authorities in foreign cities such as Mexico City have enacted hands-free driving requirements.

Many U.S. state legislators are in favor of restricting drivers' use of handheld cellular phones. For instance, Massachusetts state regulators sponsored a bill that would require drivers to keep one hand on the steering wheel while on the phone. In the late 1990s, lawmakers in Hawaii weighed a measure that would ban drivers from using cell phones as well as laptop computers and portable fax machines. Even technology-friendly California has deliberated about such measures as a bill State Senator John Burton introduced would require people with handheld phones to pull over to the side of the road if they want to talk. An interesting parallel is that Ohio legislators passed a law that would make it illegal to talk on a handheld mobile phone while hunting.

Headsets will increasingly be seen as a solution for benefiting from the convenience that wireless telecommunications allow as well as for remaining compliant with applicable motor vehicle laws. In fact, the motor vehicle code in Washington State was amended to allow the use of headsets in association with wireless communications systems.

Additional Drivers for the Growing Popularity of Headsets

Sales of telephone headsets will remain brisk as their traditional markets remain underpenetrated and as new markets unfold. According to S. Kenneth Kannappan, president and chief operating officer of Plantronics, the percentage of headsets used with handsets was less than 1 percent in 1998. And, research by Utendahl Capital Partners indicates that only about 5 percent of the 40 million American office workers that use their phones for at least three hours a day use headsets, whereas the penetration ratio for a similar number of workers in international markets is only 1 percent.

The proliferation of several technologies is likely to ignite the growth of telephone headsets. For instance:

- Voice recognition technology from companies like Lernout & Hauspie is allowing computer users to dictate (instead of type) into word processing programs. (See Chapter 12, "Voice Recognition.") Soon people will be dictating e-mails as well as instructing their Internet browsers to embark on searches. Of particular appeal is that voice recognition will make it possible for users to give commands by remote control to their computers from conference rooms or their living rooms. Headsets are important in these applications as they filter out extraneous noise.

- People who engage in Internet phone calls through their computers typically do so through headsets. Frost & Sullivan estimated that Internet telephony should account for 12.5 billion minutes of talk time in 2001, and Probe Research's analysis holds that 25 percent of all of the world's phone calls will likely be via the Internet by 2010.
- As companies like VTEL move videoconferencing to desktop computers, people are inclined to use headsets to communicate over these systems to avoid shouting into microphones.
- Headsets are a solution for people who would like to use wireless telephones but are fearful of the possibility that these phones contribute to brain cancer.

Headset Manufacturers

The dominant headset manufacturer is Plantronics followed by GN Netcom. Andrea Electronics is an aggressive player in manufacturing microphones, headsets, and handsets that are incorporated into speech recognition software. Other headset manufacturers include Motorola, Nokia, Ericsson, Sony, and NEC. Also, Hello Direct is one of the retailers with significant exposure to headsets.

CHAPTER 12

Miscellaneous Hot Sectors

In writing this book I simply tried to address the most promising industry developments occurring in the real world. However, not everything in the real world can be neatly categorized under industry headings. There are always some solid trends that lie outside of more traditional parameters. That is why I decided to discuss outdoor billboard operators who stand to benefit from technological improvements, highway congestion, and minimal competition. Also, Americans' obsession with their pets spells massive profit opportunities for pet retailers and pet health care players. Finally, companies that present solutions for quality-of-living challenges posed by noise pollution and electronic interference should be sources of exciting investment.

Outdoor Billboards

Investors should search for industries that face growing demand, especially from a captive customer base that cannot avoid patronizing the industry under review. One industry that fits this bill perfectly is the outdoor billboard advertising business.

Traffic on our nation's highways continues to coagulate. For the past two decades, the number of vehicle trips increased four times faster than the U.S. population. Passenger miles per person increased from 11,400 miles in 1970 to 17,200 miles in 1995. In terms of absolute miles traveled, the rise in automobile use overshadowed all other modes of travel, growing by over 1 trillion passenger miles during this period. The distance traveled by the average car or light truck in the United States each year equals a journey halfway around the earth. Despite this growth in travel, highway construction has increased only about 1 percent a year.

Not only are more people driving past billboards, but outdoor billboard companies provide the last captive mass audience for advertisers—it is the one medium in which viewers have no control over what they see. Unlike television viewers, motorists cannot turn the channel; unlike magazine readers, passengers cannot turn the page. Moreover, increasingly common traffic jams on the nation's highways are literally capturing viewers for billboard advertisers.

TRAP: Some analysts have opined that investors should take positions in radio station companies because longer commuting time will translate into more listening time and therefore higher advertising rates. However, radio operators have three distinct disadvantages vis-à-vis billboard operators. First, a radio station's listeners can be lost as easily as a dial can be turned. Second, billboard companies experience none of the programming headaches with which radio stations must constantly contend.

Third, competition from satellite radio providers will present a serious challenge to traditional radio station companies. Satellite radio companies such as CD Radio and American Mobile Radio are building 50-channel subscription radio systems that will deliver 30 channels of CD-quality music programming and 20 channels of talk, news, and sports directly to motorists that subscribe to their services. Satellite radio subscribers will be able to listen to their selection of these commercial-free channels while traveling anywhere in the continental United States.

Billboards Attract More Advertisers

Throughout the late 1990s, billboard advertising generated about $2 billion in annual revenue and received 2 percent of all advertising dollars. The Outdoor Advertising Association of America (OAAA) estimated that spending on billboard advertising would grow at a double-digit rate in 1998, up from a 9 percent gain in 1997. Some industry authorities believe that greater acceptance of billboard advertising will result in this segment receiving 3 percent of total advertising revenues, or a 50 percent increase in market share.

Small advertisers have long appreciated the fact that, unlike other media, billboard advertising is usually located very close to the point of purchase. The proximity and repetition that billboards offer allows for highly effective advertising campaigns. Consolidation now makes it possible for large advertisers to take advantage of the same benefits. According to the OAAA, 80 percent of the outdoor advertising sites in the United States in mid-1998 were concentrated in the hands of half a dozen companies. Instead of advertisers trying to launch a coordinated marketing campaign with dozens of billboard operators, industry consolidators such as Outdoor Systems, Clear Channel Communications, and Lamar Advertising now offer one-stop shopping for regional or nationwide billboard campaigns.

Billboards' enhanced features are attracting a more diversified customer base. Owners have transformed their flat, one-dimensional billboards into three-dimensional advertisements enhanced by fiber optics and neon effects. The Walt Disney Company, for example, promoted the release of the movie *Armageddon* by creating the illusion of a meteor striking a downtown Los Angeles building. The appearance of a sky blue hole in the middle of the building proved so captivating that traffic officials prevailed on Disney to remove its outdoor display for fear of causing accidents. In 1998, Dayton Hudson Corporation advertised a Valentine's Day candy on billboards that wafted a mint scent for blocks in downtown Minneapolis.*

Computer painting—in the forms of ink-jet, electrostatic, and digital airbrushing—is proving to be much more appealing than physically painting the signs. In addition, computer painting on vinyl allows for greater consistency in the blends of colors used, because computers make identical prints whereas manually blended paints inevitably result in some variation. Consistency is imperative for advertisers like apparel designers who obsess over every aspect of the visual presentation of their advertisements.

Not only does computer printing on vinyl make billboards look better, but the speed of vinyl application on billboards allows advertisers to change boards more frequently with less cost. Vinyl can be applied in less than an hour by inexpensive and unskilled workers, whereas painting requires hours of work by expensive, skilled professionals. The faster response times vinyl offers allow billboard operators to serve new industries, such as movie studios that need to advertise their products precisely two weeks before their release. The use of vinyl is also improving billboard occupancy rates as installation requires less downtime. Furthermore, advances in the durability and weatherability of inks and vinyl substrates prevent billboard images from fading for a longer time than is the case with painted wood or steel panels.

Billboard Ad Rates Are Positioned to Rise

Billboard advertising revenues will rise with higher ad rates that result from greater demand for outdoor advertising, the relative low cost of billboard impressions and consolidation within the industry reducing the incidence of discounted advertising rates. Because billboard advertising is relatively inexpensive, billboard companies like Obie Media and Bowlin have leeway to raise prices. As of early 1998, billboards imparted their impressions at a cost-per-thousand rate (a

---

*Ronald Grover, "Billboards Aren't Boring Anymore," *Business Week*, Sept. 21, 1988, p. 86.

term for the cost of reaching 1,000 people) that was just one-third of the cost of advertising on radio (the next cheapest medium) and less than one-eighth the cost of airing a commercial on prime-time television.

Billboard companies should be able to close the ad rate disparity as they are favorably positioned with their captive audiences, which is especially appealing to advertisers in light of the challenges besetting competing media. Newspaper readership is aging and declining as only 64 percent of the adult population reads newspapers on weekdays, down from 77.6 percent in 1970. Radio prices are rising due to consolidation in that industry resulting from the liberalization of ownership limitations. Traditional broadcast network television has been losing market share over the past 10 years as television viewing continues to fragment and lose share to the Internet. The average number of available television channels is in excess of 50 compared to only nine in 1980. Also, a survey by A. C. Nielsen revealed that America Online's 17 million subscribers (in early 1999 and growing at the rate of 8,200 a day) watch 15 percent less television.

Other attractions that outdoor billboard companies offer investors are discussed below.

A marked decrease in tobacco advertising on billboards has occurred. The OAAA reports that advertisements for tobacco products accounted for roughly 40 percent of outdoor advertising revenues in the late 1980s but that percentage fell to the single digits by the late 1990s. Several billboard companies have expressed relief that regulations are restricting tobacco advertising on billboards, not only because of reduced liability risks, but also because replacing tobacco ads allows operators to lease their billboards to new advertisers at higher rates.

Billboard advertising is not technology intensive. Operating outdoor billboards is relatively easy—there are no capital expenditures, no investments in research and development, and no risk of technological obsolescence. Rather than being threatened by technology, billboard operators benefit from technology. For instance, satellite lighting systems allow outdoor companies to adjust, by remote control, billboard lighting to change with seasons and daily light variances. These lights can also be programmed to turn off at the end of an advertiser's contract, and two-way communication informs outdoor companies when power outages occur or when fluorescent bulbs for backlighting need to be replaced.

Another electronic device—barcode identification—tracks an advertiser's campaign from poster production through shipping, display, and removal. In this way, advertisers can verify the status of their campaign through online communication with the outdoor companies. Also, computer-mapping systems help advertisers combine demographic and geographic market research data with outdoor locations to determine optimal advertising locations.

Looking further into the future, Harry Blount of CIBC Oppenheimer has noted that billboards are eventually going to become digital and that operators will be able to change electronic advertisements by remote control. With global positioning of satellite navigation systems, messages will be customized in accordance with oncoming traffic. For instance, when a bus carrying a high school football team approaches, the screen may flash advertisements from a nearby pizza restaurant.

Billboard operators also benefit indirectly from technological advances when they charge cellular phone companies rent to place their equipment on billboard structures. The growing number of moratoria on cellular tower construction is actually a boon for billboard operators as at least 170 communities in mid-1998 restricted the installation of wireless telephone stations.

Restrictive zoning laws make it difficult to erect new billboards. President Lyndon B. Johnson signed the Highway Beautification Act of 1965 (HBA) into law in October 1965. This watershed legislation continues to allow the federal government to impose strict limits on the number of outdoor billboards along 306,000 miles of interstate and National Highway System roads. Although states and localities may enforce stricter ordinances than those dictated by the HBA, states not complying with the provisions of the HBA are subject to a 10 percent reduction in their federal highway allocations. The combination of rising demand for outdoor advertising and the stagnant supply of billboards allows billboard operators to raise their rates.

The outdoor billboard industry typically enjoys long-term contracts with its clients. These contracts provide investors with good revenue visibility because contracts are sold well in advance and often are in force for one year with options to renew.

Pet Care

The old adage about dogs being a man's best friend may be an understatement today. Millions of Americans have replaced their ties to family, religious institutions, and social groups with slavish devotion to their pets.

America's obsession with pets is as widespread as it is intense. Roughly 58 million households, or 58.9 percent of all U.S. households, own at least one pet, and 40 percent of these households own more than one type of pet. The United

Nations' 1998 Human Development Report calculated that Americans and Europeans spend $17 billion a year on pet food—$4 billion more than the estimated annual additional total needed to provide basic health and nutrition for everyone in the world. In America alone, pet owners lavish $3 billion worth of other pet products on the 57 million dogs and 70 million cats they own. Pet owners' deep attachment to their pets is resulting in a growth of expenditures on pet care and pet supplies of about 20 percent a year.

Demand for pet products and veterinary care should continue to rise at a steady rate because the popularity of pets is based on the following solid demographic underpinnings. Pets have always been popular with young children, partly because parents believe that caring for pets instills a sense of responsibility in their children. Working parents have a propensity to provide pets to their latch-key children (see Chapter 1 for statistics showing the growth of households with children).

The growing number of single people are inclined to rely on pets for docile companionship. U.S. Census Bureau data indicate that the number of women living alone has doubled during the past 20 years to 15 million, and the number of solitary men has tripled to 10.3 million. Also, the percentage of women from 50 to 54 who remarried after divorce from their first husbands fell to 63 percent in 1990 from 74 percent in 1995. Pets are patient, nonjudgmental listeners who never talk back and who keep all secrets. Pets actually help their owners become more socially integrated because it is easier to strike up a conversation with a stranger while walking a dog than walking alone.

Pets are especially important companions for the aging populations in the United States, Europe, and Japan as they are conducive to seniors maintaining their cognitive and physiological faculties (see Chapter 8, "Assisted Living Facilities"). The Delta Society reports that 84 percent of senior dog owners tell their dogs about their problems; 73 percent relate everyday experiences to their canine companions; and 49 percent read aloud from newspapers and magazines. A study conducted in the late 1990s of 938 Medicare enrollees found that dog owners make fewer visits to the doctor and have fewer health complaints than non–dog owners. In another study, animal-assisted therapy programs attracted the highest voluntary attendance of inpatients for occupational therapy. On a similar note, you may have noticed that people with even the worst stammering problem never stutter when speaking to their animals.

Wealthier households evidence a higher incidence of pet ownership. Only 55.6 percent of households with incomes between $12,500 and $24,999 own pets, whereas 64.6 percent of households with incomes above $60,000 own pets.

Owners' Attachment to Their Pets Knows No Bounds

One of the primary reasons Americans are now more attached to their animals than ever before is due to increased proximity. In the earlier agrarian economy, animals were filed away in chicken coops and barns—far from their owner's living quarters. Ranchers, farmers, and crop growers regarded animals as nothing more than income-producing machinery. Throughout the ensuing decades, as animals moved closer to the home, the owner-pet relationship became more intimate. As families moved from farms to cities, their animals relocated from barns to backyards. As people began relying on their animals for companionship—jogging mates, for example—and began moving into apartments without yards, pets migrated into their master's home. Now, many pets and their owners sleep side-by-side. This physical intimacy is complemented by owners' attaching an elevated sense of importance to their pets. According to a report by the American Animal Hospital Association:

- 70 percent of pet owners surveyed thought of their pets as children.
- When asked what one companion they would want on a desert island, 53 percent listed a dog or cat.
- Nearly one-half of female pet owners said they rely more on their pet than a spouse or child for affection.
- Nearly two-thirds of dog owners have traveled with their pets—a growing trend facilitated by the more than 23,000 lodgings that accept such guests.
- 27 percent of pet owners have taken their pet to a photographer for inclusion in the family portrait.
- More than 60 percent of pet owners include news about their pets in their holiday greeting cards.

This fealty toward animals throughout so much of American society has resulted in animals' lives being valued more than human life. In some states, animal abuse laws are as harsh as those for drive-by shootings and domestic assault. In mid-1998, 22 states treated animal abuse as a felony and 11 more states were considering raising such offenses to a felony, up from 5 states that classified such behavior as a felony in 1986.

The Pet Industry Joint Advisory Council reported that owners spent $41.7 million on dog toys sold in pet stores in 1997. Owners are paying $59.95 for pet canopy beds, and Melia Luxury Pet Products makes six flavors of tennis balls for dogs, ranging from zesty orange to peanut butter and jelly. At least one upscale New York pet retailer sells $90 Chanel sweaters and $95 custom-made harness-and-leash sets. Grooming at Doggie-Do and Pussycats, Too! costs as much as $250 and requires an entire month's notice to book an appointment.

Traditional services such as grooming and canine day care centers, and less traditional services, such as limousine services exclusively for dogs, pump an estimated $500 million a year into the New York City economy alone. Some of these canine daycare centers are in such demand that their waiting lists are more than one year long and pet owners try to advance in the queue by insisting on their pooch's ability to get along with other dogs. Not all pet owners are this eccentric, but pet supply stores like PETsMART and PETCO Animal Supplies, and their suppliers such as Ralston Purina Group and InnoPet Brands Corporation, are clearly positioned to benefit from the largesse that Americans are all too eager to shower on their pets.

Veterinarians Are Becoming the Medical Providers' Cat's Meow

Although pet owners lavish money on pet supplies, they are even more willing to go to any extent necessary to maintain the health of their pets—a boon to veterinarians, who now see their patients more frequently than people visit their doctors. In fact, between 1983 and 1996, the number of visits per household for dogs increased 3.7 percent a year and 7.9 percent a year for cats. This surge in demand is allowing veterinarians to increase their rates for office visits. The average cost for a veterinarian visit for cats rose from $44.81 in 1991 to $66.58 in 1996, increasing at an 8.2 percent compounded annual rate. For dogs, the price for veterinarian visits rose from $49.96 to $73.60, an 8.1 percent compounded annual rate. By way of comparison, inflation grew just 2.9 percent over the same period.

Veterinarians perform most human medical procedures on animals, with common procedures including chemotherapy, artificial hip replacement, and open heart surgery. Veterinarians provide kidney dialysis for cats and prescribe Prozac and Valium for pets that suffer from such psychological problems as separation anxiety.

Veterinarians are able to increase their fees by extending their range of services to include a host of specialties and alternative therapies. While there were no specialties recognized by the American Veterinary Medical Association until 1951, as of the beginning of 1998, there were 20 board-certified specialties; and the number of veterinarians who had additional schooling and taken examinations to become certified has grown from 2,700 in 1984 to more than 5,600. The infrastructure is firmly in place for the trend to specialize to continue. For instance, the University of California at Davis is renowned for animal kidney care, Michigan State University's Veterinary Teaching Hospital is recognized for open heart surgery, and Colorado State University's Veterinary Teaching Hospital is highly regarded for animal bone cancer treatment. Also, the American Veterinary Dental College teaches all aspects of veterinary dentistry, including placing crowns, orthodontics, endodontics, and periodontics.

Alternative animal practices have been available for several years; their procedures range from acupuncture to chiropractics, and from homeopathy and nutritional therapy to botanical medicine. These therapies are used to treat everything from arthritis and skin problems to gastrointestinal ailments, hernias, and behavioral disorders. As veterinarians have increasingly realized that these specialties are a way to supplement their income, membership in the American Holistic Veterinary Medical Association soared from 30 in 1982 to 700 members in mid-1998.

Expenditures on veterinary care rose at a 9.5 percent annual growth rate to total more than $12.5 billion in 1997, up from $7.3 billion in 1991. I believe these expenditures will continue to rise rapidly as better veterinary care is resulting in longer lifespans for animals, which in turn generates more demand for medical attention. Pet insurance, already a $100 million a year industry in the United Kingdom, is emerging as a source of funding for animal medical treatments in the United States. RewardsPlus of America reported in 1998 that pet insurance from the likes of the Veterinary Pet Insurance Company is the second most popular benefit bought by employees who are offered supplemental benefit plans. And the growing array of specialty and alternative therapies is testimony that owners will do virtually anything necessary to increase the longevity of their pets, since most of these nontraditional regimens are resorted to only after more conventional methods have been exhausted.

Television programs, such as the cable show called *Emergency Vets* that is broadcast five days a week, increase awareness of pet care. Unlike physicians, veterinarians are neither exposed to government reimbursement risks nor to limitations that managed care imposes on the array of services that physicians may offer. Companies such as Veterinary Centers of America are perfectly positioned to prosper from these developments.

Animal Medications Are Lucrative

Compared to developing pharmaceuticals for humans, the costs and time associated with bringing medication to market for animals are infinitesimal. It takes roughly $5.5 million to develop new drugs for animals, whereas the General Accounting Office estimates that it costs an average of $360 million and takes some 12 years to bring a pharmaceutical for human consumption to market. Animal vaccines take approximately 4 years and $1 million to develop, and point-of-care diagnostics can be developed and approved in about 2 years and under $500,000.

The main reason for such disparity is that human medicine is first tested on animals and then, if believed to be safe, tested on humans. However, veterinary medicines are only required to be effective for animals and do not require human testing, which is the most time-consuming and expensive element of human drug development. Another important distinguishing point is that, unlike human pharmaceuticals, approval of animal drugs does not require demonstrating benefits over existing therapies.

Companies like Heska Corporation and Symbiotics are pure plays in animal pharmaceuticals, but units of Merck & Co. and Pfizer are also committed to developing medicine for animals. Diagnostic companies such as IDEXX Laboratories play a critical role in treating animals given the limited ability of animals to articulate their health history to an attending veterinarian.

Photovoltaics

The sun's power is increasingly being harnessed to electrify economic activity throughout the world. The conversion of sunlight into electricity is called photovoltaics and is often referred to as PV. Electricity producers are attracted to photovoltaic systems for their low construction costs and absence of related regulatory oversight, while users enjoy minimal maintenance requirements and high reliability associated with PV. Environmentalists favor photovoltaics over fossil fuels because sunlight is both infinite and pollution-free. Many energy-deficient governments are encouraging the use of photovoltaics because there are no adverse balance-of-trade ramifications as is the case with imported oil.

As a result of support from all of the affected constituencies, it is no surprise that more than 1 billion handheld calculators, several million watches, and millions of portable lights and battery chargers are already powered by PV cells. The late 1990s marked the emergence of photovoltaics to provide homes, cars, telephones, and computers with inexpensive and reliable power. The dawn of the next millennium will usher in the photovoltaic era by powering the Athletes Village at the 2000 Olympic Games in Sydney.

How Sunlight Is Converted into Electricity

Photovoltaic systems are semiconductor devices that convert sunlight directly into electricity. In fact, the term *photo* stems from the Greek word *phos,* which means light, while *volt* is named for Alessandro Volta (1745–1827), a pioneer in the study of electricity. Accordingly, photovoltaics literally means "light-electricity."

The direct conversion of light into electricity is accomplished by means of a solid-state device called the photovoltaic cell. Sunlight is composed of infinitesimally small packets of radiant energy called photons. When photons strike a photovoltaic cell, some packets are absorbed by the PV cell, which sparks the generation of electricity. The energy of a photon is transferred to an electron in an atom of the semiconductor device. When electrical contacts are attached to the semiconductor layers and the circuit is completed, an electrical current flows. To protect the circuits from weather and the environment, cells are linked together and encapsulated in modules, which are used in various applications.

These modules are typically incorporated into solar electric power systems. Such systems may include some form of energy storage for systems that require nighttime operation, such as a battery, as well as associated control equipment to measure the power output and convert electrical direct current (DC) into electrical alternating current (AC) required to operate electrical devices.

Industry Growth

According to PV Energy Systems, over the 18-year period since 1980, PV industry shipment volumes (in terms of megawatts) have grown at a compound annual rate of approximately 22 percent, and industry revenues for solar electric power are estimated to have been $1.8 billion in 1997. Despite such dramatic growth, the contribution that all of these PV solar cells have made toward meeting the world's growing demand for electricity has been only a minuscule fraction of its potential. Although enough sunlight falls on the earth's surface each minute to meet world energy demand for an entire year, the total world output of PV solar cells from 1980 to 1998 was equal to just 10.3 minutes of U.S. electric utility generation during 1996. While still not nearly reaching its full potential, PV shipment volumes are predicted to grow by 24 percent annually through 2005.

Investments in PV are being spurred partly by tax incentives. For instance, the Energy Policy Act of 1992 allows investors in, or purchasers of, qualified solar energy property to take an energy investment tax credit on up to 10 percent of their investment or purchase price and installment amounts. Section 1212 of the same act applies an electricity production incentive of 1.5¢ per kilowatt hour for solar energy generation sold by municipal electric utilities, rural cooperative utilities, and other public agencies. In the late 1990s, Vice President Al Gore proposed a tax credit equal to 15 percent of the cost of a rooftop solar system—up to $1,000 for water-heating systems and up to $2,000 for photovoltaic panels. This tax credit would apply to systems put in service starting in 1999 and would extend through 2003 for water-heating systems and 2005 for photovoltaics.

As of the late 1990s, approximately 35 states had official policies encouraging the development of solar energy and provided financial incentives for investment in the use of solar thermal collectors and photovoltaic modules and cells. Among the most common incentives were property tax exemptions and income tax credits for both the residential and business sectors. Also, states such as Arizona have a sales tax exemption for purchases of solar goods.

Attractions of Photovoltaics

The following are among the advantages associated with photovoltaic-generated power:

High reliability. PV systems are highly reliable as they are built to last as long as 20 years and are essentially maintenance-free. Interestingly, PV cells were originally developed for use in space shuttles, where the costs and logistics of repair are prohibitive. Today, nearly every satellite circling the earth is powered by photovoltaics.

Durability. PV systems are manufactured to withstand the most rugged conditions. Modules are designed to endure extreme temperatures, any elevation, high wind, and any degree of moisture or salt in the atmosphere.

Minimal operating costs. Because sunlight fuels PV cells, there are no fuel costs. The lack of moving parts in PV systems reduces associated maintenance requirements.

Environmental benefits. PV systems are clean because they neither burn fuel nor create pollutants, and they are silent because they have no moving parts. In comparison, mining coal with explosives sets off deafening blasts and burning coal emits sulfur, nitrous oxides, and carbon dioxide. PV-generated electricity presents neither balance-of-trade deficits nor the risk of oil spills, as does imported oil. Users of PV energy are not at risk for explosions as is everyone in proximity to natural gas pipelines. Unlike fossil fuels, PV is unaffected by inflationary pressures, and no nuclear waste issues are associated with electricity derived from the sun. Finally, by reducing the amount of fossil fuels burned, the use of PV can alleviate global warming. In a speech to the United Nations Special Session on Environment and Development, President Clinton said: "By capturing the sun's warmth, we can help turn down the earth's temperature."

Americans have consistently shown that they support the development of renewable energy sources and are appreciative of the environmentally friendly nature of PV. According to results of a poll by Research Strategy Management, more than 70 percent of Americans recognize global warming or climate change as a threat and more than three-quarters of the American population want to do something about U.S. dependency on foreign oil. Three out of four people surveyed indicated a willingness to pay more for electricity generated from renewable sources.

Other polling has revealed that 82 percent of Detroit Edison's customers believe that renewable energy options should be considered before any other technology for new electric generating capacity, and 89 percent of Hawaii Electric Light Company customers thought that that utility should offer solar electric service rather than line extensions. PV Pioneers, a group of homeowners in Sacramento, backed their preference for naturally derived electricity with their own money. These homeowners provided roof area for solar panels and agreed to pay a 15 percent surcharge on their electric bill for the "satisfaction of generating clean, renewable energy." This initiative was so popular that a waiting list resulted from the more than 700 customers volunteering for the first 100 PV systems.

TRAP: The only noteworthy drawbacks of PV power are that many cells contain potentially harmful substances—such as arsenic and cadmium—that may be hazardous to handle during production. These substances may also be a hazard to firemen should a PV cell catch fire.

Modularity. PV systems can be built in whatever size is believed best suited to meet the application's desired energy requirements. For instance, homeowners can add solar modules as their finances permit. Also, PV systems are lightweight and can be easily relocated as evidenced by disaster agencies' common practice of bringing solar panels to hurricane sites.

Low construction costs. Because PV systems are typically placed in close proximity to where electricity is consumed, much shorter power lines are required than if such power was brought in from the electric utility grid. Less wiring translates into lower costs, reduced construction time, and fewer regulatory burdens.

Photovoltaics Have a Wide Range of Applications

The simplest PV systems—those that power small calculators, for example—have long been part of the developed world's landscape. More sophisticated permutations of solar-powered electricity generation are used as alternative sources of power where electric utility grids are not available. Solar power is now being used to provide electricity to remote villages in developing countries and to generate the electricity needed to power secluded vacation homes of the wealthy. Solar electric power is also used by electric utilities as an alternative to burning fossil fuels. Other critical applications of solar power are found in pumping water, communications switching, and rural electrification.

Photovoltaic Electricity Is a Boon to the Telecommunications Industry

Telecommunications providers require electricity—which can be generated from photovoltaics—to power both their fiber-optic systems and the repeater stations necessary for relaying cellular, personal communications services, and radio signals. Direct broadcast satellite networks also need ground-based power. Customer convenience, plummeting per minute usage costs, and subsidized handset prices have driven the tremendous growth these businesses have experienced in the developed world.

Wireless telephone subscribers are projected to grow from 58 million in 1998 to 108 million in 2002 in the United States, a country in which at least 94 percent of the population has reliable landline telephone service. However, the economics of wireless communications are even more compelling in the developing world. With little or no existing landline phone service, developing nations are designing their phone systems from a clean sheet of paper. These countries, which collectively represent the 50 percent of the world's population that had yet to make its first phone call by 1998, can either deploy landlines or wireless telephone service. The choice is obvious, because it is dramatically easier, more expedient, and less costly to establish wireless towers, antennas, and repeater stations sporadically within a nation's borders than it is to lay telephone wires through deserts, jungles, swamps, lakes, lagoons, minefields, and the like.

Transportation infrastructure is another business segment for which PV solar cells are well suited. Emergency call boxes, highway hazard signals, telemetry and actuation devices, and navigation aids are all high-tech communications capabilities that need relatively small quantities of electricity and are usually situated in areas without access to an electricity grid.

Photovoltaics Illuminates Villages and Homes

The second significant market segment is the village and home market. Traditional means of supplying electricity to developing nations has proven insufficient. For instance, the World Bank has reported that even though Americans consume 12,900 kilowatt-hours of electricity a year, Indians only consume 373. The average electricity generation per person is highest in Canada at 15.4 megawatt-hours, which is nearly 39 times Africa's average generation per person at 0.4 megawatt-hours.

Huge infusions of lending for energy infrastructure have averaged $40 billion every year over the past 20 years and have resulted in crushing debt loads for many developing countries. Separately, even if a standstill in nuclear energy projects were to come to an end, the possibility of diverting nuclear raw materials such as plutonium from electricity generation into weapons production would prove to be a risk unacceptable to many world leaders. With more than 2 billion people in the developing world without electricity, PV technology delivers the safest and most cost-effective form of energy for remote, rural, or suburban villages. With international lending agencies and politicians beginning to realize the efficiency with which PV energy can be delivered to the underserved masses, the following are among the early examples of photovoltaics being used to electrify developing parts of the world:

- Farmers and herdsmen in China's Gansu Province received 800 solar electric home-lighting systems from the nonprofit Solar Electric Lighting Fund headquartered in Washington, D.C.
- With help from the U.S. Initiative on Joint Implementation of the Climate Change Action Plan, more than a combined 800,000 photovoltaic systems were slated to be installed in Sri Lanka and in 400 households in Bolivia in 1998. The recipients of these PV systems were not serviced by their national electricity grid.
- Amoco/Enron Solar Power Development signed a 25-year power purchase agreement with the Rajasthan (India) State Electricity Board for the sale of up to 50 megawatts of photovoltaic electricity-generating capacity from what is expected to be the world's largest photovoltaic power plant to be built in the Thar desert in Rajasthan State.

While photovoltaics can be relied on to supply remote villages in the developing world with electricity less expensively and more expediently than extending power lines, a growing number of homeowners in the developed world are turning to PV systems. In fact, by mid-1998 more than 200,000 homes worldwide depended on PV to supply all of their electricity.

PV commercial rooftops can be integrated into traditional roofs without additional supporting structures and can be installed by commercial roofing companies. Another attraction of PV is that many homeowners benefit from net metering. In the more than 20 net-metering states, the meters attached to PV houses measure power purchased from the electric utility (electricity inflows) and power sold to the electric utility (electricity outflows). When homeowners export more electricity than they import, they become entitled to a refund from the electric utility. Such refunds reduce the impact of initial outlays for PV systems. In addition, homeowners who sell power to their utility get the satisfaction of knowing that the electricity they harness from the sun reduces the amount of fossil fuels the electric utilities would otherwise burn in the production of electricity.

TIP: Other developments allow homeowners to derive more of their electricity from the sun. For instance, the Florida Solar Energy Center has designed a residential photovoltaic-powered water heater; and Sun Frost has designed a sun-powered refrigerator that functions without an outside source of electrical power. Sun Frost's refrigerator does not produce the common and annoying humming sound; and because the compressor is on top rather than on the bottom of the unit, it keeps the kitchen cooler.

Photovoltaic Electricity to Flow over Electricity Grids

The third major PV solar market segment is the grid-connected power segment. This means that solar-generated electricity flows across utilities' networks like electricity produced from nuclear power, coal, natural gas, or oil. According to PV Energy Systems, approximately 22 MW (19 percent of total shipments) were shipped to the grid-connected market in 1997. However, government bodies in many countries (notably the United States, Germany, and Japan) have provided subsidies in the form of cost reductions, tax write-offs, and other incentives to promote the use of solar energy in grid-connected applications and to reduce dependence on other forms of energy. Also, the desire for better living standards, especially a cleaner environment, is driving PV demand in this segment. The Kyoto Climate Summit held in December 1997 in Japan attracted scores of nations from around the world and focused worldwide attention on concerns of environmental activists. Similar summits should help sustain such programs as the Clinton administration's Million Solar Roofs Initiative, which targets placing at least a million solar energy systems on the roofs of buildings and homes across the United States by 2010. This order was born when President Clinton signed Executive Order 12902, which called for the federal government—the world's largest owner of buildings, with 500,000 rooftops—to accelerate the purchase of solar energy power systems for federal buildings. The Energy Department estimates that the Million Solar Roofs program will generate the same amount of electricity produced by three to five coal-fired plants and will reduce pollution equivalent to what is now produced by 850,000 cars annually. Former Secretary of Energy

Federico Pena noted: "By putting solar cells on the roof, we are going to send solar sales through the roof." As a result of this initiative, a consortium of more than 80 public utilities pledged to buy $500 million worth of solar energy panels by 2003.

A similar program is the Residential PV Rooftop Program in Japan, under which the Japanese government allocated $109 million for a solar rooftop program and shifted funds from research and development toward increased market development. The "1,000 Rooftop Program" in Germany was launched in 1990, and by early 1998 had exceeded its goal fourfold as approximately 4,000 households had purchased solar systems funded through federal and state subsidies.

Photovoltaics to Benefit from Electric Utility Deregulation

I believe that photovoltaic power will be especially appealing to the electric utilities in a more competitive, deregulated environment.* PV will reduce the utilities' required capital investments, reduce expenditures associated with upgrading electric power lines, and will help utilities meet peak demand. More specifically, PV arrays can be installed and begin operating in months instead of the years required for conventional power plants. Also, photovoltaic arrays can be installed in small or large quantities and can closely match the electricity needs of the user. Rapid installation and deployments designed to closely match customer needs decrease capital expenditures for a utility and result in superior service to the utility's customers.

Again, the cost of transmitting and distributing (T&D) power to a utility's customers is often higher than the cost of producing the power. When a utility has new demand (as a result of new customers or increased demand by existing customers) and T&D lines are operating at their maximum capacity, the utility would normally build additional lines, which can be very expensive. An alternative is to use PV arrays at the customer end of the system to provide the additional power, thereby removing the need to upgrade the T&D lines.

A third way that photovoltaic power can benefit utilities stems from the fact that PV electrical output closely correlates with the daily load pattern of many utilities, which generally increases during daylight hours—when people are most active and when intense heat renders air-conditioning essential—and decreases again at night, after the sun sets. This means that PV systems can help alleviate peak loads, thereby reducing the chances of a blackout induced by an overloaded electricity grid. The economic benefits of on-site PV solar-generated electricity

---

*To learn about deregulation in the electric utility industry, see David Wanetick, *Bound for Growth*.

are becoming more pronounced from new rate structures such as time-of-day rates—where the highest rates are charged during hot summer afternoons—that are resulting from electric utility deregulation.

New Applications Drive Demand for Photovoltaics

Solar power will be a beneficiary of an increasingly mobile society. Photovoltaic cells and modules can already be found producing power for boats, cars, and recreational vehicles. In fact, solar cells from many different automakers have been shown off at 3,010 kilometer World Solar Challenge races in Australia.

Solar-powered chargers for laptop computers and solar battery chargers for radios and flashlights are among the photovoltaic products that are already available. The use of PV applications to keep these devices working does more than untether their users. Because photovoltaic systems provide a small but constant current to batteries, they prove to be a good solution to the self-discharge problem—whereby batteries' capacity gradually diminishes if they are not used from time to time. (Similarly, solar auto battery chargers are in demand to keep recreational vehicle and boat batteries charged up while they sit unused for months at a stretch.) Also, in view of the reliability of PV systems, the Solar Energy Industries Association has noted an increase in demand for PV-powered flashlights and radios when major floods and other disasters loom.

TRAP: One of the major drawbacks with PV is that direct sunlight is required to generate electricity. On partly cloudy days, total power generation drops to 70 percent of maximum generation. On cloudy days this number can fall to around 50 percent, and on rainy or overcast days, this number may be as low as 30 percent. Also, seasonality causes variance in power generation.

Other sources of demand for solar-powered niche products include solar sidewalk lights that now come in more than 30 designs and solar-powered watches rolled out by Seiko and Swatch. Crete has hosted numerous solar-powered concerts, and some television and radio broadcasts in Greece are powered with solar energy. Also, the U.S. military is interested in using photovoltaic material for communications and other electronic field equipment. Finally, another suitable application for PV systems is remote monitoring as most of these systems—which are used for gauging electricity consumption as well as for monitoring the weather, water temperature, flow rates, factory emissions, and pipelines—use less than 200 watts of power.

Investment Vehicles

Demand for PV solar power is growing at a faster rate than the industry is capable of delivering because of pent-up demand for electricity and a cleaner environment. I expect the growth of the PV industry to continue into the next millennium, driven by an expanding base of infrastructure selling, financing, and servicing of PV systems, and rising PV production. These developments should make it possible to extend sales into new market areas. Some of the electric utilities that are employing photovoltaics include Tucson Electric Power, New Century Energies, and Idaho Power Company. Companies that are engaged in manufacturing solar cells and modules include AstroPower, Golden Industries, Siemens, Kyocera, Solarex, Energy Conversion Devices, and Advanced Energy Systems.

Noise Pollution

With car alarms blaring, jet engines breaking supersonic sound barriers, boom boxes blasting, and construction teams drilling into concrete, it should be no surprise that noise is by far the most common quality-of-life lament. According to a report issued in December 1997 by *The Daily News,* New Yorkers filed 100 complaints about noise pollution for every complaint filed for other annoyances. Also, in a fall 1998 survey of 2,000 Long Island Rail Road commuters, passengers cited noisy cell phones as one of their major annoyances.

Lawmakers are reacting to their constituents' dissatisfaction with their sonorous environs by enacting a growing number of quality-of-life ordinances that target noise pollution. Greater enforcement of these acts, together with the public's yearning for quiet surroundings, bodes well for the companies that can soundproof homes, dampen noise emissions, and filter out background sounds.

TIP: One beneficiary of increasingly prevalent noise pollution is HEARx Ltd. This publicly traded company operates hearing care centers that offer audiological products as well as testing, diagnosis, and rehabilitation services for the hearing impaired.

Noise Pollution Is More Than Annoying

Noise is more than a nuisance: it causes substantial physiological damage. According to Dr. Linda Rosenstock, director of the National Institute of Occupational Safety and Health, 30 million employees are at risk of hearing loss. However, damage caused by noise is not limited to workers employed in clangorous workplaces. Noise—by far the most pervasive environmental hazard in urban areas—is linked to hearing loss and sleep deprivation. And noise contributes to surges in blood pressure, cholesterol, and stress hormones. Thus, Dr. Ken Roy, Armstrong World Industries' principal acoustics scientist, stated that "noise reduction is a proven method of reducing stress, increasing workspace effectiveness, and aiding the healing and learning processes."

In fact, exposure to excessive noise inhibits childrens' learning progress. For instance:

- Gary Evans, an environmental psychologist at Cornell University, found that schoolchildren living near airports suffer from reading deficiencies and impaired long-term memory.
- In the high-rise apartment buildings straddling the Manhattan approach to the George Washington Bridge, children living on the lower floors scored worse on 1997 reading tests than did children above them.
- At an elementary school next to elevated train tracks in Inwood, New York, the average reading level of sixth-graders on the noisy side of the school was a full year behind the students on the quiet side. After acoustic engineers muffled the train noise, the reading scores on both sides of the school were the same.

Policymakers Hear Antinoise Chorus

Politicians are responding to the constant bombardment of noise the public has been condemned to withstand by writing laws designed to foster a more tranquil environment. Regulators are aggressively enforcing these statutes, even going so far as indemnifying those who sustain injury from excessive noise. The courts have generally ruled that forbidding the playing of loud music and the like does not violate one's freedom of speech. Finally, sensitivity to noise is not strictly an American phenomenon as evidenced by the European Court of Justice's ruling that member states may impose stricter noise limits on aircraft engines than required under European Union law.

Big cities have been leaders in combating noise pollution. As a result of New York City Mayor Rudolph Giuliani signing a noise pollution bill in November

1997 that gave the city new prevention and enforcement tools, the number of summonses issued for noise violations increased 22 percent from October 1997 to January 1998. Also, New York City's Taxi and Limousine Commission ruled that taxi passengers should be discouraged from tipping if the driver honks his horn for any reason other than to avoid an accident. Similarly, in early 1998, Los Angeles banned the use of leaf blowers in residential neighborhoods. Separately, Chicago impounded 4,764 vehicles in 1997 for violating that city's noise ordinances.

Smaller cities are joining the metropolises in making noise polluters pay. Police officers in Montgomery, Alabama, issued 3,975 tickets to people in violation of its noise ordinances between May 6, 1996, and March 18, 1998, for fines totaling $463,595.71. Small communities in Washington State have been joined by the U.S. National Park Service in passing ordinances that ban personal watercraft, such as jet skis, from their nearby waters as well as from national parks.

TIP: Watercraft on which Bombardier's D-Sea-Bel Noise Reduction System have been installed may be able to skirt many antinoise ordinances.

Governments have demonstrated that they are willing to help reduce noise levels when overbearing noise is caused by government decree. For instance, the Federal Aviation Administration (FAA) dispersed over $1 million to pay for soundproofing 25 houses near Baton Rouge's Metro Airport in 1998. In the same year, the Quebec government announced a $35 million plan to erect sound barriers along its Highway 25.

Investment Vehicles

Just as noise pollution is caused by a variety of factors, a variety of weapons are available in the antinoise arsenal. First, buildings can be constructed with sound-deadening properties. Because most sound enters homes through windows and doors, holes, and the wooden framework of the house itself, noise can be blocked by sealing holes around windows, electrical service entrances, and vents with caulking and weatherstripping. A relatively inexpensive sound barrier can be made by replacing single-pane windows with double-pane or triple-pane glass. Building materials companies that supply caulking, weatherstripping, and glass panes include ABT Building Products, Jannock Ltd., and Morgan Products. H. B. Fuller is a manufacturer of sound-ending mastics, which are sealants used in soundproof walls. And Solutia developed Safeplex, which is a plastic layer placed on glass that has soundproofing characteristics.

Offices, too, must strive to lower their noise levels. According to the American Society of Interior Designers, over 70 percent of U.S. office workers say their productivity would increase if their workspaces were less noisy. In addition, over 70 percent of contemporary office spaces are based on "open plan" environments, where the din of routine activities can negatively impact worker productivity. One leading company in reducing office noise is Armstrong World Industries, which manufactures noise reduction commercial ceiling tiles. Also, Johnson Controls offers its PersonalEnvironments system that gives individual employees the ability to select their own settings for background noise masking.

TIP: ATCO Noise Management designs and constructs buildings and acoustic barriers to reduce noise emissions from industrial facilities.

Another category of antinoise products is found in telecommunications applications. In an increasingly competitive environment, clarity of telephone calls has become imperative. Thus, AT&T's True Voice and Sprint's Pin Drop ad campaigns boast their carriers' transmission quality. The following are among the other drivers for the deployment of noise cancellation technology by the telecommunications companies:

- Echo cancellation is a critical function in wireless networks as background noise, acoustic echo, and electrical echo are very common problems on these networks.
- As more data and video are delivered over the phone lines, the risks of distortion rise.
- Noise cancellation technology is needed to act as a filter and to remove background noise that tends to degrade the quality of Internet-based voice conversations.
- Speech recognition systems will not function if excessive noise is detected.

Companies that offer solutions to these problems include Tellabs' Coherent unit, Andrea Electronics, and NCT Group.

The following are additional vehicles for playing the antinoise trend:

Airplane hushkits. Realizing the noise that airplanes produce, the FAA has mandated that airlines flying into the United States must have complete Stage 3 fleets by December 1999. (Canada and Europe have rough deadlines of April 2002.) To meet these antinoise criteria, airlines can either retrofit their existing fleets with hushkits or replace their fleets. Hushkits cost $1.5 million versus $30 million for a new plane, and hushkits burn less than 0.5 percent more fuel as they are lightweight. Thus, hushkits should be the preferred option, which will be a boon to their hushkit manufacturers, such as United Technologies' Pratt & Whitney unit.

Chemical plays. Dr. Allan Cohen, managing director at First Analysis Securities Corporation, points out that many chemical companies are involved in producing noise cancellation products. For instance, Material Sciences manufactures "quiet steel" (which precludes noise when being struck) and disk brake dampers (which eliminate screeching when brakes are applied). Also, M. A. Hanna produces rubber gasketing that allows car doors to be shut quietly, and Lydall makes foams for similar applications.

Hearing protection. NCT Group offers its ProActive line of noise-reducing earmuffs and communications headsets for use in higher-noise, commercial, and industrial environments.

Noise measurement. Vallen Corporation manufacturers a wide array of instruments used to measure noise levels.

Antisnoring. Somnoplasty companies such as Somnus Medical Technologies eliminate snoring by sculpting human airways through the application of radio-frequency energy.

Antistatic. NCT Group manufacturers a chip that cancels static on radio stations and on intercom systems found at drive-thru restaurants.

Electronic Interference

Electronic interference from the proliferation of semiconductors is extremely problematic. Semiconductors can be found almost everywhere you look—your VCR, computer, digital camera, telephone, garage door opener, and home security system. The problem is that computer chips and their associated circuitry inadvertently function as tiny radio broadcasting and receiving stations. And any device with a microprocessor radiates radio signals in a frequency band that can overlap with other radio signals.

Consequences include pacemakers that malfunction when their wearers walk past electronic antitheft systems; cellular phones that corrupt airplanes' electronic controls; and automobiles' cruise control functions that are compromised by electronic signals emanating from industrial equipment. The seriousness of such instances of electronic interference should spur the demand for antielectronic interference devices from such companies as Hewlett-Packard, Ansoft Corporation, and Thermo Voltek.

Microprocessors Permeate Society's Landscape

According to the Semiconductor Industry Association, worldwide sales of semiconductors should soar from $137.2 billion in 1997 to $222.4 billion in 2001. (However, the actual unit volume of semiconductors sold will be much higher as prices of semiconductors remain locked in a long-term, precipitous downward spiral.) Also, while the average proportion of semiconductors incorporated within electronic devices between 1975 and 1979 was only 7 percent, the proportion rose to 17 percent in 1995.

At least one semiconductor circuit is connected with just about every electrical device or motor on the earth. Semiconductors are found everywhere: from pay phones to vending machines and from computer modems to electronic books. Other innovative uses of semiconductors include these:

- Pet owners are placing chips in their peregrinating animals' necks in order to claim them if they are caught by animal protection agencies.
- Electronic wristbands are used to monitor children in child care. Similarly, radiofrequency identification technology is used to keep Alzheimer's patients from going astray in nursing homes.
- Surgeons place computer chips in breast implants that contain information about the procedure (e.g., the date of the procedure and the contents used in the implant) in case further work is required.
- Marathon races sometimes require all runners to wear chips on their shoes so that any deviation from the course will be detected.
- According to META Group, by the year 2001 there will be almost 3.5 billion computer chip–laden smart cards used to perform over 100 billion transactions worldwide.
- Some municipalities are attaching electronic tags to trash containers to keep track of how much garbage is picked up at each stop.

Microprocessors are Inherently Susceptible to Electronic Interference

As semiconductors become ubiquitous, the risk of electronic interference rises exponentially because semiconductors emit and receive radio signals. For instance, the speed of microprocessors in portable computers is measured in megahertz, the same unit of frequency used to identify FM radio stations. Megahertz chips in one electronic device can read radio signals of similar frequencies in other electronic devices. In fact, compact disk players operate at 28 megahertz, and because of harmonics (progressively weaker multiples of a given frequency), they can interfere with navigation systems that operate at 112 megahertz. Similarly, many electronic lighting products emit frequencies in the AM band and have been reported to interfere with nearby appliances.

Other factors resulting in electronic interference prompted the Federal Communications Commission (FCC) to strictly prohibit the use of cell phones while travelers are airborne. According to Robert Lilley, director of the Avionics Engineering Center at Ohio University, the issue of cell phone/plane safety is determined by the electromagnetic relationships among three variables: the plane, the cell phone, and the sky. The primary problem is that the electromagnetic qualities of each of the variables are either unpredictable or changeable. No two planes are exactly alike—the slightest difference in a plane's configuration can result in different electromagnetic characteristics. Each cell phone handset may be different. And the sky is a veritable quilt of electromagnetism.

The following are among other factors that cause electronic interference:

- Electronic devices from some foreign countries do not meet U.S. standards for errant radio waves.
- Electronic devices such as wireless phones and laptop computers that have been dropped or modified are dangerous if the shielding designed to prevent emissions has been damaged.
- Radio transmitters can transmit spurious emissions on a frequency not assigned to that transmitter. Also, all telephones contain electronic components that are sensitive to radio frequencies.

Health Care Concerns

Many of the advances in medicine are attributable to breakthroughs in semiconductors. While pacemakers have been available for several decades, newer health care applications of semiconductors are found in hearing aids, prosthetics, and even retinal implants to help the blind regain vision. The risks of patients becoming the subjects of electronic interference are real and the consequences could be fatal.

Many hospitals have banned cellular phones after suspecting that signals from those devices caused breathing machines and heart monitors to shut down. The FCC also warned hospitals that digital television stations could interfere with some types of wireless heart, blood pressure, and respiratory monitors and "endanger the heath and safety of the patients." This proved to be a little-heeded warning: When engineers at WFAA-TV in Dallas began broadcasting digital television signals in the summer of 1998, a dozen wireless heart monitors stopped working at the nearby heart surgery recovery center at Baylor University Medical Center.

Research by Michael McIvor of the St. Petersburg Heart Institute in Florida has shown that the acoustomagnetic signals transmitted by modern antitheft systems cannot be screened out by pacemakers. A separate medical study presented in 1997 showed that Sensormatic Electronics' antishoplifting systems changed the heart rate of 49 of 50 people wearing pacemakers. Similarly, the Food and Drug Administration has warned pacemaker wearers to move quickly through electronic security gates to avoid problems. Finally, research from the University of Oklahoma has shown that digital wireless phones interact with some hearing aids, creating a buzzing noise that reduces speech intelligibility for many wearers.

Other Concerns with Electronic Interference

The following are additional concerns related to electronic interference:

- From 1982 to 1997, pilots recorded at least 137 incidents that they believed were caused by electromagnetic interference, according to the Federal Aviation Administration. Similarly, NASA documented more than 50 incidents in which computers, Nintendo sets, and other devices may have interfered with avionics gear.
- A Pentagon review indicated that the U.S. military had about 90 missile systems installed around the world in 1997 without making sure they did not conflict with local phone frequencies.
- According to *Defense Week,* in 1997, radar in Saudi Arabia interfered with telecommunications equipment, while Patriot missiles in South Korea were grounded because their frequencies were the same as those of mobile phones.
- In the late 1990s, General Motors lost lawsuits in which drivers claimed that their cruise controls caused accidents because internal wires were not appropriately shielded from outside electromagnetic waves. It was asserted that these unprotected wires activated the cruise control systems. The plaintiffs' expert witnesses showed that a Buick's cruise control was sensitive enough to be set off by simply running a power drill near the car.

Investment Considerations

In 1996, companies spent $17 billion worldwide to make products more resistant to electromagnetic interference. Demand for these products will grow in lockstep with the accelerating proliferation of semiconductors.

Thermo Voltek manufactures products that allow electronics manufacturers to check for resistance to electronic pollution. These devices perform both immunity and emissions testing that verify that completed electronic products are not only immune to electromagnetic interference but also are not emitting electromagnetic interference. Ansoft Corporation and Hewlett-Packard offer similar products.

Voice Recognition

Increasingly, people will use their voices for operating software programs, accessing and composing E-mail, and directing Web browsers as well as controlling car navigation, dialing phones, and activating security systems. In fact, at Microsoft's Windows Hardware Engineering Conference in 1998, Bill Gates said he believed that voice, not fingers tapping on keyboards, would eventually become the primary user interface for computers. Robert Stone of SG Cowen estimated that the potential market for natural speech interfaces was $8 billion in late 1998. Companies positioned to seize this opportunity include interactive voice-response solutions providers such as Periphonics and speech-to-text application providers such as Lernout & Hauspie.

However, major companies such as IBM and Microsoft are also committed to delivering voice recognition products to the market. For instance, Microsoft's NT 5.0 system has the ability to read text out loud, and future operating systems will allow people to dictate into most Windows applications. Finally, all variations of voice recognition technology allow users to work more efficiently and save substantial amounts of time.

Interactive Voice Response Providers

Interactive voice response (IVR) technology allows people to access databases of information by Touch-Tone phone, speech input, fax, and Web browsers. Thus, IVR technology enables companies and other entities to realize substantial savings by eliminating or reducing the number of their call center agents. Broker Charles Schwab, for example, estimated that its IVR system handles as many calls as 300 operators would.

The following are examples of IVR deployments:

- United Parcel Service uses IVR technology to allow customers to obtain package status information via telephone, using speech input.
- American Express has implemented an IVR system to provide customers with airline schedule information and flight reservation capability via telephone.
- Charles Schwab used IVR systems to provide stock quotes for more than 14,000 issues to over 45,000 callers each day in 1998.
- Utilities such as NUI and Washington Water and Power have deployed IVR systems to enable customers to check their accounts.
- Many universities are establishing IVR to allow students to register for courses and to retrieve their grades.

Interactive Voice Response Players

The major IVR companies include Periphonics, Voice Control Systems, Brite Voice, Intervoice, and TALX.

Speech-to-Text/Text-to-Speech

Many exciting applications for speech-to-text/text-to-speech technology are emerging. First, most computer users would prefer to dictate rather than type, and speech-to-text applications are already helping active computer users avoid repetitive motion injuries. Motorists would be well served to have their E-mail and favorite Web sites read aloud rather than reading while driving. Also, the fact that more technology is being designed for portable use (e.g., wireless phones and handheld computers) results in users having no keyboard through which information can be entered into their computers. Thus, it would be very practical for users to be able to dictate a memo or an E-mail as easily as they speak on wireless phones.

Another emerging application that is well suited for text-to-speech applications is interactive educational programs. For example, programs that read aloud with children could help youngsters learn how to read. Of course, the traditional dictation markets continue to present enormous opportunities for speech-to-text technology.

Speech-to-Text/Text-to-Speech Players

The dominant company in the speech-to-text/text-to-speech industry is Lernout & Hauspie. Other competitors include IBM, General Magic, and Dragon Systems. Medquist is a pure play on transcription for the medical industry.

Index